Cognitive English Grammar

Cognitive Linguistics in Practice (CLiP)

A text book series which aims at introducing students of language and linguistics, and scholars from neighboring disciplines, to established and new fields in language research from a cognitive perspective. Titles in the series are written in an attractive, reader-friendly and self-explanatory style with assigments, and are tested for classroom use at university level.

Executive Editor

Günter Radden
University of Hamburg

Editorial Board

René Dirven
University of Duisburg-Essen

Suzanne Kemmer
Rice University

Kee Dong Lee
Yonsei University

Klaus-Uwe Panther
University of Hamburg

Johanna Rubba
California Polytechnic State University

Ted J.M. Sanders
University of Utrecht

Soteria Svorou
San Jose State University

Elżbieta Tabakowska
Cracow University

Marjolijn H. Verspoor
University of Groningen

Volume 2

Cognitive English Grammar
Günter Radden and René Dirven

Cognitive English Grammar

Günter Radden
University of Hamburg

René Dirven
University of Duisburg-Essen

John Benjamins Publishing Company
Amsterdam / Philadelphia

 The paper used in this publication meets the minimum requirements of American National Standard for Information Sciences — Permanence of Paper for Printed Library Materials, ANSI Z39.48-1984.

Library of Congress Cataloging-in-Publication Data

Radden, Günter.
   Cognitive English grammar / Gunter Radden, Rene Dirven.
       p. cm. -- (Cognitive linguistics in practice, ISSN 1388-6231 ; v. 2)
Includes bibliographical references and index.
1. English language--Grammar. 2. Cognitive grammar. I. Dirven, René. II. Title.
PE1106.R33   2007
415--dc22   2007012165
ISBN   978 90 272 1903 9 (EUR) / 978 1 55619 663 8 (US) (Hb; alk. paper)
           978 90 272 1904 6 (EUR) / 978 1 55619 664 5 (US) (Pb; alk. paper)

© 2007 – John Benjamins B.V.
No part of this book may be reproduced in any form, by print, photoprint, microfilm, or any other means, without written permission from the publisher.

John Benjamins Publishing Company • P.O. Box 36224 • 1020 ME Amsterdam • The Netherlands
John Benjamins North America • P.O. Box 27519 • Philadelphia PA 19118-0519 • USA

Table of contents

Preface VII

Introduction XI

Part I: The cognitive framework 1

1. Categories in thought and language 3
2. Cognitive operations in thought and language 21
3. From thought to language: Cognitive Grammar 41

Part II: Things: Nouns and noun phrases 61

4. Types of things: Nouns 63
5. Grounding things: Reference 87
6. Quantifying things: Quantifiers 115
7. Qualifying things: Modifiers 141

Part III: Situations as temporal units: Aspect, tense and modality 171

8. Situation types: Aspect 175
9. Grounding situations in time: Tense 201
10. Grounding situations in potentiality: Modality 233

Part IV: Situations as relational units: Sentence structure 267

11. Event schemas: Sentence patterns 269
12. Space and extensions of space: Complements and adjuncts 303

Glossary 335

References 349

Index 361

Preface

Since the publication of Ron Langacker's monumental, two-volume *Foundations of Cognitive Grammar* in 1987 and 1991, the cognitive approach to grammar has established itself as a viable and attractive model of linguistic description. An increasing number of linguists from all over the world have become dissatisfied with the still widespread view of language as a separate module that is detached from all other cognitive faculties. Cognitive Grammar, by contrast, claims that language is part and parcel of our overall cognitive and human make-up. This book is an attempt at showing how Cognitive Grammar may help to better understand the grammar of English.

This book is intended to be used as a textbook in classes of English grammar and linguistics and in courses of general linguistics. The book should ideally be used with advanced undergraduate students or graduate students, i.e. with students who are familiar with the basic notions of linguistics and English grammar. It presents a balanced view of cognitive linguistic theory and selected problem areas of English grammar. Essentially, it seeks to give students a deeper insight into the nature of grammar as a human achievement and into the cognitive principles that motivate its structure. The traditional approach to grammar focuses on forms, structures and rules. Not surprisingly, this approach tends to have a deterrent effect on students. By contrast, the cognitive approach to grammar focuses on language as a tool of conceptualisation and hence on the meaningfulness of language. Students learn to see the study of language as a fascinating and challenging field of human experience.

Language, and grammar in particular, has by now been studied extensively by many cognitive linguists. However, it is also characterised by diverse strands of research. The authors of this book mainly adhere to the model of Cognitive Grammar developed by Ronald Langacker. This book is also indebted to George Lakoff's conceptual metaphor approach, Len Talmy's gestalt-oriented analyses, Gilles Fauconnier and Mark Turner's mental space theory, the cognitive-functional approach developed by John Haiman and Talmy Givón, and many other cognitive linguists as well as precursors of Cognitive Linguistics, such as Zeno Vendler. As a rule, these and other authors are not cited in the body of the text, but the many references in the further reading sections to each chapter will give hints as to the various sources used.

This book is the result of many years of planning and trials. The authors would like to express their gratitude to the colleagues who in the first pioneering stage were willing to co-operate in a multi-authorship and to the many people who read the manuscript and gave us invaluable ideas, in particular Susannah Ewing Bölke, Elizabeth Matthis, Jane Oehlert, and Allan Turner. We would also like to thank Birgit Smieja, Evgenia Sokolinskaja, Angela Heidemann, and Lukasz Tabakowska, who embellished the book with illustrations. Our special thanks go to the instructors of many classes who worked with earlier versions of the book and gave us suggestions and constructive criticisms as well as tokens of empathy. We would especially like to express our thanks to the many students who toiled through the book manuscript at the universities of Hamburg, Kraków, Warsaw, Murcia, Budapest, Debrecen, and Bergen. The student input gave us the satisfying impression that the book was written and re-written with its future users looking over our shoulders and somehow writing the book with us.

Günter Radden and René Dirven

List of typographical conventions used in the book

Italics are used to show that a phrase is cited as a linguistic expression, e.g. the words *gold dust*.

An **asterisk** in front of a sentence is used to indicate an ungrammatical or non-existing sentence, e.g. **The book is had by Jennifer.*

A **question mark** in front of a sentence is used to indicate its doubtful grammaticality or acceptability, e.g. *?The book is liked by Jennifer.*

A **hash sign** in front of a sentence or sequence of sentences is used to indicate pragmatically inadequate utterances, e.g. *#When a cat ran in the yard, we were having lunch.*

Single quotation marks put around a word or phrase are used to indicate a concept or the meaning of a linguistic expression, e.g. *brain* 'intelligence'.

Bold print is used for important linguistic terms at their first occurrence. These key words are repeated in the summary of each chapter and defined in the glossary.

Introduction

It quickly becomes clear to any careful observer that the grammar of a language is not just a long list of formal rules. A grammar may be seen as a cognitive achievement: it is the solution that generations of speakers of a speech community have found to structure their thoughts with the intention to communicate them to other people. As human products, the words and grammatical structures of a language reflect the physical, psychological and social experiences of its human creators. The distinctions made by the lexicon of a language reflect important specific experiences of our lives, while the distinctions made by its grammar reflect recurrent and generalised experiences. Like the words of a language, the grammar of a language is meaningful, too. Part of the cognitive approach to grammar is to detect the motivation underlying grammatical structures.

The main functions of language are to enable people to symbolise their experiences in a perceptible form and to communicate them to others. In expressing their thoughts, speakers constantly need to decide which words and grammatical constructions to use. Both the inventories of words and constructions of a language provide a set of options which the speaker has to choose from in communicating her thoughts. A cognitive approach to grammar is therefore "usage-based": it looks at the structural choices available and the speaker's reasons for choosing one alternative over the other.

A Cognitive Grammar is based on the following assumptions, which will be elaborated in the course of this book:

- The grammar of a language is part of **human cognition** and interacts with other cognitive faculties, especially with perception, attention, and memory. For example, in the same way that we focus on a bird we see flying in the sky and not on the sky surrounding the bird, we describe the situation as *a bird in the sky* and not as *the sky around the bird.*
- The grammar of a language reflects and presents **generalisations** about phenomena in the world as its speakers experience them. For example, tense as a grammatical form is used to express general notions of time (present, past and future) but not specific notions such as years, hours or days, which are expressed by lexical material.
- Forms of grammar are, like lexical items, **meaningful** and never "empty" or meaningless, as often assumed in purely structural models of grammar. For example, the element *to* of a *to*-infinitive as in *I'd like to hear from you* indicates that my wishes are directed towards a goal.

- The grammar of a language represents the whole of a native speaker's **knowledge** of both the lexical categories and the grammatical structures of her language.
- The grammar of a language is **usage-based** in that it provides speakers with a variety of structural options to present their view of a given scene. For example, I might describe the same scene as *I'm running out of time* or *Time is running out*.

As a students' grammar, this Cognitive English Grammar seeks to provide students with insights into grammar as part of human cognition and to open up new avenues for further study and research. It does not intend to be a comprehensive reference grammar of English, but specifically addresses those areas of grammar that are relevant and interesting from a cognitive point of view and difficult for learners of English as a foreign language. It is therefore unavoidable that many areas of English grammar are not, or only cursorily, dealt with in this book. For example, for reasons of space, the authors had to dispense with the treatment of complement clauses and adverbial clauses.

As a textbook, *Cognitive English Grammar* aims at clarity and insightfulness as its guiding principles. For reasons of readability, each chapter starts with an overview introducing the topic of the chapter, and ends with a summary recapping the main ideas and key notions. Linguistic terminology is kept to a minimum. Important terms are printed in bold in the text and defined in the glossary. The authors are aware of the fact that each of the areas presented in the book deserves a deeper and more intensive discussion. The reference section at the end of each chapter gives selections of books and articles where more information on a given topic might be found. Along with the descriptive sections, the study questions are the most important part of each chapter, since they allow the user to test her understanding of the chapter and to apply the notions presented in it. The solutions to the study questions can be downloaded from the Benjamins website www.benjamins.com/.

The book is organised into twelve chapters, which are arranged into four larger parts.

Part I "The cognitive framework" presents the cognitive-linguistic theory which guides the approach to grammar adopted in this book. Chapter 1 introduces the basic units of thought and language, i.e. categories, and shows how these conceptual units relate to our experience and culture. Chapter 2 looks into a number of cognitive operations that are at work in producing and understanding language. It is shown that cognition, perception and language are closely interrelated. Chapter 3 demonstrates how conceptual units and their linguistic counterparts are combined, giving rise to complex ideas and grammar.

Part II "Things: nouns and noun phrases" deals with conceptual entities and their expression in language as nouns and noun phrases. In Cognitive Grammar, conceptual entities which typically have a certain stability in time are described as "things". Grammatically, things are coded as nouns. Chapter 4 distinguishes between different types of things and the corresponding subcategories of nouns, focusing on the distinction between "objects", which are coded as count nouns, and "substances", which are coded as mass nouns. We normally talk about particular instances of things, which are expressed as noun phrases. Chapter 5 deals with the ways instances of things are "grounded" in discourse in acts of reference. Chapter 6 is devoted to the quantification of things by means of quantifiers.

Chapter 7 looks at the qualification of things by means of modifiers. A major issue of the discussion of things and their instances will be to show how, in an act of communication, the speaker ensures that the hearer can call up the same instance of thing that the speaker has in mind.

Part III "Situations as temporal units: aspect, tense and modality" is concerned with temporal information which the speaker supplies to the hearer in describing a situation. Specifically, the speaker needs to provide information on the type of situation, its time of occurrence, and its reality status. Grammatically, this information is expressed in the verb complex as aspect, tense and modality. Chapter 8 distinguishes between basic situation types according to their internal temporal structure. Situation types may be viewed externally or internally and, accordingly, expressed by using the non-progressive or progressive aspect. Situations are, moreover, anchored with respect to time and potentiality. Chapter 9 investigates the ways situations are grounded in time by means of tense. Chapter 10 studies the grounding of situations in the world of potentiality, which is achieved in English by means of expressions of modality.

Part IV "Situations as relational units: sentence structure" is concerned with the conceptual structure of situations and their structure as sentences. The core of a situation consists of participants related to each other in a particular way. The participants perform certain "roles" like actors of a play. Configurations of central roles constitute meaningful "event schemas". Chapter 11 concentrates on basic event schemas like that of an action, which are encoded in language as simple sentences. Chapter 12 looks at roles that normally do not belong to the core of a situation. They relate to the domain of space and its metaphorical extensions into temporal, circumstantial and causal domains. They typically provide information needed in order to locate a situation in a setting.

The twelve chapters of the book provide a wealth of linguistic data and offer a balanced view of present-day Cognitive Linguistics. Each chapter is designed to be dealt with as a self-contained unit in a course. Depending on the level and duration of the course, the book may be used as a textbook in one term or in two consecutive terms. For a one-term course, a sensible goal might be to introduce the student to the methods and principles of Cognitive Grammar. In this case, we recommend concentrating on the general issues presented in the first section of each chapter and illustrating them by way of selected linguistic problems. For a two-term course, each chapter can be studied in-depth. In this case, Part I and Part II establish a coherent block to be covered in one term: they introduce the student to the cognitive framework and present various aspects of things and nouns. Part III and Part IV form another coherent block to tackle in the second term: they deal with situations and their expression in language.

The cognitive view of English grammar presented in this book may not meet with every reader's unconditional approval. The field of grammar is too burdened with centuries of theorising to satisfy everybody's taste. What we hope to have achieved with this book, however, is to show that taking a fresh look at grammar as a product of human conceptualisation may be worth the reader's time and effort.

Part I

The cognitive framework

A Cognitive Grammar is based on the insight that grammar is the product of human cognition. Therefore we must first understand the principles of cognition that determine grammar. This cognitive framework also requires a new terminology. The first three chapters are intended to introduce readers to the cognitive framework adopted in this book and familiarise them with notions, principles and methods necessary for an adequate description and understanding of the grammar of English.

Chapter 1 "Categories in thought and language" introduces the reader to the basic units of thought and language: categories. Categories are conceptual units, and those categories that are relevant to a community's culture are laid down in language as linguistic categories. Both words and forms of grammar are based on conceptual units. In order to make the cognitive approach to language easier to understand, we will illustrate some of the cognitive processes by using lexical examples. We will see that the inventory of linguistic categories is not sufficient to meet all our conceptual and communicative needs. The meanings of linguistic categories are therefore continually extended by conceptual shifts, in particular metonymy and metaphor.

Chapter 2 "Cognitive operations in thought and language" looks at the cognitive operations we perform in producing, communicating, and understanding language. There are a number of cognitive operations that shape the final product of our thought as it is expressed in language. Typically, the speaker can choose among many possible "construals", i.e. alternative ways of conceiving and expressing a situation. For example, we may describe a situation from our point of view or from that of the hearer. Another type of cognitive operation relates to the speaker's packaging of information as "mental spaces". As a rule, a considerable amount of information which the speaker intends to convey is not expressed explicitly. The hearer therefore needs to infer the meanings the speaker wants to communicate. The hearer is thus not just the recipient of a message but takes an active part in understanding an act of communication.

Chapter 3 "From thought to language: cognitive grammar" explores the ways thoughts are expressed in language. We need to identify the conceptual units and trace their expression as linguistic units. The basic conceptual units are "things" and "relations", which form the "conceptual core" of a situation. Situations and their participants need to be "grounded" in the speech situation so that the hearer can identify them. Furthermore, the speaker may want to provide background information about the situation, especially about the time, the place and the circumstances surrounding a situation. In language, all these conceptual units are expressed as linguistic units within the grammatical structure of a sentence. Finally, the speaker is confronted with the task of combining situations into coherent discourse. In language, complex thoughts find expression in various kinds of complex sentence structure. At all these levels, the conceptual and linguistic units are shown to be inseparably intertwined.

Chapter 1

Categories in thought and language

> 1.0 Overview
> 1.1 Categories and their internal structure
> 1.2 Conceptual groupings of categories
> 1.3 Category extension by means of metonymy and metaphor
> 1.4 Summary

1.0 Overview

Human thought and its expression in language are intimately interrelated. This chapter seeks to show how cognitive processes mediate between the world of concepts and their linguistic crystallisation in the lexicon and grammar of a language. Three types of cognitive processes will be dealt with in this chapter: the formation of **categories**, the conceptual grouping of categories, and the extension of conceptual and linguistic categories by means of **metonymy** and **metaphor**.

1.1 Categories and their internal structure

> *The practical world is not a world of clear-cut distinctions.* (Bloomfield 1933)

1.1.1 Categories

We can only make sense of the world of our experiences and communicate our thoughts by means of what philosophers and linguists call categories. A **category** is the conceptualisation of a collection of similar experiences that are meaningful and relevant to us, i.e. categories are formed for things that "matter" in a community. Categories are conceptual in nature, and many, but by no means all, of our conceptual categories are also laid down in language as linguistic categories. Let us think of an everyday situation that may give rise to a meaningful category for which we do not have a linguistic category.

Imagine the situation of driving to college or work every morning. Whenever you approach a particular junction, the road is clogged. The traffic situations you experience at this junction are, of course, different ones each day: the traffic jams occur at different times, the tailbacks are of different lengths, the cars and the drivers stuck in the jam are different, etc. Yet all these situations appear to be similar enough for you to group them together in one and the same collection of experiences. Since you need to get to college or work in time, these are also highly relevant situations to you. You have now, according to the above definition, formed a category, which may be described as 'prone to traffic jams', and whenever you come across a similar situation, you may subsume it under this category.

Categories which we have formed on the basis of our own individual experiences such as 'prone to traffic jams' are "private" conceptual categories. People who do not drive may never have experienced traffic jams and therefore not formed this category. If I want to communicate my thoughts to other people, I need linguistic signs symbolising these thoughts or conceptual categories. These are linguistic categories, whereby the exact relation between conceptual and linguistic categories is far from clear, but this will not concern us here. Most linguistic categories are shared by the members of a speech community: they are "public" categories. The most commonly found linguistic categories are lexical items, i.e. words. However, if I want to warn my friend that road junction 65 is 'prone to traffic jams', there is no simple word available in English to express this idea. However, English provides linguistic categories for parts of the idea: the compound word *traffic jam*, the adjective *prone*, and the preposition *to*. *Prone* followed by *to* is used in expressions such as *prone to infection* or *prone to error*, where the prepositional object (*infection, error*) describes something unpleasant which is likely to happen. The situation of traffic jams fits in with this familiar mode of expression, and I can now communicate my thoughts by means of a particular grammatical structure and three lexical categories: *prone, to,* and *traffic jam*.

Any category is part of an overall system of categories. Language is sometimes seen as an **ecological system** in which linguistic categories occupy an "ecological niche" like living beings in nature. The special meaning of a linguistic category is defined relative to its neighbouring categories and the system at large, and the introduction of a new category affects other categories. For example, in the old days we only had one word for 'posted items': *mail*. The introduction of airmail affected the system with the result that traditional postal deliveries came to be named *surface mail*. The new category 'surface mail' only makes sense in contrast to its opposite category 'airmail', and this is also brought out in its label *surface* (of the earth). The introduction of e-mail has given rise to a new ecological niche for its opposite category, non-electronic mail. Non-electronic mail comprises both surface mail and airmail and is informally described as *snail mail* — the label *snail mail* reflects its opposition to e-mail. These lexical developments are diagrammed in Table 1.1. The arrows point to an ecological niche which originated as a result of the introduction of a new lexical category.

Table 1.1. Ecological subsystem of 'mail'

The grammar of a language is also an ecological system whose constructions occupy ecological niches. For example, English, unlike many other European languages, has developed a progressive aspect. As a result, the ecological niche of the simple, or non-progressive, form is defined relative to the progressive aspect. Events that go on at present time are described in the present progressive, as in (1a), not in the simple present. The simple present tense can be used, as in (1b), but its ecological niche is restricted to describing habitual events (for aspect see Chapter 8).

(1) a. Howard is playing football in the yard. [event in progress]
    b. Howard plays football. [habit]

The process of establishing categories within an ecological system is known as **categorisation**. Categorisation means drawing "conceptual boundaries" and giving structure to an unstructured world around us. The structure which our linguistic categories provide is, however, deceptive: linguistic categories only cover a very small fraction of our conceptual distinctions. Moreover, linguistic expressions are typically associated with more than one concept and hence tend to be vague or, to use the technical term, "fuzzy". In short, language can hardly be said to reflect reality. Different cultures often categorise the world differently and lay this down in their linguistic categories. Anybody who has ever studied a foreign language will have noticed that words in that language and the range of meanings associated with seemingly equivalent words are often different from those in one's own language.

Let us look at the way different cultures deal with the phenomenon of weather conditions of poor visibility. In the objective world, there is an undifferentiated gradual transition from dense fog caused by evaporation to dry haze. Languages, however, have only a few words which cut up this conceptual continuum at certain points and, moreover, the distinctions made by each language tend to be different. Table 1.2 illustrates lexical categories expressing weather conditions in the languages of three cultures. The English-speaking and Dutch-speaking cultures have three lexical categories for weather conditions, but make distinctions at different points on the weather continuum, while German only provides two categories.

Table 1.2. Culture-specific lexical categorisations

weather continuum			
English culture	*fog*	*mist*	*haze*
Dutch culture	*mist*	*nevel*	*waas*
German culture	*Nebel*		*Dunst*

We might speculate that the differences in the way the weather continuum is cut up relates to the prevailing climatic conditions and hence is meaningful to each of these three cultures. The predominantly maritime climate in Britain and the Netherlands may have favoured a more differentiated three-way distinction of weather conditions while the continental climate in Germany could be sufficiently described by a two-way distinction. Whatever the reason for the differences may be, we can state as a fact that, when talking about visibility and air moisture, speakers of English and Dutch have to place their experience under one of three lexical categories provided by their language, while speakers of German choose between two categories. In this sense, a language imposes its own conceptual grid upon our world of experience.

Just like lexical categories, grammatical categories are based on meaningful experiences of the world. Imagine the following situation. A gold digger who hits upon a sizeable piece of gold will think to himself that he has found a precious gold nugget. Most of the time, however, all he finds at the bottom of his pan after washing out the sand is, at most, minute flakes of gold, which he calls *gold dust*. His experience as a gold digger tells him that gold dust is pretty worthless. So the distinction between the categories 'gold nugget' and 'gold dust' is meaningful and relevant to the gold digger. He can tell the difference between gold nuggets and gold dust from the size and the shape of the pieces of gold: gold nuggets are bigger, have a distinct shape, are discrete particles and can therefore be counted; gold dust, by contrast, is composed of small particles which lack contours and cannot be counted or are not worth the trouble. We tend to take the existence of gold nuggets and gold dust for granted as if they were part of objective reality, but the distinction between them is, in fact, purely man-made. This becomes clear when two speakers find that their respective distinctions differ: one gold digger may become much more excited about a particular find than his companion. We mentally cut the continuum of sizes of pieces of gold at some point and mark the conceptual distinction both lexically and grammatically: lexically, larger-sized pieces are categorised as *nuggets* and smaller-sized pieces as *gold dust*; grammatically, larger-sized pieces are categorised as count nouns and smaller-sized pieces as mass nouns. Count nouns may be pluralised, as in *ten gold nuggets*, while mass nouns cannot be counted, as in **ten gold dusts*. A conceptual continuum may thus be split up both lexically and grammatically, as shown in Table 1.3.

Table 1.3. Lexical and grammatical categorisation

"gold" continuum	○ ○ ○ ○ ○ ₀○ ₀°₀ ° °.	
lexical categories	*gold nugget(s)*	*gold dust*
grammatical categories	count noun	mass noun

The fundamental conceptual distinction between count nouns and mass nouns will be looked at more closely in Chapter 4. Here it is important to note that categories do not describe objective reality but that they are based on a community's experience and conception of reality. Our conception of reality makes us "see" the many different traffic situations at a road junction as being sufficiently similar in nature so that we may categorise them together. The case of nuggets and gold dust, on the other hand, demonstrates that our conception of reality also makes us "see" similar entities as different and, consequently, makes us categorise them differently. To put it simply, we can only see reality in relation to us as part of it.

1.1.2 Internal structure of categories: Prototype and periphery

A category such as 'car' is composed of various similar members. For example, a sports car, an estate car (AmE. *station wagon*), a jeep and a saloon car (AmE. *sedan*) are completely different types of cars but are, nonetheless, understood as being similar enough to count as members of the same category 'car'. However, we intuitively feel that some of these types of cars fit the idea of the category 'car' better than others. Probably, for most people, a saloon car is the best type of car, and an estate car is a better type of car than a jeep. Thus, a saloon car would

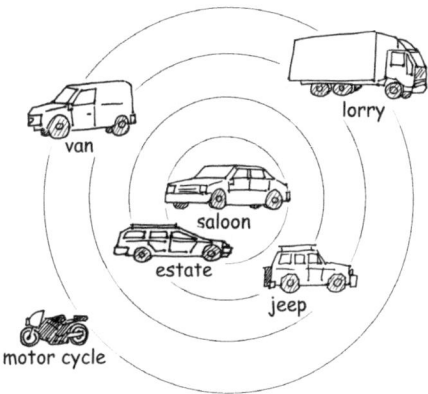

Figure 1.1. The category 'car'

be considered a prototypical member, or **prototype**, of the car category, while other types of cars such as a jeep would be considered to be less prototypical members of this category. In English, a van and a lorry would be seen as peripheral members of the category 'car', or even not cars at all, because they are used to transport not people but goods. A motor cycle would be outside the category 'car' altogether because it only has two wheels.

In the same way that lexical categories have prototypical and peripheral members, grammatical categories display different degrees of membership. This holds true for any grammatical category such as 'noun', 'verb', 'transitive verb', 'passive', etc. For example, transitive verbs are usually characterised as taking a direct object, while intransitive verbs do not. But this is only part of the story. Within these two grammatical categories, some types of verbs are obviously better members of their category than others. This can be shown in their syntactic behaviour. For example, sentences with prototypical transitive verbs can be freely passivised as in (2a), sentences with less prototypical transitive verbs can only marginally form a passive (2b), and sentences with peripheral transitive verbs do not allow the passive at all (2c):

(2)   *Active*   *Passive*
       a.   Sally *bought* the book.   a'.   The book *was bought* by Sally.
       b.   Sally *liked* the book.   b'.   ?The book *was liked* by Sally.
       c.   Sally *had* the book.   c'. * The book *was had* by Sally.

The issue of transitivity will be further explored in Chapter 11. At this point we may, however, already note the impact of prototype structure in grammar. An action verb like *buy* is obviously a better member of the category of transitive verbs than an emotion verb such as *like*; and *like* in its turn is a better transitive verb than a possession verb like *have*.

1.2 Conceptual groupings of categories

Categories form part of larger groupings of categories. In particular, categories

i. are included in a hierarchy, or *taxonomy*, of categories (e.g. 'car' is a member of the category 'means of transport');
ii. may be a part of another category, i.e. may be included in a *partonomy* (e.g. 'wheels' are parts of the category 'car'); and
iii. form part of a coherent area of conceptualisation, especially *frames* and *domains* (e.g. the 'car' frame and the domain of 'combustion').

1.2.1 Taxonomies

Categories are included in hierarchies of categories. They are normally included as members of a higher category and in their turn subsume members of a lower category. Such conceptual hierarchies are known as **taxonomies**. For example, the category 'car' — along with 'train', 'bike' and 'plane' — is a member of the higher category 'means of transport' and has as its members the categories 'sports car', 'jeep', 'saloon', 'estate car', etc. The members of a higher category are prototypically structured. Thus, 'car' or 'train' is a better member of the category 'means of transport' than 'bicycle' or 'plane'. We might arrange all these categories in a three-level hierarchy in which the lower categories are members, or kinds, of a higher category, as illustrated in Table 1.4. Thus a 'sports car' is a kind of 'car', and a 'car' is a kind of 'means of transport'. We express such *kind of*-relations by simply saying *is a*: *A train is a means of transport*. Note that a taxonomy is purely conceptual in nature: there is no such hierarchical order of categories in reality. Taxonomic hierarchies also apply to words and are known as *hyponymies*. The superordinate word is described as a *hyperonym*, the subordinate word as a *hyponym*.

Table 1.4. Taxonomy of the category 'means of transport'

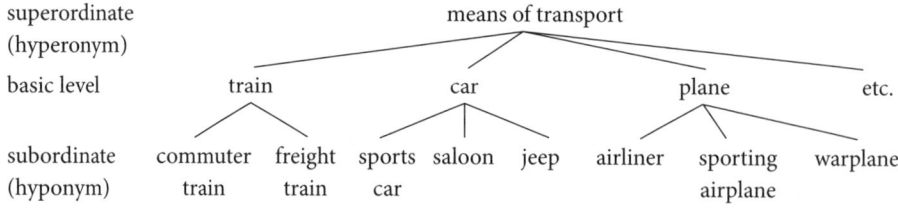

The types of category that come to our mind most readily in our daily interaction with the world belong to the middle, or **basic level**. Categories at the basic level such as 'car', 'train' and 'plane' are conceptually much more salient than either their superordinate category 'means of transport' or any of their subordinate categories. As a result, terms which denote basic-level categories, i.e. **basic-level terms**, have special properties: they are simple in form, are used frequently, are learned early by young children, and evoke rich images.

1.2.2 Partonomies

Taxonomic hierarchies have to be distinguished from part-whole hierarchies, in which categories are interrelated by *part of*-relations. Part-whole hierarchies are known as **partonomies**, or meronymies. Table 1.5 illustrates a partonomy of the category 'car' and some of its parts, which include the wheels, the engine, the body, and the interior. All of these main parts consist of further parts: the wheels have tyres and hubcaps, the engine has amongst others a crankshaft and cylinders, etc. A specialist would even be able to identify about 15,000 separate components that make up a car. All of these *part of*-relations are expressed by using *have*, as in *This engine has six cylinders.*

Table 1.5. Partonomy of the category 'car'

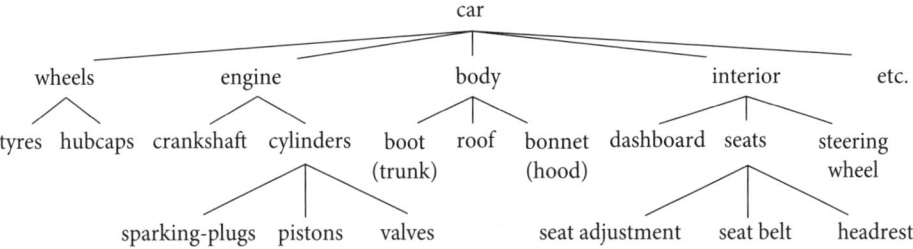

Partonomies refer to whole entities and parts of them in the real world as we conceive of them. Each part is unique in that it has its own place and function within the total structure.

1.2.3 Frames and domains

1.2.3.1 *Frames*

The parts of a thing are not just loosely put next to each other as Table 1.5. might suggest, but they are conceptually integrated within a structured whole. Thus, the body of a car provides the frame of the vehicle, the engine produces the energy to propel the car, the wheels allow its motion along a road, and its interior is designed to carry and protect its passengers. In thinking of a car, we activate knowledge of the functional uses of these parts; but we also think of cars within their taxonomy of means of transport, we see prototypical and peripheral cars, and we also visualise scenes involving cars such as 'driving', 'parking', 'accidents', etc. This coherent "package of knowledge" that surrounds a category and is activated when we use or hear a word is known as a conceptual **frame**. As we will see in the following chapters, all our coherent bits of knowledge are structured in conceptual frames. Thus, we have a 'marriage' frame, a 'party' frame, a 'university' frame, etc. All the situations described so far involve frames: a 'traffic' frame, a 'mail' frame, a 'weather' frame, and a 'gold digging' frame. The 'gold digging' frame, for example, includes our encyclopaedic knowledge of the gold rush in 19th century America, fortune hunters looking for gold using a pan, etc.

Our knowledge of frames enables us to understand the coherent "nature" of things in which each part has its place and function within its global structure. For example, when the car won't start, our knowledge of the 'car' frame makes us look for problems in the battery or petrol supply. Our shared knowledge of frames also governs communication. For instance, in the sentences under (3) and pictured in Figure 1.2, we immediately "know" that a particular main part or parts of a car are meant, although only the car as a whole is named:

(3)   *Whole*   *Parts*
   a. Can you lubricate *the car*?   [*parts easing smooth motion*]
   b. Can you start *the car*?   [*engine of the car*]
   c. Can you wash *the car*?   [*body of the car*]
   d. Can you hoover *the car*?   [*interior of the car*]

Our knowledge of the 'car' frame tells us that the parts of a car that are lubricated are those that move such as the wheels, that we start a car by starting its engine, that the part of a car that gets washed is the body, and that the part of a car that is vacuumed is its interior. The wheels, the engine, the body and the interior are the parts of the car that are directly and crucially involved in each of the situations described under (3). Such parts of a whole are known as an entity's **active zone**. Speaking of a whole thing but meaning its active zone is

Figure 1.2. Active zone parts of a car

a very common phenomenon. In fact, this way of speaking comes to us so naturally that we have to think twice before we realise that we are not using the words at their face value. For example, we speak of "a printer running out of ink" when we mean its cartridge, or of "eating a banana" when we mean its pulp but not its peel. What these examples are meant to show is that recognising an active zone is a major cognitive achievement by the hearer. We can see this when we look up the word *car* in a dictionary: among its meanings listed there, we will not find the senses 'wheels', 'engine', 'body', and 'interior' of a car, which we so easily supply in our understanding. More generally, this phenomenon reveals an important aspect of language in use: we always understand acts of communication with respect to our knowledge of frames.

1.2.3.2 Domains

Categories relate not only to taxonomies, partonomies and frames, but also to conceptual domains. A conceptual **domain** is the general field to which a category or frame belongs in a given situation. For example, a knife belongs to the domain of 'eating' when used for cutting bread on the breakfast table, but to the domain of 'fighting' when used as a weapon. Whereas frames are specific knowledge structures surrounding categories, conceptual domains are very general areas of conceptualisation. Some typical domains are those of 'space', 'time', 'emotion', 'sports', 'travelling', etc. Conceptual domains crosscut with frames and thus allow us to link frames to one another. For example, the 'car' frame may be linked to the 'house' frame by means of the shared domain 'combustion': both the engine of a car and the heating system of a house use fossil energy. Such links may be represented as shown in Figure 1.3.

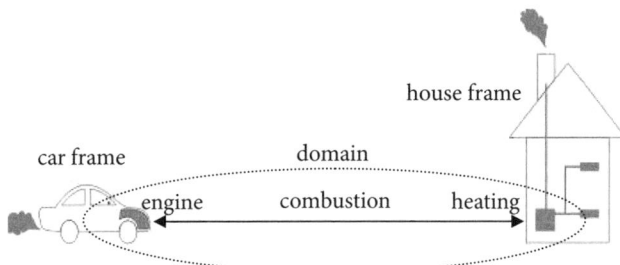

Figure 1.3. Interaction of frames and domains

The dotted ellipse in Figure 1.3 indicates the conceptual domain 'combustion', which is shared by the 'car' and 'house' frames. The domain 'combustion' may be further linked to the domain of environmental pollution, so that both combustion engines and combustion heating systems are seen as environmental polluters. The possible links of categories and frames by means of domains are myriad. For example, the 'traffic' domain links cars to other transport systems and allows us to compare different means of transport with respect to comfort, efficiency or costs of travelling.

1.3 Extension of categories by means of metonymy and metaphor

Our human ability to evoke frames and domains allows us to extend our inventory of conceptual and linguistic categories substantially. We are constantly being confronted with innovations and changes in the world, which we need to categorise conceptually and which we often express as linguistic categories. One way of dealing with these new experiences is to create new, especially compound words — something we do all the time. For instance, the heightened threat of terrorist attacks led to the introduction of security personnel on airliners, for which the new word *air marshal* has been coined. However, the sheer number of new words that would have to be coined would soon exceed the capacity of our memory and render communication impossible. A more elegant and efficient solution to deal with new experiences and innovations is to make use of our existing linguistic categories and extend their meanings, i.e. the conceptual categories associated with them. There are various means of extending the senses of a linguistic category; here we will only concentrate on the two most powerful conceptual shifts that lead to meaning extension: metonymy and metaphor.

1.3.1 Conceptual shifts

Extensions of the sense of a word are not just a matter of language, but a matter of cognition. Let us illustrate conceptual shifts of the word *brain*. According to a dictionary definition, the brain is 'the organ inside your head that controls how you think, feel, and move'. In the following examples, *brain* is obviously used in other senses:

(4) a. The company is hiring new *brains*.
 b. The microprocessor is the *brain* of a computer.

Most people immediately understand *brains* in (4a) to mean 'intelligent persons' and *brain* in (4b) to mean 'microchip of a computer'. We thus need to account for the shift in meaning from 'organ inside your head' to 'intelligent person' on the one hand and to 'microchip' on the other hand. The cognitive process that relates literal meanings to extended meanings is known as mapping. **Mapping** is the projection of one set of conceptual entities onto another set of conceptual entities.

The conceptual shift in (4a) involves a mapping between 'brain' and 'intelligent person'. Since a brain is a body part of a person, both categories belong to the same frame. In using the word *brain*, we give prominence to this particular body part of a person. Moreover, we know that the brain is the seat of a person's intelligence and that we are obviously not talking about the brain as an organ but its prominent property of intelligence. Thus both the body part 'brain' and the property 'intelligence' are mapped onto 'person' so that we arrive at the interpretation of 'intelligent person' for *brain*. This kind of conceptual shift within the same frame or domain is an instance of **metonymy**.

The conceptual shift in sentence (4b), *The microprocessor is the brain of a computer*, is of a different kind. We are no longer talking about people but computers. People and their brains belong to the conceptual domain 'human being', which comprises human aspects such as consciousness, rationality, emotions, etc. Microchips belong to the conceptual domain 'electronics', which comprises computer technology and other digital equipment such as mobile phones and DVD. The structure of the domain 'human being' is mapped onto the structure of the domain 'electronics' and, as part of the structures, the 'brain' as a body part is mapped onto 'microchip' as a part of a computer. Thus, the way a microprocessor functions in a computer is understood in terms of the way a brain functions in a human being. This kind of conceptual shift across domains is an instance of **metaphor**.

In cognitive linguistics, the two conceptual domains linked in a metaphorical mapping are known as **source domain** and **target domain**. In the *brains* metaphor, the 'human being' serves as the source domain and 'electronics' as the target domain.

Figure 1.4 illustrates the two types of conceptual shift: a metonymic shift, which operates within the same frame or domain, and a metaphorical shift, which operates across two different domains. Metonymy is therefore often said to involve contiguity, while metaphor is said to involve similarity.

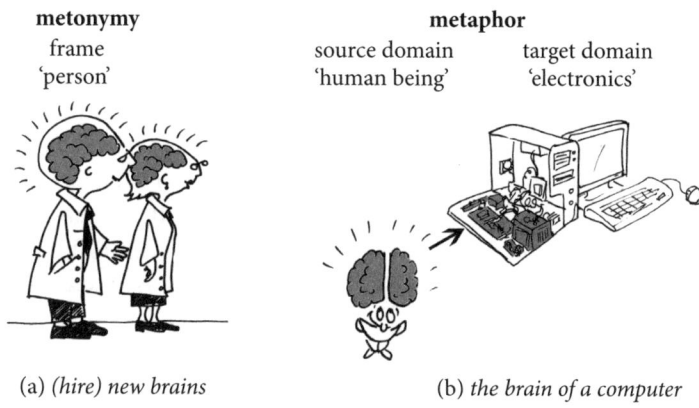

(a) *(hire) new brains*   (b) *the brain of a computer*

Figure 1.4. Metonymy and metaphor

In the metonymic mapping (a), the word *brains* is used to stand for persons, but we may also make use of other body parts within the 'person' frame. For example, the coach of a soccer team might say something like *We need fresh legs* when he wants to bring in a new player. In the metaphorical mapping (b), the brain of the human being is mapped onto the microchip of a computer; but we may also project other elements that belong to the human domain onto the domain of 'electronics'. For example, expressions such as *memory, virus* or *brood* in *The computer is brooding over the problem* describe the computer in terms of humans. We will now look more closely at metonymy and metaphor and the functions these two conceptual shifts have for thought and communication.

1.3.2 Conceptual metonymy

Let us look at an everyday expression of metonymy:

(5) *The Crown* never rejects a bill approved by Parliament.

The Crown in sentence (5) is used to stand for a 'monarch' in a frame which might be described as 'monarchy' frame. A crown is that part of a monarch's attire which most attracts our attention. If we were asked to draw a king, the part which we would certainly not leave out would be his crown: it is *the* distinguishing feature of a king. Its importance is reflected in the expressions *to crown someone king* and *uncrowned king*. The crown has also become the conventionalised symbol of its royal wearer and, more abstractly, of the monarchy.

Figure 1.5. Metonymic reference point and target

We described metonymy as a conceptual shift, and we can now see what its conceptual impact is. We mentally trace a path from a conceptually salient conceptual entity, such as 'crown', to another conceptual entity, 'monarch'. The notion of *salient* or *salience* is understood here in the sense of 'conspicuously standing out conceptually'. Technically, we will refer to the salient entity in this conceptual shift as a **reference point**. Metonymy thus involves speaking about a salient reference point which allows us to access another conceptual entity, the target. In processing the PART FOR WHOLE metonymy in (5), we thus mentally access a whole ('monarch') via a salient part ('crown'). This situation is illustrated in Figure 1.5. We also find the reverse situation of a WHOLE FOR PART metonymy, in which a whole serves as a reference point for accessing one of its parts, as in sentence (6):

(6) *Our school* won the cup.

Here, *our school* refers to a team of our school. The school is a conceptually salient reference point in that it is a permanent institution, possibly has its own outfit and songs, and wins fame by winning the cup. The team is a fully independent part of the school. In this respect this WHOLE FOR PART metonymy is different from the active-zone examples discussed in Section 1.2.3.1 above.

Both the PART FOR WHOLE metonymy and WHOLE FOR PART metonymy are conceptual in nature because they have a very general application, i.e. many more instances of these metonymies can be found in language, and even outside language. There are many other types of conceptual metonymies, some of which are listed below (conceptual metonymies and metaphors are conventionally printed in small capitals):

(7)   *Conceptual metonymy*   *Metonymic expression*
    a. POSSESSION FOR OWNER   *The Porsche* left without paying.
    b. INSTITUTION FOR PERSON   She phoned *the hospital*.
    c. CONTAINER FOR CONTENTS   *The kettle* is boiling.
    d. ORGAN OF PERCEPTION FOR PERCEPTION   Our warning fell on deaf *ears*.

In all these cases, the metonymic expression highlights a facet of a frame that, for some reason or other, serves as the salient reference point. In (7a), a thing possessed, namely the car, serves as the reference point for accessing its owner, the driver, whom we do not know. In (7b), we need a doctor but do not know who will pick up the phone: the receptionist, a nurse or a doctor. In (7c), the kettle is visible while the water boiling in it is not. Similarly, in (7d), a person's ear is tangible but the person's hearing ability is not.

The cases of metonymy looked at so far have had to do with extensions of lexical categories. We will see later on that metonymy also operates in the grammar of a language. The following examples illustrate a few such instances of grammatical metonymy:

(8) *Conceptual metonymy*   *Metonymic expression*
   a. OBJECT FOR SUBSTANCE   We had *octopus* for lunch.
   b. RESULT FOR ACTION   *Win* two weeks' vacation!

In (8a), the count noun *octopus*, which commonly refers to the invertebrate that inhabits the oceans, is used as a mass noun and describes the food substance acquired from an octopus (see Chapter 4.3.1.2). In (8b), the verb *win*, which normally describes a punctual event, is used to describe a preceding action, such as playing in the lottery, which may lead to winning two weeks' vacation as a result (see Chapter 8.5.1).

1.3.3 Conceptual metaphor

> *A good metaphor implies an intuitive perception of the similarity in dissimilars.* (Aristotle, *Poetics*)

Many people, including literary critics, often assume that metaphor is a rhetorical device used by poets to achieve an aesthetic effect. While this may be true for highly imaginative metaphors, it is not true for the kinds of metaphor we commonly use. These metaphors are less striking and often described as "dead" because we are no longer aware of them as metaphors. Let us look at an example of what may be called a dead metaphor:

(9) Amanda was *overcome* by grief.

Sentence (9) may not appear to be metaphorical at first sight: the expression *be overcome* simply means 'be overwhelmed emotionally'. As its use in the famous song *We shall overcome* attests, the word *overcome* originally belongs to the domain of fighting and means 'come out on top in a contest or struggle', i.e. 'defeat someone'. Many emotions, particularly negative ones such as grief or anger, are metaphorically seen as physical opponents with which we have to struggle. Thus we use metaphorical expressions such as *wrestle with one's anger* or *struggle with one's conscience*. We may describe this particular metaphor conceptually as EMOTIONS ARE OPPONENTS. The metaphor has developed because we have no direct way of understanding our emotions; it is almost impossible even to find literal expressions capable of describing such strong emotions. Metaphor thus provides a means of understanding abstract domains such as emotions by relating them to better-known domains and experiences in the physical world. Here are some more conceptual metaphors and their manifestations in language:

(10) *Conceptual metaphor*   *Metaphorical expression*
    a. TIME IS MONEY   I've *invested* a lot of time in her.
    b. LOVE IS MADNESS   I am *crazy* about her.
    c. BELIEFS ARE POSSESSIONS He *clings* to his beliefs.
    d. UNDERSTANDING IS SEEING I don't *see* your point.

A particularly widespread and productive set of metaphors are "orientational metaphors". These metaphors have as their source domain spatial relations such as up–down or front–back. Such basic spatial structures are known as image schemas. **Image schemas** make particularly good source domains because they have developed from our earliest bodily and spatial experiences and hence are immediately meaningful to us. For example, we constantly experience up and down movements in the physical world: the force of gravity makes things like rain come down, while heat makes things like smoke go up. Hence we have developed a deeply entrenched UP–DOWN image schema. In exploring the world around us we grasp objects and develop a CONTACT schema. The fact that we interact in the world with the front of our bodies has given rise to the FRONT–BACK schema. Some objects have a hollow space which may be filled with other objects or substances, such as a bowl filled with milk. This experience gives rise to a CONTAINER schema, which is characterised by a boundary setting an interior apart from an exterior. The MOTION schema has developed from our perception of objects moving past our eyes and the experience of our own motor activities when we move around. All these embodied image schemas provide rich sources for conceptual metaphor:

(11) *Conceptual metaphor*   *Metaphorical expression*
    a. MORE IS UP   Oil prices are *rising* again.
    b. CONNECTION IS CONTACT   Please *hold* on!
    c. THE FUTURE IS IN FRONT I look *forward* to seeing you.
    d. STATES ARE CONTAINERS   He is *in* a mess.
    e. CHANGE IS MOTION   The telephone *went* dead.
    f. CAUSES ARE FORCES   His nagging *sent* me into a frenzy.

The above image schemas serve as source domains for our understanding of various abstract domains: the MORE IS UP schema in (11a) describes more in quantity, the CONTACT schema in sentence (11b), said on the phone, is used here to describe an action, the

FRONT-BACK schema in (11c) serves to describe future time, the CONTAINER schema in (11d) describes a state, the MOTION schema in (11e) describes a change of state, and the FORCE schema in (11f) makes us see a relation of cause and effect in terms of a human being deliberately setting an object in motion.

1.4 Summary

This chapter dealt with categories and the cognitive processes operating on categories. **Categories** are conceptual units; they represent collections of similar experiences that are meaningful and relevant to us. A comparatively small number of categories are crystallised in language as lexical and grammatical categories. Linguistic categories such as the new word *e-mail* occupy an ecological niche in the overall **ecological system** of a language. The cognitive process by means of which linguistic categories are established is known as **categorisation**. Categories have members. Some members are better instances of a category than others, the best instance being the **prototype**. Thus a 'saloon car' is a prototypical member of the category 'car'.

Categories are also part of conceptual groupings: they form parts of taxonomies, partonomies, frames and domains. **Taxonomies** are conceptual hierarchies whose categories are related by *kind of*-relations, as between 'car' and 'saloon'. The conceptually most salient level in a taxonomy is the middle, or **basic level**. **Basic-level terms** such as 'car' are simple in form, frequently used, acquired early, and evoke rich images. **Partonomies** are conceptual hierarchies whose categories are related by *part of*-relations, as between 'car' and 'engine'. Conceptual **frames** are larger coherent packages of knowledge that are prompted with every word. Our knowledge of the 'car' frame, for example, allows us to understand the use of *car* in *Can you start the car?* in the sense of its **active zone** 'engine of the car'. Conceptual **domains** are the general fields to which categories or frames belong in a given situation, such as that of 'combustion', which relates engines and heating systems.

Extensions of linguistic categories are made possible, amongst other things, through the conceptual shifts of metonymy and metaphor. These conceptual shifts involve projections of one set of conceptual entities onto another set of entities. Technically, these conceptual shifts are referred to as **mappings**. In **metonymy**, one conceptual entity is mapped onto another within the same frame or domain; e.g. *crown* may stand for 'monarch' within the frame 'monarchy'. Conceptually, 'crown' serves as a salient **reference point** for mentally accessing 'monarch'. In **metaphor**, we map the structure of one domain onto the structure of another domain; e.g. in *I am crazy about her*, the domain 'madness' is mapped onto the domain 'love'. 'Madness' is the metaphorical **source domain**, and 'love' the metaphorical **target domain**. The source domains of many metaphors are image-schematic. **Image schemas** are basic schematic structures that are directly meaningful, such as UP and DOWN or FRONT and BACK.

> **Further Reading**

The foundations of cognitive linguistics are laid down in the important monographs by Lakoff (1987) and Langacker (1987a, 1991a, 2000). Introductions to cognitive linguistics are presented by Dirven & Verspoor, eds. (²2004), Ungerer & Schmid (²2006), Lee (2001), Croft & Cruse (2004), Taylor (2002), and Evans & Green (2006). A complete survey of cognitive linguistics is the handbook by Geeraerts & Cuyckens, eds. (2007). Readers are Geeraerts (2006) and Evans, Bergen & Zinken (2007), and fields of application are presented in Kristiansen et al., eds. (2006).

Cognitive issues of categorisation are dealt with in Rosch (1977, 1978, 1999), Lakoff (1987), Tsohatzidis (1990), Zerubavel (1991), and Taylor (³2004). The view of language as an ecological system is developed in Lakoff (1987), Taylor (2004) and Violi (2004).

The notion of 'frame' was introduced to linguistics by Fillmore (1982) and Fillmore & Atkins (1992). An extensive discussion of frames and related notions is found in Ungerer & Schmid (²2006). Recently the notion of 'frame' has been applied to the language of politics by Lakoff (2004). The concept of 'domain' is discussed by Langacker (1987a, 1991a) and Croft (1993), who applies it to the distinction between metaphor and metonymy. The notion of 'active zone' goes back to Langacker (2000).

Metonymy as a cognitive phenomenon is discussed in Croft (1993), Langacker (1993), Gibbs (1994), Panther & Radden, eds. (1999), Barcelona, ed. (2000), and Dirven & Pörings, eds. (2002). The cognitive theory of metaphor has been developed by Lakoff & Johnson (1980) and elaborated in Lakoff (1987, 1993), Johnson (1987), Lakoff & Turner (1989), Kövecses (1990, 2002, 2005), Gibbs (1994), Gibbs & Steen (1997), Lakoff & Johnson (1999), Barcelona, ed. (2000), and Dirven & Pörings, eds. (2002).

The issue of image schemas is discussed in Lakoff (1987), Johnson (1987), Krzeszowski (1993), Gibbs & Colston (1995), and Hampe, ed. (2005).

> **Study questions**

1. What do the following examples reveal about conceptual and linguistic categories and language as an ecological system?
   a. A reader puts a question to the Dr. Wordsmith column in *The Independent*:
      "Sometimes when we yawn it makes a very loud noise and sometimes it is totally silent. Does the English language have a pair of words that usefully distinguishes between the two?"
      Dr. Wordsmith writes: "If it ever did, it does not now."
   b. A boy tells his girl-friend:
      "I didn't want to be in love. I only wanted to be in like."

2. What do the linguistic categories (printed in italics) reveal about categorisation?
   a. Would you like your coffee *white* or *black*?
   b. Technically, *crayfish*, *jellyfish*, *starfish* and *shellfish* are not fish.

c. Some people call *graffiti* vandalism, others call it *art*.
d. I don't consider marijuana a *drug*. It's a *plant* like tea. Cocaine is a *drug*.

3. Which part of the house is meant as the active zone in the following examples?
   a. I'm having the house painted.
   b. Have you locked the house?
   c. He entered the house.
   d. I'm cleaning the house.
   e. They are having an open house today.

4. Identify the conceptual metonymies in the following italicised expressions.
   a. He drank the whole *bottle*.
   b. Arthur married *money*.
   c. Einstein was one of the most creative *minds* of the last century.
   d. There are too many *mouths* to feed.
   e. *Own* land in the great American West. (advertisement)
   f. *Brussels* has been negotiating with *Boeing* for months.
   g. *My wife* has been towed away.
   h. Where are *you* parked?

5. Identify the conceptual metaphors and indicate whether their source domain is image-schematic. The last three metaphors have not been dealt with in the chapter.
   a. Do you *see* my point?
   b. Socrates was reputed to *hold* knowledge in high esteem.
   c. *Budget* your time carefully.
   d. Sports car sales are *soaring*.
   e. It's *going* to rain.
   f. I've just *turned* thirty.
   g. I'll get in *touch* with you.
   h. These tiring exercises *sent* me to sleep.
   i. He is *boiling* with anger.
   j. This is *central* to the issue.
   k. Cognitive linguistics is linguistics with a *human face*.

Chapter 2

Cognitive operations in thought and language

2.0 Overview
2.1 Construals
2.2 Mental spaces
2.3 Inferences
2.4 Summary

2.0 Overview

A number of cognitive operations determine the way language is used. This chapter will present three types of cognitive operations: the construal of one's thoughts in speaking, the building of mental spaces in communication, and the drawing of inferences by the hearer. **Construals** are operations that help select the appropriate structural possibility among various alternatives. Construals are strikingly similar to principles of perceptual organisation. **Mental spaces** are packages of information that are built and evoked in the current discourse. Mental spaces draw upon our wider encyclopaedic knowledge about things in the world. **Inferences** are cognitive operations in which conclusions are drawn from a set of premises. The hearer's inferential process in arriving at the meaning of an utterance is known as **conversational implicature**.

2.1 Construals

But men may construe things, after their fashion,
Clean from the purpose of the things themselves.
(Shakespeare, *Julius Caesar*)

There is, as a rule, more than one way of thinking of a particular scene and describing it in language. In choosing one conceptual or linguistic alternative rather than another, the speaker "construes" her thoughts in a specific way. This is what is meant by the notion of

construal. Construals are cognitive operations which are often strikingly similar to principles of visual perception. For example, I may describe the contents of a bottle of whisky as being *half full* or *half empty*. In describing it as *half full*, I am looking at the drink that is (still) left in the bottle, and in describing it as *half empty*, I am thinking of the drink that is gone. The descriptions clearly differ with respect to the perspective adopted: from the perspective of a full bottle or from the perspective of an empty bottle. Adopting a particular perspective is one of many possible construal operations. Here we will look at nine dimensions of construal that are relevant in grammar. The first six relate to viewing operations: (i) viewing frame, (ii) generality vs specificity, (iii) viewpoint, (iv) objectivity vs subjectivity, (v) mental scanning, and (vi) fictive motion; the latter three relate to prominence: (vii) windowing of attention, (viii) figure and ground, and (ix) profiling.

2.1.1 Viewing frame

In viewing a scene I may take a more distant or a closer position giving me a wider or more restricted **viewing frame**. Imagine the scene of a train travelling from Norwich to Peterborough. An observer looking at the scene from an aeroplane has a *maximal viewing frame*: she has the whole train route in her view, including its termini in the two cities and the surroundings. We also have a maximal viewing frame of the train route when we study a map of the railway network and trace the connection between the two towns with our finger. When travelling on the train, however, the view from the window of our compartment only lets us see that part of the route which we are passing at any given moment. The endpoints of the section fall outside the viewing frame, even though of course we know that the train journey has a beginning and an end. We now have a *restricted viewing frame*. These two viewing situations are evoked by the grammatical structures used in sentences (1a) and (1b) and are sketched in Figure 2.1.

(1) a. This train *goes* from Norwich to Peterborough.
    b. This train *is going* from Norwich to Peterborough.

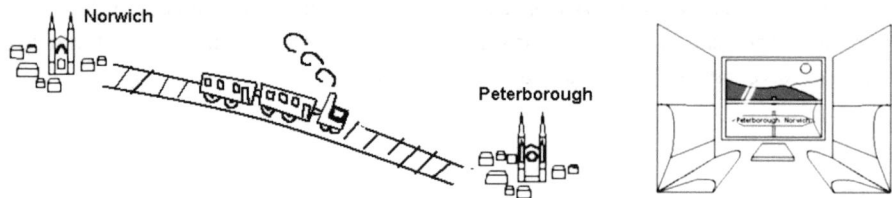

Figure 2.1. Maximal and restricted viewing frames

The use of the non-progressive in sentence (1a) makes us see in our mind the whole route and schedule of the train in the British railway network; it is a construal which provides a maximal viewing frame of a scene. The use of the progressive aspect in sentence (1b), by contrast, only lets us see part of the scene: it is a construal which provides a restricted viewing frame. The issue of different viewing frames evoked by forms of aspect will be taken up in Chapter 8 on situation types.

2.1.2 Generality vs specificity

The notions of generality and specificity relate to the degree of precision with which a scene is viewed or conceived. A distant view normally gives us a general impression of a scene while a close view or the use of a microscope or binoculars enables us to discern in-depth details. In cognition and language, taxonomic hierarchies reflect different levels of generality and specificity (see Chapter 1.2.1). By using higher-level categories, the speaker construes a situation in a more general way; by using lower-level categories, the speaker construes the situation in a more specific way. We will describe these construals as **generality** and **specificity** (also called *granularity*). In the examples under (2), cars are referred to by means of the most general term *vehicle* in (2a), the basic-level term *car* in (2b), the more specific term *Mitsubishi* in (2c), the even more specific term *Ferrari 612* in (2d), and the still more specific term *VW Convertible* in (2e), in which the specification is achieved by using the adjective *yellow*:

(2) a. Several *vehicles* collided on High Street last night.
 b. Most of the *cars* drove way too fast.
 c. A *Mitsubishi* struck another car.
 d. The *Ferrari 612* was driven by a drunk driver.
 e. The *yellow VW Convertible* was sandwiched between two lorries.

As with all construals, each of the alternative ways of expression has its own contextual meaning. Thus, the superordinate term *vehicle* in (2a) might be used by the Department for Transport or found in traffic reports. Basic-level terms such as *car* are used to describe situations in the most usual and common way as in (2b). Subordinate terms like *Mitsubishi* or *Ferrari 612* might be used by automobile experts like mechanics or car fanatics. The same thing may thus be "seen" in different detail by different people and in different situations.

As already pointed out in the Introduction, lexical categories tend to be used to make specific distinctions, while grammatical categories tend to express very general, or schematic, notions, such as those of present, past and future time. But grammar also allows us to distinguish different levels of specificity. For example, in Chapter 1.1.1 we distinguished between two specific types of nouns, count nouns and mass nouns. We will see in Chapter 4.2 how a thing's level of generality or specificity may be relevant for its expression as a count or mass noun.

2.1.3 Viewpoint

In visual perception I necessarily look at a scene from my **viewpoint** or vantage point, i.e. from the point where I, the observer, am positioned. In cognition we may also adopt another person's point of view. For example, the same newly published book may be announced as a *new release* or a *new arrival*. The difference between these two expressions resides in the different viewpoints adopted. In using the term *new release*, we take the publisher's point of view, whereas in using the term *new arrival* we take the bookseller's point of view. In this way, the publisher might say (3a), the bookseller (3b):

(3) a. *Publisher*: "Have we sent out the new *releases*?"
    b. *Bookseller*: "Have we displayed the new *arrivals*?"

We typically look at the world and describe it from our viewpoint. A good illustration of this is found in arguments such as in the following example, in which two children give their own versions of the same event:

(4) a. *Bill*: "Mum! Joe tripped me up with his foot."
    b. *Joe*: "No I didn't, Mum! Bill just tripped over my foot."

Some expressions have a built-in viewpoint on a situation. The motion verbs *come* and *go* as well as *bring* and *take* inherently adopt the speaker's viewpoint and designate motion towards or away from the speaker, respectively. Verbs like *come* and *go*, whose usage is dependent on the speech situation, are known as *deictic verbs* (Greek *deiktikos* from *deiknynai* 'show, point'; for deixis see Chapter 5.3.1). Compare the following sentences:

(5) a. My parents are *coming* to my graduation.
    b. I'm *going* to my sister's graduation.

If the motion is directed towards the speaker as the goal as in (5a), the speaker's viewpoint is typically described by using the verb *come*. If the speaker is not the goal of motion as in (5b), where motion is directed away from the speaker's location, the verb *go* is used. These two sentences thus take the speaker's point of view, i.e. the speaker is the *deictic centre*.

If the hearer is mentioned, we have two options. In using *go* as in sentence (6a), the speaker keeps her own viewpoint relative to the hearer. This construal sounds neutral, or under certain circumstances almost threatening, for example when I am known for misbehaving at official celebrations. The speaker may, however, also mentally switch her viewpoint as in sentence (6b).

(6) a. I'm *going* to *your* graduation.
    b. I'm *coming* to *your* graduation.

In using *come* in sentence (6b), the speaker takes the hearer's viewpoint, i.e. the hearer becomes the deictic centre. This is, of course, not possible in perception: we cannot take any other viewpoint but our own. In our conception of a scene and its expression in language, however, we may put ourselves into someone else's position, and we mainly do so because this has the effect of sounding sympathetic and polite.

The two construals of speaker-centred and hearer-centred viewpoints are sketched in Figure 2.2, where the circles printed in bold indicate the deictic centres and "S" and "H" speaker and hearer, respectively.

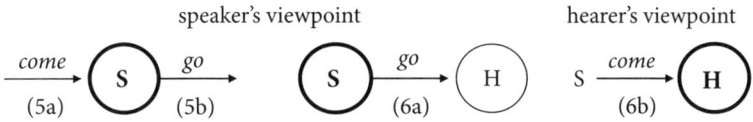

Figure 2.2. Construals of the deictic verbs *come* and *go*

Yet another type of viewpoint is typically found in authority relations such as between mother and child, doctor and patient, or policeman and driver. Parents, doctors or nurses often express their patronising sympathy towards their child or patient, and policemen may feign empathy with a traffic offender by identifying with her, i.e. by taking jointly their own and the hearer's viewpoint, as in the following examples:

(7) a. *Mother to child*: "And now *we*'re going to sleep."
    b. *Nurse to patient*: "*We* must take our tablets again."
    c. *Policeman to driver*: "*We* don't want to park here, do we?"

2.1.4 Objectivity vs subjectivity

We tend to believe that we see the world objectively as it is; at the same time, however, we are part of the world we perceive and inevitably bring in our own relation to the world. A speaker may also construe a scene more objectively or more subjectively. **Objectivity** refers to the construal of a scene as detached from the speaker, **subjectivity** refers to the construal of a scene in which the speaker is involved. Compare the following political statements:

(8) a. "The President is determined to fight a war on terrorism."
    b. "I will hunt down the terrorists."
    c. "There may still be weapons of mass destruction."

Sentence (8a) might be said by the spokesman of the White House, who describes the President's policy in objective terms: the speaker is not part of the scene described. The same wording might, however, also be used by the President in speaking of himself as *the President*. In doing so he gives an "objectified" view of himself as the institutionalised representative of the country. In using the speaker pronoun *I* in sentence (8b), the speaker includes himself as a participant of the scene described — in this respect the perspective is subjective. At the same time, however, the speaker describes his role like that of any other participant in the scene — in this respect the perspective is also objective. Sentence (8c) involves a maximally subjective perspective of the scene: the speaker gives his subjective view of the situation described without overtly mentioning himself. This is achieved by using the modal verb *may*, which expresses the speaker's assessment of the situation as being potential (see Chapter 10 for modality).

2.1.5 Mental scanning

In the same way that we may visually scan a mountain range, we may mentally scan a situation. **Mental scanning** refers to the construal of a situation with respect to its phasing in time. The sentences below illustrate two modes of mental scanning:

(9) a. The couple next door *have adopted* a baby.
 b. Another couple down the road want to *adopt* a baby, too.
 c. *Adopting* a baby can be a joyful experience.
 d. Older couples cannot apply for the *adoption* of a baby.

In sentence (9a), we mentally "scan" the whole process of adopting a child as it unfolds in time. This mode of viewing a situation in its successive phases is described as **sequential scanning**. In language, sequential scanning is manifested in the use of tense, i.e. any situation that is described by a tensed verb form involves sequential scanning. In sentence (9a), the present tense verb *have* prompts sequential scanning of the phases of the situation.

The other three sentences involve **summary scanning**. Summary scanning applies to a mode of viewing in which all the phases of a situation are activated simultaneously, i.e. the situation is seen as timeless. In language, summary scanning is manifested in the lack of tense, i.e. situations whose descriptions do not contain a tensed verb involve summary scanning. In (9b) and (9c), the timelessness of the infinitive *adopt* and the gerund *adopting* invokes summary scanning, in (9d), the timelessness of the noun *adoption* has this effect (see also Chapter 4.4.1).

2.1.6 Fictive motion

Fictive motion, also known as abstract, mental, virtual or subjective motion, is a special kind of mental scanning. It is the construal of a static scene in terms of motion. In physical motion, the moving object continually changes its location in time; in fictive motion, our eyes mentally scan an imaginary path, as in the following examples:

(10) a. The gate *leads into* the garden.
 b. The cliff *drops down* 600 feet.

Like physical motion, fictive motion involves directionality. In sentence (10a) we mentally follow the path from the gate into the garden, and in sentence (10b) our eyes roam from the top of the cliff down to the sea.

2.1.7 Windowing of attention

We cannot possibly attend to all the stimuli around us; our brain subconsciously selects those stimuli for our **attention** that are salient or important to us. A well-known case is the so-called "party phenomenon". At a party there may be several conversations going on around you at the same time; nevertheless you understand what the person you are talking to is saying or you might hear your name spoken by another person who you were not listening to. This is because you mentally filter out all the irrelevant bits of conversations. You may become aware of this mental on-line achievement when you listen to a tape-recording of such a conversation: all you hear is garbled snatches of conversation, and you can no longer focus on any one speaker. Focusing one's attention is a cognitive operation which "windows" our attention on selected elements of a scene and downplays other elements. In our linguistic construal of a scene we also window our attention on selected elements. The very fact that something is explicitly mentioned in discourse means that the speaker directs at least some attention to it. We might even say that all of language is an inventory of attention-directing devices.

To a certain extent language preselects the possibilities for our windowing of attention. For example, in sentence (1a), *This train goes from Norwich to Peterborough*, we window our attention on the whole route, including the starting-point and endpoint of the train journey. We may also window the final stretch of the journey to its endpoint, as in *This train goes to Peterborough*, or window the starting-point from the viewpoint of the goal, as in *This train comes from Norwich*. English does not, however, allow us to select the starting-point alone from another viewpoint, i.e. we cannot say **This train goes from Cambridge*.

A single scene may often be described in different ways by windowing our attention on particular elements of it. A well-known example which nicely illustrates this point is a commercial transaction. The 'commercial event' frame comprises the following elements: a buyer, a seller, goods, money, and the exchange of the goods and money. When a speaker wants to describe a commercial transaction, she can bring any of these elements into focus by using different verbs: *buy, sell, pay, spend, charge,* and *cost*. Each of these verbs evokes the 'commercial event' frame, but does so in different ways. By choosing a given verb, attention is focused on some of the elements of the frame, while others are downplayed, i.e. they are not mentioned at all or their inclusion is optional. In the following examples, the optional participants are indicated by parentheses.

(11) a. The cowboy *bought* a horse (from the sheriff) (for $500).
 b. The sheriff *sold* (the cowboy) the horse (for $500).
 c. The cowboy *paid* (the sheriff) $500 (for the horse).
 d. The cowboy *spent* $500 (on the horse).
 e. The sheriff *charged* (the cowboy) $500 (for the horse).
 f. The horse *cost* (the cowboy) $500.
 g. $500 *buys* (you) a good horse.

The main attention in each case is directed towards the entity expressed by the subject, and only secondarily towards the object entity. Here we can observe how the semantics of a verb interacts with the grammatical structure of a sentence. The following pair of sentences shows that the event is viewed from the perspective of the person who is expressed as the subject of the sentence:

(12) a. The cowboy *bought* the horse for a good price.
 b. The sheriff *sold* the horse for a good price.

What *a good price* means depends on the subject participant. For the buyer in (12a) it means paying very little money, whereas for the seller in (12b) it means getting a lot of money. Thus, if we want to draw attention to the buyer and secondarily to the goods, we use *buy* as in (11a) and (12a), if we want to draw attention to the seller and secondarily to the goods, we use *sell* as in (11b) and (12b). As illustrated in Figure 2.3, English has verbs for just about any of the relations which may hold between the four elements of a commercial event and which may thus become the focus of our attention.

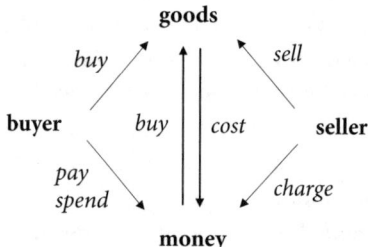

Figure 2.3. Elements and relations of the 'commercial event' frame

Still, there are constraints on the combinations of elements that can be windowed in a sentence. For example, the verbs *spend* and *cost* do not allow us to open a window for the seller — although a seller is of course conceptually present in a commercial event. Thus, we cannot say **The cowboy spent $500 to the sheriff* and **The horse cost $500 from the sheriff*.

2.1.8 Figure and ground

In focusing our attention on something, we automatically give prominence to some elements of a scene and downplay others. As gestalt psychology has demonstrated, we automatically arrange the elements of a visual scene into a salient **figure** and a non-salient background, or simply **ground**. When we look out of the window, we may see trees silhouetted against the sky. Here, the trees are the figure and the sky serves as the background. When a bird comes flying by and perches on the treetop, the bird becomes the figure and the tree recedes into the background. The figure tends to be more conspicuous, more mobile, better delineated and smaller in size than the ground. It therefore attracts our particular attention and interest.

Figure 2.4. Figure and ground

The principle of figure/ground alignment also applies to language. For example, just as there is a preferred way of seeing the spatial location of a bird relative to a treetop as shown in Figure 2.4, there is a preferred way of construing and describing this situation. Thus, it is more natural to say *The bird is on the treetop* than ?*The treetop is under the bird*. The former description conforms to our normal figure/ground alignment while the latter description might apply to a scene in which a big bird holds a little tree in its claws.

If the two entities are of about equal size and prominence, we may switch between figure and ground. The reversal of figure and ground is a well-known phenomenon in perception. For example, Figure 2.5 may be seen as a white vase at one moment and as two black faces in profile the next moment, but we never see both a vase and the two faces at the same time. Likewise, in language, we can speak of either *the cinema near the supermarket* or *the supermarket near the cinema*. Here either the supermarket or the cinema serves as the ground for locating the figure entity. English expresses the ground in such spatial situations by means of prepositional phrases.

Figure 2.5. Reversal of figure and ground

In the structure of a simple transitive sentence, the entity described by the subject is the figure, and the entity described by the direct object is the ground. In the commercial transaction scene considered in the sentences under (11), the human participant, i.e. the buyer or seller, almost always functions as the figure, while the non-human participant, i.e. the goods or the money, normally functions as the ground. If there are no humans that are windowed for attention, it is normally the goods that are typically more prominent than the money and are chosen to become the figure as in (11f), *The horse cost $500*. We may, however, reverse figure and ground to give more prominence to the money, and express it as the figure, as in (11g), *$500 buys a good horse*.

Likewise the events described in complex sentences also divide into figure and ground. Consider the following pair of sentences:

(13)   Figure   Ground
      a.   We got married   *after*   we had children. [$event_2 - event_1$]
      b.   We had children   *before*   we got married. [$event_1 - event_2$]

Both sentences describe the same sequence of events, which is indicated by the subscripted numbers with each event: we first had children and then got married. In general, the function of a subordinate clause is to provide the ground for the figure event, which is described by the main clause. In sentence (13a), having children is the ground event relative to which the figure event of getting married is located in time, while in sentence (13b), getting married is the ground event relative to which the figure event of having children is located in time. These sentences thus display figure/ground reversal and, concomitantly, mean different things. Our knowledge of the 'marriage and having children' frame allows us to read more than purely temporal meaning into sentence (13a): we tend to understand it in the sense that 'we got married *because* we had children'. Sentence (13b), by contrast, can only be interpreted in a temporal sense; a causal interpretation is ruled out because the figure event, our having children, occurred later than the ground event, our getting married, and thus cannot possibly have been caused by the latter.

2.1.9 Profiling

A special kind of figure/ground relation is the relation between an expression and its conceptual base. **Profiling** means designating a conceptualisation by means of a linguistic expression, and the **base** is the immediate larger conceptual content characterising it. For example, when we speak of *Sunday*, we profile this particular day relative to the base 'week'. Likewise, *elbow* profiles the joint between the upper and lower arm and evokes the conception 'arm' as its base, and *arm* profiles one of the two upper limbs and evokes the conception 'human body' as its base. We can test whether a conceptual unit is an immediate base or not by applying the test for *kind of-* or *part of-*relations (see Chapter 1.2). Thus, we may say *a human body has two arms, an arm has an elbow and a hand, a hand has five fingers, fingers have nails*, but not **a body has an elbow* or **an arm has five fingers*.

2.2 Mental spaces

> *At an exhibition of Franz Marc's paintings:*
> *Lady to Marc: "Horses aren't blue, are they?"*
> *Marc: "But this is not a horse. This is a painting."*

2.2.1 Building mental spaces

In speaking about things in the world we constantly evoke all kinds of knowledge associated with these conceptual units. These short-lived packages of knowledge evoked on-line in communication are known as **mental spaces**. Let us illustrate the notion of mental space by discussing the knowledge we utilise in understanding the following joke.

(14) *First Spaniard*:   "All Brazilians are either tarts or football players."
      Second Spaniard: "My wife is Brazilian."
      First Spaniard: "Which team does she play for?"

In analysing the joke, we see that the first sentence evokes the idea of the country of Brazil, which constitutes a frame. Once a mental space for the 'Brazil' frame has been opened in discourse, we can go into any of its elements and open sub-spaces typically associated with countries such as its culture, its history, its inhabitants, its stereotypical characteristics such as a craze for football, etc. In the case of the joke, the inhabitants of Brazil are characterised by no more than two properties. We know that this is a gross oversimplification of reality and hence activate the mental sub-space of national stereotypes. The second Spaniard exploits the stereotype space by forcing the first Spaniard to apply his oversimplified view to his Brazilian wife. The normal reaction to expect from the first Spaniard would be an apology or a modification of his extreme view, for example by saying, "Oh, I didn't mean it seriously, but many people are like this." In this case he would have abandoned the claim to absolute validity and adopted a space of relative validity. In the given reply, however, the first Spaniard sticks to the oversimplified stereotype space built up in his first sentence: of the two options left to characterise a Brazilian he can of course, for reasons of politeness, only choose the second one.

Mental spaces are typically evoked in communication by so-called **space-builders**. Expressions such as *I think* and *may*, as in *This may be true*, build a potentiality space, temporal adjuncts such as *last week* or *recently* open a time space, conditional clauses such as *If you were here* create a counterfactual space, etc. Let us, by way of illustration, analyse the space-builders used in the following little piece of discourse:

(15) a. On April 15, 1912, the "Titanic" sank on her maiden voyage.
 b. If the ship had slowed down, it would not have sunk.
 c. Such catastrophes *could* also happen in our times.

In sentence (15a), the prepositional phrase *on April 15, 1912*, seen from the present time, builds up the factual historical space for the sinking of the luxury passenger liner; the conditional conjunction *if* and the past perfect in (15b) prompt a counterfactual space, i.e. the opposite of what actually happened; and the modal verb *could* in (15c) opens a potentiality space (see Chapter 10). These mental spaces are specially marked in language. When we talk about things in reality, which we do most of the time, we do not as a rule need to inform the hearer about this explicitly by using "reality space-builders". This is the case in a sentence such as (16):

(16) *Monica Lewinsky to Attorney*:
 "I've never had sex with the President."

Here we are dealing with a mental space constituting a case of extreme reality, which in legal terms is described as affidavit, i.e. 'a declaration under oath'. As a witness, the ex-intern Monica Lewinsky is committed to speaking the truth and cannot evade this obligation. This example illustrates another interesting instance of space-building in the expression *the President* rather than, say, *Bill Clinton*. The use of the noun phrase *the President* evokes a public frame and opens a corresponding space of the duties and functions associated with a head of state. The use of the expression *having sex* evokes a private, even intimate frame and opens such a mental space, and hence is in conflict with the public head-of-state space. The two spaces, i.e. the public and private ones, are conceptually "blended" and give this sentence its special delicate flavour.

2.2.2 Conceptual blending

The integration of two or more spaces into a "blended space" is known as **conceptual blending**. A blended space inherits partial structure from its input spaces and has emergent meaning of its own. Blending is well-known as a word formation process. For example, the word *brunch* is morphologically composed of *breakfast* and *lunch*. Semantically, certain elements of the input spaces 'breakfast' and 'lunch' are projected into the blended space and some additional meanings emerge. For instance, a brunch is typically served in a restaurant and may include alcoholic drinks such as champagne.

Conceptual blending is also found in grammar. Sentence (17) illustrates a syntactic blend, which might be graphically represented as in Figure 2.6:

(17) In France, a sexual affair would not have harmed Clinton.

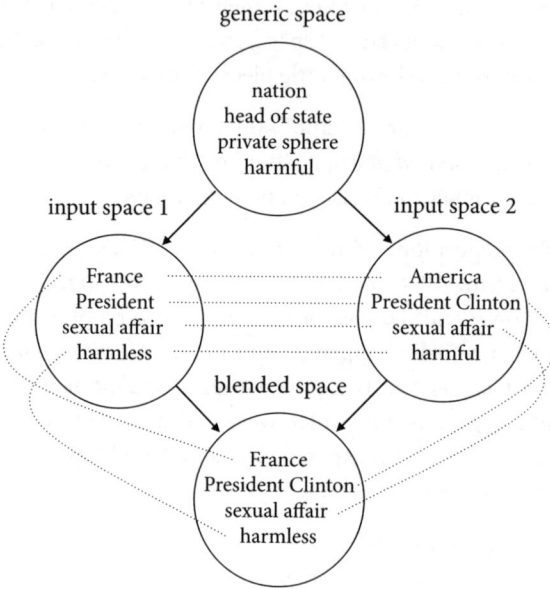

Figure 2.6. Conceptual blending

The two input spaces share a number of properties which establish the generic space. Input space 1 is opened by the space-builders *in France* and *would not*. In this counterfactual space of France, an unnamed president has a putative sexual affair, which is judged to be harmless because in France the two spheres are strictly kept separate. Input space 2 is opened by the space-builders *Clinton, sexual affair* and *harmed*. In this reality space of the United States, former President Clinton had a sexual affair, which in the context of Anglo-American culture was and is considered harmful for a public figure. In the blended space, President Clinton is seen as the President of France and had a sexual affair which, however, was evaluated as harmless. This new blended space is, of course, a counterfactual one.

We can now also analyse fictive motion, which we discussed in 2.1.6, in terms of conceptual blending. Thus, in sentence (10b), *The cliff drops down 600 feet*, the verb *drop* evokes a motion space while the situation described evokes a static space. The incompatibility of the two input spaces is resolved in the blended space, where a static scene is motional. Psychological studies on people's eye movement have, in fact, shown that we mentally simulate motion when we process fictive motion sentences.

2.3 Inferences

Thus far we have mainly focused on mental operations performed by the speaker. This section will also consider the hearer's mental contribution in comprehending a communicative act. Most people assume that the hearer simply "decodes" the message sent to him by the speaker. In this naive view of communication, the hearer would only have to extract the meaning of the words transmitted to her by the speaker. The study of language in interaction, which is known as the field of pragmatics, has shown that speakers in everyday discourse usually mean more than they actually say, and sometimes even different things. In this case the hearer has to "infer" the information which the speaker intended to convey.

In logic, the notion of **inference** applies to valid conclusions drawn from a set of premises by means of deductive reasoning. An example of deductive inference was given under (14): The premises that "all Brazilians are either tarts or football players" and that "the second Spaniard's wife is a football player" (which follows from the question "Which team does she play for?") lead to the logical conclusion that she is not a tart.

2.3.1 Conversational implicatures

Most inferences we encounter in everyday conversation are, however, different from logical inferences. The hearer needs to recover the assumptions underlying the speaker's utterance and makes use of her background knowledge and contextual cues available in the speech situation. Let us first consider some examples, often used as standard sayings:

(18) a. Boys will be boys.
  b. Business is business.

From a logical point of view, these statements are tautologies, i.e. they are necessarily true and hence uninformative: what else should boys be but boys and business be but business? But people don't expect speakers just to spout meaningless sentences, so they will search for some meaning. In the two examples of (18) this meaning belongs to the common stock of folk wisdom, but it is important to see how it comes about. In sentence (18a), our knowledge of boys and their stereotypical behaviour probably makes us think of *boys* as unruly, loud and intemperate; likewise, our stereotypical knowledge of the business world makes us understand *business* in sentence (18b) as being competitive and uncompromising or as financially rewarding. We thus understand such "conversational tautologies" by using metonymical reasoning: a person or thing is used to stand for a stereotypical attribute. Which particular attribute or attributes we infer largely depends on the context: stereotypical business may be seen in a positive or negative way; boys, on the other hand, are almost exclusively associated with a negative stereotype. Of course, these interpretations are standard ones, typically linked with sayings.

In everyday communication, the inferences drawn by the hearer are not necessarily valid conclusions, but only plausible guesses. They normally "enrich" the literal information conveyed by the utterance. Let us illustrate this point by using the following examples.

(19) a. Have you read *The Times*?
b. Have you read *Pride and Prejudice*?

The hearer is likely to understand question (19a) as asking whether I have read *The Times* today, while question (19b) is likely to be asking whether I have read *Pride and Prejudice* at all, at whatever time. The enriched inferences drawn about the time of reading are, of course, based on our encyclopaedic knowledge of newspapers and books. This knowledge also allows the listener to draw further inferences: newspapers are read to be informed about current events; novels are read for pleasure or exams.

The plausible inferences which the hearer feels "invited" to draw about the intended meaning of an utterance are known as **conversational implicatures**. The notion of implicature thus relates to implicitly communicated information, which is nevertheless as much part of our comprehension as explicitly stated information. This becomes especially clear in misunderstandings. Consider the following dialogue at a hotel reception desk:

(20) a. *Visitor*: "How much is a king-size room?"
b. *Receptionist*: "I'm sorry, we're completely booked up."
c. *Visitor*: "No, I didn't want a room; I was just asking the price."

The visitor in (20a) explicitly asks about the price of a type of hotel room. However, the receptionist in (20b) gives an answer not to the literal question but to its supposedly implicated meaning, i.e. the receptionist assumes that the visitor's question is aimed at more than just the price. His experience at the reception desk tells him that people routinely ask the price of a hotel room before they book it because the price is a relevant criterion for deciding whether to take it. To the receptionist, the visitor's question about the price in (20a) therefore invites the implicature that she intends to stay in the hotel provided the price is reasonable. The receptionist's assumptions turn out to be wrong and, to avoid miscommunication, the visitor then rejects the implicature of wanting to book the room by clarifying her intended meaning in (20c).

The dialogue above illustrates fundamental aspects of communication. A first aspect is a cognitive one: any utterance evokes a variety of assumptions which yield "contextual effects". Contextual effects are created by conceptual frames as well as personal and situational aspects. In the above inquiry about the hotel room price, an adequate contextual effect is the customer's booking a room. If the same question had been asked by the hotel manager, an adequate contextual effect might be that the room is offered too cheaply and the price should be raised.

A second aspect is a communicative one: the hearer assumes that the wording chosen optimally expresses the speaker's communicative intention in a given communicative situation and does not require any unnecessary processing effort. An act of communication that conforms to these two aspects is said to be optimally relevant: it creates assumptions of adequate contextual effects and assumptions about a minimally necessary processing effort. This important principle of human communication has been described as the **principle of relevance**, and the theoretical framework elaborating this principle is known as relevance theory.

The principle of relevance allows us to understand why implicated meanings can be communicated. The wording used to express an idea implicitly may create the same, or at least similar, contextual effects as an explicit wording. At the same time, it has the advantage of requiring less processing effort than the wording necessary to express the full, explicated meaning. Thus, the tautological statement in (18a), *Boys will be boys*, is assumed to be a relevant piece of information and, moreover, creates adequate contextual effects with a minimum of wording. Similarly, asking the price of an object may be enough wording to show that the speaker intends to buy the object. The principle of relevance implies that we do not need to use direct and literal wordings in order to express our intentions but can make use of shortcuts all the time. Indirectness is, in fact, the rule rather than the exception in everyday communication. It is when people want to be taken literally that they often need to say so. For example, in order to be understood literally, i.e. without any implicatures allowed, our visitor in (20a) might have said something like: "Just for the sake of curiosity, what's the price for a king-size room?"

Implicatures are thus balancing acts between achieving maximal contextual effects and requiring minimal processing effort. Since implicatures are only based on assumptions, it is not surprising that the hearer may fail to recover the speaker's intended meaning and that miscommunication results as in (20b). An important characteristic of conversational implicatures is, therefore, that they can be rejected, or "cancelled", as in (20c).

Implicatures that are so often made that we draw them more or less routinely may eventually become conventionalised, a phenomenon that is known as *pragmatic strengthening*. For example, the formula *can/could you* ... as in *Could you keep an eye on my luggage?* literally means 'are you able to do X'. However, this question invites the implicature 'will you keep an eye on my luggage'. This implicated meaning has become conventionalised to such an extent that *could you* is almost exclusively understood in the sense of a polite request.

2.3.2 Grammaticalisation

The extensions of the lexical meanings of words or expressions induced by implicature may result in new conventionalised grammatical forms and meanings. Such linguistic changes are described as **grammaticalisation**. The following examples illustrate processes of grammaticalisation in which the lexical sources are still recognisable:

(21) a. *Supposing* you won the big prize, what would you do?
b. Dickens died in 1870 *following* a collapse.

The present participle *supposing* in (21a) has adopted the grammatical sense of condition; its meaning thus corresponds to that of the subordinating conjunction *if*. Its grammaticalisation is motivated by implicature: something that I suppose invites the implicature that this is also hypothetical. However, this is not always the case; for example, *I suppose you're right* expresses my grudging agreement.

The present participle *following* in (21b) has adopted the grammatical sense of causation, i.e. 'because of (his collapse)'. The implicature that gave rise to this meaning relates to the common observation that an event that follows another event in time, like the case of having children and marrying afterwards in (13a), is often caused by this event. This principle was already known in antiquity: *post hoc, ergo propter hoc* 'after that, therefore because of that'.

The original lexical sources of many grammaticised forms are no longer transparent. To name just a few examples: the preposition *between* derives from 'by + two', the modal verb *can* goes back to a lexical verb meaning 'know', the indefinite article *a(n)* evolved from the numeral *one*, and the conjunction *that* has developed from the demonstrative pronoun *that*. In the process of grammaticalisation, the original lexical meanings and the phonological forms tend to be reduced, or "bleached". Thus, in the development of *a(n)*, the numeral meaning has been bleached and the quality of the vowel has been reduced to a schwa.

Also with already existing grammatical forms, further steps of grammaticalisation may occur. For example, expressions denoting notions of time may give rise to various implicated meanings. Thus, the conjunctions *since, as soon as* and *while* originally had purely temporal meanings and have adopted the meanings of 'reason', 'condition', and 'contrast', respectively:

(22) a. *Since* you're here, you'd better go and see your tutor.
b. We will send you the tickets *as soon as* we receive your payment.
c. I do all the work *while* you do nothing.

Since in (22a) means much the same as *because* due to the principle *post hoc, ergo propter hoc*, which we already mentioned above. This principle also accounts for the implicature of a condition in *as soon as* in (22b): you first have to pay and then the tickets will be sent. The implicature invited by *while* in (22c) may be explained as follows. Stating that two situations simply occur at the same time is not a highly relevant piece of information. We therefore look for a more relevant aspect of meaning which the simultaneity of two situations may give rise to. A possible meaning that is optimally relevant here is that of contrast: 'I do all the work whereas you do nothing'. These examples of grammaticalisation show that the same mental operations are at work both in actual communication and in historical changes.

2.4 Summary

This chapter presented three types of cognitive operation that govern successful communication: the construal of one's thoughts in speaking, the building of mental spaces in communication, and the drawing of inferences.

The notion of **construal** relates to the fact that, as a rule, there are different ways of imagining and portraying a situation but only one of these alternatives is chosen. We distinguished nine dimensions of construal. Six of these dimensions relate to viewing operations: the notion of **viewing frame** refers to the scene, or part of a scene, which the speaker and hearer perceive or conceive; the distinction between **generality** and **specificity** applies to the construal of a situation in a more general or more specific way; the notion of **viewpoint** refers to the speaker's point of view of a scene; the distinction between **objectivity** and **subjectivity** refers to the extent to which the conceptualiser takes part in the scene described; the notion of **mental scanning** refers to the construal of a situation in its phasing in time; and the notion of **fictive motion** refers to the construal of a static scene as motional. Three dimensions of construal relate to prominence. Windowing of **attention** refers to the speaker's focusing on selected aspects of a scene, **figure** and **ground** refer to the division of a scene into salient and non-salient elements, and **profiling** refers to the speaker's designating a conceptual and linguistic unit, e.g. *elbow*, thereby implying its **base**, i.e. 'arm'.

Any situation described in discourse evokes short-lived knowledge structures called **mental spaces**. Many expressions of language such as *I believe...* specifically function as **space-builders** in that they serve to open certain mental spaces. Mental spaces may be conceptually integrated and give rise to blended spaces, such as the **blending** of 'brunch' from the input spaces 'breakfast' and 'lunch'.

A mental operation that is primarily associated with the hearer's contribution is that of drawing **inferences**. Inferences about the speaker's intended meanings which the hearer feels invited to draw are known as **conversational implicatures**. As a rule, the hearer reads more meaning into an act of communication than it literally conveys. The hearer does so by appealing to the **principle of relevance**, according to which an optimal act of communication creates adequate contextual effects for a minimum of processing effort. Implicatures arise in acts of communication and may eventually become conventionalised. The historical process of deriving grammatical forms and meanings from lexical forms by conventionalised implicature is known as **grammaticalisation**.

Further Reading

The notion of construal is dealt with at various places in Langacker's publications, in Talmy (1988b/2000), and in Ungerer & Schmid (²2006). The notions of objectivity and subjectivity are, in a slightly different way, discussed in Langacker (1990, 2002). The notion of fictive motion is discussed in Langacker (1991b), Talmy (1996b/2000), Fauconnier (1997), Matlock (2004a, 2004b), and Matlock, Ramscar & Boroditsky (2005). The notion of windowing of attention in language has been developed in Talmy (1996a/2000), the commercial event frame has been analysed by Fillmore (e.g. 1977), Lawler (1989), and Croft *et al.* (2001), and the impact of figure and ground in language is demonstrated in Talmy (1978/2000), Wallace (1982) and Hayase (1997).

The theory of mental spaces and conceptual blending was first developed in Fauconnier (1985) and refined in Fauconnier & Sweetser, eds. (1996), Fauconnier & Turner (1996), Fauconnier (1997), and Fauconnier & Turner (2002).

One of the first studies on inferring is provided by the psychologist Herbert Clark (1977). The notion of conversational implicature was first developed by the language philosopher Grice (1975). The interesting issue of "conversational tautologies" is discussed in Wierzbicka (1991: Ch. 10), Gibbs (1994: Ch. 7), and Miki (1996). A fully fledged theory of relevance in communication is presented in Sperber & Wilson's important monograph *Relevance* (1986) and in Blakemore (1992). Recent papers on relevance theory are collected in Carston & Uchida, eds. (1998) and Rouchota & Jucker, eds. (1998). Further references are found in Yus, http://www.ua.es/dfing/rt.htm.

Studies on various aspects of grammaticalisation are found in Heine, Claudi & Hünnemeyer (1991), Hopper & Traugott (²2003), Traugott & Heine, eds. (1993), Heine & Kuteva (2002), and Traugott & Dasher (2002).

Study questions

1. Identify the dimensions of construal in the following sentences.
    a. The Eiffel Tower is in front of you.
    b. Europe is no longer cut off thanks to the Channel Tunnel.
    c. The Rocky Mountains flew by.
    d. Mother to son: "Don't lie to your mother!"
    e. The sun disappeared behind the clouds.
    f. I'm coming with you.
    g. Doctor to patient: "Now we're taking these pink tablets for the night."
    h. The road runs past the factory, continues through the tunnel and goes on to London.
    i. A pedestrian hit me and went under my car.
    j. Sign in public buses in New York City: "If you see something, do something."

2. Explain the following jokes in terms of conceptual blending. For the first it is important to know that Descartes' philosophy is based on the rationalist principle *Cogito, ergo sum* 'I think, therefore I exist'.

a. Descartes walks into a bar, orders a martini. He drinks it down.
   The bartender says, "Another?"
   Descartes replies, "I think not," and disappears.
b. Two goats are out behind a movie studio eating old movie film.
   One goat says to the other, "Pretty good, huh?"
   The second goat says, "Yeah, but it's not as good as the book."
c. Two Inuit fishermen sitting in a kayak were chilly; but when they lit a fire in the craft, it sank, proving that you can't have your kayak and heat it.

3. What conversational implicatures do the following utterances invite?
   a. "Where can I wash my hands?"
   b. A caller asking a child answering the phone: "Is your daddy there?"
   c. "The tea burnt my tongue."
   d. "What academic degree do you have?" — "I have an MA."
   e. "If you come home late, the front door will be locked."
   f. "Are you going to Chomsky's lecture?" — "I have to finish my paper."
   g. "I ate some of the biscuits."

4. Explain the following dialogue in terms of implicature:
   a. Cessna: "Jones tower, Cessna 12345, student pilot, I am out of fuel."
      Tower: "Roger Cessna 12345, reduce airspeed to best glide!! Do you have the airfield in sight??!!"
      Cessna: "Uh … tower, I am on the south ramp. I just want to know where the fuel truck is."
   b. Farmer Joe's cow is ill. He asks his neighbour, "What did you give your cow when she was sick?" — "Soda water."
      Farmer Joe gives his cow soda water, and after three days, the cow dies. He says to his neighbour, "The cow died after three days," and the neighbour says, "Mine too."

Chapter 3

From thought to language

Cognitive grammar

> 3.0 Overview
> 3.1 Conceptual and linguistic structure: Things, relations and conceptual cores
> 3.2 Situations: Sentences
> 3.3 Combining situations: Independent and complex sentences
> 3.4 Summary

3.0   Overview

This chapter aims to show how units of thought relate to language. At the level of thought, we need no more than two basic types of conceptual units: things and relations. **Things** are autonomous conceptual units that are typically expressed as nouns; **relations** are dependent conceptual units that are typically expressed as verbs and adjectives. A relation and things combine to form a **conceptual core** and ultimately a **situation**. The linguistic counterpart of a conceptual situation is the **sentence**, the basic independent unit of grammar. The chapter will also look at the ways in which situations are combined and expressed either as independent sentences or as **complex sentences**.

3.1   Conceptual and linguistic structure: Things, relations and conceptual cores

> *Concepts are the coinage of thought.*
> (Johnson-Laird & Wason, 1977)

3.1.1   Things and relations

The most fundamental distinction which the grammar of English or any other language makes is the distinction between the two word classes of nouns (e.g. *bicycle*) and verbs (e.g.

ride). It is no coincidence that these two basic grammatical categories are found in every language: they reflect our structuring of the world as we experience it into two basic types of conceptual units: things and relations.

For lack of a better name we will use the term **thing** for a conceptual unit that is expressed in language as a noun. Things appear in our conceptual world as autonomous, or independent, conceptual units that have a certain stability in space and time. The most prototypical things in our experiential world relate to physical objects such as cows and computers. Less prototypical things are abstract units such as illnesses and joy.

In our world of thought, things are usually related to other conceptual units. For example, I may think of a bicycle as the vehicle I am riding, as an object that always needs to be fixed, as a birthday present I want to buy for my son, etc. Situations such as these are held together by relations such as 'ride', 'fix', 'buy', etc. **Relations** are dependent conceptual units that link two or more things and tend to be short-lived, i.e. have a lower degree of time stability than things. Relations are expressed as verbs, adjectives, adverbs, prepositions, and conjunctions.

We might assume that these two types of conceptual units, i.e. things and relations, neatly classify all our categories, but this is an illusion. In fact, not only is the distinction between things and relations blurred, but we may also conceptually switch from things to relations and from relations to things. Thus, the stable things 'iron' and 'microwave oven' may be conceptually re-categorised as relations and expressed as verbs, as in *Dad ironed his shirt* and *Mum micro-waved the chicken*. In this way, we have created new relational categories: 'press clothes with a hot iron' and 'cook in a microwave oven', respectively. Conversely, the short-lived relational units 'cut' and 'explode' may be re-categorised as more or less stable things and expressed as the nouns (*a*) *cut* and (*an*) *explosion*. By expressing a relational concept as a noun, we can quantify it, as in *many explosions*, or qualify it, as in *a gigantic explosion*.

The flexibility between things and relations can also be seen in the multifunctional use of the word *thing* itself: we describe not only physical objects as *things*, but also abstract entities such as an issue, an experience, an action, a state of affairs, a thought, etc., as illustrated in the following examples.

(1) a. Let's not make a big *thing* out of it. [*issue*]
    b. Flying is an amazing *thing*. [*experience*]
    c. Do the wrong *thing* and you're a dead man. [*action*]
    d. How are *things* today? [*state of affairs*]
    e. I have *nothing* to tell you. [*thought*]

3.1.2 Conceptual cores

Both things and relations are conceptually needed to form and express our thoughts. We will describe the conceptual unit that consists of a relation and things related by it as a conceptual core. Such conceptual cores are illustrated in examples (2a-c). Example (2d), however, shows that conceptual cores may, in their turn, also be composed of other conceptual cores, which are expressed as clauses. We therefore describe the conceptual units related more generally as **conceptual entities**. We can now define a **conceptual core** as a relation combined with two or more conceptual entities participating in it.

(2) a. Joe *kicked* the garbage can.
 b. Jane *is fond of* Reggae music.
 c. the goldfish *in* the pond
 d. Joe invited Jane *because* he likes her.

Grammatically, the four examples under (2) involve different kinds of relational expressions: in (2a) it is a verb, in (2b) an adjective (together with the copula *is* and the preposition *of*), in (2c) a preposition, and in (2d) a conjunction. Conceptually, these different structures are, however, on a par: the relational expressions describe conceptual relations that hold between entities within a conceptual core. The structure of the conceptual core is not random, but is based on the principle of figure and ground: one entity in a conceptual core is the figure, while the other serves as the ground. The order of figure and ground is determined by the nature of the relation. Thus, in sentence (2a), *Joe* is the figure entity and *the garbage can* the ground entity. The conceptual structure underlying the four different grammatical constructions under (2) is illustrated in Table 3.1.

Table 3.1. Conceptual cores with two explicitly expressed conceptual entities

	figure entity	relation	ground entity
(a)	Joe	kicked	the garbage can.
(b)	Jane	is fond of	Reggae music.
(c)	the goldfish	in	the pond
(d)	Joe invited Jane	because	he likes her.

The relations here clearly involve two conceptual entities. In the structure of language, the relational expressions also require two linguistic entities. If a second conceptual entity, i.e. the ground, is not expressed, the linguistic structure often becomes ungrammatical: **Joe kicked*; **Jane is fond of*; **the goldfish in*; **Joe invited Jane because*.

There are, of course, thousands of examples in which only one conceptual entity, the figure of a conceptual core, is expressed in the structure of language. This is typically the case with adjectives as in *Sylvia is tall* and intransitive verbs as in *The baby is sleeping*. In these examples only one conceptual entity is expressed: *Sylvia* and *the baby*. In accordance with our definition of a conceptual core as consisting of a relation with two or more conceptual entities participating in it, there should also be a second conceptual entity which, however, does not surface in language. What is this entity that stands for the ground and why can it remain implicit?

3.1.3 Implicit ground entities in conceptual cores

Let us first consider adjectives and ask ourselves what they mean in sentences such as:

(3) Our daughter Sylvia is *tall*.

Is there a ground entity in (3) that relates to the adjective *tall*? Here we can find the ground in the domain of height relative to a certain type of people, i.e. relative to specific frames. We can make such a frame explicit by adding a phrase with *for*: *Our daughter Sylvia is tall for a young girl*. Even if such a frame is not explicitly mentioned, it is nevertheless part of our understanding. Thanks to our 'human person' frame we know how tall people on average are at a certain age, and thanks to our 'young girl' frame we know that the height of a young girl who is described as tall is above this implicit norm on a scale of height. As Figure 3.1 shows, a second entity, the 'young girl' frame, is conceptually present and invoked as a ground in our understanding of the meaning of the property *tall*.

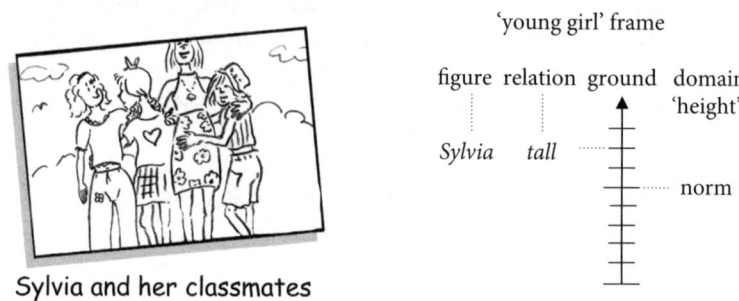

Figure 3.1. Conceptual core underlying *Sylvia is tall*

We will now, as another challenge, examine intransitive verbs, i.e. verbs that do not require a ground to be expressed as a second entity. We need to distinguish between two groups of intransitive verbs: those that can be used both transitively and intransitively such as *smoke*, *drink*, and *bite*, and those that are inherently intransitive such as *swim*, *laugh*, and *cry*.

We will first look at the group of verbs that can be used both transitively and intransitively, and consider the verbs *drink* and *bite*. The verb *drink* can be freely used transitively, as in (4a), and intransitively, as in (4b) and (4c):

(4) a. Lizzy drank a milkshake. [*past event*]
    b. Lizzy drank. [*past habit*]
    c. Lizzy drinks. [*present habit*]

The transitive sentence (4a) describes an actually occurring event of Lizzy drinking a milkshake in the past. In the intransitive usage of *drink* in (4b) and (4c), the beverage drunk remains implicit. We, of course, know that we are not talking about *any* beverage such as a milkshake or a cup of coffee but about alcoholic drinks. Moreover, we understand the sentences to mean that Lizzy drinks alcohol habitually. Sentence (4b) describes Lizzy's drinking habit in the past, which she has presumably stopped, while sentence (4c) describes her present drinking habit. The habitual sentences (4b) and (4c) thus invoke 'alcoholic drinks' as the second conceptual entity. A person's habitual behaviour is comparable to a stable property such as 'be tall', which we discussed above.

Not all transitive verbs behave like *drink* when they are used intransitively. Compare the two following transitive and intransitive usages of the verb *bite*. *Bite* behaves like *drink* in permitting the transitive use (5a) and the intransitive use in the simple present (5c), but its intransitive use in the past (5b) is ruled out.

(5) a. Our dog bit the postman.   [*past event*]
     b. ?Our dog bit.   [*past event?, past habit?*]
     c. Our dog bites.   [*present habit*]

Conceptually, the event of a dog's biting requires an object bitten. There are many possible objects a dog may bite, and they all relate to a particular domain: a dog's biting of bones relates to the 'eating' domain, a dog's biting of a cat relates to the 'fighting' domain, a dog's biting of a burglar relates to the 'guarding' domain, and a dog's biting of ordinary people such as the postman in (5a) relates to the 'aggression' domain. As in the situation of people's drinking habits, we can omit the object in the sentence structure when we are talking about habitual behaviour, as in sentence (5c), *Our dog bites*. The sentence is unequivocally understood in the sense of 'our dog bites people'. This meaning is determined by the principle of relevance: the domain that gives the most noteworthy contextual effects in speaking about a dog biting is the domain of 'aggression towards humans'. Everybody has had this scary experience. Saying things like ?*Our dog bites people* explicitly would therefore not be very informative and may even sound strange.

We still need to explain why sentence (5b), ?*Our dog bit*, sounds odd whereas sentence (4b), *Lizzy drank*, sounds fine. As in the drinking situation, the grammar forces us to see the past situation described by *Our dog bit* as a habit which no longer holds. Our knowledge of the world tells us that people can kick their habits, but animals cannot: their behaviour is instinctual and hence unalterable. We therefore normally only speak of an animal's instinctual behaviour in the present tense. If we described it in the past tense, the only interpretation of *Our dog bit* would be that the dog has died.

Let us now examine inherently intransitive verbs, such as *swim*. Grammatically, intransitive verbs do not take a direct object; at the conceptual level, however, they also require a ground entity.

(6) a. Peggy swam across the lake.   [*past event*]
     b. Peggy swam.   [*past habit*]
     c. Peggy swims.   [*present habit*]
     d. Peggy is/was swimming.   [*present/past event in progress*]

Sentence (6a) describes a past event in which the ground entity is explicitly mentioned: *across the lake*. Sentences (6b) describes a past habit of Peggy's which she has probably stopped, and sentence (6c) describes a present habit. As with Lizzy's habit of drinking in (4b), we readily supply a second conceptual entity with Peggy's habit of swimming: she swims, or used to swim, in water in which people normally swim, as in pools or in the sea. Moreover, we assume that she probably swims, or used to swim, for fun or for sport.

Interestingly, we can also omit the second conceptual entity when we use the progressive aspect, as in (6d), *Peggy is swimming* or *Peggy was swimming*. The progressive sentences do not describe habits but specific events of swimming. As with habitual swimming, we "know" that Peggy is or was not swimming in a giant bath tub or in a beer tank but in a pool or in the sea. The progressive aspect thus behaves just like the habitual present or past: it allows us to suppress a second conceptual entity that is routinely associated with the event described by the verb. With habits this is possible because they reoccur and gain the status of a property; with the progressive aspect this is possible because its restricted viewing frame makes us focus on the progression of an event, thereby defocusing other parts of the scene (for viewing frames see Chapters 2.1.1 and 8.1.2). The following examples show that this phenomenon applies widely. Not only intransitive sentences such as (7a) and (7b), but also transitive sentences such as (7c), which can hardly be said in the simple present, are fully grammatical in the progressive aspect:

(7)   *Progressive*   *Non-progressive*
  a. Mark is eating.   a'. ʾMark eats.
  b. Phil is kissing.   b'. ʾPhil kisses.
  c. The dog is biting a bone.   c'. ʾThe dog bites a bone.

Table 3.2 summarises the observations made in this section about ground entities that are present in the conceptual core but suppressed in the sentence structure. The implicit ground entity with adjectives and habitual situations is dependent on a domain.

Table 3.2. Conceptual cores with one implicit ground entity

	figure entity	relation	implicit ground entity
(a)	Our daughter	is tall.	above norm; *domain*: people's height
(b)	Lizzy	drinks.	'alcoholic drinks'; *domain*: habitual behaviour
(c)	Our dog	bites.	'humans'; *domain*: dogs' instinctual behaviour
(d)	Peggy	swims.	'in water'; *domain*: fun or sports
(e)	Peggy	is swimming.	'in water'; *domain*: fun or sports

All these examples are meant to show that conceptual and linguistic structure do not neatly match. On the one hand, conceptual structure can make do with just two basic types of conceptual units, relations and entities, while language provides a great diversity of linguistic categories and ways of combining them. On the other hand, conceptual structure typically contains entities which do not surface in linguistic structure, i.e. language tends to underspecify.

3.2 Situations: Sentences

Thus far we have looked at conceptual cores without linking them to other conceptual units. The conceptual core is at the heart of any situation. The term **situation** is understood here in the sense of events that happen or states that things are in. Thus, *Peggy is swimming* describes a typical event and *Peggy is happy* a typical state. However, the distinction between events and states is not always clear-cut. In the preceding section, we came across examples of habitual behaviour as in *Peggy swims*, which are midway between events and states and which, as we will see in Chapter 8, are categorised in English as states.

3.2.1 Conceptual core: Grammatical core

Let us illustrate the notions of conceptual core and its grammatical equivalent by way of the following example:

(8) My fiancé bought the wedding rings.

This sentence expresses a situation whose conceptual core consists of the relation 'buy' and the two conceptual entities 'fiancé' and 'wedding rings'. Two such entities are required with the relation 'buy', and they play a specific role in the conceptual core: 'fiancé' as the buyer plays the role of an "agent" and 'wedding rings' as the goods bought plays the role of an object — which we will later refer to as "theme" (Chapter 11). Conceptual entities which form part of the conceptual core are known as **participants**. Participants have a privileged status in a situation.

In its grammatical structure, this sentence consists of several syntactic units. The basic grammatical tools needed to analyse the structure of a sentence are the following notions, most of which are known from traditional grammar:

- **noun phrase**, also described as **nominal** (*my fiancé* and *the wedding rings*): a grammatical unit that denotes an instance of a thing or other entity in a situation (for the notion 'instance' see Chapter 4.1.1);
- **predicate** (*buy*): the grammatical unit of a sentence (a verb or copula with an adjective) that denotes a relation in a situation and states something about the subject participant;
- **subject** (*my fiancé*): the noun phrase of a sentence that denotes the primary participant, or figure, in a situation, from whose perspective the situation is viewed (see Chapter 2.1.7);
- **object** (*the wedding rings*): the noun phrase within a verb phrase that denotes the secondary participant, or ground, in a situation;
- **complement**: the subject, object and any other obligatory grammatical unit of a sentence other than the predicate;
- **verb phrase** (*buy the wedding rings*): the part of a sentence that includes the predicate and complements;

- **adjunct** (*at Tiffany's*): an optional grammatical unit within the structure of a sentence;
- **grammatical core** (*my fiancé — bought — the wedding rings*): the skeletal part of the sentence that combines subject, predicate and complement(s) if present.

The conceptual core of a situation and the grammatical core of a sentence can now be contrasted as shown in Figure 3.2. To indicate that we are not yet concerned with a fully-fledged sentence, we will only look at the main structural elements of the sentence.

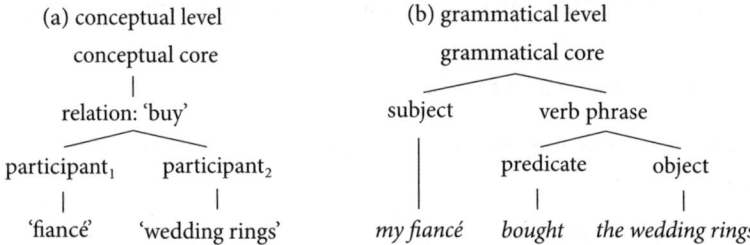

Figure 3.2. (a) Conceptual core and (b) grammatical core

Diagram (a) in Figure 3.2 presents a possible structuring of a conceptual core. The only thing we can say for sure is that the relation 'buy' has several participants, at least a buyer and a thing bought (see Chapter 2.1.7). Grammatically, these two participants can be connected to the predicate *buy* in different linear orders. The English word order is SVO (subject — verb — object); other languages may have different linear orderings. Latin, Turkish and Japanese have the order SOV, Welsh and Arabic have the order VSO. While the position of the verb is variable cross-linguistically, the subject precedes the object in most languages of the world. As will be shown in Chapter 11, this word order reflects a natural conceptual order: the subject typically denotes the primary participant, which acts upon another participant.

In addition to its linear order, every sentence exhibits a hierarchical structure as displayed in the tree diagram (b) of Figure 3.2. The hierarchical order links the subject of the sentence to the verb phrase, and the predicate of the verb phrase to the object. Not only do people intuitively feel that these hierarchical relations exist within a sentence, but we can also support this analysis by means of the "substitution test": the predicate *buy* and the object *wedding rings* may be replaced by a single superordinate verb such as *shop*; hence they must be linked to the same node in the tree diagram.

3.2.2 Grounding: Grounding elements

The notion of **grounding** refers to the speaker's "anchoring" of a situation and its participants in the speech situation shared by speaker and hearer. The particular situation described and its participants can be seen as figures and the speech situation as the all-dominating ground. In grounding a situation, the speaker provides information about who or what he is talking about, when the situation happened in relation to the present moment of speaking, and whether it really happened. Grounding is so important to successful communication that the grammar of English forces its speakers to use grounding elements in every sentence. In the following sentence, the grounding elements are italicised:

(9) *My* fiancé *bought the* wedding rings and *may* also buy *a* necklace.

We will first look at the grounding elements in the noun phrases. By using the possessive pronoun *my*, the speaker enables the hearer to identify the participant *fiancé*. Since the speaker is present in the communicative situation, she herself makes a good reference point to ground the participant 'fiancé' in the current discourse. By choosing the definite article *the* with the participant *wedding rings*, the speaker assumes that the hearer is familiar with the 'marriage' frame and the custom of buying rings long before the wedding day. In choosing the indefinite article *a* with *necklace*, on the other hand, the speaker reveals that neither she herself nor the hearer can as yet identify the necklace. All these grounding elements, which serve to indicate whether the things talked about are or are not identifiable in the current discourse, are determiners. **Determiners** are function words such as *the*, *this*, *every*, etc. which ground the thing described by the noun in the current discourse. Their function is to make the things talked about accessible to the hearer as *referents*. The important notion of *reference* will be discussed in more detail in Chapter 5.

Let us now turn to the grounding elements in the predicate. In using the past tense form *bought*, the speaker locates the situation in the past time before the present moment of speaking. By using the modal verb *may*, the speaker communicates to the hearer that the situation is a potential one. Conversely, not using a modal verb is meaningful, too. Thus, the first part of the sentence, *My fiancé bought the wedding rings*, conveys to the hearer that the speaker assesses the situation as a real one. The grounding elements of both tense and modal verbs thus provide information about the reality status of a situation. We will discuss the grounding of situations in time and factual reality in Chapter 9 and their grounding in potential reality in Chapter 10.

Grounding elements have two important characteristics which link them to the grammatical core: subjectivity and nucleus status. The subjective nature of grounding elements arises from the point of view taken by the speaker: the speaker assesses whether the situation described is real or potential, and whether the hearer can or cannot identify the participants talked about. For example, the speaker of sentence (9) assumes that the hearer does not know that her fiancé is going to buy her a necklace.

Grounding elements have nucleus status: they are obligatory grammatical forms linked to the noun(s) and the verb in the sentence and are thus tightly intertwined with the grammatical core of the sentence. We therefore use the term **nucleus** as a cover term encompassing both the grammatical core and grounding elements.

3.2.3 Setting: Setting elements

The nucleus of a sentence is set off against the setting and, just like the conceptual core, is based on an all-pervasive figure/ground configuration. This means that the notion of **setting** refers to the background against which a situation is set. Setting elements provide information such as where and when the event happened, why it happened, the condition under which it happened, etc. To provide this type of information, the speaker uses lexical resources which specify the factors surrounding a situation in more detail. Unlike grounding elements, setting elements do not give the speaker's subjective assessment of the situation and are not obligatory grammatical forms. In the structure of the sentence, setting elements are optional, as illustrated in the expressions put in parentheses in the following example:

(10) (After ten years of engagement) my fiancé bought the wedding rings (at Tiffany's) (last night).

The setting elements in a sentence are expressed as adjuncts. The adjunct *after ten years of engagement* expresses both a temporal and circumstantial setting, the adjunct *at Tiffany's* specifies the spatial setting, and the adjunct *last night* provides specific information about the temporal setting, i.e. the specific time when the event occurred relative to the moment of speaking. At a very general level, the time of the event as occurring before the moment of speaking is indicated by the grounding element of past tense. Once the setting of a situation has been established in the current discourse, it need not be repeated with each sentence. Speaker and hearer keep it in mind unless it is changed. Thus, if the description of the event in (10) was continued by *He also had our names engraved on them*, we would understand this event as occurring within the same setting, i.e. as taking place at Tiffany's last night.

3.2.4 Situations: Sentences

The situation underlying sentence (10) contains a conceptual core and a setting. The conceptual core consists of the relation 'buy' and two participants; the setting specifies the place, time and circumstances in which the situation is set. When the situation is expressed as an act of communication, it occurs within a speech situation shared by speaker and hearer. The speech situation allows the speaker to ground the situation and the participants. The situation is grounded in past reality, and its participants 'fiancé' and 'wedding rings' are grounded as definite referents. The structure of such situations may be represented as shown in Figure 3.3.

The linguistic counterpart of a situation is the grammatical unit known as the sentence. The **sentence** is a grammatically complete and independent unit. Its minimal structural elements are a grammatical core, consisting of a subject, a predicate and possibly further complements. Moreover, a sentence may contain adjuncts as optional setting elements. The situation described by a sentence is grounded in time: it is **temporal**. Sentences in fact always contain the grounding element tense or a modal. With respect to the presence of a

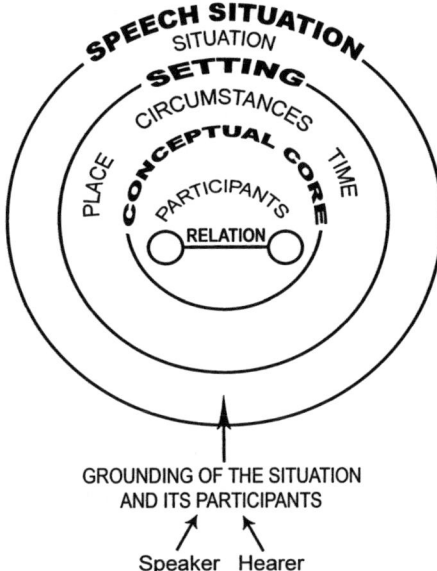

Figure 3.3. Structure of a situation

tensed verb, sentences are also described as **finite**. Most people also see the sentence as a linguistic unit that expresses a "complete thought". This, of course, cannot be verified. In an idealised and simplified model relating situations and sentences, conceptual and grammatical units correspond as shown in Figure 3.4.

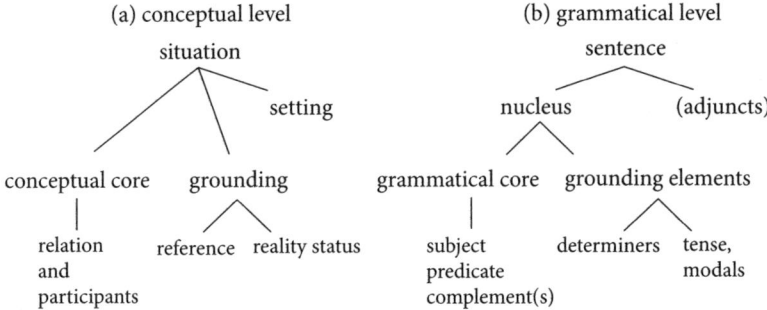

Figure 3.4. Situations and sentences

In linking the grammatical structure of a sentence to its meaning, the term *proposition* is often used. A **proposition** is that part of the meaning of a sentence or clause that is constant, irrespective of the form it takes. Thus, the sentences *My fiancé bought the wedding rings*, *The wedding rings were bought by my fiancé*, *Did my fiancé buy the wedding rings?*, *(I asked) my fiancé to buy the wedding rings* have the same proposition: 'my fiancé — buy — the wedding rings'. The notion 'proposition' will be relevant in the discussion of modality in Chapter 10; the conceptual structure of situations and the grammatical structure of sentences will be elaborated more explicitly in Chapter 11.

3.3 Combining situations: Juxtaposed and complex sentences

Thus far we have dealt with simple situations and simple sentences. In discourse, situations and the sentences describing them do, of course, not occur in isolation but form part of a coherent piece of discourse. Although the scope of this book is confined to the conceptualisation of simple sentences, we will conclude this survey on the cognitive framework by briefly touching upon the ways in which situations are combined and expressed in the structure of English. This will also give us the opportunity to introduce some of the cognitive principles that account for textual coherence.

3.3.1 Conceptual and grammatical linking of situations

A crucial aspect of producing and understanding texts is our ability to relate situations in a meaningful way. In discourse the conceptual link between situations may be expressed explicitly, but typically it is implicit and has to be inferred. The linguist Charles Fillmore gave the following convincing example to illustrate the importance of textual coherence:

(11) a. I had trouble with the car yesterday. The carburettor was dirty.
 b. I had trouble with the car yesterday. The ash-tray was dirty.

We immediately interpret the relation between the two sentences in (11a) in a causal sense. We could, of course, have made the connection explicit by saying *I had trouble with the car yesterday because the carburettor was dirty*, but thanks to our knowledge of the 'car trouble' frame we do not have to say so explicitly; in fact, the use of *because* here even sounds rather meticulous since it does not give any additional contextual effects. The sequence of the sentences in (11b), by contrast, requires some extraordinary context to be interpreted meaningfully, but still we would probably search for some causal connection. If the conjunction *because* is added, the hearer is as it were "forced" to find a meaningful relation, e.g. I could not drive my boss with such a dirty ash-tray.

The joining of two independent sentences without the use of a conjunction as in the examples under (11) and (12a) is known as juxtaposition or parataxis. English also provides other structural possibilities for joining two situations, some of which are shown in the examples (12b–d) below.

(12) a. I saw the burglar. He ran away. [*juxtaposition*]
 b. I saw the burglar and he ran away. [*co-ordination*]
 c. I saw the burglar as he ran away. [*subordination*]
 d. I saw the burglar run away. [*complementation*]

Co-ordination, subordination, and complementation involve clauses within complex sentences. **Clauses** contain a grammatical core, or a proposition, but not necessarily the grounding elements tense and modals. **Complex sentences** may consist of either two main clauses as in (12b) or of a main clause and one or more subordinate clauses as in (12c) and (12d). Main clauses are always temporal, i.e. have a tensed verb; subordinate clauses may be temporal as in (12c) or atemporal as in (12d), i.e. they do not contain a tensed verb.

In expressing a sequence of situations, the speaker has to decide which of these grammatical options best renders her communicative intentions. The speaker's choice of the structure to use is not arbitrary but mainly governed by the joint interaction of three general cognitive principles: (i) the iconic principle of proximity/distance, (ii) the iconic principle of sequential order, and (iii) the cognitive principle of figure and ground.

The two iconic principles of sequential order and proximity/distance relate to the observation that language is, at least to a certain extent, motivated and not, as has often been claimed, an arbitrary system of signs. One of the main motivating factors of language is iconicity. **Iconicity** in language refers to the similarity between conceived reality and language structure. The notion of iconicity is often associated with so-called onomatopoeic words such as *cuckoo* and *crack*, whose sound shapes are suggestive of their meanings. Iconicity has, however, a much wider application in the area of grammar than in the lexicon.

i. The iconic **principle of proximity/distance** says that conceptual units that belong together conceptually tend to be closely integrated in the structure of language; conversely, conceptual units that do not belong together tend to be distanced in the structure of language. This principle accounts for the difference in meaning between the phrases *his third unfinished book* 'the third of his three unfinished books' and *his unfinished third book* 'the third of his books which is unfinished'. In each case, the syntactic distance between the past participle and the noun reflects a conceptual distance between their conceptual units. In complex sentences, this principle accounts for the degree of grammatical integration of the sentences or clauses.

ii. The iconic **principle of sequential order** says that the temporal order of events in the conceived world is mirrored in the order of clauses describing them. A classic illustration of this principle is Caesar's famous exclamation *Veni, vidi, vici* 'I came, I saw, I conquered', when he described his victory over King Pharnaces II of Pontus. The chronological order of these three events is iconically reflected in the order in which they are uttered or written. A modern version of this principle would be the shopping slogan *Eye it, try it, buy it*. The principle of sequential order also accounts for the order of fixed expressions such as *now and then, sooner or later,* and *hide and seek*.

iii. The perceptual **principle of figure and ground** applies when two or more units of different salience are related. In this chapter, we saw that the subject participant is a figure relative to the object participant; the conceptual core is a figure relative to the ground and the setting; the situation or setting is a figure relative to the overall speech situation; and we may surmise that, where two situations are combined, the more salient situation will stand out as the figure relative to the other situation, which will function as its ground.

We will apply these principles to the complex situations described in (12). The combined situations and the clauses expressing them will be discussed in the order from their weakest to the tightest link.

3.3.2 Degrees of conceptual and grammatical integration

There are many gradations in how loosely or tightly two situations are integrated. A weak conceptual link between two situations is matched by a weak grammatical link and typically finds expression in **juxtaposition**. According to the principle of conceptual distance, juxtaposed sentences are separated from each other and constitute independent grammatical units. Their separation is clearly signalled by falling intonation and an intonation break in spoken language, as in the juxtaposed sentences "I saw the burglar ↘‖ He ran away". In written language, juxtaposition is marked by a full stop.

The temporal relation between juxtaposed sentences is not explicitly stated, but is inferable from the principle of sequential order: the first sentence denotes the earlier event, the second sentence the later event. When the order of the sentences is reversed, as in (13), their temporal order changes too.

(13) a. I saw the burglar. He ran away.
b. The burglar ran away. I saw him.

The speaker may opt for construing two situations as juxtaposed when they are distanced in time, i.e. when they occur, or at least start to occur, at different times. In this case, both successive situations are salient in their own right: neither of them is foregrounded. Juxtaposed sentences may also convey other than purely temporal meanings. Thus, we may see a causal connection between the situations. In this case, we divide the complex situation into figure and ground: the first event is seen as describing the causal ground for the second event, which is seen as the resulting figure. Sentence (13a) would then be understood to mean 'I noticed the burglar and, because of being detected by me, he ran away', and sentence (13b) 'The burglar ran away and therefore I noticed him'. The causal interpretation in the juxtaposed sentences arises by implicature due to the principle *post hoc, ergo propter hoc* (Chapter 2.3.2).

Since juxtaposed sentences are only loosely linked to each other, they may convey many meanings. Thus, both (13a) and (13b) may also be interpreted in a contrastive sense: the first sentence provides the "ground" for our expectation about events which could happen next, while the second sentence, the "figure", expresses the unexpected real event. The counter-expectation can be paraphrased by *but*: in (13a) 'I saw the burglar but he ran away', in (13b) 'The burglar ran away but I saw him'. Sentence (13b) may also be understood as an afterthought and as evidence for what is said in the first sentence: 'The burglar ran away. I know this for a fact because I saw him'. Here, the first sentence describes the figure and the afterthought serves as its ground.

The conceptual link between situations that are coded by means of **co-ordination** is slightly stronger than that between juxtaposed situations. An indication of the stronger link between co-ordinated situations can also be seen in the more restricted range of meanings associated with this construal.

(14) a. I saw the burglar *and* he ran away.
b. The burglar ran away *and* I saw him.

As in juxtaposition, we tend to infer a temporal link between the past events and, by further implicature, a causal link. However, none of the other meanings (i.e. contrastive and evidential) found with juxtaposition is compatible with co-ordination. A speaker who decides to construe two situations as co-ordinated thus mainly wants to highlight their strong temporal and/or causal connection.

Subordination is the construal to be chosen if the speaker wants to draw attention to the particular type of link between the situations by naming it explicitly. Different kinds of temporal relations may thus be signalled by means of subordinating conjunctions such as *when, as, while, after*, etc. At the same time, the two combined situations are clearly divided into figure and ground: the main clause always constitutes the figure and the subordinate clause is always the ground. In choosing the construal of subordination, the speaker thus also communicates which of the situations is foregrounded (F) and which one is backgrounded (G), as in the following complex sentences:

(15) a. I saw the burglar (F) *as* he ran away (G).
 b. *As* the burglar ran away (G), I saw him (F).

The complex sentence (15a) and its reversal (15b) roughly mean the same: 'The burglar first started to run away and then I saw him'. We can note two general aspects of subordination. Firstly, the meaning of subordination is even more restricted than those of juxtaposition and co-ordination — here the subordinating link has only one meaning, i.e. a temporal one, though it may invite all kinds of implicatures, e.g. causal ones. Secondly, the order of events is not iconically reflected in the order of the clauses, but in the grammatical form of the clause: the subordinate *as*-clause always describes the event that began first, the main clause describes the event following it. The sequential order of events described by main and subordinate clause is thus grammatically fixed.

The difference between iconic sequential order, as in juxtaposition and co-ordination, and grammatically fixed sequential order, as in complex sentences with subordination, is presented in Table 3.3. Event "A" represents my seeing the burglar and event "B" the burglar's running away.

Table 3.3. Iconic sequential order vs grammatically fixed order

iconic order			grammatically fixed order	
event A	*and*	event B (14a)	event A *as* event B (15a)	
event B	*and*	event A (14b)	*as* event B, event A (15b)	
A/B = 1st event		B/A = 2nd event	Ground = 1st event	Figure = 2nd event
*I saw the burglar **and** he ran away.*			*I saw the burglar **as** he ran away.*	
*The burglar ran away **and** I saw him.*			***As** the burglar ran away, I saw him.*	

The tightest conceptual link between clauses is established by **complementation**, as in the examples under (16):

(16) a. I saw the burglar *run away*.
 b. I saw the burglar *running away*.

Here, the times of the burglar's running away and my seeing this coincide. The burglar's running away is in fact understood as the object of my observation and no longer as an event of its own. According to the principle of proximity, the tightly integrated events of the burglar's running away and my seeing this should motivate the tight grammatical integration of the clauses. This is in fact the case. The main clause and the complement clause are not separated by a conjunction or intonation break, the complement clause is the direct object of *saw* and hence part of the grammatical nucleus of the main clause, and it lacks tense. As we saw in Section 3.2.2, tense serves to ground a situation in time. Since the time when the complement event occurred is identical with that of the main event, there is, of course, no need for separately grounding the complement event in time — it is already grounded in time by the main clause.

Within the field of complementation, the structure of English provides the speaker with further options. The speaker may decide to focus on the completion of the perceived event by using the bare infinitive, as in (16a), on its progression by using the present participle, as in (16b), or on its factuality by using a *that*-clause, as in *I saw that the burglar ran away*. In this case, the wider conceptual distance between the two situations is reflected in the use of the intervening particle *that* and the use of tense in the complement clause, i.e. the clause is grounded on its own.

3.4 Summary

This chapter has dealt with the processes of combining conceptual units and their counterparts in language. Human thought is organised around two basic types of conceptual units: things and relations. **Things** are autonomous and fairly stable conceptual units, **relations** are dependent and short-lived conceptual units. In language, the conceptual division into things and relations is reflected in the main word classes: things are coded as nouns; relations are coded as verbs, adjectives, adverbs, prepositions, and conjunctions.

A relation combined with two or more things or other conceptual entities forms the **conceptual core** of a situation. The notion **situation** comprises events that happen or states things are in. Things or other conceptual entities which form part of a conceptual core are **participants**. Participants hold a privileged position in a situation and play a specific role in it, such as that of an agent in *Peggy was swimming*. The conceptual core of a situation corresponds to the **grammatical core** of a sentence; a relation corresponds to the **predicate** of a sentence, participants correspond to grammatical functions such as **subject** and **object**, and a situation corresponds to the **sentence**. That part of the meaning of a sentence or clause that is constant, irrespective of the form it takes, is known as a **proposition**. Situations and their participants need to be grounded in the current discourse so that the hearer can identify them. **Grounding** is an essential feature of any situation and is grammatically expressed by determiners, tense and modal verbs. **Determiners** ground things in the current discourse, tense grounds situations in time and reality space, and modal verbs ground situations only in potentiality space. Optionally, situations can be located within a spatial, temporal and circumstantial **setting**. The setting is specified by **adjuncts**. A simple sentence thus consists of a grammatical core, grounding elements, and optionally adjuncts.

Situations do not normally occur in isolation but in combination with other situations. Complex situations are expressed either as juxtaposed or as **complex sentences,** which are made up of one main clause and another main clause or a subordinate clause. The choice between these different grammatical constructions is governed by principles of iconicity and the principle of figure and ground. **Iconicity** refers to the reflection of conceptual structure in linguistic structure. The iconic **principle of proximity/distance** says that conceptual units that belong together are more closely integrated in language structure. The iconic **principle of sequential order** says that the temporal order of events is mirrored in their linguistic order. The perceptual **principle of figure and ground** accounts, among others, for the coding of situations as a main or a subordinate clause.

The principle of proximity/distance determines the strength of the grammatical integration of the sentences or clauses according to the conceptual integration of their situations. A weak conceptual link between situations tends to be matched by **juxtaposition**, i.e. two independent sentences. Due to their weak link, juxtaposed sentences allow many interpretations. If the speaker wants to communicate a slightly stronger link between situations, she can opt for **co-ordination**, i.e. two main clauses conjoined by *and*. If the link is still stronger, the speaker may use **subordination**, i.e. a sentence that is made up of a main clause and a subordinate clause. If the link is tight, she may use **complementation**, i.e. a complement clause that is fully integrated into a main clause. The meanings associated with these linguistic construals are motivated by the principles of sequential order and figure and ground as well as implicatures.

Further Reading

The conceptual distinction between things and relations is extensively dealt with in Langacker (1987b, 1991a, 1991b, Ch. 3). On nouns and verbs see also Gentner (1981) and Hopper & Thompson (1985), on the conceptual status of word classes see Givón (1984, 1993, Vol. 1) and Wierzbicka (1988a: Ch. 9), and on the conversion of nouns into verbs see Clark & Clark (1979).

The notions of 'grounding' and 'setting' are part of Langacker's model of cognitive grammar. An in-depth study of grounding is Brisard, ed. (2003). The notion of 'nucleus' (of the sentence) stems from functional grammar, especially from Dik (1989) and Mann & Thompson (1988).

Relevant work on iconicity is found in the volumes edited by Haiman (1985), Landsberg (1995), Simone (1995), and Fischer & Nänny (2001).

Study questions

1. Analyse the following humorous observation in terms of ground entities and frames:
   I just realised how old I am: People stopped telling me *I look good* and started telling me *I look good for my age*.

2. Identify the meanings associated with the noun *thing* in the following sentences (see the examples under (1) in Section 2.2):
   a. A *thing* of beauty is a joy forever. (Keats)
   b. The first *thing* I want to say is this.
   c. I'm afraid we can't change *things*.
   d. Our car broke down, and to make *things* worse, we had run out of money.
   e. That was a nice *thing* to do.
   f. I don't have a single *thing* to wear.

3. Supply one or more ground entities that do not show up in the following sentences as a participant and/or a domain or frame:
   a. *Harry Potter* is really good.
   b. The fish is really good.
   c. The fish smells.
   d. Our children behave.
   e. I exercise every day. (two conceptual entities)
   f. Francis was reading. (two conceptual entities)

4. Identify the conceptual core, the grammatical core, the grounding elements and the setting elements for each of the following sentences:
   a. My husband left his glasses on the train.
   b. Tomorrow he may lose his wedding ring.

5. Which iconic principles operate in the first sentences of the following pairs of sentences as opposed to the second sentences?
   a. I heard Sue come home. *versus* I heard Sue when she came home.
   b. The ambulance came and rescued the child. *versus* ?The ambulance rescued the child and came.

6. Young children tend to understand sentence (a) correctly, but not sentences (b) and (c). How would they interpret them and why?
   a. John played before Mary sang.
   b. John played after Mary sang.
   c. Before Mary sang, John played.

Part II

Things: Nouns and noun phrases

This part is concerned with "things" and their function in our conceptual world. In Cognitive Grammar, things are understood as types of entities that have an autonomous and stable existence in the world as we see it. In language, things correspond to the word class of nouns. Things, and the nouns describing them, are characterised by a number of conceptual and linguistic properties which distinguish them from other conceptual and linguistic units. In particular, things may be referred to, they may be quantified, and they may be qualified by spelling out their properties or by assigning properties to them in predications. The chapters of this part on things will deal with each of these characteristics of things and the expression of things as nouns and noun phrases in English.

Chapter 4 "Types of things: nouns" looks at things as conceptual categories and the way things are expressed as nouns. It will be concerned in particular with the fundamental conceptual distinction between two classes of things: objects and substances. In English, this distinction is reflected in two classes of nouns: count nouns such as *car(s)* and mass nouns such as *water*.

Chapter 5 "Groundings things: reference" deals with the intriguing problem of how the things the speaker has in mind and talks about can be made accessible to the hearer. We normally talk about particular instances of a thing and need to ensure that the hearer can identify them — otherwise, miscommunication may arise. The speaker therefore needs to "ground" the particular instance of a thing which she has in mind in the current discourse. Such a grounding is achieved by means of various referring expressions, especially determiners.

Chapter 6 "Quantifying things: quantifiers" is concerned with the quantification of things. In fact we systematically quantify instances of a thing whenever we use the singular or plural with nouns. These morphological markings of number express quantification at a very general level. We may also quantify instances by using more specific quantifying expressions such as *all*, *every*, *many* and *a few*. We will see that quantifiers are divided into two groups: set quantifiers that denote a magnitude relative to a set, such as *all* and *every*, and scalar quantifiers that denote a magnitude along a scale, such as *many* and *a few*.

Chapter 7 "Qualifying things: modifiers" looks at the qualification of things by means of modifiers. We may qualify instances of a thing for the purpose either of referential identification or of categorisation. In its referential function, qualification provides a means of restricting a reference mass to the particular instance which the speaker wants to refer to, as in *the book over there*. In its categorising function, qualification provides an efficient means of subcategorising things, as in *book on tape*, which describes a special type of book, namely one that can be listened to rather than read.

Chapter 4

Types of things: Nouns

> 4.0 Overview
> 4.1 Classes of things: Classes of nouns
> 4.2 Objects versus substances
> 4.3 Blending of objects and substances: Hybrid nouns
> 4.4 Reified things: Abstract nouns
> 4.5 Summary

4.0 Overview

The conceptual category 'thing' finds its parallel in the linguistic category 'noun'. The distinction between the two main classes of things, i.e. **objects** and **substances**, is reflected in the linguistic distinction between **count nouns** and **mass nouns**. But, due to the prototype structure of all conceptual and linguistic categories, the distinction between objects and substances tends to be blurred: objects may shade into substances and substances may shade into objects. The problem of fuzziness is even more intriguing with abstract nouns. Abstract nouns are the result of a conceptual shift known as **reification** by means of which relational concepts like 'be married' are construed as things, in this case 'marriage'.

4.1 Classes of things: Classes of nouns

4.1.1 Things and instances of things

The notion of **thing** has already been introduced in Chapter 3.1. There we focused on the conceptual stability of things in space and time, but we also noticed that many things, especially abstract things such as 'explosion', are certainly not time-stable. The main characteristic of things is their conceptual independence or autonomy. Like other conceptual entities, things are defined relative to a conceptual domain and extend over a certain region within this domain. For example, each of the three weather terms *fog*, *mist* and *haze*, which we discussed in Chapter 1.1.1, extends over a certain region within a domain that may be called 'weather of reduced visibility'. Each term touches its neighbouring term or, as shown in Figure 4.1, may even overlap with it.

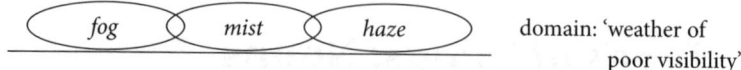
domain: 'weather of poor visibility'

Figure 4.1. Things extending over regions in a domain

In a similar way, the nouns *father*, *mother*, and *uncle* designate relatives as "regions" in the domain 'kinship'. Abstract nouns also denote things that extend over a region in some domain: the abstract noun *explosion* denotes a thing within a domain which may be called 'rapid expansion', and the region it extends over contrasts with those of *blast* and *detonation*.

In Cognitive Grammar, the term *thing* is used in the sense of an abstract **type**. Things are expressed as nouns, and all the nouns listed in a dictionary denote types of things. For example, the noun *tree* denotes the thing 'tree' as a type. Types are to be distinguished from particular **tokens** of a type. The type-token distinction applies to all levels of linguistic description. For example, phonology deals with types of sounds, i.e. phonemes such as /p/, while phonetics deals with tokens of sounds, or phones, as they are actually pronounced in speech, such as the aspirated [pʰ]. In Cognitive Grammar, tokens are called instances. An **instance** of a thing may be chosen to become a referent and is then expressed as a noun phrase. For example, the noun phrase *the tree* describes a particular instance of the type 'tree'. In talking about *the tree* I may have the one in mind that is growing in my front garden. The distinction between things and their instances is crucial for reference and will be taken up in Chapter 5. This chapter deals with things and classes of things, and their linguistic expression as nouns and classes of nouns.

4.1.2 Distinguishing objects from substances

In Chapter 1.1.1 we already drew attention to the distinction between two classes of things, objects and substances, which are coded in English as count nouns and mass nouns, respectively. The notions *object* and *substance* are also understood as types. Examples of objects are 'car', 'lake', and 'gold nugget'; examples of substances are 'traffic', 'water', and 'gold dust'. We can distinguish objects from substances on the basis of three criteria, which are closely interrelated: (i) boundedness, (ii) internal composition, and (iii) countability.

4.1.2.1 Boundedness

Things such as 'car' have clear perceptual outlines which give them their characteristic gestalt. Such well-delineated things appear to us as discrete, individuated objects. In order to recognise something as an object, we normally need to see the thing as a whole. We can do so by adopting a maximal viewing frame (see Chapter 2.1.1), which allows us to discern the object's boundaries. The criterion of **boundedness** is thus an essential characteristic of objects and their expression as count nouns such as *car*.

Substances such as 'water', by contrast, have no inherent boundaries and, as a result, are continuous rather than discrete and individuated. When we come home and are shocked to find water all over the basement, we may describe this situation as *The basement is flooded with water*, i.e. by using the mass noun *water*. Water appears to us as an unbounded, shapeless liquid. This is the impression we typically gain from taking a restricted view of a thing: all we see is an unlimited substance. If there was only a small pool of water, we would have been able to discern its boundaries and see it as an object; we would then use a count noun describing an amount of water such as *puddle*: *There is a puddle of water in the basement*.

4.1.2.2 *Internal composition*

Things are also distinguished with respect to their internal **composition**. Things whose internal compositions are heterogeneous are seen as objects and therefore coded as count nouns. A car is composed of many different parts which are arranged so that they function in an integrated way. If a car is taken to a salvage-yard and all its useful parts are removed, its structure as a car is destroyed — it is no longer a car but a car wreck and may eventually turn into scrap, i.e. be seen as a substance and expressed as a mass noun.

Things whose internal compositions are homogeneous are seen as substances and therefore coded as mass nouns. This applies to water, dust or scrap. From a physical or chemical point of view, these substances are composed of particles and are therefore, strictly speaking, heterogeneous rather than homogeneous. In our daily experience of water, dust or scrap, however, we do not discern separate particles with the naked eye, or if we do, they are simply not relevant to us. One portion of a substance is made up of much the same kind of material as any other portion of it. Water, dust or scrap can therefore be expanded, contracted or divided without destroying their identities, i.e. each portion will still be thought of as water, dust or scrap. Since substances, but not objects, are divisible into portions, we can speak of *a drop of water, a puddle of water, a lot of scrap*, and *a bit of dust*, but not of **a bit of (a) car*.

4.1.2.3 *Countability*

Entities which are similar in their appearance or equivalent in their function may be subsumed under the same category and be counted. For example, the *Bible*, the *Oxford English Dictionary* and Shakespeare's *Sonnets* are equivalent in their function: they are to be read. They can therefore be subsumed under the same category 'book' and may be counted as *three books*. We would, however, not think of counting highly dissimilar entities for which we lack a common category, such as a car, a mouse and a cloud. **Countability** thus means being able to recognise different entities as members of the same category so that they can be conceptually replicated and counted. If there is only one entity as in *a tree*, it is described as *uniplex*, if there are more equivalent entities as in *three trees* or *forest*, which is comprised of many trees, they are described as *multiplex*.

As argued above, most substances are non-individuated and only divisible into portions of the same kind. Water, for example, cannot be separated into discrete, individuated parts because, even if divided into portions, all these portions of water contain the same material. We can only see one mass of water at a time, so there is nothing to count.

The three criteria of boundedness, internal composition and countability allow us to distinguish objects from substances. For ease of reference they are summarised in Table 4.1.

Table 4.1. Criteria distinguishing objects from substances

		objects (e.g. 'car')	substances (e.g. 'water')
(i)	boundedness:	discrete, individuated	non-discrete, non-individuated
(ii)	composition:	heterogeneous, integrated into a whole	homogeneous, divisible into portions
(iii)	countability:	multipliable, uniplex or multiplex	non-multipliable

These three criteria tend to go together in categorising a given thing either as an object or a substance. Some non-prototypical objects and substances may, however, only be characterised by two of the three criteria. We will come across such borderline cases in the course of this chapter.

4.1.3 Count nouns and mass nouns

> *Not everything that can be counted counts,*
> *and not everything that counts can be counted.*
> (Albert Einstein)

In the grammar of English the conceptual distinction between objects and substances is reflected in the distinction between **count nouns** and **mass nouns**. The conceptual criteria that distinguish objects from substances also account for the grammatical behaviour of these two types of nouns. Count nouns and mass nouns differ with respect to a number of grammatical phenomena, which are listed in Table 4.2: (i) possibility of taking a numeral, (ii) possibility of forming a plural, (iii) use of quantifiers, (iv) use of articles, and (v) absence of article.

Table 4.2. Grammatical behaviour of count nouns and mass nouns

		count nouns	mass nouns
(i)	numerals:	*one* car	**one traffic*
(ii)	plural:	*five* **cars**	**five traffics*
(iii)	quantifiers:	There aren't **many** cars.	There isn't much traffic.
		There are **few** cars today.	There is little traffic today.
(iv)	use of articles:	**a** car / **the** car	**a traffic / **the** traffic*
(v)	absence of article:	**Car is a problem today.*	**Traffic** is a problem today.
		Cars are a problem today.	**Traffics are a problem today.*

The first three criteria distinguishing count nouns from mass nouns relate to countability, the last two criteria to reference. The notion of reference as a grounding operation will be discussed in Chapter 5. Here we will only point out its impact for the use of articles.

(i) *Numerals* and (ii) *plural*: It follows from our characterisation of objects as either uniplex or multiplex entities that count nouns can be combined with numerals and are marked for number (singular and plural). Mass nouns cannot be combined with a numeral, so that they typically only appear in the singular. They are therefore also described as *singularia tantum*, i.e. 'singulars only'.

(iii) *Quantifiers*: Quantities are typically specified by means of quantifiers such as *many* and *much*. Objects and substances are quantified by means of different quantifiers. Objects are quantified by adding up a number of individuated items of the same kind. Thus, *many cars* and *few cars* describe an unspecified number of cars. Substances are quantified by extracting a larger or smaller amount of the same homogeneous substance. Thus, *not much traffic* and *little traffic* describe an unspecified amount of 'traffic'. We will therefore refer to these two types of quantification as *number quantification* (for objects) and *amount quantification* (for substances). The issue of quantification will be dealt with in Chapter 6.

(iv) Use and (v) absence of *articles*: In referring to a single instance of an object, we use a determiner, as in *a car* or *the car*. The indefinite article *a* historically derives from the numeral *one*, and it still requires its noun to be countable. Since substances are not countable, they cannot be referred to with the indefinite article *a*, i.e. we do not speak of *a traffic. Both count and mass nouns may, however, take the definite article *the*. With count nouns as in *the car*, the definite article singles out one definite single instance of an object. With mass nouns, the definite article singles out a definite portion of a substance. Consider the following examples of definite substances:

(1) a. *The traffic* on the M25 is rather dense this morning.
    b. Can you pass *the salt*?

The traffic in (1a) refers to that particular portion of traffic that clogs the M25 this morning. The portion is still the same internally homogeneous substance as traffic in general. The definite article does not turn the substance into a discrete entity. When there is also a traffic jam on the M4, we do not describe the situation as **The traffics on the M25 and M4 are rather dense*. In (1b), *the salt* conventionally refers to the salt which is in the salt cellar on the dinner table. The amount of salt is delimited by the inside of the salt cellar, yet it is still seen as a portion of the substance and not as an individuated object. Thus, we can pass several salt cellars, but not several salts.

Plural count nouns often behave like mass nouns, as illustrated in Table 4.3. The phrases under (i) describe situations which only apply to a single instance of an object and which therefore cannot be expressed by plural count nouns and mass nouns, while the phrases under (ii) describe situations which only apply to several individual elements of an object or to a substance and which therefore cannot be expressed by singular count nouns.

Table 4.3. Similar grammatical behaviour of plural count nouns and mass nouns

	singular count nouns	plural count nouns	mass nouns
(i)	the **whole** car	*the whole cars	*the whole traffic
	day **in**, day **out**	*days in, days out	*time in, time out
	take a bus	*take buses	*take transport
(ii)	***full of** car	**full of** cars	**full of** traffic
	*a **shortage of** worker	a **shortage of** workers	a **shortage of** labour
	***collect** a coin	**collect** coins	**collect** money

The grammatical behaviour of singular count nouns on the one hand, and plural count nouns and mass nouns on the other hand, is of course motivated. In the expressions under (i) of Table 4.3, the quantifier *whole*, the particles *in* and *out*, and the verb *take* relate to bounded things, while the expressions under (ii), i.e. the quantifier *full*, the noun *shortage*, and the verb *collect*, relate to unbounded things.

The common behaviour of plural count nouns and (singular) mass nouns is also not haphazard but motivated. It reflects a conceptual affinity of multiplex objects and homogeneous substances, which we also find in perception. When we look at a group of people or objects from a distance they tend to shade into each other and appear as a mass. For example, when hundreds of cars are rushing by on the motorway, we no longer see the outlines of each individual car but have the impression of an unbounded, homogeneous flow of traffic. The cars may therefore be referred to by the mass noun *traffic*.

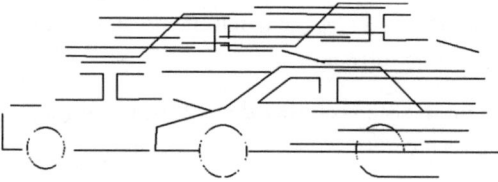

Figure 4.2. Objects (cars) shading over into a substance (traffic)

Because of their conceptual affinity, both plural count nouns and mass nouns may sometimes express very similar sorts of things. For instance, certain strips of pasta are seen as countable objects, namely *noodles*, while others are seen as uncountable substances, namely *spaghetti*. Likewise, small stones may be seen as objects, namely *pebbles*, or as substances, namely *gravel*. This also applies to cross-linguistic differences. For example, the mass noun *news* in English — we have *little news* and not **few news* — corresponds to a plural count noun in French (*les nouvelles*) and German (*die Nachrichten*).

4.2 Objects versus substances

We categorise the phenomena in the physical world as objects or substances, not so much on the basis of their objective properties, but primarily on the basis of their appearance and relevance to us. However, phenomena in the world do not always come to us neatly as clear instances of either objects or substances. This section will mainly be concerned with the sometimes puzzling area of fuzziness between objects and substances.

As illustrated in Chapter 1.1.2 for 'car', categories tend to have prototypical members and more or less peripheral members. This also applies to the categories 'object' and 'substance'. Prototypical physical objects are bounded, internally heterogeneous and countable physical objects, such as cars. More peripheral objects may lack one of these properties. For example, sunflower seeds, coffee beans and peppercorns are usually too many to count, but they are big enough to be recognizable as separate particles and appear to be heterogeneous in having a hard surface and a soft interior so that we express these things as count nouns. Grass seed, sand, salt, rice and wheat also consist of particles, but these are too small to be worth counting. Moreover, their internal composition appears to be homogeneous so that we see them as substances and express them as mass nouns. Particles thus occupy a mid-position on a continuum between objects and substances. Sunflower seeds are relevant to us as individual things — we eat them and plant them, whereas grass seed is not — we only sow it in large amounts.

Prototypical physical substances are unbounded, homogeneous and uncountable. Good examples of substances are fluids such as oil and blood, gases such as air and steam, fabrics such as cotton and wool, and materials such as steel and wood. More peripheral substances would be wild plants such as moss, grass or ivy, and plants that are cultivated in vegetable beds such as mint, rhubarb and lettuce. Although these plants may be counted, they are seen as substances and expressed as mass nouns because the individual plants grow exuberantly and proliferate in the vegetable beds so that their boundaries become obscured. We may even subsume a number of very different objects such as tables, chairs, beds and chests of drawers under the mass noun *furniture*. Here, basic-level objects are grouped together under a superordinate substance.

Let us look more closely at the ways the superordinate and basic levels of a taxonomy interact with objects and substances. There are four possible combinations, and English does in fact make use of all four possibilities, as illustrated in Table 4.4. The hierarchies under (a) and (b) represent the expected symmetrical situation involving either objects or substances on the two levels of the taxonomy, while the hierarchies under (c) and (d) represent asymmetrical situations in that objects and substances co-occur within the same hierarchy.

Table 4.4. Objects and substances in taxonomies

	(a) object	(b) substance	(c) object	(d) substance
superordinate level	*toy(s)*	*food*	*beverage(s)*	*furniture*
basic level	*doll swing ball* object	*bread fish meat* substance	*milk beer juice* substance	*table(s) chair(s) bed(s)* object

The object taxonomy in (a) and the substance taxonomy in (b) involve *kind of*-relations between the lower and the higher categories: dolls, swings and balls are (kinds of) toys, and bread, fish and meat are (kinds of) food. Further examples of object taxonomies as in (a) are established by superordinate terms such as *flower, tool, vehicle, animal, bird*, etc.; further examples of substance taxonomies as in (b) are established by superordinate terms such as *art (music, literature, painting), literature (poetry, drama, prose), merchandise, produce*, etc.

Why do we also find the asymmetrical hierarchies under (c) and (d)? Hierarchy (c) involves object terms such as *beverage* or *drink* at the superordinate level and substance terms such as *milk, beer* and *juice* at the basic level. Beverages typically come in small and bounded amounts, i.e. in packed forms such as bottles or cans or in drinking-vessels such as cups, mugs, wine glasses, etc. Their difference is also highlighted by the special vessels we use for different types of drinks. In talking about beverages or drinks at the superordinate level, we are thinking of them as coming in a bounded form and as comprising various substances as their members. The superordinate terms *beverage* or *drink* thus have all the characteristics of objects and are therefore expressed as count nouns. The basic-level terms *milk, beer* and *juice*, by contrast, describe homogeneous substances so that, although they are bounded by the vessel they come in, they are expressed as mass nouns. Further examples of such asymmetrical hierarchies include the superordinate object terms *metal(s)* (and basic-level terms such as *iron, lead* and *copper*) and *material(s) (linen, cotton* and *paper)*. Abstract things are also conceptualised as objects or substances (see Section 4.4). For example, the superordinate term *emotion(s)* behaves like an object and its basic-level terms (*anger, happiness* and *jealousy*) are conceptualised as substances.

Hierarchy (d) has the opposite structure: it involves substance terms at the superordinate level and object terms at the basic level. Apart from *furniture*, this group includes the superordinate terms *cutlery* (BrE) or *silverware* (AmE) (and basic-level terms such as *knives, forks* and *spoons), money (dollar, dime* and *cent), jewellery (ring, bracelet* and *necklace)* and some others. The basic-level terms in these hierarchies, *a table, a knife, a dollar* and *a ring*, represent clear instances of discrete objects; but why should their superordinate terms be mass nouns? Furniture, jewellery, cutlery, etc. combine aspects of both objects and substances. They are object-like in that they include a limited set of different, well-defined things: the category 'furniture' includes pieces of furniture such as chairs, tables, beds, cupboards, sideboards and bookshelves, 'cutlery' comprises a small set of eating utensils like knives, spoons and forks, 'money' comes in banknotes and coins, etc. These superordinate terms are thus multiplex. It will be recalled that, in our discussion of countability in Section 4.1.2, we assumed that only objects are multiplex. Here we are obviously dealing with an exceptional class of substances. The superordinate terms are substance-like in that the things they are composed of are not seen as individuated but as somehow interrelated. Pieces of furniture are typically arranged in a household in a specific, often complementary, or interdependent, way. Moreover, all pieces of furniture have the same overall function in the house: they are designed to put things in or on. In this respect pieces of furniture lose their distinct individuality and 'furniture' is seen as a substance. Similarly, knives, spoons, and forks are placed together on the table and have the common function of being used for eating with. A nation's different banknotes and coins share the same, important property of being legal tender. In English, this aspect of homogeneity prevails and accounts for categorising these superordinate terms as mass nouns. In other languages, the aspect of multiplexity may predominate, as in the Swedish word for 'furniture', *möbel*, which is a count noun.

4.3 Blending of objects and substances: Hybrid nouns

> *Here and there we find anomalies in the use of number-forms which are difficult to explain, but which at any rate show that people are not absolute rational beings.* (Jespersen, *Philosophy of Grammar*)

The discussion of multiplex substances such as 'furniture' illustrated that things may involve aspects of both objects and substances. We will refer to nouns in which aspects of objects and substances are blended as **hybrid nouns**. Hybrid nouns are best described along a continuum. Hybrids such as 'furniture' vacillate between the object and substance ends of a continuum of things, and the way they are seen in a given language determines their linguistic categorisation as a count noun or a mass noun. Another group of hybrids fluctuates between the uniplex and multiplex ends of a continuum of objects. This applies to a noun such as *board (of directors)*, which is singular in form but describes a multiplex entity, i.e. a group of people. We will therefore speak of (i) an "object-substance continuum" of things and (ii) a "uniplex-multiplex continuum" of objects.

4.3.1 The object-substance continuum of things

The conceptual distinction between objects and substances as defined by the criteria in Table 4.1 is more flexible than it may appear. A thing which is usually understood as a substance such as 'beer' may be viewed as an object and expressed as a count noun and, conversely, a thing which is usually understood as an object such as 'apple' may be viewed as a substance and expressed as a mass noun. Let us first look at substances which are viewed as objects.

4.3.1.1 *Substances viewed as objects*
Substances often come to us in smaller portions which take an individuated form: they have a bounded shape, which we typically associate with objects. For example, rain is seen as a substance in the domain of weather conditions, as in *We had nothing but rain during our vacations*, but when we experience rain when it starts raining, it comes to us in the shape of drops of rain. English usually expresses such portions of a substance by means of a partitive construction consisting of a count noun expressing a form, container or measuring unit, the relational expression *of*, and a mass noun expressing the substance. Thus,

we may describe the portion of a substance as *a piece (of salami), a drop (of rain), a cup (of tea), a pint (of beer), a lump (of sugar), a bar (of chocolate), a gust (of wind)*, etc.

The conceptual link between a substance and the characteristic form, container or measuring unit it comes in may become so conventionalised that we may describe the thing by naming either the form of the portion or the substance. When I order a glass of beer by saying *Can I have another pint?*, I only name the unit of measure but am of course interested in getting a pint of beer. When I say *Can I have another beer?*, I name the substance but, in using *beer* as a count noun, treat it as if it was an object. Both construals are metonymic: in the former case, a characteristic measuring unit (*pint*) is used to stand for a portion of the substance (*pint of beer*); in the latter case, a bounded substance (*another beer*) is used to stand for a portion of the substance.

Once a substance is construed as an object, the noun it describes can, of course, be pluralised like any other count noun. Thus, we may order *three beers* and expect to be served 'three glasses of beer'. We may also understand a substance construed as an object in the sense of a variety, sort or brand. For instance, we are likely to interpret *a whisky* in (2a) and *whiskies* in (2b) to mean 'different variety/ies' or 'brand(s) of whisky':

(2) a. This is *an* excellent Scotch *whisky*.
 b. They have excellent *whiskies* in Scotland.

Table 4.5. Levels of varieties

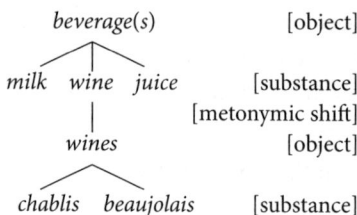

These usages involve a different metonymic shift: here, a bounded and individuated substance (*a whisky/whiskies*) stands for a variety of the substance (*brand of whisky*). More or less any mass noun can, in fact, be used as a count noun and is then typically understood in the sense of 'variety'. Thus, the plural nouns *cheeses, waters, wines, chocolates, sands, metals, furs*, etc. make us think of different varieties of the substance: sorts of cheese such as cheddar, brie and gouda, sorts of water such as Evian and Montpellier, sorts of wine such as chablis and beaujolais, etc. The different varieties of food, drinks and other kinds of substances tend to be associated with distinct qualitative characteristics that are relevant in each specific domain. Unlike "genuine" objects, substances construed as objects are thus not bounded by their limits in space but by their different qualities, which set off one variety from another. And, unlike the varieties subsumed under superordinate terms such as *beverage* (see Table 4.5), the varieties found here are subordinate terms (*wines* such as *chablis* and *beaujolais*) that are subsumed under a basic-level term (*wine*), which is construed as an object (*wines*). The subordinate terms may in their turn be viewed as objects as in *three beaujolais*, pronounced ['bəʊʒəleɪz], which will then, however, be seen as bounded substances of the same kind (*three glasses of beaujolais*).

4.3.1.2 Objects viewed as substances

The reverse process of viewing an object as a substance is less common although almost any object can be mentally transformed into a substance. When we construe an object as a substance, we restrict its essence as a thing to one particular domain, as illustrated in the examples under (3):

(3) a. We had *octopus* for lunch. [*domain*: food]
     b. We did (pages of) *Shakespeare* today. [*domain*: reading]
     c. The whole neighbourhood is full of *skunk*. [*domain*: smell]
     d. You will get a lot of *car* for your money. [*domain*: comfort]
     e. This is a lot of *garden* for one man to do. [*domain*: work]

Lifting the conceptual boundaries of an object has the effect of destroying, or moving the focus away from, both its whole and its internal composition. When we are served octopus, we can no longer identify the invertebrate's body parts, some of which, apart from its sucker-bearing arms, will even have been removed. More importantly, it is no longer alive and frightening. As a substance, the octopus in (3a) is reduced to the domain of food.

an octopus *We had octopus for lunch.*
Figure 4.3. Object, and object viewed as substance

Similarly, the substance 'Shakespeare' in (3b) belongs to the domain of reading and text analysis. While the usages of 'animals' as 'food' and 'authors' as 'reading material' have become conventionalised, the shifts in examples (3c-e) have a feel of deliberate anomaly: in (3c), the substance 'skunk' is understood in the domain of smell, in (3d), the substance 'car' pertains to the domain of comfort, performance or size depending on what is relevant to the buyer of the car, and in (3e), the substance 'garden' relates to the domain of work to be done in the garden. All these shifts are metonymic: an object is used to stand for a domain of that object, and domains are seen as substances.

4.3.1.3 The object-substance continuum of things

The object-substance continuum of things may be represented as shown in Figure 4.4. In between bounded, heterogeneous objects at the one end and unbounded, homogeneous substances at the other end we have two types of blended categories: substances which are seen as objects and objects which are seen as substances.

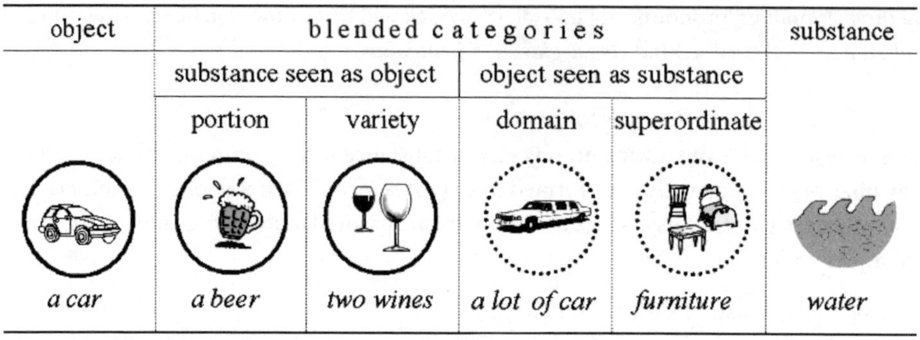

object	blended categories				substance
	substance seen as object		object seen as substance		
	portion	variety	domain	superordinate	
a car	a beer	two wines	a lot of car	furniture	water

Figure 4.4. The object-substance continuum of things

The three solid circles to the left indicate bounded things, i.e. objects (*a* car) and substances seen as objects (*a beer* and *two wines*); the three dotted circles to the right indicate unbounded things, i.e. substances (*water*) and objects seen as substances (*a lot of car* and *furniture*). Things like a car at the left end of the continuum are prototypical objects, and things like water at the right end are prototypical substances. The things in the midfield represent different types of blended categories.

4.3.2 The uniplex-multiplex continuum of objects

Uniplex things consist of one element and should ideally be expressed by a singular noun, while multiplex things consist of more than one element and should ideally be expressed by a plural noun. Often, however, a multiplex thing may be seen as uniplex and a uniplex thing may be seen multiplex. The former situation is found with nouns such as *football team*, the latter with nouns such as *scissors*. A football team is multiplex with respect to its individual players and uniplex with respect to the team as a whole. The uniplex aspect predominates in the English singular noun *football team*. Scissors, on the other hand, are uniplex as a single object and multiplex with respect to their two blades. Here, the multiplex aspect predominates in the English plural noun *scissors*. We will now look more closely at both types of hybrid nouns.

4.3.2.1 *Multiplex objects viewed as uniplex: Collective nouns*

Nouns such as *football team* or *jury* are known as **collective nouns**. Collective nouns denote groups of individual members composed as a set. We mentally group together individuals as members of a composed set if the set is seen as a distinct entity of its own within a certain domain. Thus, the players of a football team can be seen as forming a group because they follow a common goal in the domain of sports.

Collective nouns describe multiplex objects which can be seen in two ways: we may either foreground the group as a whole and background its members or foreground its individual members and background the group. In British English, these two perspectives lead to two possible grammatical construals, as illustrated in the following pair of sentences:

(4) a. The jury *which has* been selected in the murder trial *is* likely to be unanimous in *its* verdict.
b. The jury, *who are* meeting today, *are* still undecided about *their* verdict.

Sentence (4a) foregrounds the jury as a collective group and backgrounds the individual jurors. We may therefore describe this collective construal as "group construal". In this construal, the collection is no longer viewed as composed of individuals but is conceived of as a single entity. This can be seen in the verb's singular agreement with the collective noun. At the same time, the group of humans is mentally transformed into an inanimate object. This can be seen in the choice of the relative pronoun *which* and the possessive pronoun *its*. In varieties of English which provide an alternative construal to that of (4a), the group construal suggests that the collection in its totality is affected.

Sentence (4b) foregrounds the individual jurors without losing sight of the group as a whole. The singular subject *the jury* profiles the jury as a group, while the verb *are* and the pronoun *their* profile its individual members. Moreover, the pronoun *who* reflects the human character of the individuals. This collective construal can be described as "individual construal". As an alternative to the group construal, the individual construal focuses on the members as individuals. In American English, the individual construal is not used, i.e. the grammar of American English forces its speakers to see collections in their totality only.

As shown in Figure 4.5, both collective construals involve conceptual blending. One of their input spaces comprises individuals which are mentally grouped together — notice that there is no boundary in reality demarcating the group. In the group construal, the second input space is a schematic inanimate object; in the individual construal, the second input space contains individuals.

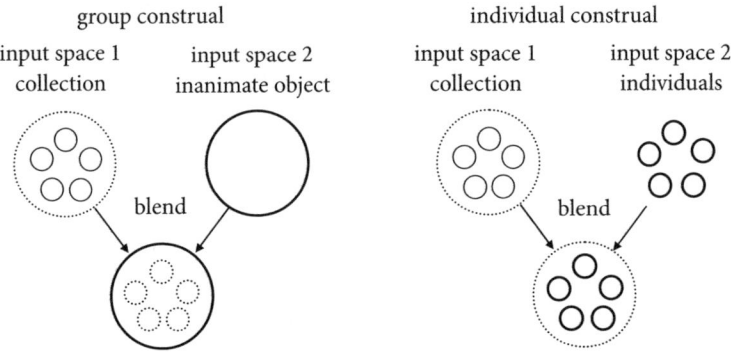

(a) *The jury is unanimous in its verdict.* (b) *The jury are undecided about their verdict.*

Figure 4.5. Two types of collective construal

In Figure (a), the bold lines of the blend circle indicate that the collective group is in profile and seen as an object — except for the fact that its internal composition does not consist of parts but of individual members. In Figure (b), the bold lines of the small circles in the blend indicate that the individual members are profiled. However, the notion of the group is still present in the blend and indicated by the dotted circle surrounding the members.

As is well known, there are a few collective nouns in both British and American English that are used only in the individual construal. In the sentences under (5), the singular collective-noun subjects require a plural verbal concord — an idiosyncrasy of English that often puzzles speakers of other languages.

(5) a. The police *were* injured.
b. The cattle *are* grazing in the corn field.

The types of objects which we tend to see collectively are, as shown in Table 4.6, mainly (i) groups of human beings that are united with respect to a certain domain, (ii) animals of a similar kind that live together, (iii) salient collections of artefacts that belong together, and (iv) configurations of natural objects.

Table 4.6. Types of multiplex objects and collective nouns

	groups	collective nouns
(i)	human groups:	*army, orchestra, committee, jury, family*
(ii)	groupings of animals:	*a flock* (*of sheep*), *a herd* (*of cattle*)
(iii)	collections of artefacts:	*a batch* (*of papers*), *a pack* (*of cards*)
(iv)	configurations of natural objects:	*a constellation* (*of stars*), *a bunch* (*of flowers*)

We group humans as in (i) together much more readily than animals as in (ii) or inanimate objects as in (iii) and (iv). This is, of course, due to the fact that humans are organised in all kinds of social groups. The groups are normally defined by certain goals within a domain, such as playing music. The prominent position of human groups is also reflected in the possibility of using human collective nouns without expressing the members that constitute the group. Thus, we speak of *an army* or *an orchestra*, but we would not, as a rule, speak of ?*an army of soldiers*, ?*an orchestra of musicians*, etc., which would be felt to be tautological. With non-human collective nouns, by contrast, phrases such as *a bunch of flowers* are normal rather than exceptional.

4.3.2.2 *Uniplex and amassed objects viewed as multiplex: Pluralia tantum*

A number of objects are in English viewed as multiplex and expressed as plural nouns like *measles* or *glasses*. Unlike count nouns, these plural nouns can normally not be counted by means of numerals. Thus, *ten measles cannot be said to describe ten cases of this disease, and *three glasses* can only be said in reference to wine glasses or other containers made of glass, but not to three pairs of eyeglasses. This class of inherently plural nouns is traditionally described as **pluralia tantum** (from Latin 'plurals only'). There may be different motivations for viewing a thing as multiplex.

The most obvious motivation for conceiving of a single thing as multiplex is its apparent, unmistakable composition of many discrete elements. *Measles* and *mumps* are names of infectious diseases which show as spots on a person's skin, *billiards*, *draughts* and *darts* are names of games which are played with several balls, pieces or darts, *the United States*, *the Netherlands* and *the Balkans* are names of countries or geographical areas which are, or were once, composed of separate states or countries, and the evening news on television is composed of many news items and hence described as *news* (plural of *new* as a translation of Latin *nova* 'new things'). Words ending in *-ics* such as *gymnastics*, *politics* and *linguistics* are historically plural (as adaptations from Greek or Latin neuter plural forms in *-ika* or *-ica*). These nouns describe fields of study which subsume many branches. The blended character of these multiplex things manifests itself in their linguistic behaviour: the nouns are plural in form but take singular verb agreement as in:

(6) a. The Balkans *is* a powder keg.
b. This *is* the nine o'clock news.

This group of *pluralia tantum* leans toward the uniplex end of the uniplex-multiplex continuum. The singular agreement of these nouns indicates that the things they denote are felt to constitute a unitary entity.

Another group of *pluralia tantum* has plural agreement and thus leans toward the multiplex end of the continuum. This group includes names of dual objects, multiple objects and amassed objects along a cline of multiplexity.

Objects that consist of two prominent symmetrical parts may be seen as multiplex. Such "dual objects" are typically expressed as plural nouns (*glasses*, *scissors*, *pants*, *lungs*, etc.). Notice, however, that it is not sufficient for objects to consist of two identical parts — these must also be prominent. If this is not the case, they are rendered as regular count nouns such as *shirt*, *blouse*, *jacket* and *coat*. The two parts of underwear are normally not prominent, as in *bra* and *slip*. Loanwords such as *bikini* and *bicycle* are less transparent and tend to show an element of arbitrariness in their grammatical behaviour.

Objects that encompass several individual elements may also be viewed as multiplex. The individual elements of "multiple objects" can normally be quantified and sometimes also be counted. Thus, we can speak of *many belongings*, *many valuables*, *many surroundings* and *many groceries*. We may also have *three belongings* and *five valuables* but, for no apparent reason, not ?*three surroundings* and ?*five groceries*, unless we mean five grocery stores. The plural noun *wages* also describes a multiple object; its elements, however, are not quantifiable like normal quantities because they are seen along a scale of 'high' and 'low'. When *wages* is quantified, as in *Her wages are below poverty level*, it refers to wages along the scale of verticality.

Certain amassed things which are only loosely lumped together are also seen as forming multiple objects and expressed as plural nouns. The individual elements are easier to discern in some "amassed objects" than in others. Horse-droppings, for example, may be spread all over the road as individuated pieces of horse dung. They are perceived as multiplex and therefore expressed as a plural noun, while a cow pat is seen as a uniplex object and expressed as a normal count noun. We rarely feel the need to quantify or count the elements an amassed object is composed of, but the grammar of English often allows us to do so. Thus we can speak of *many* or *three horse-droppings* and *tea-leaves*, of *many leftovers, oats, grounds* and *basics*, but only of *guts* and *ashes*.

We can now locate the different types of objects along the uniplex-multiplex continuum as shown in Figure 4.6.

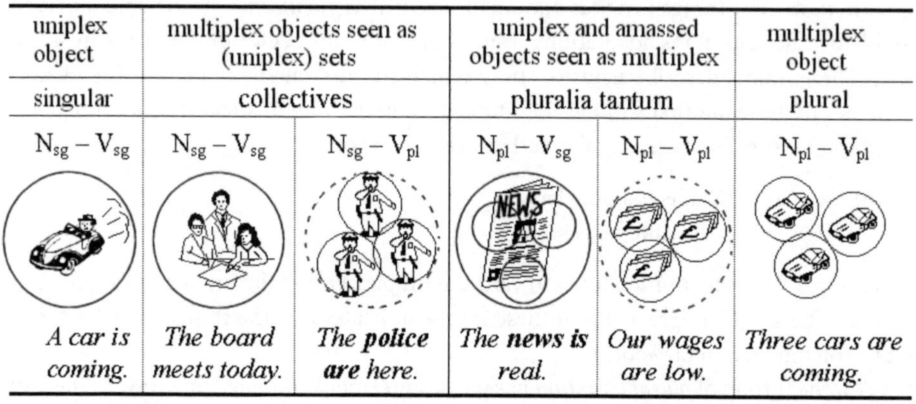

uniplex object	multiplex objects seen as (uniplex) sets		uniplex and amassed objects seen as multiplex		multiplex object
singular	collectives		pluralia tantum		plural
$N_{sg} - V_{sg}$	$N_{sg} - V_{sg}$	$N_{sg} - V_{pl}$	$N_{pl} - V_{sg}$	$N_{pl} - V_{pl}$	$N_{pl} - V_{pl}$
A car is coming.	The board meets today.	The **police** **are** here.	The **news is** real.	Our wages are low.	Three cars are coming.

(N_{sg} = singular noun form, V_{pl} = plural verb form, etc.)

Figure 4.6. The uniplex-multiplex continuum of objects

The entities encircled in bold lines at either end of the continuum indicate straightforward objects; the presence of smaller circles within a big circle indicates the blended status of an object. Aspects that predominate in a blend are printed in bold lines, while aspects that are backgrounded are printed in broken lines. English makes use of all possibilities of combining number in nouns and the verbs that agree with them. The hybrid nouns printed in bold do not agree with the number of their verbs.

4.4 Reified things: Abstract nouns

4.4.1 Reification and nominalisation

Our discussion of things has so far concentrated on concrete things and the way they are expressed as concrete nouns. Concrete things like the object 'tree' or the substance 'water' are prototypical things: they belong to the physical domain and can be seen, touched and manipulated. This section will consider abstract things and their linguistic expressions as abstract nouns. A very large number of abstract things, if not most, are based on relational concepts viewed as thing-like. For example, the relation 'be married' is treated like an object when we speak of 'marriage'. The conceptual shift from a relational concept to a thing is known as reification (from Latin *res* 'thing').

Reification involves a metaphorical shift from a relational entity into a thing. It makes us see a relation as having some kind of "ontological" existence (from Greek *óntos* 'being'). This type of metaphorical shift has therefore been named **ontological metaphor**. Since relations are essential to conceptual cores and situations, ontological metaphors allow us to understand events and states in terms of things. For example, the state expressed by *We* *are married* is expressed as a thing in *our marriage* — and is thus treated on a par with concrete things as in *our house* so that we can predicate the same attributes to them: *Our house/Our marriage is in order/stands firm/is in shambles.*

The conceptual shift from relation to thing, or reification, has its linguistic counterpart in what is called nominalisation. **Nominalisation** refers either to the process of deriving abstract nouns from other word classes or to the resulting abstract noun itself. Nominalised abstract nouns are typically derived from verbs, adjectives or nouns: *marriage* derives from the verb *marry* or *be married*, *happiness* from the adjective *happy*, and *friendship* from the noun *friend*.

Not all abstract nouns are, however, morphologically derived forms. For example, the abstract nouns *horror* and *theft* are not derived from the verbs **horror* or *thieve* — the verb *thieve* does exist (as an informal synonym of *steal*) but is derived from the noun *thief*. The linguistic notion of 'nominalisation' is obviously too restricted to allow us to account for all abstract nouns. At the conceptual level, however, we need not worry about lexical gaps and idiosyncrasies of a particular language. Conceptually, the abstract thing 'horror' is reified from the conceptual relation lexicalised by a Latin stem **horr-* 'fright', also found in *be horrified*; 'theft' is a reification of the conceptual relation symbolised by a stem *thiev-* 'steal'; and 'accident' is the ontological equivalent of a relation expressed by the Latin verb *accedere* 'approach by coincidence' and narrowed down to 'crash into another car' or some similar situation.

Reification does not, or not substantially, affect the conceptual content of the original relational concept, which is largely preserved in the reified thing. The conceptual impact of reification is in giving relational concepts the kind of stable existence that we typically associate with things. We can, in particular, refer to reified things as in *this marriage* in the same way that we refer to *this computer*, we can modify them as in *my new marriage* just like *my new computer*, we can quantify them as in *many marriages* just like *many computers*, and we can treat them as either objects or substances. Thus, *marriage* is used as a count noun in *Each of my three marriages ended in divorce* and as a mass noun in *There are various forms of marriage*. At the same time, however, reified things preserve some aspects of their relational, and often processual character: they may have a beginning, a duration and an end, which can be brought out by means of temporal expressions. Thus, we can speak of a marriage or friendship which began in 1955, lasted for fifty years, and ended in 2005, but we cannot speak of a friend, a wife or a tree that began in 1955 or lasted for fifty years. The conceptual difference between a thing, a relation, a situation and a reified thing may schematically be represented as sketched in Figure 4.7. Here, the circles stand for things, in this case two people; the line connecting them indicates a relation, bold lines indicate profiled conceptual units, and the arrow stands for the passage of time.

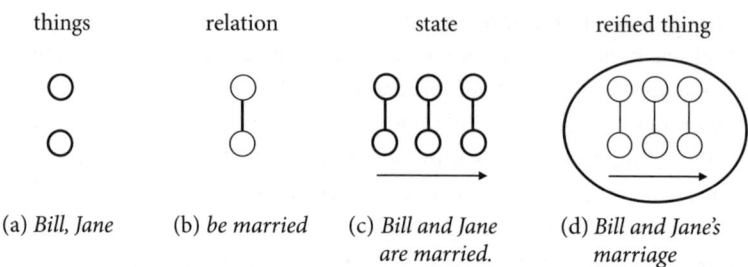

Figure 4.7. Things, relation, situation (state) and reified thing

The two things depicted in diagram (a), Bill and Jane, exist independently of each other. The bold line in diagram (b) represents a relation, 'be married', between two things. In diagram (c), the relation 'be married' links Bill and Jane as a conceptual core, and the succession of an indefinite number of such identical cores, or component states, forms a state. In processing the temporal state described by *Bill and Jane are married*, we mentally "scan" all its component states through time. As pointed out in Chapter 2.1.5, such temporal situations are characterised as involving sequential scanning. In diagram (c), this is indicated by three conceptual cores as component states and the time arrow. The reification in diagram (d) converts the temporal situation into an atemporal thing, indicated by a bold circle. Internally the succession of identical component states is still present in the reified thing 'marriage'. But, since things do not pertain to time, we do not scan their internal component states sequentially but see all of them accumulated. Atemporal conceptual units are therefore characterised as involving summary scanning. The component states inherent in 'marriage' may, however, still be invoked, for example by means of a temporal expression as in *Our marriage has lasted for sixty years*.

4.4.2 Abstract objects and substances: Abstract count and mass nouns

Like concrete things, abstract things may be construed as objects or substances, and hence be expressed as count nouns or mass nouns. However, with abstract nouns the dividing line between count and mass nouns is far less clear-cut than with concrete nouns. Abstract things lack distinct physical properties and are therefore open to variable categorisation. For example, the abstract thing 'pain' can be seen in either way: as an object in (7a) or as a substance in (7b):

(7) a. She has a terrible pain in her back.
    b. She is in great pain.

The count and mass nouns in (7) convey differences in meaning which are reminiscent of the ones we encountered with concrete count and mass nouns. The count noun *pain* in (7a) refers to the feeling of pain in a localised area of one's body. This feeling of pain is bounded in space and therefore coded as a count noun. It should be mentioned, though, that the count noun *pain* does not have all the characteristics of concrete count nouns. Thus it can be pluralised (*pains*), but it cannot be counted as in **I have three pains*. The mass noun *pain* in (7b), on the other hand, refers to a general, undifferentiated state of bodily or emotional suffering. This feeling of pain is unbounded in space and therefore seen as a substance.

Let us, as a further challenge, look at the abstract nouns *war* and *peace*. Both *war* and *peace* may be used as mass nouns as in (8a) and (8b), but *war* may also occur as a count noun as in (8c), while *peace* may not, i.e. we do not speak of **a peace* or **two peaces* like we do of *a war* or *two wars*:

(8)   a.   Former Yugoslavia has been ravaged by *war*.
       b.   Western Europe has seen *peace* for over half a century.
       c.   Britain fought two *wars* in the 20th century.

Both *war* and *peace* describe the unbounded state a country is in, which explains their usage as mass nouns in (8a) and (8b). But why should *war*, but not *peace*, also occur as a count noun in (8c)? A war, even a hundred years' war, is viewed as lasting for a limited period of time and involving intensive military actions. In this respect, a war corresponds to the bounded and heterogeneous internal composition of objects. Peace, on the other hand, even a very short period of it, is thought of as an undifferentiated state that lasts indefinitely. Peace thus corresponds to unbounded and homogeneous substances. The conceptual difference between these count and mass nouns also shows up in their temporal usages. Due to its bounded nature, the count noun *war* may be used to describe the time during which events happen, as in *All we had to eat during the war was cabbage*. Due to its unbounded nature, however, the mass noun *peace* excludes this temporal usage: **There was plenty of food to eat during (the) peace*.

4.4.3 Types of reification

Most reified things can be expressed as count nouns or mass nouns. Dictionaries usually provide examples of both usages. One of these usages may, however, be predominant for a given abstract noun.

The abstract nouns *war, attack, protest, problem, doubt* and *desire* are generally used as count nouns. What these abstract count nouns have in common is that they describe **episodic situations**, i.e. situations which, due to their limited duration, are seen as discrete episodes. Episodic situations are typically events that take place or come up (*attack, protest, objection*), but also certain states that can suddenly arise are seen as episodic (*disease, idea, doubt*).

In contrast, the abstract nouns *peace, knowledge, happiness, information, help* and *advice* are mostly used as mass nouns. They describe **steady situations**, i.e. situations which are seen as lasting indefinitely or holding in general. Steady situations are typically states (*peace, knowledge, happiness*), but also certain events are seen as steady (*information, help, advice*).

Table 4.7 summarises these observations and shows how the relational concepts discussed so far — here described as situations — are reified as either objects or substances and hence coded as count nouns or mass nouns. The typical "routes of reification" are printed in bold. Words that may be reified as either objects or substances are indicated by subscripts.

Table 4.7. Situations reified as things

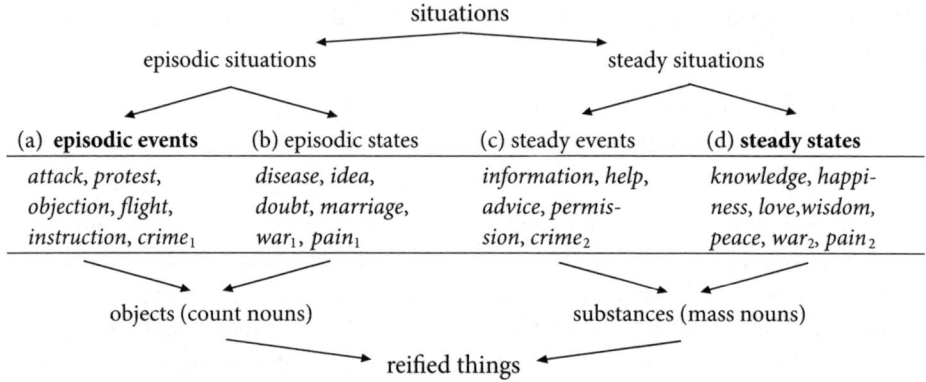

These four types of reification may be stated as ontological metaphors:

(9) a. EPISODIC EVENTS ARE OBJECTS: They gave us no *instructions*.
b. EPISODIC STATES ARE OBJECTS: I have *doubts* about this.
c. STEADY EVENTS ARE SUBSTANCES: I need some *help*.
d. STEADY STATES ARE SUBSTANCES: I only have little *knowledge* of computers.

(a) Episodic events are bounded in time, internally heterogeneous, and may reoccur: they are therefore typically reified as objects. For example, the safety instructions given by a stewardess take a limited time before take-off, point to different measures to be taken in case of emergency, and are given over and over again with each flight. Episodic events typically involve a beginning, a process phase and a result. Abstract nouns describing episodic events may refer either to the process phase or to its result. In (10a), the noun *instructions* refers to the process of instructing, in (10b) to the result of instructing:

(10) a. The stewardess gave the safety *instructions*. [process]
b. The *instructions* are on the leaflet in the seats. [result]

The result of an event belongs to the same conceptual domain as the event itself; hence the result meaning in (10b) is due to the metonymic shift EVENT FOR ITS RESULT. This metonymic shift is in fact so common with nouns describing episodic events that people are hardly aware of their systematic polysemy.

(b) Episodic states that are reified as objects are normally transient states such as diseases, wars or even marriages (in their bounded senses), which are coded as count nouns: *a disease*, *an idea* and *a marriage*.

(c) Steady events that are reified as substances include the social acts of advising, informing, permitting and helping, which are expressed by the mass nouns *advice*, *information, permission* and *help*, as in *We need some help*. Any event may, however, be reified as a substance by using the gerund as in *Smoking is hazardous to your health* and *Dancing is fun*.

(d) Steady states that are reified as substances include fairly permanent attributes such as being strong (*strength*), being healthy (*health*), or being wise (*wisdom*), mental and emotional states such as knowing something (*knowledge*), loving someone (*love*), being happy (*happiness*) or having fun (*fun*), and general, culturally and socially given states such as *peace, war, patriotism* and *justice*. In fact most abstract notions are thought of in English as substances and expressed as mass nouns such as *science, education, work*, etc. Given the appropriate context, however, more or less all abstract things may also be viewed as object-like. Their conceptual bounding has the same effect we encountered with concrete substances viewed as objects (see 4.3.1.1): they are understood in a 'variety' sense. For example, the noun *strength* is normally used as a mass noun, but when it is used as a count noun as in *His strengths are mathematics and tennis*, it refers to different kinds of strength.

4.5 Summary

Things as conceptual units are divided into objects and substances, which are the conceptual counterparts of the linguistic categories 'count noun' and 'mass noun'. They are distinguished on the basis of the three criteria of boundedness, internal composition and countability. **Objects** are bounded in some domain, internally heterogeneous and countable; **substances** are unbounded, internally homogeneous and uncountable. Count nouns and mass nouns display different grammatical behaviour with respect to taking numerals, forming a plural, use of quantifiers and presence or absence of articles.

The majority of concrete nouns clearly belong to one of these conceptual categories. Prototypical **count nouns** have the properties of objects, prototypical **mass nouns** have the properties of substances. A great many nouns, however, vacillate between these poles. Such nouns are treated here as **hybrid nouns.** Hybrid nouns are to be placed along two conceptual continua: an object-substance continuum of things and a uniplex-multiplex continuum of objects. Hybrid nouns along the object-substance continuum describe substances viewed as objects, as in *three beers*, and objects viewed as substances, as in *a lot of car*. Hybrid nouns along the uniplex-multiplex continuum describe multiplex objects viewed as uniplex and uniplex and amassed things viewed as multiplex. The former group is expressed as **collective nouns**, which describe members of a composed set as in *jury*. These nouns are morphologically singular and may, in British English, take singular verb agreement as in *The jury is unanimous in its verdict* or plural verb agreement as in *The jury are undecided about their verdict*. A few collective nouns such as *people* and *police* require plural agreement. Another group of nouns only occur in the plural form. These nouns are known as **pluralia tantum**. Some of these nouns take singular verb agreement as in *The news is real*, others take plural verb agreement as in *The surroundings of the town are* *beautiful*. The group of *pluralia tantum* also includes plural mass nouns expressing amassed things such as *groceries*, which take plural agreement as in *The groceries are there*.

The majority of **abstract nouns** are derived from verbs, adjectives or nouns by means of a morphological process known as **nominalisation**. For example, the abstract noun *marriage* is derived from the verb *marry*. There are, however, also many non-derived abstract nouns, such as *peace*, which are conceptually no different from nominalised forms. Conceptually, all abstract nouns are treated alike as **reifications**, i.e. as ontological metaphors, which allow us to understand relational concepts or situations in terms of things. Like concrete nouns, abstract nouns fall into count nouns and mass nouns. Their distinction is, however, less clear-cut. As a rule, **episodic situations**, i.e. situations that are thought of as holding for a limited time, are converted into objects and hence coded as abstract count nouns, such as *attack*, while **steady situations**, i.e. situations that are thought of as lasting indefinitely, are converted into substances and hence coded as abstract mass nouns, such as *knowledge*.

Further Reading

The conceptual basis of nouns as things is developed in Langacker (1991a: Ch. 1). The distinction between count and mass nouns has been studied in Moravcsik (1973), Pelletier (1979), Allan (1980), Mufwene (1984), Markman (1985), Bunt (1985), Wierzbicka (1985, 1988a), Talmy (1988b/2000), Wilckens (1992), Svensson (1998) and Middleton, Wisniewski, Trindel & Imai (2004) as well as in many reference grammars of English, such as Quirk *et al.* (1985) and Huddleston & Pullum (2002). The use of collective nouns in British English is studied by Depraetere (2003).
A classic on nominalisation is Lees (1960); cognitive approaches to nominalisation are Nikiforidou (1999) and Heyvaert (2003a,b, 2004). The analysis of abstract nouns as ontological metaphors goes back to Lakoff & Johnson (1980: Ch. 6); in the afterword to the second edition (2003: 264), they argue that all metaphors are structural; all are ontological and many are orientational. The notion of 'conceptual reification' is developed in Langacker (1991a); for a critique of reification see Sinha (1999). A recent cognitive treatment of abstract nouns is Schmid (2000).

Study questions

1. Decide whether the following nouns are (i) count nouns, (ii) mass nouns, or (iii) both. When in doubt, check the word in a dictionary.
   a. *literature*
   b. *champagne*
   c. *character*
   d. *show*
   e. *love*
   f. *position*

2. Give the collective nouns for the following collections of "things".
   a. soldiers
   b. sheep
   c. stars
   d. the common people in the court of law judging the defendant's guilt
   e. believers in church
   f. rulers of the country
   g. ministers of the church
   h. people of nobility
   i. organization of workers

3. Provide the missing noun in the following sentences.
   a. *A sudden … of wind came up.*
   b. *We were greeted with a … of applause.*
   c. *It's your turn to shuffle the … of cards and deal.*
   d. *There is a … of fish over here at this side of the boat.*
   e. *I felt a sudden … of guilt.*
   f. *Do you want a good … of advice?*
   g. *There was no … of evidence of his murder.*

4. Analyse the meaning of the final -s in the following nouns provided its meaning as a morpheme can be identified.
   a. books
   b. fruits
   c. *physics*
   d. *scissors*
   e. *draughts*
   f. *sugars*
   g. *ashes*
   h. *wines*
   i. *summons*
   j. *weathers*
   k. *DTs (delirium tremens)*
   l. *brains*

5. Comment upon the usages of the italicised nouns in the following sentences.
   a. I am campaigning against early retirement for married men. It appears to me that it means twice as much *husband* on half as much money.
   b. Northern Ireland will have a little sunshine, a little *cloud* and a number of showers.
   c. Heineken refreshes the parts other *beers* cannot reach.
   d. His work as a reporter gave him a detailed *knowledge* of London and its inhabitants.

Chapter 5

Grounding things: Reference

5.0 Overview
5.1 Reference, referents and referring expressions
5.2 Indefinite reference
5.3 Definite reference
5.4 Generic reference
5.5 Conclusion
5.6 Summary

5.0 Overview

The various instances of things brought up in discourse need to be shared by speaker and hearer. The speaker therefore tries to make the things she has in mind accessible to the hearer. She may relate them either to the ongoing speech situation or to the hearer's state of knowledge, as assessed by the speaker. Technically, the speaker "grounds" the instance of a thing in an act of **reference**. If the speaker deems that the hearer has as yet no access to the instances meant, she uses **indefinite reference** expressed in indefinite noun phrases. If the hearer can be supposed to be able to access the instances of the things meant, the speaker uses **definite reference**. A special case occurs when the speaker refers to the class as a whole, which is called **generic reference**.

5.1 Reference, referents and referring expressions

5.1.1 How we refer

When thinking or talking to people, we have all kinds of things in our minds: my friend Sue, the ticket I have just bought or the cup of cappuccino I am dying to drink. Usually, these are particular instances of a thing (for the notions *type*, *token* and *instance* see Chapter 4.1.1). When we want to talk about such instances, we need to draw the hearer's attention to them and ensure that the hearer will have the same instance in mind as we do.

Technically, the particular instance of a thing we draw attention to in speaking is known as a **referent**, and the communicative act of directing the hearer's attention to a referent is known as **reference**. An act of reference is achieved by using a **referring expression**, by means of which the speaker "anchors", or grounds, a referent in the current discourse situation. Referring expressions are noun phrases, i.e. phrases composed of a grounding element and a noun (for grounding see Chapter 3.2.2). For example, in the noun phrase *your dog*, the grounding element *your* anchors the referent 'dog' in the speech situation.

Successful acts of reference are performed so automatically that we are hardly aware of the complexities of referring. Let us therefore illustrate reference by considering a typical example of referential failure:

(1) Gerald to Harry: "We'll meet at *the pub* in Greek Street."
(Gerald goes to the 'Coach and Horses', while Harry is waiting in the 'Three Greyhounds'.)

The instruction was obviously not "precise" enough for Harry to call up the same pub that Gerald had in mind. But what exactly went wrong? As a first piece of information, Gerald provided the name of the category, 'pub', so that Harry would only have to look for a pub and not for other things like shops. As a second piece of information, Gerald specified the pub's location in Greek Street so that Harry would not look for a pub in Gower Street. As a third piece of information, Gerald used the definite article *the* in the referring expression *the pub in Greek Street*. He hereby expressed his double assumption that the instance of a pub he had in mind, the 'Coach and Horses', was the only pub in Greek Street and that for this reason it was also accessible to Harry, i.e. that Harry would be able to call up the same pub that he had in mind, possibly because they had been to this pub before. Unfortunately, the use of the definite referring expression also confirmed Harry in *his* belief that the referent he was thinking of, i.e. 'Three Greyhounds', was also the one that Gerald meant, possibly because they had talked about it.

We may now generalise these observations as conditions for successful acts of reference. The speaker normally has to perform the following four tasks:

Firstly, the speaker has to specify the *type* of thing to which the particular referent belongs. In our example, the relevant type is the thing 'pub'.

Secondly, the speaker wants to direct the hearer's attention to the particular token, or *instance*, of the thing he has in mind. This instance becomes the referent. The number of potential instances within a thing's **reference mass** is infinite, and of course there is not a name for each one of them. Normally, therefore, an instance remains unnamed.

Thirdly, the speaker has to assess the instance with respect to its *reality status*, i.e. whether it belongs to the world of reality or non-reality, and with respect to the *hearer's knowledge*, i.e. whether or not the hearer already knows the instance meant by the speaker. In our pub example, Gerald obviously assumed that Harry knew which pub he meant.

Fourthly, the speaker has to decide on the appropriate *referring expression* to ground the referent in the speech situation. In the pub example, he chose the referring expression *the pub* with the definite article. He might as well have chosen a possessive determiner (*our pub*), a modifying phrase (*the pub with the new dart board*), or the proper name *Coach and Horses*. In this case, the choice of the definite article turned out to be misleading because it suggested to the hearer that he knew which pub the speaker had in mind.

These steps in a normal act of referring are sketched in Figure 5.1. First the speaker thinks of a category, such as 'pub'. If it is named, it is expressed as a noun: *pub*. He then wants to draw attention to the particular instance of 'pub' among the reference mass of pubs. He does so by grounding the referent in the speech situation by means of the referring expression *the pub*. In a successful act of reference, both speaker and hearer establish mental contact with the same instance, which is indicated by dotted arrows pointing to the particular instance printed in bold.

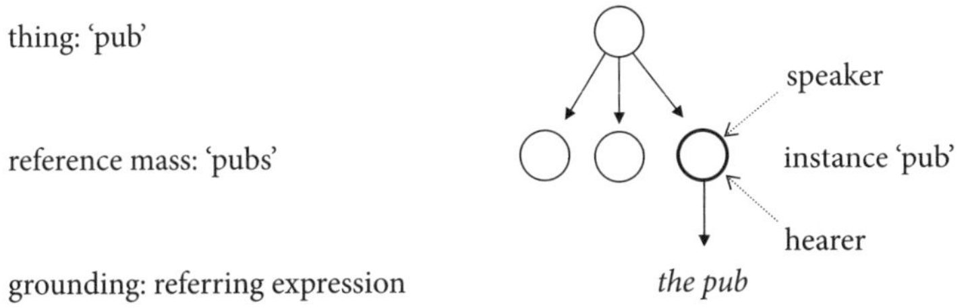

thing: 'pub'

reference mass: 'pubs'

speaker

instance 'pub'

hearer

grounding: referring expression   *the pub*

Figure 5.1. An act of reference: *the pub*

Like many other linguistic phenomena, reference can be seen as a problem-solving strategy: how can we talk about all the things, real and imaginary, that we lack names for? Languages provide a large number of proper names (see Section 5.3.3), but we would need billions of proper names to cover all potential individual referents in the world. The solution is to use common names of higher-order types for particular instances of them and ground the particular instance in the speech situation. Grounding is achieved by using grounding elements in the referring expression, which anchor the instance in the current discourse and thus make it accessible to the hearer. This chapter will mainly be concerned with the possibilities available to the speaker in grounding a referent.

The main function of referring expressions is usually seen as that of identifying a referent, but this is only one aspect of it and, as we will see, does not even apply to all types of reference. Reference is a cognitive phenomenon, and the entities invoked by referring expressions are conceptual in nature. This can be seen from the fact that I can say things like "I have no money", where the referent 'no money' has no existence in the real world. Referents are always part of larger knowledge structures. The knowledge structures set up by referring expressions in an ongoing discourse are short-lived packages of knowledge, which we have already described as mental spaces in Chapter 2.2. The notion of 'mental space' will be fundamental in understanding the conceptual basis of the different types of reference.

5.1.2 Types of reference

The most basic distinction between types of reference is that between individuative reference and generic reference. **Individuative reference** is used in speaking of an individuative instance, where an 'individuative instance' is not restricted to *one* particular token but can also mean any number of tokens singled out for referential purposes, as in (2a). **Generic reference** is used in speaking about a class as a whole, as in (2b)

(2) a. *These lawyers* are crooks. [*individuative reference*]
    b. *Lawyers* are crooks. [*generic reference*]

We use individuative reference when we talk about things that are occurring, have occurred, or may occur. Thus the statement about the particular lawyers in (2a) may be based on my personal experience, e.g. in a family lawsuit case over an inheritance. We use generic reference when we talk more generally about the world as we perceive it to be structured. Thus the generalisation in (2b) is meant to hold true for the world at large, present, past and future. Most people's concern is with events and states that actually occur, and hence with individuative referents.

Both individuative and generic reference may be indefinite or definite. Let us look at individuative reference first and illustrate the functions of indefinite and definite reference by way of a joke, taken from a British book on national stereotypes. The referring expressions used in this short piece of discourse are typical of the beginning and continuation of referents in a narrative.

(3) (a) A Belgian found a monkey and asked a gendarme what he should do with it. (b) The gendarme told him to take the animal to the zoo. (c) The next day, the gendarme saw the man walking along holding hands with the monkey. (d) "Look," said the gendarme, "I thought I told you to take the monkey to the zoo." (e) "Yes," said the Belgian, "We went to the zoo yesterday. (f) Today we're going to the cinema."

Narratives typically start out by introducing to the hearer instances of things. Here, three participants in a situation are introduced in the first sentence: a Belgian, a monkey and a gendarme. Since these instances are not yet accessible to the hearer, the speaker has to open a mental space for them in the hearer's mind. This is achieved by using the indefinite article *a* in their referring expressions. This type of reference is called **indefinite reference**.

Once the speaker can assume that the hearer has a mental space available for an instance, she uses **definite reference**. After hearing the first sentence (3a), the hearer has opened a mental space for each of the three instances introduced there, and the speaker can therefore assume that both of them share the same instances. In the following sentence (3b), the speaker therefore uses the definite referring expressions *the gendarme*, *him* and *the animal*. *The zoo* and *the cinema* are also referred to by definite referring expressions, but these instances are available to hearers within their shared frames of a metropolis.

With generic reference, referring expressions also distinguish between indefiniteness and definiteness as in (4a) and (4b). However, their functions are different, as will be shown in Section 5.4.

(4) a. *A tiger* has a life-span of about 11 years.
   b. *The tiger* hunts by night.

The four types of reference introduced above are summarised in Table 5.1. The three main types of reference to be discussed in this chapter are printed in bold. We will present them in the following order: indefinite reference (Section 5.2), definite reference (Section 5.3), and generic reference (Section 5.4).

Table 5.1. Main types of reference

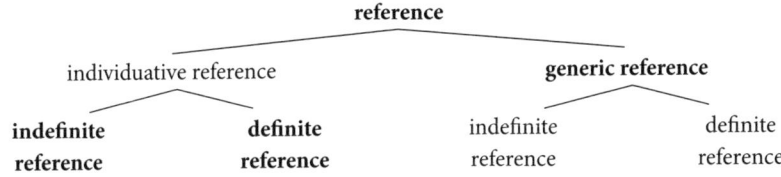

5.2 Indefinite reference

Indefinite reference involves singling out a particular element from a reference mass, or a set. A **set** is a collection of elements that forms a whole. In the case of the indefinite referent *a Belgian* in the beginning of the narrative under (3), one particular Belgian is singled out from the set of all Belgians. A set may also be implicitly defined by a pragmatic situation. For example, when we ask someone, "Can you open a window?", we are thinking of the set of windows of the room or car in which we and the hearer(s) are and would like to have one of the windows opened. If the room has only one window, we will not say "Can you open a window?" That is, indefinite reference always implies elements of a set that are singled out for reference and other elements of the set that are "excluded" from reference. Indefinite reference has therefore been characterised as "exclusive".

English has a fairly elaborate system of indefinite determiners, which we will look at first.

5.2.1 Indefiniteness and indefinite determiners

The basic system of indefinite determiners is listed in Table 5.2. The choice of the indefinite determiner depends on the type of noun (singular or plural count noun or mass noun) on the one hand and on the context (affirmative or non-affirmative) and the speaker's expectations (positive or negative) on the other hand.

Table 5.2. Indefinite determiners

	context	expectation	singular count noun	plural count noun	mass noun
(i)	affirmative, (numerals)		a(n), (some) one	some /sm/, Ø two, etc.	some /sm/, Ø
(ii)	non-affirmative	negative	any	any	any
(iii)	non-affirmative	positive	some	some	some

5.2.1.1 Affirmative context

By 'affirmative context' we mean non-negated assertions as in the following sentences:

(5) a. They're having *a friend/some friend* round to dinner. [singular]
    b. They're having *friends/some friends* round to dinner. [plural]
    c. They're having *fun/some fun*. [mass]

With singular count nouns in an affirmative context as in (5a), indefiniteness is marked by means of the indefinite article *a(n)* or the determiner *some* in its phonological form /sʌm/. The article *a(n)* has retained its original meaning, i.e. that of the numeral, and refers to one single instance; it is the unmarked determiner for indefinite singular referents. The use of the marked determiner *some* with singular count nouns conveys additional meanings. Its use in sentence (5a), *They're having some friend round to dinner*, suggests indeterminacy and vagueness of the referent: 'I have no idea who exactly it might be'. The use of *some* may also invite further implicated meanings. For example, while *They are having a priest round for dinner* is understood as a neutral statement about the guests invited for dinner, *They are having some priest around for dinner* highlights the type of person that is being invited and may give rise to all kinds of speculation about the referent or might suggest anti-clerical prejudice on the part of the speaker.

With plural count nouns (5b) and mass nouns (5c) in affirmative sentences, indefiniteness is marked by the determiner *some* in its weakened form /sm/ or the zero-form. The indefiniteness of *some* with count nouns ranges between at least 'two' and, in our normal understanding, 'not all'. With abstract nouns, *some* as in *some fun* means 'an indefinite amount of'. The indefinite number or amount described by *some* leans towards the smaller end of the set, while the indefiniteness of the zero-form is fully indeterminate between its endpoints 'more than one' and 'all'. The indeterminacy of the zero-form may be the reason why we tend to read more meaning into its use. We typically shift our attention away from the notion of indefiniteness to the frame associated with the referent. Thus the articleless referents *friends* in *They're having friends round to dinner* and *fun* in *They're having fun* evoke the frame of a 'friendly social gathering'. The ranges of indefiniteness of the three indefinite determiners *a*, *some* (+ plural noun) and zero (+ plural noun) are sketched in Table 5.3.

Table 5.3. Ranges of indefiniteness of indefinite determiners

one	two	three	.....	all
a friend				
		some friends		
		friends		

5.2.1.2 *Non-affirmative context, negative expectation*

Non-affirmative contexts are typically evoked by grammatical constructions such as *yes-no* questions (6a), negated sentences (6b), conditional clauses (6c), and comparative clauses (6d). Certain lexical expressions also evoke non-affirmative contexts, like those in (6e–h).

(6) a. *Did* you have *any* problems with your paper?
     b. No, I did*n't* write *any* of my papers.
     c. *If* there is *anything* you need please let me know.
     d. I like smoked salmon *more than anything* else.
     e. I've *hardly* got *any* work done this year.
     f. I *doubt* that I can do *any* work with this noise.
     g. It is *difficult* to do *any* serious work at all.
     h. I can live off my savings *without* doing *any* work.

The non-affirmative contexts in the sentences above tend to be associated with negative or neutral, i.e. non-positive, expectations. English has a special determiner for such contexts, the "negative polarity item *any*". Like the indefinite article *a(n)*, *any* derives from the numeral 'one', but while *a(n)* grammaticised into an indefinite article, *any*, probably due to its adjectival suffix *-y*, grammaticised into an emphatic determiner (6a) and pronoun (6b) and is no longer restricted to count nouns, as in (6e). Unlike *a(n)*, *any* can be, and typically is, stressed, and it can be additionally emphasised by the phrase *at all*, as in *Did you have any problems at all?* This phrase provides a clue to the special usage of *any*, even if *at all* is not explicitly mentioned. *At all* refers to all elements of a pragmatically or universally defined set (for set see 5.2 and Chapter 6), of which not a single element may qualify for the given purpose. Not surprisingly, such situations are non-affirmative and tend to give rise to negative expectations. The status of the referent specified by *any* may vary. In questions (6a) and conditions (6c), the referent has potential reality, in negations (6b), it is non-existent, and in comparisons (6d), the referent has reality status. What all these different types of referents have in common is their non-affirmative context coupled with non-positive expectations. This also applies to the use of *any* with adverbs such as *hardly, barely, only,* or *too* (6e), verbs such as *doubt, forget, prevent,* or *deny* (6f), adjectives such as *difficult, hard, reluctant,* or *unwilling* (6g), and prepositions such as *without* or *against* (6h).

5.2.1.3 *Non-affirmative context, positive expectation*

Non-affirmative contexts that are associated with positive expectations take the "positive polarity item *some*" as an indefinite determiner. Compare the differences in meaning conveyed by *any* and *some* in the following sentences:

(7) a. Would you like *any* strawberry cake?
    b. Would you like *some* strawberry cake?

By using the negative polarity item *any*, the speaker does not make any assumption about the hearer's wishes: question (7a) might be uttered as a pure information question in discussing an order. By using the positive polarity item *some*, however, the speaker is guided by positive assumptions. Question (7b) might be intended as an offer, which tacitly assumes that the hearer will accept the offer or at least regards this outcome as desirable.

The choice of the indefinite polarity items *any* and *some* is thus clearly dependent on cognitive factors and cuts across linguistic categories.

5.2.2 Two types of indefinite reference

The indefinite instance a speaker is thinking of may have the status of an existing or non-existing entity, i.e. it may have factual reality or non-reality. Compare the following examples:

(8) a. I want to marry *an American*. He lives in Kalamazoo.
    b. I want to marry *an American*. He should be rich.

The American talked about in (8a) is a factually existing person in the speaker's, though not in the hearer's, mind. This type of indefinite reference is known as **specific reference**. Specific reference is typically used in introducing a new instance as in the first sentence of the narrative in (3) to single out a referent among the reference mass.

The American talked about in (8b), by contrast, is no specific real person. He may be one person among the reference mass of American males of marriageable age that matches the criterion of being rich, but there may also be no such person. The set of Americans has, of course, reality, but the dreamed-of husband does not: he has only imaginary, or virtual, reality. This type of indefinite reference is called **non-specific reference**.

The referring expressions of English do not distinguish between specific and non-specific reference: *an American* is used for both types of reference and the sentence *I want to marry an American* is ambiguous without further specification. The difference between the two meanings may be more explicitly brought out in a logical-like way as in (9):

(9) a. There is an American who lives in Kalamazoo and who I want to marry.
    b. I want there to be an American who is rich and who I could marry.

These paraphrases clearly indicate the difference between specific and non-specific reference. The reality space in which (8a) and (9a) are set is established by the existential expression *there is* in the present tense (see Chapter 11.2.2.1), while the hypothetical space in which (8b) and (9b) are set is evoked by the volitional verb *want*, on which the whole wished-for situation is dependent. We therefore find the tenseless expression *there to be* in (9b) and the modal verbs *should* in (8b) and *could* in (9b) (for modality see Chapter 10).

5.2.2.1 *Specific reference*

By using specific reference the speaker signals to the hearer that she, but not the hearer, has a referent in mind, and she "instructs" the hearer to open a mental space for this referent. A specific referent may be entirely new to the hearer as in example (8a), or it may be inferable from elements of a given cultural frame as in the following sentences:

(10) a. That's a brand-new book, and just look at this: there is *a page* missing.
b. This pub closes at 11 pm, but it's after midnight already and there are still *some customers* in there drinking beer.

Here, the specific referents can easily be inferred thanks to our knowledge of the 'book' frame and the 'pub' frame: *a page* in (10a) obviously refers to a page of the brand-new book, and *some customers* in (10b) apparently refers to customers of the pub.

In colloquial speech, especially in story-telling, specific referents are sometimes introduced by means of the demonstrative determiner *this*, as in:

(11) I looked out of the window, and there was *this* woman, and she was going to back up the car, and forgot to open the gate, and …

The demonstrative determiner *this* in (11) does not, unlike its normal deictic usage (see 5.3.1), point to a definite referent but to a referent that needs special highlighting as a story heroine. Due to its deictic meaning, *this* lends greater immediacy and vividness to the story. Here it appeals to the hearer's familiarity with the stereotypical frame of distracted women drivers.

The speaker may also express vagueness of specific reference by using determiner-supporting adjectives such as *particular, specific, given* or *certain* in expressions such as (12a) and (12b):

(12) a. *At a given point in time* they started laughing.
b. *At a certain* age you will be thankful for my advice.

The expressions *at a given point in time* and *at a certain age* do not express the speaker's certainty about a time but a rather vague time. In conjunction with specific reference, the adjectives *given* and *certain* have lost their literal meanings. This kind of shift to weaker meanings of words is known as **semantic bleaching**.

5.2.2.2 *Non-specific reference*

Non-specific referents belong to imaginary, or virtual, reality. Space-builders which typically open a space of virtual reality for non-specific referents are non-affirmative constructions such as *yes-no* questions, negations, imperatives, conditionals, and constructions involving modal verbs or verbs of want, need or desire. What these constructions have in common is that the speaker signals that she does not make any claims about the factual existence of a referent but only sees it as having virtual existence. Just as the American referred to in (8b) and (9b) is only a dreamed-of husband, the drinks talked about in the following examples are only virtual entities:

(13) a. Would you like *a cup of tea*?
 b. No, thank you. I don't fancy *tea* so early in the morning.
 c. So do have *something* else. Have *a milkshake* instead.
 d. Sorry, if I drink *a milkshake* now, *it* will upset my stomach.

There are two ways of continuing a virtual space in discourse: either the speaker stays within the world of hypotheticality or she switches to the world of reality. All the entities in the above discourse fragment (apart from the deictic words *you, me* and *my (stomach)* and *the morning*) are non-specific referents and can be referred back to as long as we stay in the realm of hypotheticality. For example, a possible answer to *Would you like a cup of tea?* in (13a) could be *Yes, make it very sweet*, where the pronoun *it* refers back to the virtual instance of *a cup of tea*.

A shift from the world of hypotheticality to the world of reality is illustrated in example (14):

(14) a. I needed *a new computer*. [*non-specific*]
 b. I went to the Mac shop and bought *one/a notebook*. [*specific*]
 c. *It*'s absolutely supersonic. [*definite*]

The non-specific referent *a computer* in (14a) becomes a specific referent in (14b). The speaker introduces it in reality space by using the pronoun *one* or the referring expression *a notebook*. Once a specific referent has been set up in the discourse, we can go further to a definite referent as in (14c).

5.3 Definite reference

While indefinite reference was shown to be exclusive, definite reference is inclusive: a definite referent includes all the elements that form its set, i.e. it does not exclude any of them. For example, in "Can you open the window?", the speaker refers to a window that is the only one of its kind or somehow attracts our attention within a given pragmatic situation, e.g. in a room that only has one window, or that has several windows but only one of which can be opened without having to remove plants or piles of paper, etc. In "Can you open the windows?", the speaker refers to all windows which form a set in a given pragmatic situation — the speaker would not be satisfied if the hearer only opened four of the six windows of a room.

In order to refer to all elements that are included in a set, the set has to be mentally shared by speaker and hearer. There are different ways of making a set accessible to both speaker and hearer, and hence making the referent definite. The referent may be found in the present speech situation, it may be evoked in the current discourse, or it may be part of the social and cultural world shared by speaker and hearer. Accordingly, we have three subtypes of definite reference, which will be discussed in the following sections: (i) deictic reference, (ii) discourse reference and (iii) unique reference.

5.3.1 Deictic reference

Referents that are accessible in the environment of the speech situation can be pointed to. This is why this type of situationally given reference is described as **deictic reference** (from Greek *deiktikos* from *deiknynai* 'show, point'). In deictic reference it is essential that the speaker reveals the deictic centre of the speech situation. We can see this in one of the sentences of the "zoo story" under (3), repeated here as (16):

(16) I thought *I* told *you* to take the monkey to the zoo.

The deictic centre in the speech situation of (16) is, of course, the speaker, who refers to himself as *I*; the secondary deictic centre is the hearer, who is referred to as *you*. To see how important deictic information is, let us imagine a situation where vital elements of it are lacking. Suppose you see a notice lying on the office floor which had probably been stuck on one of the office doors, with the following message written on it:

(17) *I'll meet you here* at *this* door *at the same time tomorrow*.

This message is, of course, incomprehensible to anybody other than the intended addressee. The forms *I*, *you*, *here*, *this door*, *at the same time* and *tomorrow* are deictic referring expressions and can only be interpreted in the context of the speech situation: we must know who the *I* is, when the note was written, on which door it was pasted, etc. Since the note is lying on the floor, we can't even identify the sender, which is the first and most important clue.

This example illustrates the three basic types of deictic reference, or deixis: person deixis (*I, you*), place deixis (*here, at this door*), and time deixis (*the same time, tomorrow*). These three types of deixis show a strong parallelism in that they each distinguish between central and distant regions of reference. In person deixis, the centre is the speaker *I*; a bit less central is the hearer *you*; and outside this central region are persons who do not participate in the ongoing conversation: *he, she* or *they*.

Similarly, in place deixis we have a central region *here* and a distant region *there*. English also has a mainly dialectal expression for still more remote regions, *yonder,* as in *the shed over yonder*. The standard English form that comes closest to remote spatial deixis is *over there*. In many other languages such as Latin, Spanish or Japanese, such remote forms are part of the spatial deictic system.

In time deixis, the central region is present time: *now*; more distant times in the past and the future are described as *then*; and times much further away in the past are described as (*way*) *back*. English has no corresponding expression for 'way ahead in the future', apart from *one day* or *some day*, which denote a vague future as in the song *One day my prince will come*. With days, however, we have complex expressions in both directions: for the past *yesterday* and *the day before yesterday*, and for the future *tomorrow* and *the day after tomorrow*. These expressions are motivated by a model of moving time. The time units are conceived of as lined up and move from the future via the present to the past so that the day before yesterday precedes yesterday and the day after tomorrow follows tomorrow. In our discussion of the future form *be going to* in Chapter 9.4.1 we will find a model of time in which the person moves into the future.

5.3.2 Discourse reference

In the progress of discourse, mental spaces for new referents are continually opened by means of indefinite referents. Once a space for a referent has been opened in the discourse, it becomes part of the set of referents shared by speaker and hearer. The speaker may therefore refer to them at any time by means of definite reference. This type of reference is dependent on the ongoing discourse and is therefore described as *discourse deixis* or *discourse reference*. Two main types of discourse reference are distinguished: anaphoric reference and cataphoric reference.

The more common type of discourse reference is **anaphoric reference** (from Greek *anapherein* 'carry up, back'). Here, the speaker refers back to entities introduced in the preceding discourse. In the zoo story under (3), the referents *the gendarme*, *him* and *the animal* in sentence (3b) illustrate anaphoric reference: they refer back to the same referents introduced earlier in the discourse.

Since an anaphoric referent is already known, its second mention carries no new information. According to the iconic **principle of quantity**, something that carries more meaning is accorded more wording and, conversely, something that carries less meaning is given less wording. Anaphoric referents are, therefore, typically expressed by third person pronouns. The main function of a third person pronoun is to refer back to an antecedent referent while keeping track of a minimum of information about the referent(s) such as number (*he, she, it* versus *they*), animacy status (*he, she* versus *it*) and sex (*he* versus *she*).

Pronouns are, however, often used in reference to entities that have not been explicitly introduced in the preceding discourse. Consider the use of the pronoun *they* in the following example:

(20) I no longer care about politics; *they* are all corrupt.

The pronoun *they* refers back to the unnamed referent 'politicians'. Such "pronouns of laziness", which would be frowned upon by very strict language teachers, are interesting phenomena to the cognitive linguist because they offer a glimpse into our cognition. Thus, the word *politics* activates the 'politics' frame, which includes 'politician' as one of its central elements. The referent 'politicians' is therefore easily accessible in the speaker's mental space and can be exploited for anaphoric reference. These pronominal usages have therefore been described as "conceptual anaphors".

In referring back to an antecedent referent by a noun phrase, the speaker may also make use of other, in particular expressive, information about the referent evoked in her mental space, as in (21):

(21) a. My car never left me in the lurch. But I had to say good-bye to *my sweetheart*.
 b. My car is a lemon. I should never have bought *that set of wheels*.

In (21a), the anaphoric referent *my car* is elaborated metaphorically, in (21b) it is elaborated metonymically.

The second type of discourse reference, cataphoric reference, occurs much more rarely. In **cataphoric reference** (from Greek *katapherein* 'carry down'), the speaker refers forward to a referent which is to be introduced in the discourse immediately following. The following fragment of a conversation illustrates cataphoric reference.

(22) "Do you know the joke about *the police officer* and *the driver*?"
 "No."
 "Well. *A police officer* pulls *a man* over for speeding …."

Here, *the police officer* and *the driver* are cataphorically referred to as definite referents before they are introduced as indefinite referents in the following discourse. The main function of cataphoric reference is that of announcing a referent or a situation that the speaker is going to talk about, as in the phrase "Let me tell you *this*…."

5.3.3 Unique reference: The case of a category with one single instance

Always remember you're unique,
just like everyone else. (Anonymous)

Speaker and hearer of the same speech community share knowledge of their immediate environment, their culture, and the world at large. Speakers start from the assumption that the people they are talking to are familiar with many referents of their shared world knowledge. Consequently they may simply refer to such entities as definite referents even if they have not been introduced before. These referents are "unique" within the shared socio-cultural world knowledge of speaker and hearer, and reference to them is known as **unique reference**. We may distinguish three subtypes of unique reference, which are illustrated in the following examples:

(23) a. Last summer we went hiking in *Yosemite Park*.
 b. Let's watch the sunset from *Jennifer's apartment*.
 c. On Sunday afternoons, I take the children to *the park*.

The use of a proper name in (23a) illustrates inherent uniqueness, the noun phrase with a possessive noun in (23b) exemplifies qualified uniqueness, and the definite noun phrase in (23c) demonstrates framed uniqueness. These three types of unique reference will be discussed below.

5.3.3.1 *Inherent uniqueness: Proper names and mass nouns*

Referents may be **inherently unique** by virtue of being the only instance of their kind or a salient, socially recognised sector of life or discipline in a given world of reference. The former type of inherent uniqueness is typically labelled by a **proper name** such as *Trafalgar Square*, while the latter type of inherent uniqueness is found with mass nouns such as *education* or *philosophy*. Grammatically, the referring expressions used for these two types of inherent uniqueness are very different: proper names on the one hand and common mass nouns on the other. Conceptually, however, the two types of referent are closely related: both are inherently definite, and the uniqueness of both is socially sanctioned — by a given social group or by society at large. Let us take a closer look at these two types of inherent uniqueness.

(i) Unique instances of an object: Proper names

Single entities that are salient and assumed to be unique are mainly limited to persons and locations. Such single entities typically have a proper name and, provided the speaker knows the name, may be referred to by their proper name. Unlike common nouns, proper names denoting persons do not involve a category but only a single instance. Therefore, proper names of persons have no or only little meaning. However, the category of which they are an instance is usually inferable. Thus, *Bill Hunter* is expected to be a male human. Since they are inherently definite, proper names need not, as a rule, be grounded by a definite determiner. This is the case with most personal proper names, which do therefore not normally take an article. We only use proper names with a stressed definite article when the person is famous or when we doubt his identity in spite of knowing his name, as in *Are you THE Bill Hunter?*, implying that there may be different persons of the same name but one is better known than the others. The definite article is therefore also used in its unstressed form with proper names that are defined in relative clauses as in *the Bill Hunter who lives in Durham Road* — as opposed to the one who lives in Cromer Avenue (for relative clauses see Chapter 7.4).

The situation is different with geographical names, or *toponyms*, which are notorious for their seemingly unsystematic use: some have no article, others have the definite article. Whether a geographical name is used with or without a definite article is often a matter of historical accident. Yet there are also factors that tend to determine the use of articles with proper names, in particular the conceptual factor of boundedness and, in the case of complex toponyms, the morphological factor of its composition.

The names of most countries such as *Canada* take no article, which reflects their conceptualisation of a clearly bounded political entity. Countries or geographical areas that are seen as collections of political units take a plural proper name with the definite article, as in *the United States, the Netherlands*, and *the Baltics*. The parts that constitute these multiplex units are (still) seen as having a certain independence and may even be discontinuous and further extensible. Therefore, the definite article is needed to mark the uniqueness of the collection.

A clear instance of a semantic opposition between the zero-article form and the definite article is found in the names of states such as *Ohio* and names of rivers such as *the*

Ohio. States are clearly bounded political entities, while rivers are natural phenomena that may stretch for hundreds, even thousands of miles so that we do not have their overall extension in mind. Most river names, therefore, require the definite article to mark an unbounded entity as a unique referent. The same applies to natural landscapes, which normally lack clear boundaries and are therefore named with the definite article: *the Midwest, the Sahara, the Black Forest, the Grand Canyon*, etc. The concept of the Midwest, for instance, is fuzzy: it roughly covers the north central states from Ohio in the East to the Dakotas in the West and Wisconsin in the North to Illinois in the South, as shown in Figure 5.3(b). Once geographical areas are demarcated by administrative boundaries, as in state parks like Yosemite Park or Grand Canyon Park, they are expressed by the bare proper name.

Figure 5.3. Geographical areas with and without clear boundaries

The principles governing the choice of proper names of buildings, bridges, etc. are more complex. As a rule, proper names consisting of noun–noun compounds are seen as denoting a well-established unique thing and take no article, as in *London Bridge, Oxford Street*, and *Buckingham Palace*. Adjective–noun compounds, by contrast, look like normal phrases with a qualifying modifier and are therefore normally seen as less unique and therefore take the definite article, as in *the Golden Gate Bridge, the British Museum*, and *the White House*. In British English, *the High Street* and *the Main Street* also follow this pattern, while in American English street names are generally used without the definite article. But we also have articleless adjective-noun proper names in British English, such as *Big Ben* for the clock tower on the Houses of Parliament.

Some abstract entities, in particular unique institutions like *the Church, the Army* and *the Government*, are referred to by proper names and capitalised in the written form. Their unique status in a society needs to be marked by the definite article to distinguish them from their corresponding common nouns. There are a few institutions that are expressed by a bare proper name like *Parliament, Westminster* and *Scotland Yard*. The latter two institutions were named after the place in which they were housed: the Palace of Westminster and the street Scotland Yard in London, i.e. their names are based on the common metonymy PLACE FOR INSTITUTION.

(ii) Instances of substances recognized as "unique": Mass nouns

A striking feature of English is the use of abstract nouns as articleless referring expressions, indicating that many abstract things are seen as inherently unique. Such abstract nouns include *life, silence, tourism, society, education, botany, medicine, science, architecture, economics, linguistics, language*, etc. The following examples illustrate their usages:

(24) a. *Life* is full of surprises.
 b. *Silence* means *approval*.
 c. *Tourism* is ruining many beautiful spots.
 d. *Society* is obliged to support all the unemployed people.
 e. Two of my best friends are in *education*.
 f. The object of *botany* is the study of plants.

The abstract nouns in the examples above denote very general notions surrounding our lives (24a, b) or sectors of organised civilisation (24c-f). These notions are familiar to all members of the English speech community and do not need to be introduced in any discourse. They are coded as mass nouns because they perfectly meet the criteria characterising physical substances: they are unbounded, homogeneous and uncountable. *Botany* as used in (24f), for example, describes an undifferentiated discipline as such and refers to the study of plants wherever botany is pursued.

In our discussion of objects and substances in Chapter 4.1.2 we noted that we can isolate a portion of a concrete substance by means of the definite article, as in *the water in the basement*. We may also isolate a portion of an inherently unique abstract entity. With abstract nouns, however, English makes a distinction between portions that are expressed by the articleless abstract noun as in (25a and b) and portions that are expressed by the definite article preceding the abstract noun as in (26a and b).

(25) a. *Education in the inner city* requires special training.
 b. *Life expectancy in the Middle Ages* was about 50 years.

(26) a. *The education of inner-city children* requires special training.
 b. *The life expectancy of women* is higher than that of men.

The noun phrases with the articleless abstract mass nouns in the examples under (25) express "genuine" portions of the substance — the *in*-phrases only restrict their general application to a certain space or time. Thus, *education in the inner city* in (25a) describes a genuine portion of 'education' in general and *life expectancy in the Middle Ages* in (25b) describes a portion of 'life expectancy' in general. The abstract nouns modified by *of*-phrases under (26), by contrast, describe reified episodic situations in which the *of*-phrase refers to a participant in an episode. Thus, *the education of inner-city children* in (26a) is about the event of educating inner-city children. Likewise, sentence (26b) is about the length of life that can be expected by specific parts of the population. These abstract nouns no longer describe inherently unique sectors of civilisation but more specific situations, which therefore require the definite article in order to become unique.

5.3.3.2 *Qualified uniqueness: Qualifying modifiers*

A frequently used possibility of establishing a referent's uniqueness is restrictive descriptive qualification, which we will describe as **qualified uniqueness**. Types of qualification and their linguistic expressions as modifiers are discussed in Chapter 7; here we will only consider their referential function.

The speaker may point to a salient qualitative aspect of the referent that allows the hearer to distinguish the referent from other referents. Such salient aspects of a referent may be one of its properties, as in (27a), circumstances such as the place where things are, as in (27b), and events in which things are involved, as in (27c).

(27) a. No, my coat is the *green* one.
 b. And the umbrella *in the umbrella stand* is also mine.
 c. This is the cloakroom ticket *you gave me*.

Reference by qualified uniqueness is often needed in deictic situations such as that of a classroom, where there may be too many "instances" of the same kind:

(28) a. *The boy in the last row*, can you read the sentence for us?
 b. *The girl with the pink sweater*, what is your question?

The speaker may also make use of a reference point, which serves as a kind of "mental bridge" allowing the hearer to access the referent (for reference point see Chapter 1.3.2). The best reference points for accessing unique referents are human beings. Thus, in the phrase *That's Lily's car*, we mentally access the referent *car* via the reference point *Lily*. Since the person called *Lily* is inherently unique in the speech situation, her car is also unique. To a certain extent non-human instances can also be used as reference points, as in *the world's languages*. However, most non-human entities are not salient enough to serve as reference points; thus ?*this car's wheels* sounds odd.

The possessive construction with the genitive is particularly well-suited with salient entities as reference points because it then iconically reflects the order of processing: the salient reference point is processed before the target referent. The task of mental processing may, however, require quite some effort if more than one reference point is involved, as in *Lily's father's friend's son's summerhouse*.

Figure 5.4. Chain of reference points

Lastly, English has a class of determining adjectives that have the function of uniquely specifying things (see Chapter 7.2.4 (iii)). For example, the adjectives in *the only solution, the main reason,* and *the very man* emphasise the uniqueness of the referent. Also superlative forms of adjectives signal uniqueness in that they select the extreme instance and therefore require the definite article, as in *the prettiest woman* (**a prettiest woman*). Interestingly, the unique referent need not have reality status, as in *I want to marry the prettiest woman*, which expresses a wished-for, i.e. non-specific, referent. Uniqueness of a referent thus does not necessitate its definiteness.

5.3.3.3 *Framed uniqueness*

People's knowledge of frames is relevant in two referential situations: situations in which a frame allows them to infer the identity of a referent, and situations in which the function or role of an element within a frame is at stake. The former situation of **framed uniqueness** will be described as *inferred uniqueness*, the latter as *functional uniqueness*.

(i) Inferred uniqueness

The immediate speech environment or the wider social situation usually provides clues for activating a conceptual frame in which the situation described is set. In Section 5.2.2.1 we saw how our familiarity with a frame such as that of books enables us to infer that *a page* in *a page was missing* refers to a page of the book. There we were dealing with specific referents. Inferring a definite referent from a conceptual frame is even more common. For example, the loudspeaker warning *Mind the gap* at a London tube station is understood to refer to the gap between the platform and the train and not to a gap in the wall. We arrive at this interpretation by inferring the unique referent from our familiarity with the 'London tube' frame.

In the following examples the italicised definite noun phrases refer to entities which are unique or at least assumed to be unique within a given frame. The increasingly larger frames from (29a) to (29f) demonstrate that a referent's uniqueness may be inferred at all levels of generality.

(29) a. Have you locked *the door*? [*frame*: house, car, etc.]
 b. The children are in *the park*. [*frame*: neighbourhood]
 c. *The boss* will be upset. [*frame*: work]
 d. *The new term* has started. [*frame*: university]
 e. I met Claire at *the bookshop*. [*frame*: town, city]
 f. Let's go to *the seaside*. [*frame*: country]

The uniqueness of the definite referents in these sentences crucially depends on people's knowledge of the conceptual frame they belong to. Once a mental space is opened for a frame, the hearer may retrieve from it relevant information allowing her to identify the intended referent. For example, sentence (29a) evokes the prototypical 'house-locking' frame and makes us think of the front door, the park in (29b) calls up the 'neighbourhood' frame and makes us think of the park nearby, etc.

(ii) Functional uniqueness
We are sometimes interested less in the identity of a referent but rather in its unique role or function within a certain socio-cultural frame. In the "zoo story" under (3), the referents described by *the zoo* (take the monkey to the zoo) and *the cinema* (Today we're going to the cinema) illustrate functional uniqueness: we are interested in the zoo or cinema as institutions. Here are some more examples of functional uniqueness:

(30) a. "Where do you know this from?" — "I read it in *the newspaper*."
 b. "How are we getting there?" — "We can take *the bus*."
 c. "It's so stuffy in here. Can't we open *the window*?"
 d. *The murderer* left his fingerprints on the knife.

Sentence (30a) evokes the frame of media and news reporting, and media that typically fulfil this function are newspapers, the radio or TV. Within this frame, the referent 'the newspaper' is functionally unique as a type and hence takes the definite article. We think of 'the newspaper' in terms of typical instances, for example as the paper most people typically read, such as *The Daily Mirror*. Notice that books are different from newspapers in this respect. Books are probably too varied in their range of topics to be associated with a particular function. Thus *I read it in the book* can only refer to an individual book, not to the function of books.

Sentence (30b) evokes the frame of public transport, which includes as typical elements trains, trams and taxis but not, for example, private cars. Thus *You can take the car* only refers to a particular car.

Sentence (30c), *Can't we open the window?*, may be said in a room that has only one window and refers to this uniquely identifiable window, or it may be said in a room that has several windows. In this situation, the speaker alludes to the function of windows as a means of regulating the room temperature, and opening any one of the windows would be consonant with this wish. Notice that the window may refer to any of the windows of a room when it is used in its functional sense, but may only refer to a particular one of several windows, like the one that can be opened, when it is used in its identifying sense (see Section 5.3).

Sentence (30d) evokes the frame of murder, which includes the unique role of a murderer as its main participant. Unlike the functionally unique referents presented in the preceding examples, the referent 'the murderer' involves only one instance: the murderer. Due to the fact that his or her identity is not known, however, many people may be suspected of being the perpetrator.

Reference to the role function of an entity is expressed by definite singular referring expressions, but it applies to a type of thing rather than to individual instances. It is thus close in meaning to reference to a class, i.e. generic reference, which is the topic of the final section.

5.4 Generic reference

5.4.1 Generic reference and class

*All generalisations are false,
including this one.* (Anonymous)

Generic reference is used in generalising about a class. A **class** is a collection of similar individual elements that are understood as forming a type and having a name. For example, the collection of all individual tigers in the world forms the class of tigers. Classes differ from sets in that they have a name. Thus, the class of tigers has the name *tigers*, but the set of three tigers in our zoo has no name. Classes differ from categories, too; they consist of individual elements, e.g. real-life tigers. Categories have conceptual entities, i.e. subcategories, as their members (see Chapter 1.1.1). Thus, the category 'tiger' has as its members subcategories such as 'Bengal tiger', 'Siberian tiger', etc., which may have further members. We can therefore speak of the *class of tigers* and the category 'tiger', but not of the *category of tigers*. The term *member*, unfortunately, is also often applied in reference to the individual elements of a class.

In generic reference, as in individuative reference, a category is "instantiated" within the discourse, and the instance of a given category is equivalent to the whole class. An act of generic reference is very similar to an act of individuative reference, which was illustrated in Figure 5.1. The speaker thinks of a category, such as 'tiger', singles out an instance of the category, which in generic reference is the class of tigers, and grounds this instance in the current discourse by means of a generic referring expression so that speaker and hearer can establish mental contact to the same referent. Figure 5.5 gives a schematic illustration of generic reference in *The tiger has stripes*, where *the tiger* is a generic referent.

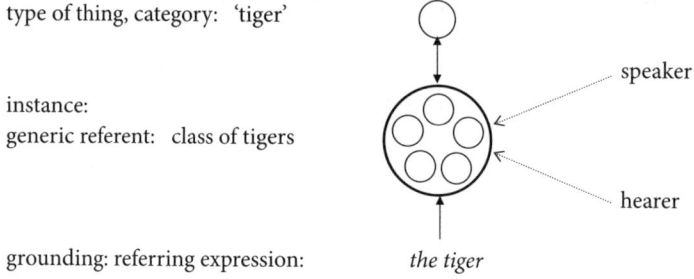

Figure 5.5. An act of generic reference: *the tiger (has stripes)*.

Ideally, all the individual elements of a class should share the same property and consequently the category should also have this property. Thus, if we discover that all the individual tigers in the world have stripes, we can generalise this observation and are justified in saying that the class of tigers, and also the category 'tiger', has the property of having stripes. Since we normally do not know all the individual elements of a class, however, we tend to generalise about a class, or a TYPE, by way of a number of its elements, or TOKENS, i.e. we make use of metonymic reasoning: TOKENS are used to stand for a TYPE. This would, for example, apply to a general statement such as *Americans are rich*.

5.4.2 Four types of generic reference

There are various possibilities of generalising about a class from individual elements. However, languages do not have specifically generic determiners but use the same referring expressions for generic reference that are used for individuative reference. Thus the same indefinite and definite determiners are used for generic reference, as already shown in the sentences under (4), which are repeated here:

(31) a. *A tiger* has a life-span of about 11 years.   [*indefinite generic*]
      b. *The tiger* hunts by night.   [*definite generic*]

The distinction between indefiniteness and definiteness, which we expounded for individuative reference, also applies to generic reference, albeit less strictly. As in individuative reference, indefinite generic referents are mainly used to open a mental space for an instance, while definite generic referents are used for instances for which a space has already been opened. In generic reference, however, indefinite and definite referring expressions are often interchangeable. Thus, we can express roughly the same idea by saying *The tiger hunts by night* or *A tiger hunts by night*. Moreover, we may generalise by using either a singular noun as in these examples or a plural noun as in *Tigers hunt by night*.

The two dimensions of definiteness (definite and indefinite) and number (singular and plural) lead to four possible generic construals, all of which are found in English. However, the generic statements below show that animal nouns (in the sentences under a) and human nouns (in the sentences under b) behave differently as subjects of a generic sentence.

(32) a. *A tiger* hunts by night.   [*indefinite singular generic*]
      b. ?*An Italian* is fond of children.

(33) a. *Tigers* hunt by night.   [*indefinite plural generic*]
      b. *Italians* are fond of children.

(34) a. *The tiger* hunts by night.   [*definite singular generic*]
      b. ?*The Italian* is fond of children.

(35) a. ?*The tigers* hunt by night.   [*definite plural generic*]
      b. *The Italians* are fond of children.

Why are animal nouns used in the first three generic construals (32a, 33a, 34a) but not in the definite plural (35a), and why can human nouns occur in the plural (33b and 35b) but not in the singular (32b and 34b)? In the following we will look at the specific meanings conveyed by these four types of generics and try to explain their divergent grammatical behaviour. Since the forms used for generic reference are the same as those for individuative reference, we may surmise that their generic meanings are also related to their corresponding individuative meanings.

(i) Indefinite singular: An element for its class
In individuative reference, indefiniteness involves singling out a particular instance from a set. In *They're having a friend round to dinner*, one element, *a friend*, is singled out from the set of their friends. Likewise, in generalising about a class as in (32a), *A tiger hunts by night*, one element, *a tiger*, is singled out from the class of tigers. However, the particular element is not singled out in order to refer to a single element but to the class as a whole. Hunting by night is evidently not unique to one particular tiger but a characteristic feature of all tigers. If an individual element may represent the class as a whole, all its elements must be of equal status, i.e. they all must share the attribute in question. In (31a) all tigers are assumed to share a life-span of 11 years, and in (32a) all tigers are assumed to hunt by night.

Attributes that are uniquely shared by all elements of a class are felt to be essential, not accidental, attributes. Such attributes are therefore particularly relevant in defining a thing — they define what we believe to be the "essence" of a thing. In definitions, the word to be defined is typically expressed in the indefinite singular. For example, I might define a "generic bird" by saying *A bird has a beak, wings and feathers*. We can now also see why sentence (32b), ?*An Italian is fond of children*, sounds odd, whereas the dictionary definition *An Italian is a native, citizen or inhabitant of Italy* does not. The singular indefinite generic would make us see 'fondness for children' as an attribute defining the "essence" of all Italians. However, groups of people such as nationalities do not have an essence, so we can hardly generalise about humans by using the indefinite singular generic.

Indefinite singulars differ from the other generic construals in that they cannot be used with so-called "class predicates". Class predicates make statements about a class as a whole, such as *extinct, die out, numerous*, or *abound*. Thus, while we can say things like *Balinese tigers have been extinct for 50 years* or *The Balinese tiger has been extinct for 50 years*, we cannot say **A Balinese tiger has been extinct for 50 years*. This grammatical restriction of the indefinite singular is due to the blended meanings of 'singularity' of the individual element and the 'class' as a whole. What is stated about a single element also holds for the class but, at the same time, it must also hold for the particular element singled out; hence one particular animal can, of course, not die out.

(ii) Indefinite plural: Indeterminate elements for their class
In individuative reference, the indefinite plural is indeterminate between 'more than one' and 'all' (see 5.2.1.1). In generic reference, the indefinite plural generalises over large segments of a class, but not all its elements, as in (36):

(36) The large majority of *Italians* are Roman Catholics and for centuries, this has affected their art. *Italians* are proud of their artistic heritage

Whereas the first sentence restricts the segment of Italians to a majority proportion, the second sentence without any quantity restriction applies very generally. We may generalise even on the basis of an indeterminate number of individual elements. I may, for example, say sentences such as (33b), *Italians are fond of children*, when I have met no more than five Italians who happened to be crazy about children: I assume that fondness for children is characteristic of a very large number of Italians. People tend to generalise on the basis of relatively few experiences, and the indefinite plural provides the adequate referring expression to do so: it conveys generalisations based on vague, impressionistic judgements and allows for exceptions.

(iii) Definite singular: Prototypical element for the class as such
In individuative reference, the definite singular refers to a single instance as the only element included in a set (see 5.3). Likewise, in generic reference, the definite singular refers to a single instance, which is the class as such. With animals, the class is a species, which is implicitly contrasted to other species within the animal kingdom. Sentence (34a), *The tiger hunts by night*, describes the behaviour of the 'tiger' as implicitly opposed to that of other types of predators. Hence exceptions are not relevant. There may be some tigers that prefer hunting by daylight, but these are disregarded in the generalisation over the type. We have a clear mental image of the species 'tiger' and have a prototypical member in mind when we think of the whole class of tigers. It is much harder to visualise a superordinate category such as 'mammal' or 'bird' as a contrastive species or class, so that with them the definite singular sounds odd, as in ?*The bird has wings and feathers*.

The notion 'species' mainly applies to categories in biological classifications, especially to kinds of animals and plants, but may also involve physical objects, especially artefacts. In this case we similarly see them in contrast to other categories. For example, in saying *The computer has changed our lives*, we are thinking of the 'computer as such', which has replaced the typewriter, enabled world-wide communication and eliminated many traditional office jobs. Biologically speaking, groups of humans are a species, too. But also cultural attributes may be thought of as species-like characteristics, as in the following contrast of groups of humans:

(37) Like *the Chinese*, *the Italian* is a born gambler. *The Italian* is gay, light-hearted and, if his fur is not stroked the wrong way, inoffensive as a child.

But unless a specific context is given, a statement like that made in sentence (34b), ?*The Italian is fond of children*, sounds odd since fondness of children is normally not understood in the sense of a species-like attribute of humans. It is only when groups of humans are seen in a certain contrastive function that they can be referred to by the definite singular. This is the case in the following examples, where husband and wife are referred to in the roles defined for them in a traditional Western culture:

(38) a. *The husband* is the head of the family.
b. *The wife* is in charge of the children.

(iv) Definite plural: Many elements for their class
In individuative reference, the definite plural refers to all elements included in a set as in *Can you open the windows?* (see 5.3). In generic reference, the definite plural generalises

over a class by referring to many elements, but not necessarily all its elements. The limited validity of a generic statement in the definite plural may even be explicitly mentioned, as in sentence (39).

(39)   *The Italians* are generally not inhibited when interacting with the opposite sex.

In English the definite plural is mainly applied to classes of humans. Since, as we have just observed, classes of people are normally seen in terms of cultural characteristics, and since the definite singular as a species-characterising generic is ruled out, the definite plural provides an adequate alternative for generalising about humans. As the following example shows, people typically generalise on the basis of many individuals that share a salient attribute.

(40)   Football is the main national sport and *the Italians* are well known for their passion for this sport. Italy has won the World Cup four times.

The definite plural, unlike the definite singular, allows for exceptions, and since humans display idiosyncratic behaviour, it is the appropriate form to choose for generalisations about humans.

Generic human groups may also be expressed in English by nominalised adjectives which describe a salient property. In English, these nominalised adjectives always refer to a class, never to a singular entity, and always take plural agreement, as in the following sentences:

(41)   a.   *The old* are still running the country.
       b.   *The young* will take over soon.

Such usages involve the metonymy PROPERTY OF A THING FOR THE THING. The nominalised adjectives describe a property that defines a class and, at the same time, focus on its individuals by taking plural agreement. For obvious reasons only characteristic and stable properties qualify for defining a class. Thus we have generic adjectives such as *the blind, the rich, the poor, the hungry, the unemployed*, etc., but not ?*the happy,* ?*the new* or ?*the thirsty*.

The four (or five) types of generic reference identified in the preceding discussion are schematically represented in Table 5.4. The first line under each diagram provides an example, the second line characterises the kind of element or elements that stands for the class, and the third line specifies the kind of attribute that characterises each type of generic reference.

The diagrams in Table 5.4 represent the relations between a generic class and its elements. With indefinite singulars, the identical small circles represent elements which share the same essential attribute, where one element is singled out to stand for the class; with indefinite plurals, the three identical circles represent an indeterminate number of elements which share a characteristic attribute and stand for the class; with definite singulars, a prototypical element and its distinct attribute are highlighted as representative for a species; and with definite plurals, either many humans sharing a salient attribute form a class, or a salient property of humans itself determines a class.

Table 5.4. Types of generic reference

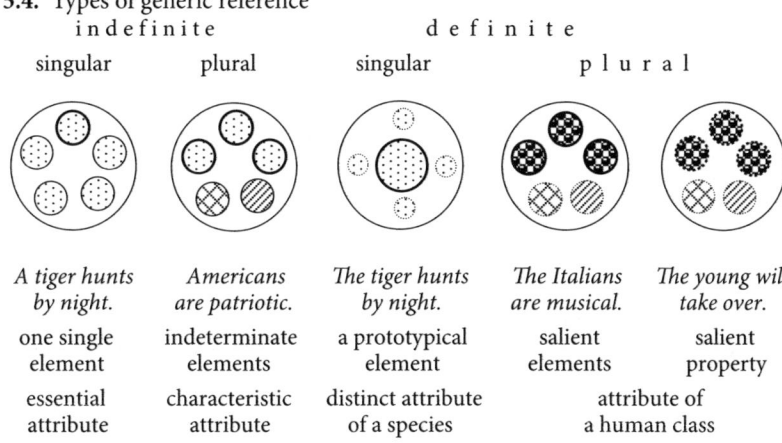

indefinite		definite	
singular	plural	singular	plural
A tiger hunts by night.	*Americans are patriotic.*	*The tiger hunts by night.*	*The Italians are musical.* / *The young will take over.*
one single element	indeterminate elements	a prototypical element	salient elements / salient property
essential attribute	characteristic attribute	distinct attribute of a species	attribute of a human class

5.5 Conclusion

We will conclude this chapter on reference by summarising all the types of reference discussed in this chapter.

Table 5.5. The main types of reference

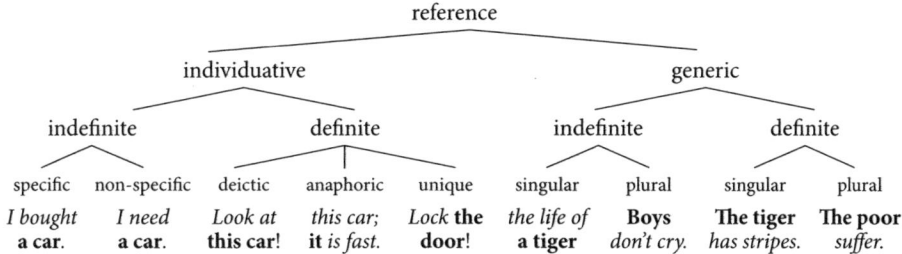

5.6 Summary

Successful communication crucially depends on the speaker's and hearer's tacit agreement on the instances of a thing talked about. This is achieved by means of reference. In an act of **reference,** the speaker grounds the instance she has in mind in the current discourse. In this way the speaker ensures that the hearer can call up the same instance. The instances referred to in an act of reference are known as referents. **Referents** are typically instances of a category such as 'the pub'. The referent is grounded in the current discourse by means of a **referring expression**. The definite referring expression *the pub* indicates uniqueness.

Two basic types of reference need to be distinguished: **individuative reference**, which applies to an individual instance of a thing, as in *The dog bit me*, and **generic reference**, which applies to a class, as in *The dog is a social animal*. There are two types of individuative reference: indefinite and definite reference. **Indefinite reference** involves singling out a particular element, or elements, from a set. If the particular instance already exists in the speaker's, but not the hearer's mind, the speaker uses **specific reference**, as in *I bought a car*. If the particular instance neither exists in the speaker's nor the hearer's mind, it has only virtual existence, and the speaker uses **non-specific reference**, as in *I need a car*.

Definite reference applies to an instance which is accessible to both speaker and hearer. There are three conditions that allow the speaker to assume that an instance is accessible to the hearer and thus definite: the speech situation, the current discourse, and shared knowledge of a socio-cultural frame. An instance that is present in the speech situation can be referred to by means of **deictic reference** as in *this book*. An instance that is part of the ongoing discourse can be referred to by means of **discourse reference**, in particular **anaphoric reference** for referents that have already been introduced in the preceding discourse. An instance that is unique within a given socio-cultural frame and therefore assumed to be known to members of a speech community can be referred to by means of **unique reference**, as in proper names.

Generic reference applies to a class as a whole. Generic reference is achieved metonymically via one or more elements of the class. The two dimensions of definiteness (definite and indefinite) and number (singular and plural) lead to four types of genericness, each of which is associated with its own specific generic meaning.

Chapter 5. Grounding things: Reference

Further Reading

Overall treatments of reference are found in Christophersen (1939), Jespersen (1949, Ch. XII), Hewson (1972), Halliday & Hasan (1976, Ch. 2), Hawkins (1978) and, most exhaustively, in Lyons (1999). Cognitive approaches to reference are presented in Chesterman (1991), Epstein (1996; 2001) and Ariel (1998). The important distinction between type and instance is justified in Langacker (1991a: Ch. 2.2).

Indefiniteness is dealt with in Hawkins (1978; 1991); the issue of the polarity items *some* and *any* is insightfully presented in R. Lakoff (1969) and Bolinger (1977). Definiteness is discussed in Hawkins (1978; 1991), Prince (1981), Clark & Marshall (1992), Birner & Ward (1994), Chafe (1976; 1994, Ch. 8) and Epstein (1996; 2001). The role of inference in definiteness is discussed in Gundel (1996). Anaphoric reference is extensively studied in various papers and a book (1997) by van Hoek. The issue of deixis in language is addressed in Fillmore (1997) and Ariel (1998); the use of deictic *this* and *that* for non-deictic purposes is treated in R. Lakoff (1974); the acquisition of deictic words is investigated in Tfouni & Klatzky (1986). Explanations for the use of proper names with and without the definite article are offered in Horowitz (1989) and Berezowski (1997 and 2001). Possessives as reference-point phenomena are discussed by Langacker (1993) and Taylor (1996). Reference to the role function of entities is discussed in Fauconnier (1985), Langacker (1991a: Ch. 2.2.5) and Epstein (2001).

Issues of generic definiteness are investigated in Declerck (1986), Krifka et al. (1995) and Langacker (2000: Ch. 8).

Study questions

1. Which types of reference (definite, specific, non-specific, generic) do the italicised noun phrases in the following joke illustrate?

    A man giving *a talk* to *a multinational audience* tells *a joke* about *the Irish*. Someone at *the back* of *the hall* jumps up and protests angrily: "*I'm Irish!*" "OK", says *the speaker*, "I'll say it again — slowly."

2. Which types of reference are involved in the italicised referring expressions and what meanings do they suggest?
    a. *My husband* and I don't get along very well any more.
    b. *He* has changed so much.
    c. *Gerald* has become so utterly conceited.
    d. *This Gerald* is not the same man that I married.
    e. But *this bloke* can still be so nice sometimes.
    f. *The little bastard* even buys me flowers every week.

3. Which of the following proper names take the definite article and why?
    a. Mississippi (state)
    b. Mississippi (river)

c. Everglades (swamps in Florida)
d. Deep South
e. British Museum
f. Waterloo Station
g. Balkans

4. Choose the most appropriate type of generic reference (indefinite singular/plural, definite singular/plural) for the following generic statements and justify your choice. Note that elements other than the referring expression and the verb may need to be adjusted.
   a. … Italian (be) quite different from … German.
   b. … car (have) changed our lives.
   c. … cat (like) fish.
   d. … dog (be) the oldest domesticated animal.
   e. … New Yorker (drop) … r's.
   f. … ostrich (be) the largest bird in the world.
   g. … Italian (eat) spaghetti.
   h. … rolling stone (gather) no moss.
   i. … customer (be) always right.
   j. … cat (sleep) most of the day.

Chapter 6

Quantifying things: Quantifiers

6.0 Overview
6.1 Types of quantification
6.2 Set quantification
6.3 Scalar quantification
6.4 Interaction of quantifiers with each other and with referents
6.5 Summary

6.0 Overview

As speakers of English we normally combine reference to an instance of a thing with information about its **quantity**. Notions of quantity are typically expressed by number (singular or plural) and **quantifiers**. This chapter concentrates on **quantification** by means of quantifiers. We may conceive of the quantity of an instance in two different ways: in terms of a set or in terms of a scale. **Set quantification** refers to the magnitude of a subset relative to a full set; it is expressed by **set quantifiers** such as *all* and *most*. **Scalar quantification** refers to a magnitude along a scale; it is expressed by **scalar quantifiers** such as *many* and *much*. Set and scalar quantifiers may interact with referring expressions in **partitive constructions** and can be combined with each other.

6.1 Types of quantification

Quantification is an all-important facet of our daily lives. We quantify both things and situations. The quantification of a thing often shades over into the quantification of a situation. Compare the following sentences:

(1) a. We *often* spent our summer in Blackpool.
 b. We spent *many* summers in Blackpool.
 c. We stayed at *three* hotels.

Sentence (1a) refers to different occurrences of the same situation at different times and quantifies them by means of the frequency adverb *often*. Sentence (1b) may also describe different occurrences of the same situation but the quantity is now expressed by means of the noun quantifier *many*. Sentence (1c) also involves three occurrences of situations at different times — it is highly unlikely that we stayed at three different hotels at the same time — but now we focus our attention on the number of hotels. Notice also that we indicate a quantity in the noun phrases (1b) and (1c) twice: by means of the lexical quantifier (*many* and *three*) and, at a very schematic level, by means of the plural marker *-s* in the noun (*summers* and *hotels*)

This chapter is solely concerned with the quantification of things. More precisely, we will speak of the quantification of instances of a thing. Only a particular instance of a thing, not a thing as a type, may have a certain magnitude. Imagine a situation in which I want to inform my parents that I can't see them this weekend because I have to study for *three tests*. In conveying this information, I first need to specify the type of thing I am talking about, i.e. 'test', then single out the particular instance of test, i.e. 'the midterm tests I have to prepare for' –which are not explicitly mentioned, and finally indicate its magnitude as 'three'. Notice that an instance of a thing, in this case the three tests, may consist of several individual elements. Speaker and hearer need to make mental contact to the same instance and its quantity — otherwise miscommunication will arise. The indication of the quantity of the instance is part of the referring expression *three tests*. The conceptual "steps" required in an act of reference involving quantification may be represented as shown in Figure 6.1.

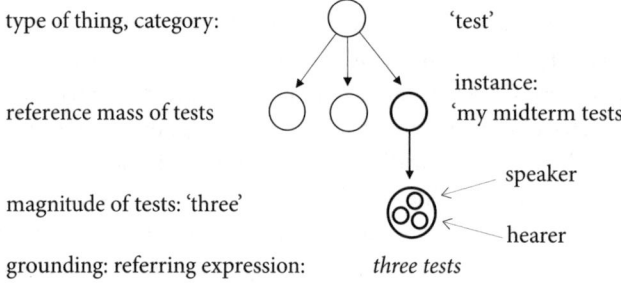

Figure 6.1. Quantification in an act of reference: *three tests*

The notion of **quantity** thus refers to the magnitude of an instance of a thing. The speaker's act of specifying the quantity of an instance is known as **quantification**. In fact, any instance of a thing is quantified in English. At a very general level, we provide information about the quantity of an instance by means of number: uniplex instances are marked by the singular, multiplex instances are marked by the plural. For finer-grained distinctions of quantities we use quantifiers.

Quantifiers are expressions that denote a quantity, such as *many, all, three, a large amount of*, etc. Quantifiers typically occur in prenominal position as in *three tests*, but may also function as pronouns as in *Many have passed* or *Three have failed*. As pronouns, quantifiers typically occur in partitive constructions such as *many of my books* (see 6.1.2 below).

In our ensuing discussion of quantification and quantifiers we need to distinguish between three types of opposition: (i) set versus scalar quantification, (ii) non-partitive versus partitive quantification, and (iii) number versus amount quantification.

6.1.1 Set quantification versus scalar quantification

We may understand a quantity of something either relative to a set or relative to a norm on a scale. The sentences under (2) illustrate these two types of quantification.

(2) a. *Most books* are fun to read.
b. *Many books* have been adapted for the screen.

Sentence (2a) makes a statement about a quantity of books relative to all books in the world. 'All books' of the world represents the overall reference mass of books. Even though the magnitude of the reference mass is not explicitly stated, it is part of our understanding. It needs to be tacitly agreed upon by speaker and hearer in order to understand the quantity described by *most books*. Technically, this kind of situation involves a set and a subset. In Chapter 5.2 we defined a **set** as a collection of elements that forms a whole. A **subset** is a collection of elements that forms part of a set, as in 'books that are fun to read'. The quantifier *most* in (2a) refers to the subset of books that are fun to read. At the same time, *most* invokes the full set of all books in the world, which of course encompasses the subset of books that are fun to read.

Quantifications that relate a subset to its set as in (2a) will be described as **set quantification** — also known as relative quantification. Note that the full set is presupposed and need not be explicitly stated. Set quantification is expressed by **set quantifiers** such as *most, all, every, each* and *any*.

Sentence (2b) describes a different situation. Here we are not dealing with a quantity relative to a full set, but with a quantity relative to an implicit norm on a scale. All we can say about the quantity described by *many books* in (2b) is that its number is higher than one might have expected for screen adaptations. **Scalar quantification**, elsewhere known as absolute quantification, thus invokes a scale with some implicit norm or standard. It is expressed by **scalar quantifiers** such as *many, much, few, little* and numerals such as *three*.

These two types of quantification may be illustrated as shown in Figure 6.2.

In Figure 6.2a, the lower semicircle indicates the quantity that establishes the subset, technically known as "proper subset". This subset$_1$ is profiled and therefore printed in bold lines. It invokes the full set, indicated by the circle. The quantifier *most* conveys that the quantity of subset$_1$ is larger than that of subset$_2$, which is out of focus.

In Figure 6.2b, the arrow on the scale pointing in both directions is meant to indicate that the scale invoked in scalar quantification is open-ended at both ends. *Many books* in the context of screen adaptations means that its quantity is located on this scale somewhere above an implicit norm. Once the scale reaches an end, as in *all books* or *no book*, we are no longer dealing with scalar quantification but with set quantification.

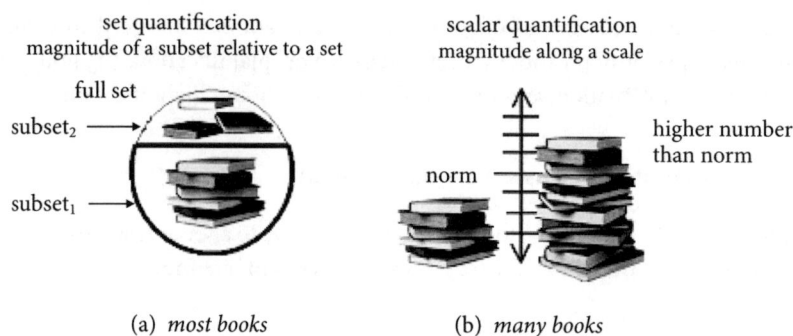

Figure 6.2. Set and scalar quantification

The conceptual distinction between set and scalar quantification shows up in their semantic and syntactic behaviour.

Firstly, set and scalar quantifiers take different types of adverbs. Since set quantification invokes the idea of a full set, we can think of the quantity of a subset approximating that of a full set as its limit and hence use the approximative adverb *almost* as in (3a). Since scalar quantification, by contrast, invokes an open-ended scale, it cannot be approximated by using *almost* (*almost many books*). A scalar quantity can only be relocated along a scale by means of an intensifying adverb such as *very* as in (3b) — which is impossible with set quantifiers (*very all books*).

(3) a. *Almost all* books are fun to read.
　　b. *Very many* books have been adapted for the screen.

The approximative adverb *almost* can modify all set quantifiers (*almost any book, almost every book*) except *most* itself (*almost most books*) because *most* already is approximative in meaning. The intensifiers *very* and *quite* express a higher degree of an implicitly assumed norm: *very many books* in (3b) means something like 'considerably more than many books', and *very few books* means 'considerably fewer books than few books' (see Table 6.5).

Secondly, set and scalar quantifiers differ with respect to their function. Like determiners, set quantifiers have grounding function: the full set invoked serves as an external reference point in the speech situation and allows the hearer to assess the subset's quantity. Thus, in *most books*, the quantity of books is still indefinite but the hearer can at least relate it to the reference mass of all the books in the world. Since they ground their referent, set quantifiers cannot be combined with other grounding elements in a noun phrase, in particular determiners. Hence phrases such as *those all people* are ungrammatical — *all* may however precede a determiner as in *all the passengers* (see sentence (11) below). The *most books* can also not be said in a quantifying function but may be used in a specifying function, as in *Of the three of us, Jane has the most books*, where *most* is used as a determining adjective (see Chapter 7.2.4(iii)). Scalar quantifiers, by contrast, have a purely quantifying function. They can therefore be combined with a definite determiner as in *the many books* (*I haven't read yet*) or *the little money* (*left after paying tax*).

Thirdly, being grounding elements in a noun phrase, set quantifiers cannot stand on their own as predicate nominals: like determiners, they need an entity they can ground. Therefore we cannot say things like *The books I still need to read are most/ all/ every*. Scalar quantifiers, by contrast, can readily stand on their own, as in *The books I still need to read are many/ few/ seven*.

6.1.2 Non-partitive quantification versus partitive quantification

In our discussion of set quantification as in *most books* we saw that the quantity of the subset is profiled, while that of the full set, of which it forms a part, is left implicit: we know, however, that it is identical to the universal set of books. Thus, in *Most books are fun to read*, the full set is all books in the world. More commonly, however, our interest is in more restricted sets and quantities thereof. For example, in *Most of these apples are rotten* or *Some of our politicians are corrupt*, we explicitly state the relation between a subset (*most apples*) to a full set (*these apples*). Such relations will be referred to as **partitive quantification**. Quantifying relations in which the full set remains unstated will, for lack of a better name, be described as **non-partitive quantification**. Non-partitive and partitive quantifications are different in structure:

(4) a. *Most books* are fun to read. [*non-partitive, universal set*]
    b. *Most of my books* are novels. [*partitive, restricted set*]

In the non-partitive phrase *most books* in (4a), the quantifier *most* functions as a determiner of its head noun *books*, and the reference of *most books* is indefinite. In the partitive construction *most of my books* in (4b), the quantifier *most* is a pronoun and functions as the head of the prepositional phrase *of my books*, which is its complement. Notice also that the referent of the full set, here *my books*, is always definite, i.e. I cannot, for instance, speak of **most of books*. This is to be expected since we cannot specify the size of a subset whose full set is not definite.

The partitive construction is particularly relevant with scalar quantifiers. As pointed out above, scalar quantification involves an open-ended scale and not a set. Speakers may, however, also want to quantify an instance along a scale within a restricted set and can do so by using the partitive construction. Let us contrast these two types of partitive quantification:

(5) a. *Most of my books* deal with Africa. [*subset of set*]
    b. *Many of my books* are detective novels. [*scale within set*]

As shown in Figure 6.3, set and scalar quantification look alike with respect to their full set (*my books*); however, set quantification involves two subsets (subset$_1$ *most books* and an unnamed subset$_2$), while scalar quantification involves a scalar quantity that is measured relative to a norm, where the norm is different for each frame: the norm of books adapted for the screen versus books that are detective novels.

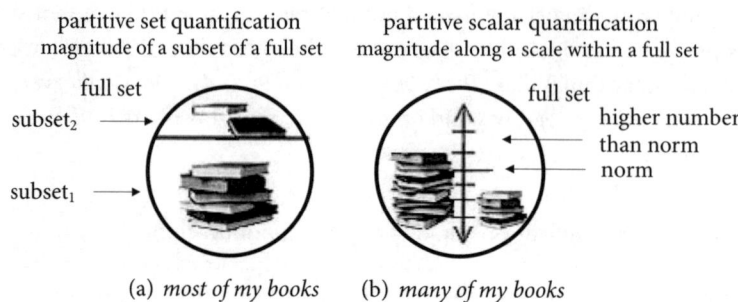

Figure 6.3. Partitive set and scalar quantification

Partitive set quantification (Figure 6.3a) is very similar to non-partitive set quantification (Figure 6.2a) and only differs from it in explicitly naming the full set, which is therefore drawn as a bold circle. Partitive scalar quantification (Figure 6.3b) combines aspects of set and scalar quantification. Internally, the scale of non-partitives is preserved: the quantity is measured against some implicit norm and can therefore only be intensified (*very many of my books*), but not approximated (**almost many of my books*). Externally, the quantity is measured against a full, definite set just as in set quantification — an indefinite *of*-phrase as in **many of books* is therefore not possible.

6.1.3 Number versus amount quantification

We may quantify both instances of objects and instances of substances. Instances of objects are quantified by adding up the number of individual elements of the same kind: thus *many jobs* are 'a certain number of jobs'. We will therefore describe this type of quantification as **number quantification**. Quantifiers that are used in number quantification such as *many*, *several*, and *three* will be referred to as **number quantifiers** — since they quantify count nouns, they are also known as count-noun quantifiers.

Instances of substances are quantified by extracting a portion or an amount of the substance: thus *much work* describes a certain amount of the "substance" work. We will therefore describe this type of quantification as **amount quantification**. Quantifiers that are used in amount quantification such as *much* and *little* will be referred to as **amount quantifiers** — since they quantify mass nouns, they are also known as mass-noun quantifiers.

Most quantifiers are restricted to either type of quantification. Thus we do not use number quantifiers with mass nouns (**many work* or **three work*) and amount quantifiers with count nouns (**much jobs* or **little jobs*).

The different types of quantification distinguished above are summarised in Table 6.1. Set and scalar quantifiers overlap in partitive quantification.

Table 6.1. Types of quantification

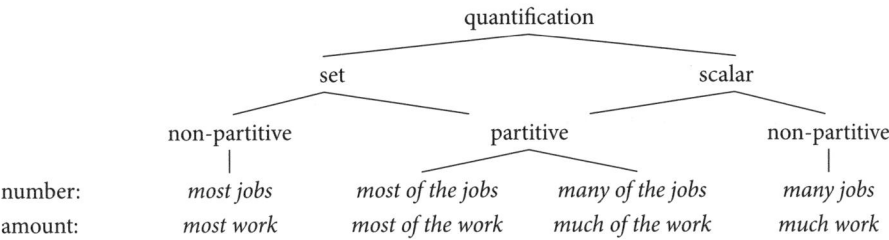

	non-partitive	partitive		non-partitive
number:	most jobs	most of the jobs	many of the jobs	many jobs
amount:	most work	most of the work	much of the work	much work

6.2 Set quantification

> *I started out with nothing and still have most of it left.* (Anonymous)

In the preceding section, we defined the quantity of a set as the magnitude of a subset relative to its full set and used the quantifier *most* as an illustration. *Most* specifies more than half the quantity of a full set. As a limiting case, the subset may be of the same size as the full set. English has four set quantifiers that describe this situation: *all*, *every*, *each* and *any*. These quantifiers comprise each and every element of a set and will therefore be referred to as **full-set quantifiers**. The set quantifiers *most*, *half* and *some*, by contrast, denote quantities of a subset that are smaller than that of the full set; they are thus **subset quantifiers**.

6.2.1 Sets: The four full-set set quantifiers *all, every, each* and *any*

We may conceive of a full set in different ways: we may focus on the collection of its elements, on each individual element, or on selected elements that are representative of the full set. The English full-set quantifiers *all*, *every*, *each* and *any* allow us to adopt these three conceptual strategies. Let us consider the following examples:

(6) a. *All* doctors have taken the Hippocratic oath.
  b. *Every* doctor uses a different method.
  c. *Each* doctor believes in his or her own method of treatment.
  d. *Any* doctor will confirm that influenza is contagious.

In using the quantifier *all* as in (6a), we visualise a collection of individuals which is equivalent to the full set. We will therefore refer to the quantifier *all* as a **collective quantifier**. *All* combines the notions of collectivity and distributiveness of its individual elements. **Distributiveness** differs from collectivity in that it picks out, and focuses on, the individual elements of a set. The use of *all* with a plural noun (*doctors*) and its plural agreement (*have*) in (6a) indicate that the notion of collectivity outweighs that of distributiveness.

In using *every* and *each* as in (6b) and (6c), we focus on the individual elements in relation to the full set. The quantifiers *every* and *each* are therefore known as **distributive**

quantifiers. *Every* and *each* make us see each of the elements of a set individually, which accounts for the singular form of their nouns (*doctor*).

In using *any* as in (6d), we assume that any individual element from the set could potentially be selected as representative of the full set. The quantifier *any* will therefore be referred to as a **selective quantifier**. Sentence (6d) thus means that 'no matter which doctor you select, he or she will confirm that influenza is contagious', implying that all doctors will confirm this. It would therefore be contradictory to say **Any doctor will confirm this but not all of them will*.

The particular meaning associated with each of these full-set quantifiers may be expressed more explicitly by additional adverbs: *together* signals 'collectivity' as in (7a), *separately* indicates 'distributiveness' as in (7b), and *whatsoever* highlights the notion of 'random selection' as in (7c):

(7) a. *All* the movie stars arrived *together*.
    b. *Each* movie star arrived *separately*.
    c. *Any* movie star *whatsoever* can play this role.

The adverbs only go with their particular quantifier. Thus, the collective adverb *together* is only compatible with the collective quantifier *all*, but is incompatible with a distributive quantifier (**Each movie star arrived together*) or the selective quantifier *any* (**Any movie star will leave together*). Likewise, the distributive adverb *separately* is compatible with the distributive quantifier *each* (and less so with *every*), and the adverb *whatsoever* is only compatible with the selective quantifier *any*. The quantifier *all* is polysemous in that, as stated above, it combines the notions of collectivity and distributiveness. In conjunction with the collective adverb *together* in (7a), *all* focuses on its collective aspect, in conjunction with the distributive adverb *separately* as in *All the movie stars arrived separately*, *all* focuses on its distributive aspect of meaning.

We can now specify the particular conceptual niches of the four full-set quantifiers.

Table 6.2. The four full-set quantifiers

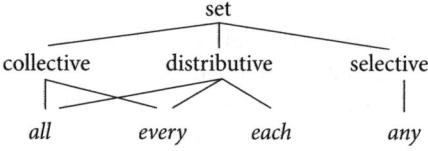

In this section on set quantifiers we tacitly assume that speakers behave according to the "logic" of quantification. In every-day speech, however, set quantifiers are often not used to designate all elements of a set exhaustively but much rather to express the speaker's emotional assessment in a hyperbolic way. If we hear somebody say things like *He'll eat anything* or *I have seen every church in Italy*, we will automatically take a "loose interpretation" of the set quantifiers for granted.

6.2.2 Collective sets: The set quantifier *all*

The collective set invoked by the quantifier *all* is typically multiplex, i.e. it is composed of individual elements, like the coins in sentence (8a). We may, however, also conceive of uniplex things as collections, such as the money in sentence (8b):

(8) a. I've spent *all my coins*.
    b. They don't need *all that money*.

The quantifier *all* with a plural count noun in (8a) makes us see a number of discrete coins as forming a collective set. The use of *all* with a mass noun as in (8b) is more problematic. As shown in Chapter 4.1.2, substances such as 'money' are non-discrete, homogeneous and uncountable; they should therefore not form a set. However, we may think of the substance 'money' as a superordinate term comprising banknotes, coins and other means of payment such as credit cards, cheques, etc. Thus, *all that money* in (8b) might evoke mental images of piles of cash or cheques.

We will describe these two types of collective set as multiplex collective sets and uniplex collective sets. Linguistically, they correspond to *all* with plural nouns and *all* with singular nouns.

6.2.2.1 *Multiplex collective sets:* **all** *with plural nouns*

Multiplex collective sets can be construed in two ways: as universal sets or as restricted sets.

(i) Universal sets: *all* with indefinite plural nouns

A universal set applies to all the individual elements of a thing in the world as in *All cows eat grass*. This statement is true of all the cows in the world in present time, in the past and in the future. In logic, this unrestricted use of a set quantifier is known as "universal quantification". Universal statements such as these can be paraphrased by the logical formula 'it is true for all x that, if x is a cow, then x eats grass'. Sentences with the universal quantifier *all* are similar in meaning to indefinite generic sentences as discussed in Chapter 5.4. Compare the generic sentence in (9a) with the "universal" statement in (9b):

(9) a. *Italians* speak Italian. [*generic reference*]
    b. *All Italians* speak Italian. [*universal quantification*]

The generalisation of statement (9a) is based on so many Italian-speaking Italians that we are inclined to generalise this finding to the whole class of Italians. The meaning of this sentence may therefore be paraphrased as 'almost all Italians speak Italian', possibly 90% of the population. The universal claim made in (9b), by contrast, does not, logically speaking, permit any exception, i.e. it is claimed that 100% of the population speak Italian. There certainly are, however, many Italians in the world who do not speak Italian — e.g. Italians who grew up in another country, or foreigners who have an Italian passport and live in Italy but speak another language — so that this universal claim is not valid. Generic and universal statements thus involve different conceptualisations of their sets.

(ii) Restricted sets: *all* with definite plural nouns

In most everyday situations, speakers do not make generic or universal statements but have a "restricted universe" in mind. Of course, it is reasonable to talk about quantities of a restricted set only if they are also present in the speaker's and hearer's mind, i.e. if they are definite. Therefore a definite referent may serve the same function as a restricted set. Compare the following two announcements at an airport, which, for most travellers, mean the same:

(10) a. Will *the* passengers for flight BA111 please proceed to gate 14.
b. Will *all* passengers for flight BA111 please proceed to gate 14.

The assumptions underlying the two construals of the announcement are, however, different. Announcement (10a) addresses the group of passengers who have booked the particular flight; these passengers are uniquely identifiable within the 'airport' frame and hence can be referred to with the definite article *the*, even if they are at different places in the boarding lounge, the snack bar or the bathroom. The announcement may, incidentally, also be made in the form *Will passengers for flight BA111 please proceed to gate 14*, in which the group of passengers is presented as not yet identified.

Announcement (10b) with the quantifier *all* refers to the same group of passengers but views them as forming a set. Portraying a group as a full set focuses on its completeness and is particularly relevant if the set is not complete. This announcement therefore implies that some passenger or passengers are still missing, possibly still wandering around the duty-free shops. It draws special attention to those passengers who have not shown their tickets yet, because without them the set of passengers that belong to the flight group would be incomplete. As a result, call (10b) is more emphatic, is likely to be made after, but not before, call (10a), and might be made repeatedly.

Since the definite noun phrase *the passengers for flight BA111* and the set quantification in *all passengers for flight BA111* express different, though similar, conceptualisations, they may be combined, as shown in:

(11) *All the passengers* have boarded now.

Sentence (11) might be said by the flight attendant to the captain following the repeated calls in (10b). It combines the notions of definiteness of the group of passengers (*the passengers*) and their collectivity and distributiveness invoked by *all*.

The quantifier *all* is, in fact, typically used in conjunction with definite referents. It is a handy way of expressing three notions of a referent at the same time: the referent is definite, collective, and composed of individual elements. Here are some further examples illustrating this usage of *all* in definite reference:

(12) a. Have you put *all the ingredients* in the soup?
b. You have *all the documents* in front of you.
c. We provide the best service to *all our customers*.
d. He has been a fisherman *all his life*.

6.2.2.2 *Uniplex collective sets: **all** with singular nouns*

Among uniplex things it is in particular substances that can be viewed as forming a set composed of elements, as in:

(13) a. Now you have spilled *all the milk*.
  b. Stop *all that nonsense*.
  c. Philosophy is central to *all knowledge*.

The "substance sets" may be concrete (13a) or abstract (13b, c), may be restricted (13a, b) or universal (13c), and may be understood as being composed of the same elements or of different elements. In the latter case, the elements of the set are interpreted as varieties in the same way that substances viewed as objects are interpreted as varieties (see Chapter 4.3.1.1). Thus, *all the milk* in (13a) might be understood in the sense of several bottles of the substance 'milk' or hyperbolically as just the whole milkjug, while *all that nonsense* in (13b) and *all knowledge* in (13c) suggest several different acts of folly and various fields of knowledge.

The central aspect of meaning conveyed by *all* in conjunction with a singular noun is that of 'wholeness of a collective set'. The collective quantifier *all* may therefore also be used with collective nouns as in (14a), where it emphasises the wholeness of the collective family elements; and it may be used with certain singular count nouns as in (14b), where it stresses the totality and length of a unit of time.

(14) a We shared our food with *all the family*.
  b. I didn't sleep a wink *all night*.

Notice that the idea of wholeness can be brought out by paraphrases with *whole*: *the whole family* and *the whole night*.

6.2.3 Distributive sets: The quantifiers *every* and *each*

In distributive sets, each individual element of the set is attended to. The quantifiers *every* and *each* are distributive in that they pick out a single representative instance of a set and thereby invoke the full set. They therefore take singular agreement as in *Every car is air-conditioned* and *Each car has its own character*. But this is about all the two distributive quantifiers have in common. Most importantly, *every* and *each* differ in the way they invoke their sets.

Every links the individual elements to each other until we ultimately reach the complete, collective set, while *each* focuses on each single element of the set by examining it individually. These are the interpretations we associate with the following sentences, which might be said by the teacher of a group of children:

(15) a. Now let's dance a ring-a-ring-o'-roses, and *every* child has to hold hands with another child.
  b. When we do ring-a-ring-o'-roses, *each* child has to hold hands with another child.

Sentence (15a) would be spoken in a situation where the teacher wants to make sure that every child is included in the game. Sentence (15b), on the other hand, might be spoken if the teacher were explaining the game to another, less experienced teacher and wanted to make sure that she pays attention to the children's individual interactions.

The conceptual difference between *every* and *each* is shown in Figure 6.4, where the bold circle with *every child* indicates that the collective set is focused upon, whereas, with *each child*, the bold print of the children indicates that the individuals are focused upon while the set recedes into the background.

Figure 6.4. *Every* child and *each* child

The difference between *every* and *each* is also nicely illustrated in the following pair of sentences:

(16) a. *Every* piece of the jigsaw puzzle fits some other piece.
     b. *Each* piece of the jigsaw puzzle fits its neighbouring pieces.

Every in (16a) makes us see the piecing together of the puzzle until it is completed, while *each* in (16b) makes us see the step-by-step work of fitting one piece to the next piece without necessarily having the completed set in view.

These general conceptual differences between *every* and *each* account for subtle differences in meaning as illustrated in the following examples:

(17) a. Liverpool gets scruffier *every day*.
     b. I didn't sleep a wink *each time* I went there.

(18) a. There is only one computer for *every four students*.
     b. There is one computer for *each student*.

(19) a. For *every problem* there is a solution.
     b. *Each problem* has its own solution.

Time units are seen as successive with *every* as in (17a) but as separate with *each* as in (17b). Due to its notion of succession, *every* may express a one-to-many relation as in (18a), whereas, due to its notion of individuality, *each* may express a one-to-one relation as in (18b). Due to its focus on collectivity, the quantifier *every* as in (19a) makes us see abstract things more generally while the quantifier *each* as in (19b) makes us see them more specifically.

These differences in meaning have further consequences. Due to its notion of succession, a set invoked by *every* has a minimum number of three elements, i.e. *every* excludes the notion of 'two'. We thus cannot say *every of these two books*, and if we speak of *every book*, we imply that there are at least three books. The set described by *each*, on the other hand, implies at least two elements. Thus we can speak of *each of these two books*. The one-to-one relation with *each* also motivates further sense extensions: the sense of 'complementarity' as in *each side of a coin*, the sense of 'reciprocity' as in *They kissed each other*, and the sense of 'back and forth motion' as in *I have to travel ten miles each way*.

Finally, since *every* and *each* involve different types of distributive quantification, they may be combined to emphasise both the collective and the individual aspect of the distributive set as in the following examples:

(20) a. The epidemic effects *each and every one* of us.
 b. *Each and every June*, the world's top cyclists get on their bikes to pedal along the roads.

6.2.4 Selective sets: The quantifier *any*

As said in the discussion of sentence (6), the quantifier *any* refers to a randomly selected element of a set and thereby invokes the set as a whole. With *any*, a collective set is thus inferred, while *all* and *every* denote a collective set as part of their established meaning. This has consequences for their grammatical behaviour. *All* and *every* may be used in both non-factual and factual situations, as in (21a) and (21b), while *any* is largely restricted to non-factual situations, as in (21a).

(21) a. *Any* trespasser(s) / *All* trespassers will be prosecuted.
 b. *All* trespassers were prosecuted.

The restriction of *any* to non-factual situations follows from its meaning of selectivity. We can, of course, only select an element from a set if we have a choice. Once we have already selected an element, we can no longer use the quantifier *any*. This is why *all* is used as the set quantifier in the past event (21b), where the use of *any* is ruled out: **Any trespasser was prosecuted*. Since *any* and *all* involve different conceptualisations, they can be coordinated. The quantifier *any* focuses on individual kinds of contributions or claims, while the quantifier *all* focuses on their collective totality.

(22) a. *Any and all* contributions are welcome.
 b. You hereby waive *all and any* claims against the company.

The order of the quantifiers reflects different viewing arrangements, but does not appear to be associated with differences in meaning: in using *any and all* we adopt a view from one selected element to the whole set, and in using *all and any*, we adopt a view from the whole set to one selected element.

Although the quantifier *any* and the determiner *any* have different grammatical status and hence are dealt with in different chapters, they are closely related conceptually. Let us consider the differences and the commonalities of the two usages of *any* in the following sentences.

(23) a. He won't drink *any wine* at all. [*determiner*]
 b. He will drink *any wine* at all, even hot wine. [*quantifier*]

The determiner *any* in (23a) is used in a non-affirmative context and conveys negative expectations (see Chapter 5.2.1.2), namely 'I don't expect him to drink wine'. The quantifier *any* in (23b) is used in an affirmative context and conveys positive expectations, namely 'I expect him to drink wine'. The two usages of *any* are thus complementary to one another. In both usages, *any* invokes a whole set from which an element may be selected: in the non-affirmative situation (23a), no element is "found"; in the affirmative situation (23b), a random element is selected.

The examples under (23) also demonstrate that, in both usages, the element may also be an amount or a kind of a "substance set". Thus, (23a) is understood to mean that 'he doesn't drink any amount of wine', while (23b) is probably understood to mean that 'he drinks any kind of wine'. In both usages, *any* can be stressed, and its relation to the set can be emphasised by using *at all*. The use of *at all* is more common with non-affirmative situations as in (23a), where it serves to highlight the contrast between a whole set and its non-existent or non-expected elements described by *any*; with affirmative sentences as in (23b), there is no such contrast because the quantity invoked by *any* corresponds to that of the set.

6.2.5 Subsets: Subset quantifiers

As pointed out in the discussion of quantification in Section 6.1.1, subset quantifiers describe the magnitude of a subset relative to the full set. The main subset quantifiers of English divide the continuum of quantities into a few vaguely defined areas of subsets, as shown in Figure 6.5.

Figure 6.5. Subsets

A subset that is identical to the full set is expressed by one of the set quantifiers, most typically *all*, decreasing magnitudes of the subset are described by the quantifiers *most*, *half* and *some*, and an empty set is described by the prenominal quantifier *no* or the pronoun *none*. The following examples illustrate usages of the subset quantifiers.

(24) a. *Most* Republicans are conservative.
 b. *Half* the Senate voted for abortion, the other half against it.
 c. *Some* senators support the President, *others* don't.
 d. *No* senator was pleased with the vote.
 d'. *None* were pleased with the vote

As these examples show, the subset quantifiers behave differently in spite of their common function. Their grammatical usages are plotted in Table 6.3.

Table 6.3. Grammatical behaviour of subset quantifiers

	prenominal		predeterminer		
	quantifier + noun		quantifier + *the* + noun		quantifier + *a* + noun
all	all people	all wine	all the people	all the wine	
most	most people	most wine			
half			half the people	half the bottle	half a dozen
some	some people	some wine			
no	no person	no wine			

As stated at the beginning of this chapter, quantifiers typically occur in prenominal position, i.e. the position preceding (articleless) indefinite plural count nouns or mass nouns — the noun may of course also be preceded by an attributive adjective, as in *all great poets*. More rarely, a quantifier occurs before a determiner; in this function quantifiers are usually described as *predeterminers*. This use was found with *all* followed by a definite determiner as in *all the people*, where the quantifier contributes the notions of collectivity and distributiveness to a definite referent (see 6.2.2.1ii). More rarely, a quantifier may precede an indefinite determiner as in *half a dozen* or *half a million*, where the quantifier *half* describes a clear subset of a well-defined set. Finally, all quantifiers, including *none*, may occur as independent nominals such as *none* in (24d') and in partitive constructions as in *none of the senators*.

Most is a "typical" quantifier: like *all*, it may quantify both count and mass nouns in prenominal position, but unlike *all*, *most* is not used as a predeterminer, i.e. we do not say **most the people* or **most the wine*. In English, the relative vagueness of the quantity described by *most* requires an indefinite referent, as in *most people*, while other languages may conceive of this quantity as definite, as in German *die meisten Leute* 'the most people'.

Half denotes a precise subset and therefore only occurs in a definite context, as in *half the people* or *half the bottle*, where *the bottle* metonymically stands for its contents. This definite character is also exhibited by similar quantifying expressions like the multipliers *twice, three times*, etc., as in *The spear was twice the size of a man*.

The quantifier *some* deserves special attention. Just like *any*, *some* is used both as a determiner and quantifier. As an indefinite determiner it has the unstressed form [sm], as in *There are some students waiting outside* (see Chapter 5.2.1). As a quantifier, *some* has the full, and often contrastive phonetic form [sʌm]. *Some* is used both as a set quantifier and a scalar quantifier. As a set quantifier, *some* means 'a certain number/amount of' and contrasts with *most, others, none*, etc. as in (24c) and (25a); as a scalar quantifier, *some* means 'a few' and contrasts with *many, several, few*, etc. as in (25b).

(25) a. *Sóme* students work very hard, *óthers* don't. [set quantifier]
b. *Sóme* students will fail, but *mány* will pass. [scalar quantifier]

The quantifiers *no* and *none* characterise a set as being empty. We cannot, however, think of something being absent without imagining a state of affairs in which the thing is present so that it may be conceived of as missing (see also Chapter 10.1.1). The subset quantifiers *no* or *none* thus also evoke the set.

The subset quantifiers we have considered so far form a small grammatical class. In addition, however, there are also many lexical expressions that also fulfil the function of subset quantifiers, such as *a third of, the majority of, the larger part of*, etc.

6.3 Scalar quantification

Scalar quantification differs from set quantification in two respects:

Firstly, scalar quantification invokes a scale with some implicit norm, whereas set quantification relates to a full set.

Secondly, scalar quantification applies to both object and substance instances, i.e. to both count and mass nouns, whereas set quantification typically applies to sets of individualised entities only, i.e. to count nouns.

We will first look at implicit norms in scalar quantification (6.3.1) and then distinguish number and amount quantification (6.3.2).

6.3.1 Implicit norms in scalar quantification

We can only quantify an instance in a scalar way if we have a standard or norm against which its magnitude can be assessed. The norm is not explicitly expressed, but we implicitly expect a certain magnitude within a given frame. For example, depending on the frame, *three* can mean either 'many' or 'few': three rhinos in a zoo or three children in a family in the Western world would be considered 'many'. Conversely, three students at a lecture course or three visitors at a pop concert would be considered 'few'.

Let us take a closer look at the way scalar quantities are computed.

(26) a. *Many anti-war demonstrators* were protesting in the street.
b. *Many of the anti-war demonstrators* became violent.

In both sentences the quantity of demonstrators is described as *many*, but their actual numbers are of course different. We estimate the number of anti-war demonstrators on the basis of our cultural knowledge of demonstrations, including anti-war demonstrations, our knowledge of violence, including violence in anti-war demonstrations, etc. *Many* would then mean 'above a norm', *few* would be 'below a norm'. If, in our interpretation of sentence (26a), our expected norm for anti-war demonstrations averaged 2,000 to 3,000 people, *many demonstrators* might be 5,000 people, while 500 demonstrators would be considered few.

In sentence (26b), our estimate of the number of violent demonstrators is based on two norms: the assumed number of demonstrators and our "knowledge" of the proportion of demonstrators who turn violent in such demonstrations, which we might assume to be around 5%. On this account, we would estimate the expected number of demonstrators who turn violent out of a whole group of 3,000 people to be about 150.

6.3.2 Number and amount quantification: Number and amount quantifiers

Number quantification applies to multiplex instances, i.e. to count nouns. Quantifying instances of an object means adding up discrete, individual elements of the same kind along a scale. Thus, *many bees* describes a number of "added up" individual bees which is higher on a scale of quantity than, for instance, *some bees*.

Amount quantification, on the other hand, applies to substance instances, i.e. to mass nouns. Quantifying an instance of a substance means extending or reducing the same kind of substance by a given amount along a scale. Thus, *a lot of garbage* specifies an amount of the same, indivisible substance.

The conceptual distinction between number and amount quantification is reflected in English in two clearly distinguished groups of scalar quantifiers: number quantifiers and amount quantifiers. The most common quantifiers used with count nouns, mass nouns and both count and mass nouns are listed in Table 6.4.

Table 6.4. Scalar quantifiers

	nmber quantifiers	both	amount quantifiers
positive	a huge number of	lots of	a huge amount of
	many, numerous	a lot of	much, a large amount of
	a great many, four		a great deal of
norm	a few, several, a number of		a little, a bit of
		some	a certain amount of
	not many		not much
negative	few		little

Scalar quantifiers are ranked with respect to each other and with respect to an implicit norm. For example, *a few, several, a little,* and *a bit of* are assumed to denote quantities slightly above an implicit norm, while *some* and *a certain amount of* denote quantities slightly below an implicit norm.

As is well-known, the quantifier *much* is freely used in questions (*How much money do you make?*) and negative contexts (*I don't earn much*). In affirmative contexts, however, the use of *much* is restricted to formal or academic registers, as in *Much money has been spent* *on the welfare system*. In everyday speech, sentences such as **I earn much money* would not be said. Why shouldn't the quantifier *much*, just like the quantifier *many*, be used in everyday affirmative contexts? An explanation might be found in the iconic principle of quantity. Unlike the two-syllable form *many*, the short, one-syllabic phonetic form *much* does not adequately reflect the meaning of a large quantity; longer expressions such as *a lot of*, *a large amount of*, etc. are much better suited to render this meaning. *Much* is, however, compatible with non-affirmative contexts, i.e. questions and negations, because here it does not convey the sense of 'a large amount of' but that of 'an unknown or small quantity'. Interestingly, *much* is more readily used with abstract mass nouns in positive contexts and in fairly high registers, as in:

(27)   There has been *much discussion* recently about the value of the Euro compared to the dollar.

Reified nouns with *much* like *much discussion* do not describe a large portion of a substance but repetitions and varieties of intense episodic events (see Chapter 4.4.3). For such notions, the quantifier *much* is apparently not felt to be counter-iconic.

The set of scalar quantifiers is a mixed bag of different expressions reflecting different degrees of grammaticalisation. Some are "genuine" quantifier words (*many*, *much*, *few*), others are numerals (*four*), and still others are grammaticised quantifiers that also function as lexical words (*little*); further types are partitive expressions (*a number of*) and quantifiers preceded by the indefinite article *a* (*a few*, *a great many*, *a little*). The last type of quantifier is particularly intriguing because here the indefinite article *a* is obviously not used in its normal sense as a determiner of a singular count noun. Let us contrast quantifiers with and without the indefinite article *a* in the examples below. The nominals with the bare quantifiers *few* and *little* under (28) denote non-specific referents, while those with *a few* and *a little* under (29) denote specific referents.

(28)   a.   There are *few* people who remember me.   [*non-specific*]
       b.   There is *little* love left for me in your heart.   [*non-specific*]

(29)   a.   There are (still) *a few* people who remember me.   [*specific*]
       b.   There is (still) *a little* love left for me in your heart. [*specific*]

The quantifiers *few* and *little* in (28) mean 'a small number' and 'a small amount', respectively. We tend to associate these quantified non-specific referents with negative expectations; they are therefore not compatible with adverbs such as *still*, *at least* and *already*, which indicate positive expectations: ?*There are at least few people who believe that*; ?*There is at least little risk in the project*.

The quantifiers *a few* and *a little* in (29) mean 'quantities slightly above the implicit norm'. Why should their combination with the indefinite article come to express larger quantities than the simple quantifiers *few* and *little*? As we saw in Chapter 5, the article *a(n)* applies to a bounded, uniplex instance of an object. Its conceptual contribution here is to make us see the unbounded referents as bounded: *a few people* in (29a) is seen as a collective group, and *a little love* in (29b) is seen as a delimited portion. Being clearly defined by their boundaries, these entities now qualify to be used as actual, specific referents. The quantifiers *a few* and *a little* also tend to be associated with positive expectations, as can be seen from their compatibility with the positive-oriented adverbs *still*, *at least* and *already*. The quantity they describe is seen as 'sufficient enough for a given purpose'. Thus, sentence (29a) might be understood in the sense that there are still more people who I can see and talk to than I might have feared. It is this positive orientation in conjunction with the specific reference that implicates a larger quantity of *a few* and *a little*.

The range of scalar quantifications is unlimited. If the speaker wants to make finer-grained distinctions about a scalar quantity than provided for by the quantifiers listed in Table 6.4, she may make use of adverbs such as *quite, very, about, rather, fairly, roughly*, etc. Thus, we can express shades of a number of people or of an amount of money more explicitly as shown in Table 6.5.

Table 6.5. Shades of number and amount quantifications

	number quantification	amount quantification
norm	quite a few people	quite a bit of money
	a few people	a little money
	few people	little money
	very few people	very little money
	very, very few people	very, very little money

Due to the norm as a reference point on the scale, the intensifying adverb *quite* increases the quantity expressed by *a few*, whereas the intensifying adverb *very* decreases the quantities expressed by *few* and *little*. Also stress and intonation may be used to move a quantity up or down the scale. For example, the stressed quantifiers in *We (only) saw a féw cranes* or *There is (only) a líttle money left* reduce the quantities below the norm. Lastly, the picture of quantifiers, in particular scalar quantifiers, is skewed by people's delight in using understatement and hyperbole, as illustrated in the following examples:

(30) a. I have been to a *few* countries. ('I have been all over the world')
 b. I spent *mountains of* money for just one drink.

As the last example shows, the class of scalar quantifiers may be expanded by using lexical expressions such as *mountains of*. Many of these lexical quantifiers are metaphorical. Since we understand MORE as UP, a large number of these metaphorical quantifiers derive from words with a high vertical extension. Since both objects and substances can be "piled up", the same metaphorical quantifiers can be used with both types of nouns. Other metaphorical quantifiers make use of other source domains such as *masses, tons, oceans*, etc. A selection of these lexical quantifiers is presented in Table 6.6.

Table 6.6. Lexical quantifiers

quantified count nouns	quantified mass nouns
loads of people	loads of fun
mountains of dishes	mountains of washing
heaps of books	heaps of time
piles of debts	piles of work
stacks of essays	stacks of money
masses of books	masses of data
tons of chocolates	tons of beer

The possibilities of creating lexical quantifiers such as these appear to be unlimited; yet there is at least one major constraint: quantities below the norm do not seem to be part of the lexical system of quantifiers. We cannot, for example, speak of *valleys of dishes* meaning 'few dishes'.

Speakers may also feel the need to limit the scale of scalar quantities in their positions, although, as we argued above, the scale is open-ended. Thus, people may combine the set quantifiers *all* and *none* with scalar quantifiers. Still other set quantifiers may be contrastively combined with scalar quantifiers, as in the following examples:

(31) a. *Many*, maybe even *most*, gamblers lost a fortune.
 b. *Many*, in fact *all*, flights were cancelled.

In (31a) the set quantifier *most* coincides with an unexpectedly higher magnitude on the scale than already denoted by *many*, and in (31b) the set quantifier *all* coincides with the positive endpoint of a scale. Thus, the distinction between set and scalar quantification, which we were at pains to keep apart, often blurs.

6.4 Interaction of quantifiers with each other and with referents

Thus far we have mainly looked at set and scalar quantifiers independently of each other. Now we will analyse how these two types of quantifiers interact with each other and with referents.

6.4.1 Partitive quantification

In the previous section, we considered example (26b), *Many of the anti-war demonstrators became violent*, concentrating on the meaning conveyed by the scalar quantifier *many*. Now we will look at the construction as a whole. Semantically, the *of*-construction describes the relationship between a part and a whole. Here, the part-whole schema is applied to a relation between a subset (*many*) and a full set (*the demonstrators*). In Section 6.1.2 we referred to this type of quantification as a *partitive quantification* and to the construction as *partitive construction*. The set in a partitive construction is always given as a restricted set, and hence expressed by a definite noun phrase. This means that the partitive construction can only relate to referents that are accessible by one of the various referential strategies at our disposal. In *many of the demonstrators*, this is done by anaphoric reference, i.e. the demonstrators have probably been introduced in the preceding discourse. The subset in the partitive construction, i.e. *many*, can only be indefinite: it introduces a new referent such as the subset of violent demonstrators. This applies both to partitive scalar quantification, as in *many of the demonstrators*, and to partitive set quantification, as in *all of the demonstrators*.

As an exercise in understanding the interaction of quantification with reference, let us analyse the complex phrase *most of the demonstrators*. In computing the quantity it describes, we first need to know the total number of demonstrators: the definite article in *the demonstrators* indicates that we are dealing with a set which includes all its individuals and which is mentally shared by speaker and hearer (see Chapter 5.3). The quantity described by the subset quantifier *most* can then be computed relative to the whole set. We can represent the composition of the phrase as a step-by-step assembling of each conceptual unit with its neighbouring unit, as shown in Figure 6.6. The compositional tree should be read from the bottom to the top.

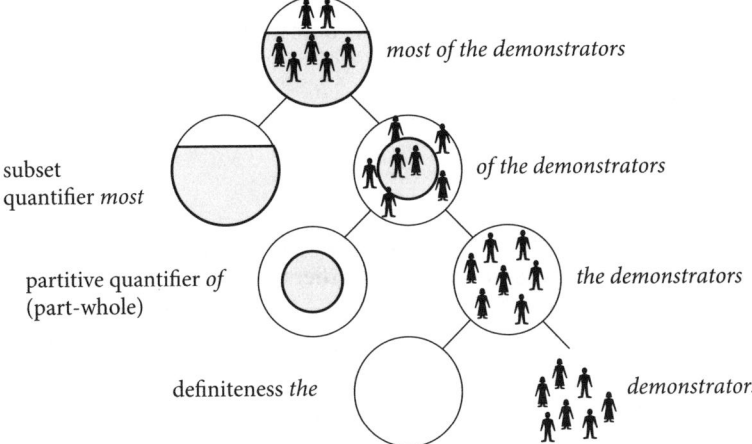

Figure 6.6. Conceptual composition of *most of the demonstrators*

We first join the schematic concept of 'definiteness' and 'inclusiveness' described by *the* with the multiplex category 'demonstrators', which gives us an agreed-upon set of demonstrators, described by *the demonstrators*. We then join the schematic 'part-whole' concept described by *of* with the whole set of demonstrators, which gives us the prepositional phrase *X of the demonstrators*. As a final step, we join the subset described by the quantifier *most* as a part with (*of*) *the demonstrators* as its whole, which gives us the quantity of the subset relative to the whole set described as *most of the demonstrators*.

6.4.2 Ordering of set and scalar quantifiers

In English, quantifiers and determiners appear in a certain order. Thus, we have a different order in the phrases *all my friends* and *my many friends*. The set quantifier *all* is a predeterminer preceding the definite determiner *my*, the scalar quantifier *many* is a postdeterminer.

Table 6.7. Ordering of quantifiers and determiner in *all my many friends*

set quantifier predeterminer	definite determiner	scalar quantifier postdeterminer	noun
all	my		friends
	my	many	friends
all	my	many	friends

The ordering of the quantifiers and determiners is determined by the iconic principle of proximity (see Chapter 3.3.1). The set quantifier *all* invokes a full set but does not add any quantitative information to the definite noun — its position is therefore distant from the noun. Scalar quantifiers, by contrast, provide essential information on the magnitude of a referent — they are thus positioned more closely to the noun. It follows from these observations that, when set and scalar quantifiers co-occur in one phrase, the set quantifier precedes the scalar quantifier.

6.5 Summary

Quantification is the assignment of a certain magnitude, or **quantity**, to an instance of a thing. Quantities are typically expressed by **quantifiers**. Two major types of quantification, and hence two types of quantifier, are to be distinguished: set and scalar quantification. **Set quantification** refers to the magnitude of a subset relative to an unnamed full set; it is expressed by **set quantifiers** such as *all, most, every, each* and *any*. **Scalar quantification** refers to a magnitude along a scale; it is expressed by **scalar quantifiers** such as *many* and *few*. Both set and scalar quantities may, as subsets, be related to a named full set by means of a partitive construction. In **partitive quantification**, the relation between the subset and the set is made explicit by means of the *of*-phrase as in *most of the books*.

Set quantifiers may denote the full set or a proper subset relative to the full set invoked. Accordingly, we distinguish more specifically between set quantifiers and subset quantifiers. The **set quantifiers** of English allow us to conceptualise the set's composition in different ways: the **collective quantifier** *all* denotes all the individual elements of a set as a collection, the **distributive quantifiers** *every* and *each* denote each single element of a set, and the **selective quantifier** *any* denotes a randomly selected element as representative for the full set. **Subset quantifiers** such as *half* and *most* denote approximate magnitudes of a subset relative to its full set.

Scalar quantifiers may quantify instances of both objects (**number quantification**) and substances (**amount quantification**). English systematically distinguishes between **number quantifiers** for object instances (*many, five, several, few*) and **amount quantifiers** for substance instances (*much, a bit, little*).

Both set and scalar quantifiers can be used in partitive constructions. Still, the difference between set quantification as in *most of my friends* and scalar quantification as in *many of my friends* looms large. The set quantifier is a predeterminer as in *all my friends*, while the scalar quantifier is a postdeterminer as in *my many friends*.

> **Further reading**

Cognitive grammar analyses of quantification and reference, especially anaphoric reference, are to be found in Langacker (1991a: 81–89), various publications by van Hoek, especially (1997), and Davidse (2004). Problems of definiteness are related to quantifier scope by Croft (1983). Van der Auwera (1980) offers a collection of papers concentrating on the various determiners and their quantifying and referential possibilities.

Quantification has traditionally been a favoured domain for logicians. Linguistic papers in this direction are those by Cushing (1982), Dryer (1989), and McCawley (1977). But Labov (1985) shows that set quantifiers like *all* and *every* are often not used literally, but in an approximative sense. Vendler (1967: 71–96) offers a detailed analysis of the four set quantifiers *each*, *every*, *all* and *any*, Langacker (2003) studies *any* in its uses as a determiner and a quantifier, and Ariel (2004) devotes an extensive article to the discussion of the subset quantifier *most*.

> **Study questions**

1. Specify the type of reference or quantification (scalar, set or subset) and quantifier (number or amount) in each of the noun phrases printed in italics. When applicable for set quantification, also further specify whether it is collective, distributive or selective.
    a. *The passengers* to the US have to fill out the immigration form.
    b. *All passengers* to the US have to fill out the immigration form.
    c. *Many passengers* haven't filled out the form yet.
    d. *Three of the passengers* are still missing.
    e. *Almost all passengers* have boarded the plane.
    f. *One* had not turned up.
    g. *Half the Senate* voted for abortion, the other *half* against it.
    h. *Some Senators* support the President, *others* don't.
    i. He was keen to drink *any wine* they offered him.
    j. *Any fool* can criticise, condemn and complain, and *most* fools do.
    k. *Every law* is a restriction of liberty.
    l. *Most cows* give more milk when they listen to music.
    m. *Most of the stuff* people worry about never happens.

2. Why can't we substitute *all the* and *any* in the following sentences for one another? Try to paraphrase the meanings of the newly made sentences.
    a. *All the* pieces of the puzzle will fit together.   [*Any piece*]
    b. *Any* piece can be put in last.   [*All the pieces*]

3. Why can we say sentence (a), but not sentence (b)?
    a. All children gathered in the school yard.
    b. *Every child gathered in the school yard.

4. Is there any reason for the soccer coach to use different set quantifiers in the following sentences?
   a. *Every* player must push himself to the utmost.
   b. *Each* player has to stick to his assignment.

5. Fill in *every* or *each* or either of them and justify your choice.
   a. E...... child likes ice-cream.
   b. E...... theory is open to objection. (Explain the different meanings.)
   c. The robber held a gun in e...... hand.
   d. E...... sow produces around six piglets.
   e. E...... man for himself. (said in a shipwreck)
   f. E...... player gets three cards.
   g. E...... king in a deck of playing cards represents a great king from history: Spades: King David, Hearts: Charlemagne, Clubs: Alexander the Great, Diamonds: Julius Caesar.

6. Analyse the quantifiers in the following joke:
   I told my psychiatrist that *everyone* hates me.
   He said I was being ridiculous — *everyone* hasn't seen me yet.

Chapter 7

Qualifying things: Modifiers

> 7.0 Overview
> 7.1 Qualifications and modifiers
> 7.2 Qualification by means of properties: Adjectives
> 7.3 Qualification by means of relations: Genitive phrases and prepositional phrases
> 7.4 Qualification by means of situations: Relative clauses
> 7.5 Summary

7.0 Overview

A thing or an instance of a thing may, in the speaker's discourse, be in need of more specific **qualification**. Qualifications have different functions: a restrictive function as in *a feminist writer*, and a non-restrictive function as in *a free gift*. Qualifications are expressed as **modifiers** of nouns. Modifiers may occupy different positions with regard to the head noun they modify. They may occur in prenominal position as in *a visible star* or in postnominal position as in *a star visible tonight*. In general, premodifiers express stable qualifications, while postmodifiers express temporary qualifications. Qualifications may be achieved in three ways: by means of a property, by means of a relation, and by means of a situation. **Qualifying properties** are expressed as adjectives, **qualifying relations** are expressed by genitive phrases and prepositional phrases, and **qualifying situations** are expressed as relative clauses.

7.1 Qualifications and modifiers

Qualifications may be used to specify things and instances of a thing — for reasons of simplicity we will use the term 'thing' to cover the type 'thing' as well as instances of a thing unless the distinction between a thing and an instance of a thing is relevant. In English, such specifying **qualifications** are expressed by means of **modifiers**, in particular adjectives, genitive phrases, prepositional phrases and relative clauses. Modifiers are grammatically part of a noun phrase and are dependent on their head noun. For example, in the noun phrase *a sweet girl*, the adjective *sweet* modifies the head noun *girl*. There are also other types of modifiers. For instance, in so-called endocentric compounds such as *alarm clock*, the first element, i.e. the noun *alarm*, typically modifies the second element, the head noun *clock*. In addition, whole sentences may be modified as in *Fortunately, he didn't knock me on the head*. These types of modification will, however, not be dealt with in this chapter on the qualification of things.

The analysis of qualification and modifiers requires two factors to be considered: (i) the function of qualification, and (ii) the type of qualification.

7.1.1 Functions of qualification: Restrictive and non-restrictive modifiers

Speakers may want to provide qualitative information about a thing or an instance for one of two reasons. The thing talked about must be specified more precisely in a given communicative situation or the referent talked about calls for some additional information. The former function of qualification is *restrictive*, the latter *non-restrictive*. The modifiers that express these two types of qualification are, accordingly, known as restrictive and non-restrictive modifiers, sometimes also called defining and non-defining modifiers.

Restrictive qualification may apply to a thing or an instance of a thing. The sentences under (1) exemplify restrictive qualifications of a thing. The thing does not refer but describes a category which includes the subject participant as its member. In English, this situation is expressed by a sentence with a copula, in particular *be*, and an indefinite predicate nominal. Sentence (1a) describes the inclusion of Simone de Beauvoir as a member in the category 'writer'.

(1) a. Simone de Beauvoir was a writer.
    b. Simone de Beauvoir was a *feminist* writer.
    c. Simone de Beauvoir was a *French feminist* writer.
    d. Simone de Beauvoir was an *influential French feminist* writer.

Sentences (1b), (1c) and (1d) increasingly restrict the category 'writer' by adding further specifications: 'feminist writer' is a subcategory of 'writer', 'French feminist writer' is a subcategory of 'feminist writer', etc. For such specific categories we lack simple names, and it is qualifications like these that allow the speaker to create subcategories whenever needed. In fact, we constantly lack simple words to express the infinite number of subcategories that we can think of and want to talk about. For example, there are no single words available in English to express subcategories such as 'law-abiding citizen', 'big surprise' or 'the man in the street'. Restrictive qualification applied to a thing thus has the function of establishing a subtype of a thing.

Applied to an instance of a thing, restrictive qualification has the function of restricting, or narrowing down, its referential range within the reference mass; it thereby gives the hearer a clearer picture of the referent or even allows him to identify it. The referential function of qualification is illustrated in the following exchange between two men at a party who want to make sure they are talking about the same person and describe the women in a typically male way:

(2) a. Do you mean the woman *with the shiny earrings*?
    b. No, I'm talking about the woman *with the low neckline*.

Both men have chosen the women's attire as the most distinct attribute to identify her. Possibly only one of the women in sight at the party is wearing shiny earrings and only one of them sports a dress with a low neckline. Each of the men at least assumes that this qualitative information enables the hearer to restrict the "reference mass of women in sight" to the one he has in mind.

Non-restrictive qualification provides additional information about a thing or instance, i.e. non-categorising or non-referential information. Descriptions of additional, often disparaging qualification are traditionally known as epithetical (from Greek *epithetos* 'added'). We will use the term **epithet** for non-restrictive qualification. A classical epithet is the stock phrase *rosy-fingered* (*dawn*) used by Homer in the opening lines of a new episode in the *Odyssey* (3a), but also speakers of present-day English take pleasure in adorning referents with epithetical qualification, as e.g. in sentence (3b).

(3) a. Now when the child of morning, *rosy-fingered* Dawn, appeared, Telemachus rose and dressed himself.
    b. That *cute little* spaniel *with its frizzy ears* is still watching us.

In (3b), the referents of *that spaniel* and *ears* are uniquely identifiable: the spaniel is present within the deictic situation and the ears are inferable as those of the spaniel. The qualifications provided by the modifiers *cute*, *little* and *frizzy* convey purely expressive information. The speaker may, for instance, emphasise these attributes of the dog because they strike her as particularly funny or noteworthy. Non-restrictive qualification thus mainly serves the purpose of providing additional, especially evaluative, information about a referent, also aptly described as editorial comment.

7.1.2 Types of qualification: Types of modifiers

We may use different types of conceptual units in qualifying a thing or an instance of a thing and, accordingly, use different types of modifiers in English. The sentences under (4) illustrate the most common usages of qualifying modifiers in English. In all of the examples, the head noun *detective* is qualified in different ways. The modifiers are printed in italics.

(4) a. Hercule Poirot is a *brilliant* detective.
    b. *Agatha Christie's* detective Poirot is a legend all over the world.
    c. The detective *with the waxed moustache* solves the *most baffling* cases.
    d. Hercule Poirot is the *famous* detective *created by the English mystery writer Agatha Christie*.
    e. Poirot is a detective *who has come to England as a war refugee*.

In sentence (4a), the adjective *brilliant* modifies the predicate noun *detective*. The qualification it describes may either be understood in a restrictive sense, i.e. as establishing a subcategory of 'brilliant detective', or in a non-restrictive sense, i.e. as expressing the speaker's personal evaluation.

Hercule Poirot

In sentence (4b), the head noun *detective* is modified by the complex noun phrase *Agatha Christie's*, where the genitive morpheme *'s* expresses the relation of possession.

In sentence (4c), the noun *detective* is modified by the prepositional phrase *with the waxed moustache*. This modifier describes a relation between the detective and his moustache, while the moustache is in its turn characterised by the property 'waxed'. The qualifying relation is probably understood in a non-restrictive sense, since the referent is already definite and the qualification does not add any new, restrictive information: the funny moustache is a well-known characteristic of Poirot's. The attribute *most baffling* in *the most baffling cases*, however, is restrictive.

In sentence (4d), two non-restrictive modifiers are added to qualify the definite referent *detective*: the adjective *famous* and the participial phrase *created by the English mystery writer Agatha Christie*. The participial phrase is atemporal and describes the result of a specific event.

In sentence (4e), *a detective* is modified by a relative clause. The relative clause is temporal and describes a specific event that is meant to restrict the category 'detective'.

The types of qualification and modification found in these examples are:

i. qualifying properties, which are expressed as adjectives, as in (4a);
ii. qualifying relations, which are expressed as genitive phrases, as in (4b), or as prepositional phrases, as in (4c);
iii. qualifying situations, which are expressed as (atemporal) participial phrases, as in (4d), or as (temporal) relative clauses, as in (4e).

Another common type of modification is *apposition*, i.e. the juxtaposition of a noun phrase to a preceding noun phrase, as in *detective Poirot* (4b), which means 'Poirot, who is a detective'. Appositions are always non-restrictive modifications; they are distinct from the system of modifiers discussed in this chapter and will not be considered here.

A special feature of the English system of qualifying modifiers is their position relative to their head noun: they occur either in prenominal or in postnominal position. These positions are associated with structural meanings: **prenominal modifiers** typically describe permanent and characteristic qualities, while **postnominal modifiers** typically describe temporary or occasional qualities. The particular meaning of a qualifying modifier is thus determined by three elements: its lexical meaning(s), its grammatical form, and its syntactic position relative to the head noun. Thus, adjectives typically occur in prenominal position and describe permanent and characteristic properties, but when they appear in postnominal position, as in (5a), the structure imposes a meaning of temporariness or occasion. On the other hand, qualifying relations are normally expressed in postnominal position, but when they are used in prenominal position as in (5b), they are seen as permanent and characteristic attributes.

(5) a. Taurus and Capella are the only stars *visible* (tonight).
    b. The limousine comes with a *five-line* cellular phone system.

The use of postmodifier adjectives like *visible* in (5a) will be discussed in Section 7.2.5. In sentence (5b), the attribute *five-line* could also be expressed as a prepositional phrase in postnominal position, *a cellular phone with five lines*. The phone in this phrase may be understood as a system that is permanently equipped with five lines or has one that can be connected to as many as five lines. The prenominal position in *a five-line cellular phone*, by contrast, only allows the interpretation of a permanent system. It makes us see the five-line cellular phone as a special kind of phone. Not surprisingly, such complex premodifiers are frequently found in languages for specific purposes.

Speakers are sensitive to the schematic meanings associated with premodification and postmodification. Many people find expressions such as *disabled person* or *blind people* offensive. Apparently, participles or adjectives in prenominal position make the qualifications sound permanent and characteristic. The politically correct usage should be *a person with a disability* and *people who are blind* or *persons with a visual impairment*. What makes these qualifications less offensive-sounding is, apart from the more general term such as *impairment*, the postnominal position of the qualifying modifier, which does not impose the idea that the person's disability is a permanent one. It should be added, though, that disabled people themselves are opposed to such euphemistic usages.

Each of these three types of qualification has a preferred structural realisation in English. Properties are coded as adjectives, relations (to an entity) are expressed as genitive phrases or prepositional phrases, and situations are rendered as relative clauses. Participles and participial phrases describe atemporal situations that are recategorised as properties; they will therefore be treated together with adjectives. For the sake of clarity, the types of qualification and their expressions discussed so far are summarised in Table 7.1.

Table 7.1. Types of qualification and modifier

qualification	property	relation		situation
modifier	adjective	genitive phrase	prepositional phrase	participle, relative clause
position	prenominal			postnominal
prototypical meaning	permanent, characteristic	possession and related senses	temporary or permanent	specific, occasional
example	a *brilliant* detective	*Agatha Christie's* detective	a detective *with a funny moustache*	a detective *who has come to England*

7.2 Qualification by means of properties: Adjectives

> *60 is not old if you are a tree.*
> (Anonymous)

7.2.1 Properties: Adjectives

When we think of properties we have in mind properties such as 'new' or 'happy'. Such properties are typically expressed as **adjectives**. In some languages adjectives are described as "property words", as in German *Eigenschaftswort*, or "quality words", as in Finnish *laatusana*. We will define **properties** as single qualitative features that are related to a thing or an instance of thing. For example, in *Jack is a dishonest person*, the property 'dishonest' is attributed to the person. The complex expression *dishonest person* is similar in meaning to the simple word *crook*. Both describe a subcategory of persons. The two terms differ, however, with respect to the number of features they contain. The property term 'dishonest' singles out one feature while the thing term 'crook' encapsulates a bundle of (negative) features which, apart from 'dishonest', may include 'criminal', 'fraudulent' and 'untrustworthy'. The phrase *dishonest person* thus defines a subcategory of 'person' along the dimension of 'honesty' only, while the noun *crook* represents an entrenched category characterised by many features. We therefore assume that someone who is a crook is dishonest, but do not assume that someone who is dishonest is a crook. Compare also the following differences in meaning between adjectives and their corresponding nouns:

(6) a. *liberal (person)* 'broad-minded, tolerant'
     a'. *a liberal* 'supporter of political liberalism' or 'member of liberal party', etc.
     b. *blond (hair)* 'blond colour of hair'
     b'. *a blonde* 'blond-haired, sexy, glamorous but dumb woman', etc.

Nouns and premodifier adjectives may be arranged on a continuum ranging from fully entrenched categories to epithetical properties, as shown in Table 7.2.

Table 7.2. Category-property continuum

entrenched category	subtype of category	categorising property	epithetical property
simple noun	compound	restrictive adjective	non-restrictive adjective
story	short story	long story	stupid story

Compounds like *short story* describe fully lexicalised (sub)categories. As a compound, ₅*short* '*story* is marked by a distinct unitary stress pattern distinguishing it from noun phrases with an adjective such as *long story*. Moreover, the adjective of a compound no longer behaves like a typical free adjective: it cannot be graded (**a shorter story*), intensified (**the very short story*) and separated from its head noun (**short interesting story*). Semantically, the literary term *short story* has many characteristics, which literary critics have been at pains to point out. For example, it is a piece of fiction, focuses on one character or event, is designed to give a single impression, is longer than an essay but shorter than a book, is short enough to be read at one sitting, etc. A *long story*, by contrast, is not (yet) a fully fledged category — it is only categorised as being long in comparison with other stories, i.e. according to a built-in scale for stories. Whereas a short story is a genre of its own and has no specific length, a long story may vary in length and even contain over a hundred pages. Finally, the phrase *stupid story*, said by a frustrated reader, is meant as a comment about the story and is based on the reader's personal taste.

Although the property denoted by an adjective only represents a single qualifying feature, its understanding typically involves complex background knowledge. In Chapter 3.1.3 we used the example *Sylvia is tall* to illustrate that the value of *tall* is computed on the scale of height relative to a norm implicitly defined by a 'young girl' frame. Let us now look more closely at the way we understand properties.

We can only assess the value of a given property if we can relate it to some reference point. Consider the italicised adjectives in the following sentences:

(7) a. Uncle Henry bought his wife an *expensive* bracelet.
    b. Charles is not just a *faithful* husband, but also a generous one.

In the normal, restrictive interpretation of (7a), we are likely to compare the price Henry paid for the bracelet with the price normally paid for bracelets, which serves as its reference point. Conceptually, we simultaneously open two mental spaces: a reality space, involving the high price paid, and a standard space, involving the price normally charged. In blending these two input spaces, we arrive at the conclusion that the price paid was higher than the price normally paid, i.e. that the bracelet was indeed expensive. The standard space represents the unmarked case in the 'shopping' frame, while the reality space is the marked case. People typically react to marked situations, e.g. they might regard Uncle Henry's purchase as a waste of money or a token of generosity, as in sentence (7b).

In our understanding of the property 'faithful' in (7b), we compare a faithful husband, not with more or less faithful husbands, but with its opposite, i.e. an unfaithful husband, which now serves as a reference point. Faithfulness in marriage is the expected "norm". It would therefore be pointless to speak of a spouse being faithful if there is not at least the possibility of his or her being unfaithful. As in the interpretation of *expensive bracelet*, we open two mental spaces, but now the reality space of 'faithfulness' represents the unmarked situation and the counterfactual space of 'unfaithfulness' the marked one. The mental space associated with a husband's unfaithfulness evokes a much more vivid scenario than that of a faithful husband. We may think of the husband having secret affairs with other women, denying having love affairs, etc. It is against the background of this highly emotion-laden scenario of marital unfaithfulness that the meaning of *a faithful husband* is understood.

The two situations of blending are sketched in Figure 7.1. The degrees on the open-ended scale of *expensive* (*bracelet*) indicate that 'expensive' is a **scalar property**, while the two endpoints in the representation of *faithful* (*husband*) indicate that 'faithful' is a **complementary property** to 'unfaithful'. Scalar properties relate to an implicit norm on the scale as their reference point, complementary properties to their opposites.

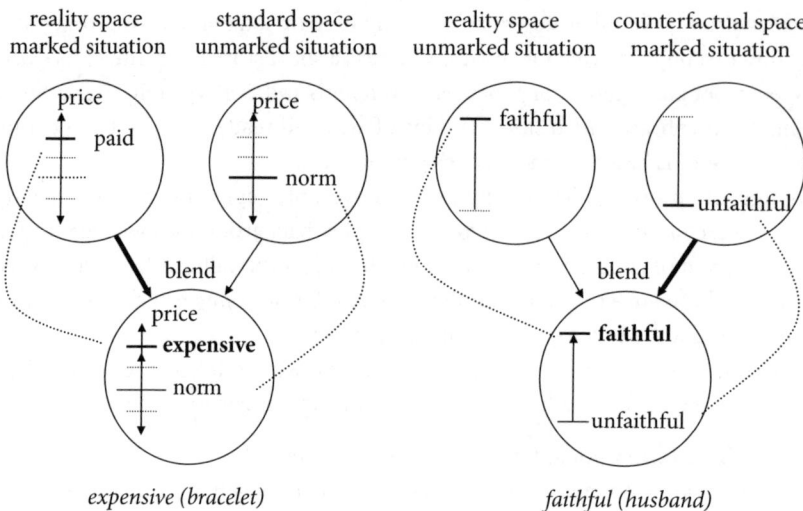

expensive (bracelet)   *faithful (husband)*

Figure 7.1. Blending with scalar and complementary properties

In their analysis of the adjective *safe*, Fauconnier and Turner (2002) have shown that even more background knowledge may be required in understanding a property. In the context of a child playing with a shovel at the beach, *safe* means that the child will not be harmed. *Safe* thus prompts a 'danger' frame in which the child is harmed. In understanding the sense of *safe*, this counterfactual scenario is blended with the factual situation. Interestingly, the same counterfactual situation is evoked when we say *The beach is safe* or *The shovel is safe*. We do not mean that the beach or the shovel will not be harmed, but that the child will not be harmed. These examples also show that adjectives do not always assign a property to their head noun but may assign a property to a metonymically related entity. *The shovel is safe* thus involves the metonymy PROPERTY OF AN INSTRUMENT FOR PROPERTY OF A PERSON USING THE INSTRUMENT.

7.2.2 Adjectives: A category between nouns and verbs

Adjectives are a grammatical category halfway between nouns and verbs. In some respects adjectives behave like nouns, in other respects they behave like verbs.

Adjectives behave like nouns in the following respects:

- Semantically, the properties adjectives describe tend to be fairly stable. Just as a dog is likely to remain a dog, also a big black dog is likely to remain big and black.
- Syntactically, adjectives may, like nominals, appear in predicative position, as in *Bill is liberal* versus *Bill is a liberal*. In attributive position, certain adjectives may also be coordinated with nouns as in *many dentistry and medical students*.
- Morphologically, adjectives in many languages (such as Latin, French and German) agree with their head nouns with respect to number and gender. In English, certain

adjectives can be used as nouns describing classes of people, as in *the blind, the sick* or *the unemployed* (see Chapter 5.4.2(iv)).

Adjectives behave like verbs in the following respects:

- Semantically, adjectives, like verbs, designate relations and are thus dependent conceptual units. As shown in Chapter 3.1.3, an adjective such as *big* in *big dog* designates a relation between the entity 'dog' and the domain 'size'.
- Syntactically, adjectives, like verbs, are typically intensifiable and gradable whereas typical concrete nouns are not. Thus, a bikini can look *very attractive* or *attract us very much* and it can be *more attractive* or *attract us more* than a one-piece bathing costume. As predicates, many adjectives can, like verbs, be used intransitively and transitively (in the sense of taking a second participant) as in *I am excited* and *I am excited about getting married*. This is one of the reasons why some models of grammar treat verbs and adjectives as belonging to the same underlying category.
- Morphologically, some English adjectives are identical in form to verbs (*open — to open, free — to free*), while others are derived from verbs as participles (*to close — closed, to amaze — amazing*) or derivations (*read — readable*). Conversely, many verbs are derived from adjectives (*new — to renew, real — to realise*).

Due to their intermediate position between nouns and verbs it therefore does not come as a surprise that adjectives constitute a heterogeneous word class.

7.2.3 Functions of properties: Functions of adjectives

Properties and the adjectives expressing them are used in two major functions: in a qualifying, or modifying, function and in an assigning, or predicative, function. Adjectives that function as modifiers of nouns are known as **attributive adjectives**, for example *visible* in *a visible star*. Attributive adjectives may occur in prenominal or postnominal position. As shown in Section 7.1.2, these positions are associated with different structural meanings: prenominal adjectives are associated with permanent and characteristic properties; postnominal adjectives are associated with temporary and occasional properties. Thus, in using the adjective *visible* as a premodifier in (8a), the speaker implies that the North Star is permanently visible to the naked eye or by telescope, at least at night time. By using *visible* as a postmodifier in (8b), the speaker suggests that the planets Jupiter and Saturn are only temporarily visible, for example in a particular month or at this moment.

(8) a. The North Star is a *visible* star. [*attributive, premodifier*]
 b. Jupiter and Saturn are the planets *visible* (in January). [*attributive, postmodifier*]
 c. Mercury is only marginally *visible*. [*predicative*]

Sentence (8c) illustrates the predicative function of adjectives. **Predicative adjectives** are usually used in conjunction with a copular verb such as *be*, *seem*, *appear*, or *sound* as predicates of a sentence.

Table 7.3. Functions of properties and adjectives

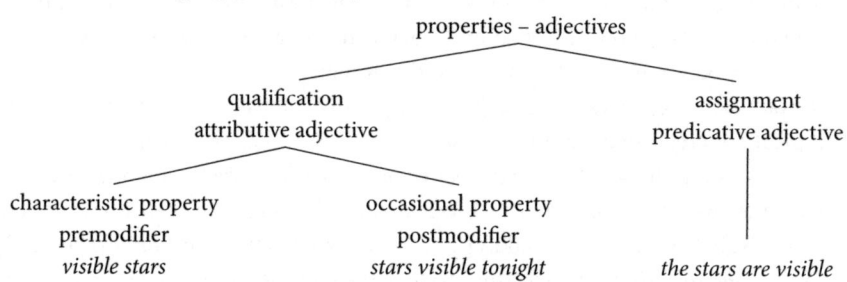

Most adjectives, but far from all adjectives, can be used in all three positions, i.e. as premodifier, postmodifier and predicative adjectives. The three positions have different functions and impose different meanings on the adjectives. Thus, *He is the right man* means 'he is the man suitable for a purpose', whereas *The man is right* means 'the man is correct with regard to what he is saying'. The challenge in the ensuing discussion will be to explain why certain types of adjectives are restricted with respect to their functions. The following sections will briefly look at these three functions of adjectives and their conceptual basis: (i) characteristic properties and their expression as premodifier adjectives, (ii) occasional properties and their expression as postmodifier adjectives, and (iii) assigned properties and their expression as predicative adjectives.

7.2.4 Characteristic properties: Premodifier adjectives

In Table 7.3 we associated the structural meaning of a premodifier adjective with 'characteristic property'. Premodifier adjectives, however, display different degrees of characteristicness, and we accordingly need to distinguish different types of premodifier adjectives. Prototypical adjectives like *intelligent* in (9a) relate to a scale and are therefore described as **scalar adjectives**. Scalar adjectives are gradable (*more intelligent*, *most intelligent*) and therefore sometimes also described as *gradable adjectives*, they are intensifiable (*very intelligent*), and they can be used in both attributive (*intelligent beings*) and predicative function (*the beings are intelligent*). Less typical adjectives cannot, as a rule, be graded, intensified, or used predicatively. If they are used in the premodifier position, the construction imposes a shift in meaning: the adjectives adopt to some extent a 'characterising' sense. We will distinguish the following types of premodifier adjectives:

(9) a. There may be *intelligent* beings on Mars. [scalar]
    b. There is *constant* talk of it. [deadverbial]
    c. *Martian* invaders may land on Earth. [denominal]
    d. Maybe all this is *total* nonsense. [determining]

The properties described in (9b) and (9c) are less typical: they relate to elements of a situation which are recategorised as a property. *Constant* in (9b) is a deadverbial adjective: it relates to a situation of talking and describes the manner of talking: 'people are constantly talking about it'; as a premodifier adjective, *constant* characterises the talk.

Martian in (9c) is a denominal adjective: it relates to a situation of Martians invading the Earth and describes the participant 'Martians'; as a premodifier adjective, it characterises the invaders. Neither *constant* nor *Martian* can be graded, intensified or used predicatively (?*The talk is constant*; ?*The invaders are Martian*) — although there seems to be considerable fluidity about such usages. For example, the denominal adjective *key* as in *key issue* is nowadays also used predicatively as in *The issue of Palestinian refugees is key to a Middle East peace plan*.

Determining adjectives such as *total* in (9d) represent an even more peripheral class of premodifier adjectives: their sole or predominant function is to specify a category or ground a referent. In *total nonsense*, the adjective *total* specifies the category 'nonsense' and stresses its validity. These latter three types of peripheral adjectives are sometimes described as *pseudo-adjectives*. Let us now take a closer look at these types of attributive adjectives.

(i) *Scalar properties: Scalar adjectives*

Properties may be placed along two kinds of scale: a scale of comparison and a scale of intensity. The comparison scale consists of three grades: positive, comparative and superlative, where the latter two may be directed towards either the positive or the negative end of the scale. With shorter adjectives like *big*, positive grades are expressed morphologically (*bigger*, *biggest*), with longer adjectives the grades are metaphorically conceived of in terms of quantity. Thus, the property 'intelligent' is "quantified" as (*much*) *more intelligent* or (*much*) *less intelligent* and *most intelligent* in the same way that money is quantified as (*much*) *more* or (*much*) *less money* and *most* (or *least*) *money*.

Degrees along the scale of intensity of a property are expressed by various adverbs such as *pretty*, *very*, *extremely*, *terribly*, and *awfully*, which describe increasing degrees of intensity. These intensifiers have largely lost their lexical meanings — they have been semantically bleached. However, the original meanings of these grammaticalised forms are still recoverable: they relate to notions such as 'sincerity' of the speaker (*very* goes back to Latin *verus* 'true' and thus means 'truly'), 'excess' (*extremely, exceedingly*), and 'fear' (*terribly, awfully*). Thus intensity too tends to be understood metaphorically.

Adjectives denoting complementary properties are less freely or not gradable and intensifiable, such as the antonyms *full* and *empty*, *dead* and *alive*, adjectives of shape like *round* and *square*, as well as the adjectives *faithful* and *safe*, which were discussed in Section 7.2.1. We seldom or never speak of ?*a fuller glass*, **the emptiest bottle* or *a very dead man because these adjectives denote extreme or "absolute" properties. We may, however, also want to express degrees between two extremes and make use of subset quantification, as in *half* (*full*), *almost* (*round*), *completely* (*dead*).

(ii) *Recategorised properties: Deadverbial and denominal adjectives*
Deadverbial adjectives relate to the manner of an action as in *constant talk* in (9b) or to the setting of a situation. The meaning of manner is found in examples such as *hard worker, early riser*, and *heavy smoker*. The distinction between scalar properties and recategorised properties may not be noticed at first sight because many adjectives can be used in both senses. For example, we have *an elegant girl* versus *an elegant dancer*, and *an intelligent boy* versus *an intelligent solution*. The second of each of these pairs relates to a manner of doing something: an elegant dancer is a person who dances elegantly, and an intelligent question is a question which shows the intelligence of the person who asks the question and her insight into the problem at hand.

Aspects of the setting that deadverbial adjectives may allude to are the time of a situation, as in *the late Marilyn Monroe* and *the former USSR*, or its reality status, as in *the possible effects* and *the likely winner*. Here too, people may not be aware of the recategorised sense of the adjective. Thus, *an old colleague* may mean 'a colleague of mine who is old in years' or 'a person who used to be a colleague of mine for some time in the past'. The first sense of *old* refers to an intrinsic, scalar property of the colleague, the second sense to some time in the past during which a situation held. Notice that *My colleague is old* only means that my colleague is old in years. The deadverbial 'past time' sense of *old* also applies to artefacts, for instance *the old newspaper, the old file* and *the old syringe*. By implicature, such things are often interpreted as no longer usable. Attributive *old* even has a third sense: *an old friend* means that I have a long-standing relationship with a friend of mine.

Denominal adjectives relate to participants of an event which are recategorised as characterising properties. Participants play a specific "role" in a given situation (see Chapter 11), and they also do so in our interpretation of recategorised properties. For example, in *presidential decision*, the president makes a decision and thus plays the role of an "agent" in the event, in *presidential adviser*, the president plays the role of the "recipient" of information, in *presidential election*, the president plays the role of the "theme" of an election, and in *presidential candidate*, the president plays the role of the "goal" of his candidature.

Denominal adjectives have a distinctly categorising function. For example, denominal adjectives are used to distinguish different kinds of advice, such as *legal advice, medical advice*, and *financial advice*. These adjective-noun phrases have the same function as noun-noun compounds such as *health advice, careers advice*, and *consumer advice*. Which of these structural construals is chosen is partly a matter of convention and partly determined by the existence of an appropriate denominal adjective. Thus we have *regional climate, continental climate*, and *global climate*; however, we say not **worldly climate* but *world climate*, since *worldly* contrasts with *spiritual*.

(iii) *Specifying properties: Determining adjectives*
Determining adjectives have the function of specifying a thing as in (10a) or grounding a referent as in (10c).

(10) a. Dick is a *true* asset to the team.
 b. Dick is the goal-getter.
 c. Dick is the *only* goal-getter.

Like the adjective *total* in *total nonsense* in (9d), the adjective *true* in *true asset* in (10a) tells us that a word means exactly what it says. The same applies to usages such as *be a regular fool, a complete idiot, a perfect stranger, a real friend*, etc. The indefinite predicate nouns *fool, idiot*, etc. denote a category, and their specification by the intensifiers *regular, complete*, etc. emphasises that the category fully applies. This usage is in fact based on an erroneous folk view of the nature of language, according to which there is a stable link between the form and meaning of a word so that the word's meaning is well-defined and fixed — whereas we as cognitive linguists of course know that word meanings are fuzzy and have prototype structure.

The determining adjective *only* in (10c) has a different function. As (10b) shows, the definite determiner in the predicate nominal *the goal-getter* already uniquely identifies Dick as having this quality. The determining adjective *only* in (10c) provides the additional information that nobody else has this quality.

The determining adjective *first* specifies the uniqueness of an instance with respect to a series. Sentence (11a) shows that this also applies to the pronoun *first*. The idea of being on top of a series tends to shade over into the notion of 'important'; this is the meaning suggested by *prime* in (11b) and *main* in (11c):

(11) a. Marie and Pierre Curie were the *first* to discover radioactivity.
 b. The *prime* suspect for the terrorist attacks is Al Qaida.
 c. The *main* reason for going to school is to learn.

Determining adjectives such as *(the) only, one, very, first, last* and *main* stress the uniqueness of a referent. This explains why these adjectives take a special type of relative clause, i.e. a relative clause with a *to*-infinitive. Sentence (11a) illustrates this construction. In processing this sentence, the word *first* makes us look for the domain in which the Curies were the first, i.e. the domain of radioactivity. The particle *to* is well-suited to express this notion: *to* has as its basic meaning 'motion to a goal'. Mental activities are often metaphorically understood in terms of motion, as in *We reached a conclusion*, and our search for the domain-related activity can therefore be conceived of as motion to a goal.

(iv) *Order of premodifier adjectives*
A given noun phrase may, of course, be qualified by more than one premodifier adjective. In this case, the adjectives follow a certain order, as illustrated in the two phrases in Table 7.4.

Table 7.4. Order of premodifier adjectives

functions:		grounding	characterising	categorising	
(a)		determining	scalar	denominal	
	the	only	reliable	economic	expert
(b)		determining	deadverbial	denominal	
	the	first	intelligent	diplomatic	solution

The order of premodifier adjectives is determined by the iconic principle of proximity (see Chapter 3.3.1). The more essentially a property functions in further specifying a thing or an instance, the closer the adjective is placed to its head noun. Denominal adjectives like *economic* and *diplomatic* in Table 7.4 play an essential function: they subcategorise a thing and are therefore placed closest to the noun. Scalar and deadverbial adjectives like *intelligent* and *reliable* have a less essential role: their function is purely characterising the referent and hence they are placed further away from the head noun. If scalar and deadverbial adjectives co-occur, they also have a preferred order: *an intelligent reliable expert* sounds more natural than *a reliable intelligent expert*. Apparently, the deadverbial property 'reliability' is more essential to expertise than the scalar property 'intelligence'. The determining adjectives *only* and *first*, lastly, have, in conjunction with the determiner, the function of grounding the referent and hence go with the article *the*.

The order among purely characterising adjectives is also determined by the iconic principle of proximity. The more relevant and stable a property is, the nearer the adjective is placed to its head noun, and vice versa. For example, the colour of a person's skin is permanent but one's intelligence much less so: *stupid white man* is therefore the natural order. Evaluative attributes are variable: evaluative adjectives are therefore placed further away from the noun as in a *pretty young girl* or *superb white beaches*.

7.2.5 Premodifier and postmodifier adjectives and participles

The two phrases *the visible stars* and *the stars visible* (*tonight*) presented in (Table 7.3) illustrate the difference in meaning between premodifier and postmodifier adjectives. Let us look at some more such contrasts:

(12) *Premodifier adjectives*
    a. drinkable water
    b. eatable game
    c. marketable products

(13) *Postmodifier adjectives*
    a. water drinkable
    b. game eatable
    c. products marketable

The premodifier adjectives in (12) designate permanent and general properties, and the noun phrases in which they occur are complete in themselves. The postmodifier adjectives in (13) describe changeable and more particular properties and are in need of further specification. Thus, the postmodifier adjectives in (13a) may refer to water drinkable when boiled, in (13b) to game eatable when roasted, and in (13c) to products marketable in winter. These adjuncts in fact describe conditions for the thing to be characterised as "*-able*."

Present participles are also used in pre- and postmodifier position, as in the following examples:

(14) *Premodifier pres. participles*
  a. drinking men
  b. lying woman
  c. queuing unemployed

(15) *Postmodifier present participles*
  a. men drinking whisky
  b. woman lying on the floor
  c. the unemployed queuing for work

Participles occupy an intermediate position between verbs and adjectives. Like verbs of a clause, participles may function as predicates and take complements and adjuncts, in fact they refer to situations. Since they are atemporal, they can, like adjectives, also function as modifiers of nouns. Let us first look at their function as predicates in the postmodifier examples under (15). Here, the present participles take a direct object in (15a) and a prepositional adjunct in (15b) and (15c). Without their complements or adjuncts, the information provided by the present participles would be felt to be incomplete. Phrases such as *a woman lying* are therefore ungrammatical. Bare present participles as postmodifiers are limited to contrastive sets such as *The man shooting was caught, while the man driving escaped.*

Sleeping Beauty

In prenominal position, the grammar of English does not permit any further specifications of participles: phrases such as *the lying on the floor woman* are in English downright ungrammatical. We may, however, use bare participles as premodifiers, as in the examples under (14). Phrases such as *drinking men, lying woman, queuing unemployed* or *sleeping beauty* are typically used as, and almost restricted to, titles of pictures, sculptures or books. The participles in these phrases do not refer to a specific situation but describe stable attributes and, like premodifier adjectives, have subcategorising function. Thus, a *sleeping beauty* may be seen in opposition to a *dreaming beauty* or a *dancing beauty*.

Past participles may also occur in either position, as illustrated in the following phrases:

(16) *Premodifier past participles*
  a. a reviewed article
  b. deposited money
  c. reduced costs

(17) *Postmodifier past participles*
  a. an article reviewed
  b. money withdrawn
  c. profits gained

Like present participles, past participles are atemporal. They refer to situations that are finished or completed, and typically describe a resultant state of an event. We may either focus on the stable result itself — and then express the property in premodifier position as in (16), or we may focus on the temporary event causing the result — and then express the property in postmodifier position as in (17). It follows from these characterisations that (16a) and (17a) mean different things: *a reviewed article* refers to an article that has been accepted for publication, i.e. it is categorised as a "stable" type of article, whereas *an article reviewed* refers to an article that may, or may not, have been accepted, as in *Of the ten articles reviewed only three were accepted*.

The phrases in (16b) and (17b) show that the semantics of a past participle may determine the preference for one or the other position. Thus, money which is deposited has stability, hence this transaction is expressed as premodification, while money that is withdrawn is no longer there, hence this transaction is expressed as postmodification. This opposition is also illustrated in the pairs *reduced costs* versus *profits gained* or *burnt-out engine* versus *engine tested*.

If we want to focus on the mere occurrence of a completed event, the past participle is used in postnominal position, as in *the gifts bought, the points mentioned, the issue brought up*, etc. Like postmodifier present participles (15), postmodifier past participles often need to be further specified by giving information about the time, the manner or circumstances of the situation, as in *the flower show held last month* (**the flower show held*), *a campaign begun in March* (**a campaign begun*) and *a friend met long ago* (**a friend met*). Postmodification by adjectives and past participles is a striking feature of English that is not shared by other Germanic languages.

7.2.6 Assigned properties: Predicative adjectives

When adjectives are used in predicative position, that is after the copular verb *be* or in some equivalent construction, they assign a property to a thing or instance. For example, in *Sirius is so bright that it is always visible*, we assign the properties *bright* and *visible* to the star Sirius. Only prototypical properties, that is characteristic or scalar properties, can be assigned, not recategorised or determining properties. In our discussion of characteristic properties in Section 7.2.4 we already observed that deadverbial (*an old friend*), denominal (*criminal lawyer*) and determining adjectives (*the only goal-getter*) cannot be used in predicative position.

The reverse also applies: a number of adjectives denoting occasional properties can only be used in predicative position — and some of them in postmodifier position, but never, or only seldom, in premodifier position. Typical examples of the exclusively predicative status of adjectives are items that designate a transient state of the body or the mind such as *ill, well, glad, content*, etc. These adjectives have counterparts that designate a more stable state such as *sick, healthy, happy* and *contented*. Compare these premodifier and predicative forms in (18) and (19):

(18) *Premodifier adjectives*
  a. Grandpa is a *sick* man.
  b. Speck is a *healthy* baby.
  c. Bonnie is a *happy* girl.

(19) *Predicative adjectives*
  a. Grandma is a bit *ill*.
  b. Juliet is *well* again.
  c. She is *glad* to see me.

The permanent nature of the adjectives in (18) can be shown by durational contexts as in *Grandpa is a sick man, and he has been sick as long as I can remember*. The transient nature of the adjectives in (19) also appears from other usages which express the beginning or end of having the property concerned, e.g. *to fall ill, to get well again, to be glad to see you now*, etc.

Scalar adjectives in predicative position are in principle ambiguous between a permanent and a temporary interpretation. This is particularly relevant with adjectives which designate a person's character or behaviour such as *nice, kind, polite, helpful, rude* or *noisy*. The following sentences illustrate such verb-like senses of so-called "behavioural" adjectives:

(20) a. You're being *obnoxious*, Howard.
 b. Please, don't be so *noisy*. I can't hear anything.
 c. Try not to be so *nervous*, will you?
 d. He had been very *rude* and was dismissed.
 e. It was very *cruel* of you to say such things.
 f. Why were you so *nasty* to your friend?

The verb-like character of these behavioural adjectives can be seen in the use of the progressive aspect in (20a), and in the speech act of request in (20b) and advice in (20c), which presuppose that the hearer is in control of his behaviour. In sentences (20d-f), the person's behaviour is seen as an action. Thus, in sentence (20d) the person's active part in his dismissal can be asked about: *What did he do?* In sentence (20e) the person is seen as the source of an action (*cruel of you*), and in sentence (20f) the person directs her actions against another person (*nasty to your friend*).

7.3 Qualification by means of relations: Genitive phrases and prepositional phrases

Qualifications by means of a relation are achieved by relating one entity to another entity. This is a very common type of qualification, used especially for referential purposes. In the structure of English, these relations are typically expressed as complex noun phrases consisting of two noun phrases and a relational expression. The relational expression can be the genitival suffix *'s* or a preposition. We will distinguish three types of **qualifying relations**: possessive relations, intrinsic relations, and schematic relations:

(21) a my father's house [*possessive relation*]
 b. the end of the tunnel [*intrinsic relation*]
 c. the water in the vase [*schematic relation*]

The relation between my father and his house in (21a) holds between a possessor and a thing possessed. In English, possessive relations are expressed by the genitive suffix *'s* or possessive pronouns. Possessors are in control of the thing possessed, hence the relationship between them is very tight. This is also reflected in the structure of language: of the three qualifying relations, the possessive relation is the only one that can be prenominal.

The relation between a tunnel and its end in (21b) is of a different kind: an end is intrinsically part of the tunnel — there is no end without a whole. Intrinsic relations typically involve a whole and a part and are expressed by means of the preposition *of*.

The relation between a vase and the water in it in (21c) is one of containment: the water is fully contained in the vase. Our notion of containment is very general, or schematic (see Chapter 12.3.2.3): it involves the structural elements of an interior, a boundary and an exterior.

As will be shown below, these three types of qualifying relations involve different degrees of conceptual integration of the two entities related: a possessive relation constitutes a very tight conceptual link, an intrinsic relation establishes a close conceptual link, and a schematic relation involves a fairly loose conceptual link.

7.3.1   Possessive relations: Genitive suffix *'s*

Possessive relations link a possessor with the thing possessed. In possessive phrases of English, the noun phrase expressing the possessor precedes the head noun expressing the thing possessed, as in *my father's house*. As shown in Chapter 5.3.3.2, the human possessor serves as the reference point for accessing the possessed thing. Thus, the speaker (*my*) serves as the reference point with respect to the target 'father', and 'my father' serves as the reference point with respect to the target 'house'. The English genitive construction iconically reflects the direction of processing from the salient reference point to the target.

The privileged position of the genitival modifier before the head noun also accounts for its unique meaning. In the phrase *the bride's father*, we tend to identify one particular referent among other potential referents, especially the bridegroom's father. In the intrinsic relation *the father of the bride*, by contrast, the father is understood in his relational role of a father to his child.

Besides its referential function in definite noun phrases, the genitive *'s* also has a categorising function in indefinite noun phrases, as in the phrase *a mother's worries*. Here the possessive relation designates a kind, or subcategory, of worries, e.g. the worries mothers may have about their children. Likewise, *a doctor's degree* is a kind of degree, *a summer's day* is a kind of day, and *a man's voice* is a kind of voice. In all these examples, the possessive qualifier is generic. These classifying genitive constructions may become so deeply entrenched that they shade over from classifying phrases into lexicalised compounds and develop new senses of their own. Thus, a *bridesmaid* is not a maid, but an unmarried young girl accompanying the bride on the day of her wedding, and a *statesman* is not just a kind of man but a wise, fair and honourable leader.

7.3.2 Intrinsic relations: Preposition *of*

With **intrinsic relations**, the meaning of the relation is determined by the entities that are related, i.e. the two noun phrases. In English, intrinsic relations are expressed by the preposition *of*, which has no other function than relating the two noun phrases. Some of the most common types of intrinsic relations are illustrated by the following sentences:

(22) a. the end of the tunnel [*part/whole relation*]
     b. the father of the bride [*relational term*]
     c. the review of the book [*reified thing*]
     d. the issue of unemployment [*identifying relation*]

The complex noun phrase (22a) illustrates a part/whole relation. Parts and wholes are complementary notions. Parts are, by definition, intrinsically related to a whole, i.e. we cannot imagine a part such as an end without thinking of the whole to which it belongs. If somebody said *Wait till we come to the end* and we didn't know what he was talking about, we would certainly ask something like "end of what?"

The intrinsic relation in (22b) is based on a *relational noun*. While relations are most of all expressed by verbs, adjectives, prepositions and conjunctions, a small number of nouns also constitute an intrinsic relation. The meaning of the term *father* intrinsically relates to another entity, namely 'child'. Other relational nouns are *president, neighbour, speaker, funeral, picture, biography, conversation*, and *history*.

The intrinsicness of the relation in (22c) is due to the abstract noun *review*. In the same way that the episodic event of *reviewing* requires both a reviewer and something reviewed, the reified thing *review* intrinsically requires these two participants. In *the review of the book*, the subject participant 'reviewer' is automatically understood while 'book' as the more salient participant is explicitly expressed. It is related to the reified thing 'review' by the preposition *of*. Like nouns such as *father*, abstract nouns are relational terms but the entities they intrinsically relate to are participants of a situation.

The complex noun phrase in (22d) illustrates an *identifying relation*, a relation involving "A is B". The noun *issue* intrinsically requires an entity which specifies or identifies the nature of the issue. The *issue of unemployment* can be paraphrased as 'the issue is unemployment', and it may be reversed as "B is A": 'unemployment is the issue' (see Chapter 11.2.1.1).

Due to their intrinsic nature, all of these types of relation are characterised by a close conceptual link between the entities related. For that reason, they can only be restrictive.

7.3.3 Schematic relations: Prepositions

A **schematic relation** relates two entities in a highly abstract, typically image-schematic way (see Chapter 1.3.3). In English, image schemas are typically expressed by prepositions. For example, the preposition *under* evokes the image schema of verticality, *on* the contact schema, *in* the container schema, *behind* the front-back schema, etc. (for prepositions see Chapter 12). The schematic meanings conveyed by the closed set of prepositions are of necessity rather indeterminate. We have all experienced situations where we can't find a street that is supposed to be "behind the station". In most everyday situations, however, we get along with schematic information very well because the relation as a whole evokes a stereotypical scene within a frame and/or domain. This applies both to concrete spatial relations as in (23a) and more abstract relations as in (23b–d).

(23) a. the plates *on* the dinner table   [*frame*: meal]
     b. a book *on* Prince Charles   [*domain*: literature]
     c. a new play *by* Alan Ayckbourn   [*domain*: drama]
     d. a donation *to* the church   [*domain*: charity]

The complex noun phrase (23a), *the plates on the dinner table,* makes us visualise a scene of plates neatly laid out on the table-top for a meal rather than scenes of plates being stacked in the middle of the table or put on the legs of a tilted table. In (23b), *a book on Prince Charles,* we expect to find a biography of Prince Charles covering the most important events of his life, rather than a book focusing exclusively on his relationship with Camilla Parker Bowles. The qualification *by Alan Ayckbourn* in (23c) makes us expect to find a hilarious boulevard comedy rather than a tragedy, and the qualification *to the church* in (23d) makes us tacitly assume that our donation will go to a good cause rather than be spent on a new bathroom for the church.

Any two entities may be linked in a schematic relation — as long as we can imagine a scene that fits the schematic meaning. The nature of the conceptual link between two schematically related entities is therefore only loose.

We may conclude this section by representing the three types of qualifying relations as shown in Figure 7.2.

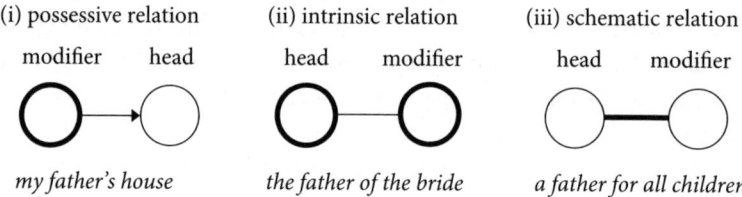

Figure 7.2. Three types of qualifications by means of a relation

In all three types of qualification, all the elements are profiled and should, according to our convention, be printed in bold. Here, the bold lines are meant to indicate the conceptual elements that are most relevant for the meaning of each relationship. The bold circle and the arrow in (i) indicate that the meaning of a possessive relation is characterised by a reference point providing access to the thing possessed. The bold circles in (ii) indicate that the meaning of an intrinsic relation is determined by the nature of the two entities related. Here, the preposition *of* cannot be substituted by another preposition. The heavy line connecting the two circles in (iii) indicates that the schematic relation is determined by the choice of the preposition. In *a father for all children,* the preposition *for* marks a relation of care and benefaction.

7.4 Qualification by means of situations: Relative clauses

Things and instances of things may be qualified by whole, temporal situations, i.e. events or states which are associated with them. Such **qualifying situations** are expressed by means of **relative clauses**. Relative clauses may qualify definite or indefinite referents and may or may not restrict them. Accordingly, we can distinguish between three types of relative clauses as illustrated in (24):

(24) a. I have friends all over the world. The friend *who lives in Tokyo* is coming to see me.
 b. A friend *who lives in Tokyo* is coming to see me.
 c. My friend, *who lives in Tokyo*, is coming to see me.

The relative clause in (24a) is restrictive in that it narrows down the range of possible referents to just one which, by its uniqueness, becomes accessible to the hearer; hence the referent of *the friend* is made definite by both the definite determiner and the relative clause. The relative clause in (24b) is also restrictive in that it narrows down the range of potential referents but not to the point that the referent is unique: the friend is just one of the friends the speaker has, perhaps even one of the friends he has in Tokyo; hence the newly introduced referent of *a friend* is indefinite. The relative clause in (24c) is non-restrictive in that it does not serve to narrow down a range of referents, since the referent of *my friend* is already definite; hence this type of relative clause only serves to provide purely additional information about an already identified referent.

We will first discuss the two types of restrictive relative clauses — restrictive relative clauses with definite and indefinite referents — and will then look at non-restrictive relative clauses.

7.4.1 Restrictive relative clauses

As with all qualifying modifiers, the predominant function of **restrictive relative clauses** is that of narrowing down the referential range of a thing. However, the use of a whole temporal situation is more complex conceptually and grammatically than the use of properties or relationships. In particular, we need to consider (i) the nature of the head of the relative clause, (ii) the relative "pronoun", and (iii) the functions of the relative clause.

(i) *Head of restrictive relative clause*
In order to be able to narrow down the range of referents, the reference mass needs to be somehow individualisable. Thus, a single inherently unique referent can, of course, not be restricted any further, but two referents carrying the same proper name may have to be distinguished, as in *I am talking about the Fred who runs the pub*. Substances are, as shown in Chapter 4, unbounded and homogeneous, but they may be restricted with respect to a portion, as in *This is water that has leaked from the radiator*, or a quality, as in *I prefer whisky that has been aged in wooden barrels*.

Some categories are so general that they do not even provide a reference mass from which a referent can be singled out without further qualification. This especially applies to superordinate categories such as 'thing', 'place', 'time', 'reason' and 'manner'. Thus, we can describe a location by saying *He lives in the mountains/in a valley/in this country*, etc., but we cannot, as a rule, say things like **He lives in a place* or **This happened at the time*, etc. The nouns *place* and *time* here mean only 'location/time in the world at large', i.e. they provide no more than redundant information. Here we must add more specific, qualifying information to the head nouns as in *He lives in the place where he always wanted to live* or *This happened at a time when I still smoked*. Since the head nouns themselves only have schematic meanings, they may be omitted altogether, as in the headless relative clauses in Table 7.5.

Table 7.5. Headed and headless restrictive relative clauses

	headed relative clause	**headless relative clause**
thing	*Show me the thing that you saw.*	*Show me what you saw.*
place	*He lives in the place where he always wanted to live.*	*He lives where he always wanted to live.*
time	*Don't you remember the time when we were still in love?*	*Don't you remember when we were still in love?*
reason	*The reason why he got married is mysterious.*	*Why he got married is mysterious.*
manner	*Tell me the way / how you can make more money.*	*Tell me how you can make more money.*

Headed and headless relative clauses are of course not interchangeable. The former have a definite head and refer to one instance only, while the latter refer to an indeterminate number of instances. Thus, *Show me the thing that you saw* refers to one thing, while *Show me what you saw* may refer to one thing or to many things.

The categories 'person' or 'people' are also so general in meaning that they normally take a further qualification, as in *The people who came were all enthusiastic*. As in the cases above, the head noun *people* is almost redundant; still, it cannot be left out in English, i.e. we cannot speak of **Who came were all enthusiastic*. Obviously, humans are too important to be left unmentioned as a head. The grammatical solution English has found is using relative clauses headed by the demonstrative pronoun *those* for plural humans (25a) and the quantifier *anyone* (25b) or the personal pronoun *he* (25c) as heads for singular humans:

(25) a. *Those who* say so are liars.
 b. *Anyone who* says so is a liar.
 c. *He who* says so is a liar. [*very formal style*]

The pronouns *those*, *anyone* and *he* have no reference of their own but can only constitute reference in conjunction with the relative clause. English, like many other languages, has its own way of construing such situations. Instead of a head, a universal relative pronoun is used, as in:

(26) a. *Whoever* says so is a liar.
　　 b. *What(ever)* they say is sheer nonsense.

In such headless relative clauses, a head is conceptually present and can be made manifest by the paraphrases *anyone who says so* and *anything they say*. The elements *ever* or *any* in *whoever, whatever* and *anyone, anything* are full-set quantifiers (see Chapter 6.2). In these compound forms, the full-set quantifiers point to the universal character of the conceptual head they modify. This universal character obviously accounts for the fact that a head need not be expressed explicitly.

(ii) *Restrictive relative pronouns*
Properly speaking, the term *relative pronoun* is a misnomer because a pronoun does not stand for a noun but for a whole noun phrase. Still, we will use the term since it is established. The function of relative pronouns is to mark the relative clause within the structure of a complex sentence. As is well known, English has different possibilities for marking restrictive relative clauses: *who(m)* for humans and *which* for non-humans, *that* and the zero-form. In distinguishing between humans and non-humans, *who(m)* and *which* are the marked forms in that they carry the highest amount of semantic content, while *that* and the zero-form are semantically neutral. These pronouns are not freely interchangeable. Compare the following sentences:

(27) a. There's the man   *who(m)* / *that* / Ø   I want to talk to.
　　 b. There's the man   *who*　　 / *that* / *Ø   wants to talk to you.
　　 c. That's all　　　　 *which / *that* / Ø   I want.
　　 d. That's the best　 *which / *that* / *Ø   can happen.

In (27a) the relative pronoun functions as the direct object of the relative clause. All three forms are grammatically possible but, due to its semantic content, the pronoun *who* is more formal and the form *whom* sounds rather stilted.

　In (27b) the relative pronoun functions as the subject of the relative clause. The grammar of Standard English requires the presence of a subject, hence relative clauses with a zero-subject pronoun are ungrammatical. In dialects of English, such sentences would be heard but the zero-form is limited to sentences in which the relative clause is clearly recognisable. This would not be the case in so-called "garden-path" sentences such as **A man wants to talk to you is at the door*, which the hearer would process in the sequence in which the constituents occur, i.e. in the sense of 'A man wants to talk to you' followed by an uninterpretable remainder.

　In (27c) the use of *which* as a relative pronoun is considered ungrammatical. This is obviously due to the full-set quantifier *all*, which excludes any other subset and therefore cannot express a contrast. Hence *which* as the relative pronoun with the highest semantic content is felt to be inappropriate. The preferred choice of the relative pronoun would be the zero form, i.e. *That's all I want*, which iconically reflects the conceptual proximity between the head (*all*) and the qualifying situation.

The same applies to heads which are characterised as unique by *only* or a superlative adjective as in (27d): here, too, the relative pronoun *which* is ruled out. The complex structure with a subject pronoun is only transparent with a relative pronoun; hence the zero-form is not possible here, leaving *that* as the only option.

(iii) *Functions of restrictive relative clauses*
The function of restrictive relative clauses we have focused upon so far was that of narrowing down the range of referents for identificational purposes as in sentences (24a) and (24b). Thereby the difference between a definite and an indefinite restrictive relative clause comes out only in the wider context of the discourse: *the friend who lives in Tokyo* typically arises in a context in which several friends are discussed, whereas *a friend who lives in Tokyo* would rather appear in a situational context in which things need to be taken to or brought back from Tokyo. This "situational function" of an indefinite relative clause is also obvious in (28a) below, whereas (28b) shows the categorising function of the indefinite restrictive relative clauses.

(28) a. I know a doctor *who lives down the road*. [*situational*]
b. I know a doctor *who can't even cure a sore throat*. [*categorising*]

The relative clause in sentence (28a) introduces a referent which is relevant in the situation at hand. This sentence might be said by a passer-by when seeing a person who has been injured in a car accident and asks, "Does anyone know a doctor in this area?"

The relative clause in sentence (28b) does not restrict the range of referents but serves to make a statement about a category: the referent is singled out because it lacks the professional quality of the category 'doctors'. It is restrictive, too, but within the category of doctors: among the members of this category there is one which I, judging from my experience, consider a poor member of this category.

The categorising function of restrictive relative clauses is typically found with indefinite heads as in (28b), which can also be paraphrased by *a kind of*, i.e. *He is a kind of doctor who can't even cure a sore throat*. But *kind of*-paraphrases are also possible with certain definite restrictive relatives as in:

(29) a. He is the player we need for the team.
b. A BMW? Yes, that's the car I would like to drive.

The categorising function of these clauses can be seen from paraphrases such as *He is the kind of player we need for the team* and *That's the kind of car I would like to drive*.

7.4.2 Non-restrictive relative clauses

The function of **non-restrictive relative clauses** is to provide either background information (30a) or expressive evaluation (30b) about a referent that is already identified and hence does not need any more referential specification. In order to pinpoint the differences between restrictive and non-restrictive relative clauses we will consider the same three properties as in the preceding section: (i) head, (ii) relative pronoun, and (iii) function of non-restrictive relative clauses.

(i) *Head of non-restrictive relative clauses*
The head of non-restrictive relative clauses necessarily describes a definite referent, i.e. a referent for which a mental space has already been opened. The referent has either been introduced in the preceding discourse or is known to speaker and hearer as in (30a). An immediately preceding situation within the ongoing discourse may also serve as a referent, which can be qualified by a non-restrictive relative clause as in (30b).

(30) a. Al Gore, *who ran for President against George W. Bush in 2000*, received half a million more popular votes.
b. Yet George W. Bush became President, *which is a political scandal*.

In (30b), the relative pronoun *which* shows that the non-restrictive relative clause modifies the whole situation expressed in the preceding main clause. Any situation that has been introduced may serve as a referent in the ongoing discourse and may, consequently, be referred to anaphorically. Since each consecutive situation establishes a new discourse referent of its own, it is natural that only the immediately preceding situation qualifies as an anaphoric referent.

(ii) *Non-restrictive relative pronouns and intonation pattern*
Non-restrictive relative clauses are introduced by the marked relative pronouns *who(m)* for human referents and *which* for non-human referents and for situations. The marked pronoun in conjunction with a caesura before and after the clause clearly sets off the non-restrictive relative clause from the main clause; in written discourse non-restrictive relative clauses are set off by commas. In this way the speaker indicates that the characterising event described in the non-restrictive clause is meant as a parenthetical aside. This intonation pattern differs strongly from the uninterrupted intonation flow of restrictive relative clauses. The relative pronouns and different intonation patterns iconically reflect the degree of conceptual integration of the events. Compare the restrictive and non-restrictive relative clauses below:

(31) a. Eve likes the shirt (*that*) *Adam is wearing*. [*restrictive*]
b. Eve likes Adam's shirt, *which is brand-new*. [*non-restrictive*]

In (31a), the shirt is identified by an event (Adam is wearing the shirt), in (31b), it is identified by a possessive relationship (Adam's shirt), and the non-restrictive event (the shirt is brand-new) is conceptually detached from the main event. The two types of relative clause thus reflect two different types of conceptual integration, which are illustrated in a simplified form in Figure 7.3. The larger ellipse in the restrictive situation indicates that a qualification by means of the relative clause is necessary in order to restrict the referent of *the shirt* among other potential referents, while the two ellipses in the non-restrictive situation indicate that the referent of *Adam's shirt* does not need further referential qualification; it is already identified and the non-restrictive relative clause only serves to provide additional qualification. Notice that the non-restrictive relative clause in (31b) may also refer to the whole event *Eve likes Adam's shirt*.

Figure 7.3. Integration with restrictive and non-restrictive relative clauses

(iii) *Functions of non-restrictive relative clauses*
The function of non-restrictive relative clauses is to provide additional information about a referent, but the reason why the speaker chooses to provide additional information about a referent is not made explicit and needs to be inferred by the hearer. In (30a), the topic of the conversation is the election results, and the hearer may assume that the speaker deems it necessary to provide some relevant background information about an event in the past which the hearer may no longer be aware of. In (30b), the hearer may assume that the speaker is expressing her personal opinion of the elections. In (31b), the hearer probably assumes that the speaker wanted to give the reason why Eve liked Adam's shirt. In short, the specific meaning associated with non-restrictive relative clauses is a matter of inference within a situational context.

7.5 Summary

Qualification refers to the specification of things or instances of things. Qualifications are expressed in language as **modifiers** of nouns or sentences. Qualifications and the modifiers expressing them have two functions. **Restrictive qualification** mainly has an identifying function, as in *the young girl* (not the older girl), and **non-restrictive qualification** has an expressive function, as in *my dear mother*. Restrictive qualification serves to "restrict" a category to a subtype as in *He is a grumpy old man*, or to "restrict" a referent among the reference mass, as in *I mean the tall guy*. Non-restrictive qualification provides additional expressive information about an already identified referent, as in *this cute baby*.

Modifiers may occupy different positions with regard to the head noun they modify. **Prenominal modifiers** as in *a visible star* tend to provide permanent and characteristic qualification, while **postnominal modifiers** as in *a star visible tonight* tend to express occasional and temporary qualification.

Qualifications are mainly achieved by means of a property, by means of a relation or by means of a situation. **Qualifying properties** are expressed as **adjectives**. Most adjectives describe **scalar properties**; **scalar adjectives** are gradable and intensifiable, as in *very expensive*. A smaller group of adjectives describe **complementary properties**, which evoke their opposites, such as *faithful*; these adjectives are not gradable. Further non-scalar types of adjectives are **deadverbial adjectives**, as in *elegant dancer*, **denominal adjectives**, as in *presidential adviser*, and **determining adjectives**, as in *perfect stranger*. Adjectives may be used attributively and predicatively. **Attributive adjectives** occur either in prenominal position, denoting stable properties, as in *drinkable water*, or in postnominal position, denoting occasional properties, as in *water drinkable (when boiled)*. **Predicative adjectives** assign properties, as in *Sirius is visible*.

There are three types of **qualifying relations**. **Possessive relations** as in *Dad's car* involve a possessor as a reference point; they are expressed by means of a genitive phrase. **Intrinsic relations** involve inherent properties such as the parts of a whole, as in *the end of a tunnel*; they are expressed by prepositional phrases with *of*. **Schematic relations** are based on image schemas such as containment as in *the flowers in the vase*; they are expressed by prepositional phrases with prepositions other than *of*.

Qualifying situations are expressed by restrictive and non-restrictive relative clauses. **Restrictive relative clauses** may help to identify a referent situationally, as in *I know a doctor who lives down the road*, or to categorise a thing, as in *I know a doctor who can't even cure a sore throat*. **Non-restrictive relative** clauses provide additional information and are clearly set off from the head noun of the main clause, as in *Eve likes my shirt, which is brand-new*.

> **Further Reading**

Adjectives have been amply studied by Ferris (1993); cognitive issues of adjectives are addressed in Thompson (1989), Taylor (1992) and Sweetser (1999). Studies of specific subtypes of adjectives are to be found in Bolinger (1967, 1977) for attributive and predicative adjectives, Górska (1994) for privative adjectives such as *moonless* and *smoke-free*, Goldberg & Ackerman (1996) for adjectival past participles, Levi (1973), Post (1986) and Wierzbicka (1988a, Ch. 9) for denominal adjectives. For differences in meaning between nouns and adjectives see Wierzbicka (1988b). The role of iconicity in the word order of adjectives is taken up in Vendler (1961) and Posner (1986). Studies of *of*-phrases are found in Vendler (1968), Langacker (1992) and Taylor (1994). The possessive genitive is analysed in Langacker (1993, 1995), Sheffer (1996) and Taylor (1996). Pre-cognitive and cognitive approaches to relative clauses are found in Tabakowska (1980), Prideaux & Baker, eds. (1986), Fox & Thompson (1990), Givón (1993, vol 2), Prince (1995), Sheffer (1996) and Gibson *et al* (2005); relative infinitives are analysed in Geisler (1995).

> **Study questions**

1. Characterise the italicised modifiers in the following sentences with respect to (i) restrictiveness/non-restrictiveness, (ii) thing or instance qualification, and (iii) type of qualification (qualifying property, relation or situation).
    a. The Japanese are *industrious* and *disciplined* workers.
    b. Let's go to "L'Escargot" *in Greek Street*. Have you ever been to that *marvellous* restaurant?
    c. We should help these *innocent* victims, *who have lost everything they had*.

2. Point out the difference in meaning conveyed by the following types of qualification:
    a. Jack is a *rich* man.
    b. Jack is a man *with a lot of money*.
    c. Jack is a man *who is rolling in money*.

3. What do the following recommendations for politically correct language reveal about different types of qualification?
    a. Negative phrase: *the blind*
       Affirmative phrases: *person who is blind*, *person with visual impairment* or *person who has low vision*
    b. Negative expressions: *cripple, lame, handicapped, deformed, physically challenged*
       Affirmative phrases: *person with a physical disability, person with a mobility impairment*

4. What kinds of adjectives (scalar, deadverbial, denominal, determining) are used in the following examples?
    a. There is no friend like an *old* friend.
    b. The *first* months of a baby's life are the most important ones.
    c. The brain is divided into two *cerebral* hemispheres.

d. The gardener is the *alleged* killer.
e. The *only* thing to do is to file for divorce.
f. He is a *distant* relative of mine.

5. Specify the role relation that is associated with the premodifier adjectives in the following phrases. Use names for roles such as agent, subject area, means, manner, material, source, goal, etc.
   a. *doctoral* dissertation
   b. *plastic* bottle
   c. *Polish* rug
   d. *financial* support
   e. *parliamentary* decision
   f. *electronic* file versus *electronic* surveillance

6. Show that the schematic relations in the following expressions (i) are understood within a given frame and/or domain and (ii) evoke stereotypical scenes.
   a. *the man on crutches*
   b. *a queue for the toilet*
   c. *a letter to the editor*
   d. *the flowers in the vase*
   e. *the water in the bathtub*

7. Specify the kind of qualifying relation in each of the following phrases.
   a. the President *of the United States*
   b. the danger *of combustion*
   c. the barking *of the dogs*
   d. her defence *of the thesis*
   e. the hub *of the wheel*

Part III

Situations as temporal units

Aspect, tense and modality

> Reality is merely an illusion, albeit a very persistent one.
> *(Albert Einstein)*

Communication is about situations, i.e. about events that happen and states things are in. Part III of this book is concerned with general temporal units of situations and the way they are communicated in discourse. The three chapters of this Part deal with temporal information which the speaker provides in describing a situation: information about the aspectual type of situation, information about the time when the situation occurred, and information about the reality status the situation is meant to have. These general notions of a situation are, at least partially, expressed in English by means of the grammatical categories *aspect*, *tense* and *modality*. These three grammatical categories share a number of linguistic properties. Grammatically, aspect, tense and modality belong to the verb complex. Semantically, aspect, tense and modality specify notions of time and related concepts that apply to a situation.

Aspect specifies the temporal structure of a situation and hence is part of the conceived situation itself. Tense and modality are external to a situation: they ground a situation in time and reality. **Tense** specifies the time of a situation and, at the same time, invokes notions about its reality status; **modality** characterises a situation as having potential reality.

Understandably, we have a fundamental interest in knowing whether a given situation has reality or not. Whenever we think of, or talk about, a state of affairs, we assess it with respect to reality. We mainly relate notions of reality to time and think of reality as evolving from the past to the present into the future. In this model of evolving reality, situations which we know occurred in the past are seen as belonging to *known reality*. Any thought, perception or emotion which we experience at the present moment is conceived of as being part of *immediate reality*. Both known reality and immediate reality are thought of as being factual, i.e. they have **factual reality**. A future situation which we can more or less safely predict from experiences in the past or present is seen as belonging to **projected reality**. Present or future situations which we judge as having the potential of becoming realised have **potential reality**. Events we have no knowledge of — which in fact applies to most events in the world, and situations which we only imagine or wish to occur belong to the world of *irreality*. Figure III.1, which has been adapted from Langacker (1991a), depicts this model of evolving reality.

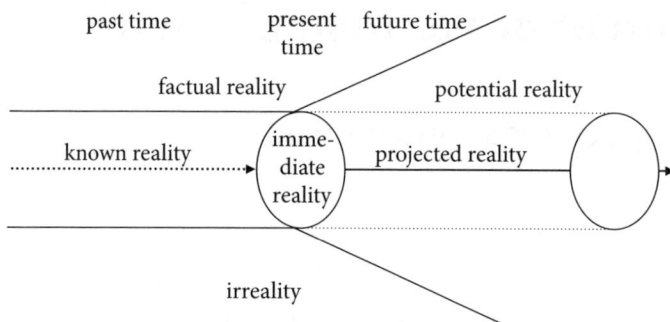

Figure III.1. Model of evolving reality

In the drawing, the cylinder represents notions of reality and the arrow its evolution through time. For example, the birth of a baby is fairly predictable from past and present circumstances and thus belongs to projected reality. As a "projected event" it is therefore described by using a future tense form: *Our baby will be born in June*. The area covered by potential reality also includes an evolutionary momentum but opens up beyond immediate and projected reality. For example, the speaker may be uncertain whether the baby to be born will be a boy or a girl. She estimates the potentiality of giving birth to a girl and expresses this in terms of modality: *It may be a girl this time*. The borderline between projected and potential realities is fuzzy. However, once we describe such "fuzzy situations", we are forced to decide on one of these realities by using either a tensed verb form or a modal verb.

Potential reality also shades over into irreality. For example, the mother may have all kinds of wishes about the baby. She may imagine a counterfactual situation, as in *I wish the baby was bigger*, which has the status of irreality, or she may imagine a hoped-for situation, as in *I wish the baby will grow up fast*, which may become reality and hence is closer to potentiality. In choosing a particular linguistic form, however, the speaker indicates the kind of reality in which her utterance is to be understood: *was* in the former sentence relates it to irreality, *will* in the latter sentence to projected or potential reality.

In the following, we will only consider situations that belong to factual, prospective and potential reality. We give expression to our judgement of the reality status of such situations in every single sentence, by using either a tense form or a modal expression. By using the past or present tense with the verb of a declarative sentence, the speaker communicates that the situation described belongs to factual reality; by using a future tense form, the speaker signals that the situation described is part of projected reality; and by using a modal verb such as *may*, the speaker informs the hearer that the situation described only has potential validity. These types of reality are summarised in Table III.1.

As already pointed out in Chapter 3.2.4 and as will be further elaborated in the following chapters, the tense forms of finite verbs and modal verbs ground the situation in one

Table III.1. The four types of reality status

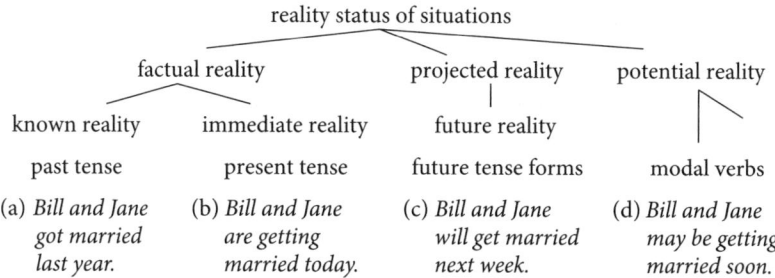

of the types of reality. We will see in Chapter 10 that grounding in potential reality is only achieved by modal verbs — this is why the right branch in Table III.1 pointing to other modal expressions is not labelled.

The three forms of aspect, tense and modality appear in a fixed order in the verb complex of English sentences. Let us first consider the order of two grammatical forms. The sentence *George was drinking* contains the past tense verb *was* and the two progressive aspect markers *be* and *-ing*. The aspect markers are closest to the main verb — the inflectional marker *-ing* is even fused with the verb stem, and the tense marker is further away from the main verb. This order is iconically motivated: aspect relates to the internal structure of a situation and forms of aspect are therefore closely integrated with the verb. The time of a situation, on the other hand, relates to an external ground and the tense forms expressing grounding are therefore further removed from the verb.

Let us now consider the sentence *George may have been drinking*. Here, the modal verb *may* expresses the speaker's judgement of the potentiality of the situation. A subjective assessment is even more detached from the situation than the time of its occurrence: the modal verb is therefore placed furthest away from the main verb. The ordering of 'modality — tense — aspect' in English is thus governed by the iconic principle of proximity (see Chapter 3.3.1). The increasing distance of the three verbal markers relative to the main verb is illustrated in Figure III.2. The anterior time in the sentence is expressed by the perfect forms *have* and *-en* (as in *be-en*), and the progressive aspect is expressed by the forms *be* and *-ing*. In the structure of the sentence, the affixes *-en* and *-ing* are attached to the verbs, i.e. as *been* and as *drinking*.

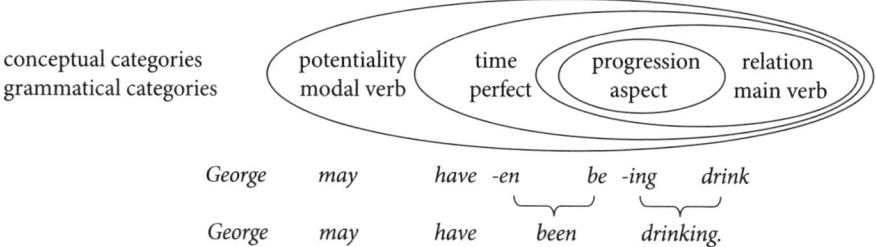

Figure III.2. Iconic order of modal verb, tense and aspect

The order of the three chapters of this Part is also organised iconically. We will first discuss the situation-internal category 'aspect' and then the situation-external categories 'time and tense' and 'potentiality and modality'.

Chapter 8 "Situation types: aspect" looks at **situation types** and their interaction with **aspect**. We will see that aspect in English is essentially a matter of viewing. In taking an internal view we see a situation in its progression. This view is expressed by the progressive aspect, as in *Bill was watching Star Trek*. In taking an external view we see a situation in its entirety. This view is expressed by the non-progressive aspect, as in *Bill watched Star Trek*.

Chapter 9 "Grounding situations in time: tense" is concerned with the grounding of situations in **time** by means of **tense**. The only point in time that is readily available to both speaker and hearer is the present moment of speaking, i.e. speech time. Tense relates the time of a situation to speech time. Tense does not affect the conceptual content of a situation: both *Bill is watching Star Trek* and *Bill was watching Star Trek* describe the same situation type.

Chapter 10 "Grounding situations in potentiality: modality" deals with situations that belong to **potentiality**. The speaker's assessment of potentiality and its expression in language is known as **modality**. Thus, the modal verb *may* in *Bill may be watching Star Trek* expresses the speaker's assessment of the potentiality that Bill is watching the TV show.

Chapter 8

Situation types: Aspect

8.0 Overview
8.1 Situations and basic aspectual classes
8.2 Types of events
8.3 Accomplishments and accomplishing activities
8.4 Bounded activities and unbounded activities
8.5 Achievements and culminating activities
8.6 Acts and iterative activities
8.7 Types of states
8.8 Conclusion
8.9 Summary

8.0 Overview

This chapter discusses the notion of **situation** and its interaction with aspect. **Aspect** is the grammatical form used by a speaker in taking a particular view of a situation. The speaker may view a situation with a maximal or a restricted **viewing frame**. Events which are viewed with a maximal viewing frame are seen externally and in their entirety. Such **bounded events** are expressed in the **non-progressive aspect**, as in *Ann cuddled the baby*. Events which are viewed with a restricted viewing frame are seen internally and in their progression, but still imply boundaries. Such **unbounded events** are expressed in the **progressive aspect**, as in *Ann is cuddling the baby*. States which are viewed with a maximal viewing frame are seen as infinite. Such **lasting states** are expressed by the non-progressive, as in *Ann lives with her parents*. Some states may also be viewed with a restricted viewing frame and, like bounded events, imply boundaries. Such **temporary states** are expressed by the progressive aspect, as in *Ann is living with her parents*.

8.1 Situations and basic aspectual classes

8.1.1 Situations

The notion **situation** has already been introduced in Chapter 3.2, where we looked at its conceptual core and its grounding and setting elements. Situations are also characterised by another important property: they have a particular temporal structure. For example, the situation described by *Grandma baked her favourite cherry pie* has a starting point, an end-point and a certain duration, while the situation described by *We just love her pies* has no starting point and no end-point and hence no specific duration. These are clearly different types of situation: the former sentence describes an event, the latter a state. We will describe such temporal structures defining types of situations as **time schemas**. We may now define a situation more explicitly as a conceptual unit consisting of a conceptual core, a time schema, grounding elements, and setting elements.

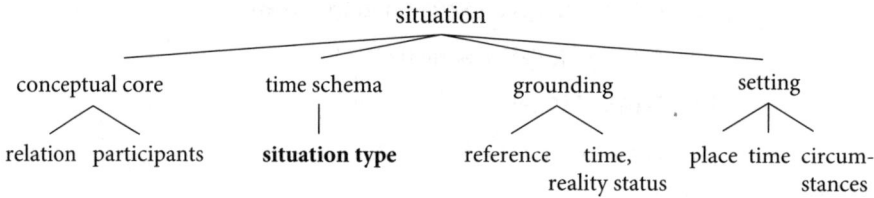

Figure 8.1. Elements constituting a situation

The relational configurations between participant roles will be discussed in Chapter 11 on event schemas. The grounding of referents was dealt with in Chapter 5 on reference; the grounding of situations with respect to their time and reality status will be examined in Chapter 9 on time and Chapter 10 on modality. The setting of situations in space, time and circumstances will be taken up in Chapter 12 on space and extensions of space. This chapter is concerned with types of situation as defined by their time schemas.

People are aware of types of situation when they speak of events, activities, habits or states; other types of situation that we need to distinguish are less familiar. In English, like in many other languages, a careful distinction between **situation types** is crucial because they interact with aspect. We will, therefore, first look at basic time schemas that characterise aspectual classes of English.

8.1.2 Basic aspectual classes: Non-progressive and progressive aspect

Basic aspectual classes are time schemas that are relevant for aspectual distinctions in language. **Aspect** is the grammatical form used by a speaker in taking a particular view of a situation. The origin of the term *aspect* nicely captures this idea: the word *aspect* derives from Latin *aspectus* 'view', which shows that earlier grammarians have already noted that aspect pertains to ways of viewing. As is well-known, English has two forms of aspect: the non-progressive and the progressive aspect. Formally, the **non-progressive aspect** is expressed by the simple verb form, while the **progressive aspect** is expressed by a construction with *be V-ing*. Traditionally, only the progressive aspect is treated as a form of aspect, the construction with the simple verb form is not, but the simple verb form has aspectual meaning as well. In Chapter 2.1 we already characterised their aspectual meanings in terms of **viewing frames**. The non-progressive aspect is characterised by a *maximal viewing frame*, the progressive aspect by a *restricted viewing frame*. Let us apply the maximal and restricted viewing frames to events and states. **Events** are dynamic situations: they involve changes and hence are heterogeneous. **States** are static situations: they do not involve a change and hence are homogeneous.

(1) a. Ann *cuddled* the baby. [*event: maximal viewing frame*]
 b. Ann *is cuddling* the baby. [*event: restricted viewing frame*]
 c. Ann *lives* with her parents. [*state: maximal viewing frame*]
 d. Ann *is living* with her parents. [*state: restricted viewing frame*]

Sentence (1a) in the non-progressive aspect describes an event seen with a maximal viewing frame. We adopt an *external view* and see the event as a whole, i.e. as a bounded event with a beginning and an end. Sentence (1b) in the progressive aspect describes an event seen with a restricted viewing frame. It only allows us to take an *internal view* of an event and see it in its progression. It is an unbounded event. However, the temporal boundaries of the event are only out of focus but implicitly still there: we "know" that Ann will not cuddle the baby forever, i.e. the event has 'limited duration'.

Sentence (1c) in the non-progressive aspect describes a state seen with a maximal viewing frame. It provides an *infinite view* of an inherently unbounded and homogeneous, or lasting, state. The sentence thus means that 'Ann lives with her parents for an indefinite time'. Sentence (1d) in the progressive aspect describes a state seen with a restricted viewing frame. Like unbounded events as in sentence (1b), some states may be seen with a restricted viewing frame and allow us to take an *internal view*. However, the portion of the state we see is comparable to a portion of a substance like water: a portion of a state is still an unbounded and homogeneous state in the same way that a portion of the substance water is still water. If the progressive aspect contributed nothing else but denote a portion of a state it would not be informative and not be needed in the ecology of the language. The progressive with states makes us conceive of the state as having implicit boundaries in the same way that the progressive with events makes us see implicit boundaries. Sentence (1d) thus means that 'Ann is living with her parents temporarily'.

The English progressive aspect thus has one unitary meaning for events and states, which may be described as 'unboundedness with implicit boundaries'. This meaning is, though, the result of different conceptual processes: with events, the temporal boundaries are defocused, with states, implicit temporal boundaries are imposed. The two viewing frames applied to events and state give rise to three aspectual classes:

i. bounded events, which are expressed by the non-progressive aspect;
ii. lasting states, which are expressed by the non-progressive aspect;

iii. unbounded events and states with implicit boundaries, which are expressed by the progressive aspect.

The time schemas defining these three aspectual classes are diagrammed in Figure 8.2. The boxes printed in bold represent the viewing frames, the heavy lines indicate the situation or the part of the situation that is profiled, the light lines extending beyond the viewing frame indicate implied continuations of the situation and its boundaries, and the arrows stand for the passage of time.

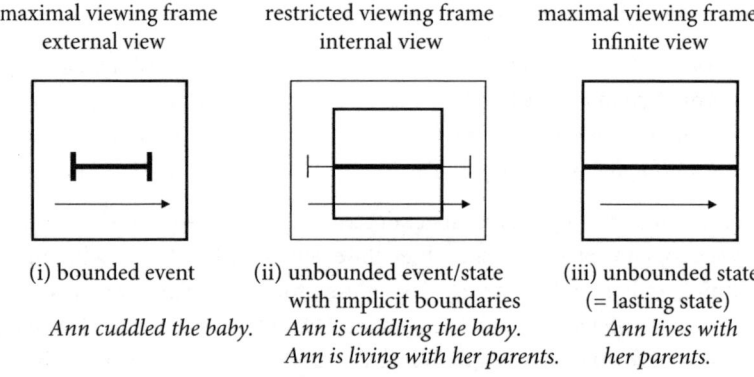

Figure 8.2. Time schemas of the three basic aspectual classes

(i) **Bounded events** are viewed externally and in their entirety. They are internally heterogeneous and comprise many successive sub-events. The speaker's main focus is on the boundaries of the event, in particular its end. We will see that the end-point of an event is particularly relevant in English. Bounded events are therefore often described as *perfective*. In order to avoid confusion with the term *perfect* (see Chapter 9), however, we use the term bounded event.

(ii) (a) **Unbounded events**, also described as *imperfective*, are viewed internally and provide a close-up view on the progression of the event. The progressive therefore often conveys greater immediacy to an event as it unfolds. Thus, in the progressive sentence (1b), *Ann is cuddling the baby*, we may see Ann in the process of nestling, hugging and kissing the baby. It is, however, not the particular activity actually performed at the moment that matters in the progressive but the activity "as such". For example, in the middle of changing the baby's nappy Ann might receive a telephone call and be asked what she is doing at the moment, and she could reply that she is changing the baby's nappy even though in fact she is talking on the phone. She could of course be doing both at the same time in this age of speaker phones. Once we focus on the internal progression of an event it is only natural that we lose sight of its beginning and end. However, the progressive presupposes overall boundaries of the event, as shown in viewing frame (ii) of Figure 8.2. This explains why the meaning of the progressive has often, and correctly, been identified as expressing 'limited duration'.

(ii) (b) Unbounded states with implicit boundaries are, in fact, **temporary states**. These states only last for a limited duration. A fairly small number of states are typically thought of as being short-lived and hence are construed in the progressive, as in *She is sleeping; I am waiting; The cushion is lying on the floor*, etc. Some states like 'living at a place' can be construed as temporary or lasting, but the majority of states are seen as lasting

(iii) **Lasting states** are seen as infinite, i.e. as having no beginning and end. This typically applies to uncontrolled states of affairs, as in *Ann loves the baby* or *I know my wife*, which are thought of as lasting indefinitely. The progressive is therefore normally ruled out here. Interestingly, the non-progressive aspect applies to bounded events and lasting states, i.e. it is used for two diametrically opposed aspectual classes. It is probably their very opposition that has licensed the use of the same form for these different conceptual categories.

The preceding discussion has shown that the notion of **boundedness** is fundamental for the distinction between aspectual classes and situation types in English. We have already used 'boundedness' in distinguishing between objects and substances in Chapter 4. The same notion distinguishes types of things and types of situations: bounded events correspond to objects; lasting states correspond to substances. Unbounded events and temporary states occupy an intermediate position: with respect to their internal focus they are unbounded, with respect to their implied boundaries they are bounded.

The following sections will mainly be devoted to the intriguing issue of bounded and unbounded types of events; the distinction between types of states is less dramatic and will be addressed in the final section.

8.2 Types of events

8.2.1 Bounded and unbounded events

8.2.1.1 *Bounded events*

Bounded events can be distinguished by means of two criteria: duration and telicity. **Duration** refers to the length of time an event lasts; the criterion of duration distinguishes durational from punctual events. The event described by *Ann changed the baby's nappy* is durational: changing a nappy takes a certain length of time, which may be specified as in *Ann changed the baby's nappy in a minute*. The event described by *The baby burped*, by contrast, is conceived of as involving no duration at all: burping is thought of as punctual or instantaneous even if, strictly speaking, the passing of gas from the baby's stomach through his mouth involves at least a minimal duration.

Telicity (from Greek *télos* 'end') refers to the inherently conclusive and definitive endpoint of an event. The criterion of telicity distinguishes telic events, which possess a conclusive end-point, from atelic events, which lack a conclusive end-point. Whether an event has, or does not have, a conclusive end-point is determined by the conceptual structure of the situation. The event described by *Ann changed the baby's nappy* has as a conclusive and definitive end-point, namely the baby's wearing a new, clean nappy. It is immaterial whether the end-point of a telic event is ever reached (see 8.3.2 for accomplishing activities). When the end-point is reached, the event is completed, or finished. We can then, for instance, truly say that *Ann has finished changing the nappy*. The event described by *Ann cuddled the baby*, on the other hand, has no conclusive end-point; it is atelic. Atelic events can only be said to be *stopped*, not *finished* in the sense of 'completed': *Ann finished cuddling the baby* (see 8.3).

The two criteria of duration and telicity allow us to distinguish four types of bounded events, which are presented with their time schemas in Figure 8.3. These four event types are usually referred to as accomplishments, activities, achievements, and acts.

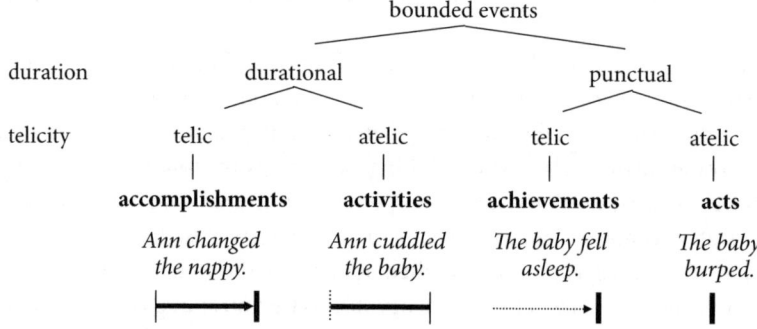

Figure 8.3. Types of bounded events and their time schemas

Accomplishments are bounded telic events that take a certain duration for their completion. They require an energy source, typically an intentionally acting human being, that propels the event to its conclusion. This is indicated in the time schema by the bold arrow leading to the event's end-point. The focus of accomplishments is on their conclusion, which is indicated by the bold end-point.

Activities are durational and atelic events, i.e. they do not have a conclusive end-point. Activities may be bounded or unbounded. Bounded activities are typically bounded with respect to the moment they stop. In the time schema of bounded activities, the durational phase is highlighted by bold print and the end-point by a light line.

Achievements are bounded events that focus on the punctual moment of the event's termination and invoke a preceding culminating, or "build-up", phase. This is indicated in the time schema of achievements by the dotted arrow for the culminating phase and a bold line for the terminal point.

Acts are punctual, atelic events. The punctual, or momentary, character of acts is indicated in their time schema by a single vertical line.

8.2.1.2 Unbounded events

The use of the progressive makes us view all four types of bounded events in their internal progression, i.e. as *unbounded events*. Unbounded events have the time schema drawn in Figure 8.2(ii). The restricted viewing frame allows us to see only part of the event, its beginning and end are only implicitly there, and since the viewing frame has at least some extension, the internal part which we see in an unbounded event necessarily has duration. It goes without saying that this time schema is incompatible with the time schemas of bounded events — a punctual event cannot have duration. We will see in the ensuing sections that such conceptual conflicts have been elegantly resolved by the language users. While the overall meaning of unbounded events corresponds to its time schema, particular meanings associated with each of the unbounded events derive from imposing a restricted viewing frame on the corresponding bounded event. The four types of unbounded events are diagrammed in Figure 8.4, where the boxes indicate the restricted viewing frames and the dotted lines show implicit boundaries. The four types of unbounded events are described as activities corresponding to their respective bounded situation type.

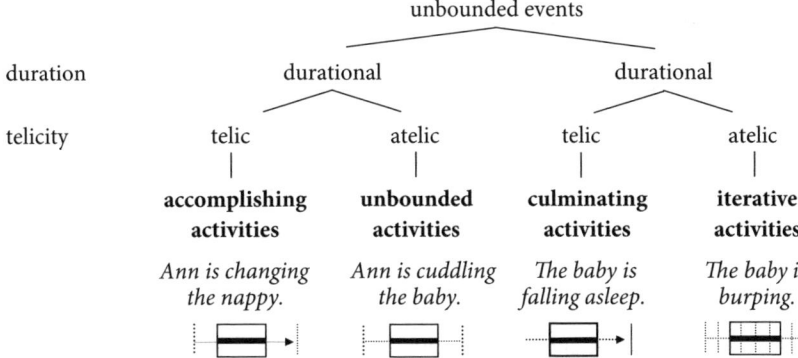

Figure 8.4. Types of unbounded events and their time schemas

All unbounded events are durational, i.e. the notion 'duration' no longer distinguishes situation types — it has only been kept to show the parallelism between bounded and unbounded events. The time schemas of the two unbounded telic events, i.e. accomplishing and culminating activities, in fact look almost identical, and those of the two unbounded atelic events, i.e. unbounded and iterative activities, are very similar as well.

Accomplishing activities focus on the durational phase of an accomplishment. Like accomplishments, accomplishing activities are telic in having an inherently conclusive end-point (the change of the nappy), but this is only expected to come about and need not actually occur.

Unbounded activities differ from bounded activities in that they focus on the progression of the event, which, as will be shown in Section 8.4.2, results in subtle differences in meaning.

Culminating activities are the unbounded counterparts of achievements. As punctual events, achievements cannot easily be extended in time. But we may focus on the build-up phase preceding the achievement, which, however, describes a different type of situation. As in accomplishing activities, an end-point is expected to be reached but need not occur.

Iterative activities are quick successions of punctual acts, which are conceived of as constituting a single durational event.

8.3 Accomplishments and accomplishing activities

8.3.1 Accomplishments

Accomplishments are telic events, i.e. they consist of a series of cumulative phases leading to a conclusive end-point. Each of the cumulative phases, or sub-events, contributes to the completion of the event as a whole, which therefore takes a certain amount of time to be realised. For example, changing a nappy involves successive cumulative sub-events such as untying the old nappy, disposing of it, cleaning the baby, getting a new nappy, putting it on, tying it, etc. Likewise, laying the table involves putting a table-cloth on the table, arranging the plates, glasses and silverware, etc. Only when all these sub-events have been carried out cumulatively can I proudly announce that "the nappy is changed" or "the table is laid". The successive sub-events that an accomplishment consists of are thus understood as part of an overall event leading to its completion. Since its completion is essential, an accomplishment can be said to be "finished" when it is completed, as in sentence (2a). When an event stops midway it is not an accomplishment; hence an accomplishment cannot be said to be "stopped". Sentence (2b) therefore describes an accomplishing activity (see 8.3.2 below).

(2) a. Ann *finished* changing the nappy. [*accomplishment*]
    b. Ann *stopped* changing the nappy. [*accomplishing activity*]

The possibility of using *finish*, but not *stop*, with an event is diagnostic for accomplishments. Another test relates to the time span an accomplishment takes from its beginning to its completion. We can therefore ask about the duration of an accomplishment by using the question *How long did X take to ...?* as in (3a) and can specify its duration by using a time adjunct with the preposition *in* as in (3b).

(3) a. *How long did* Ann *take* to change the nappy?
    b. She changed it *in less than a minute*.

Both the question *How long did X take to ...?* and the time-span preposition *in* can also be used with achievements, as in *How long did the baby take to fall asleep?* However, here the time-span expressions do not refer to the duration of the achievement, which is a punctual event, but to the phase preceding it (see 8.5 below).

Accomplishments can be brought about by humans as well as non-human entities. Typically, humans act intentionally and have a goal in mind which they intend to accomplish. Such goals may be to write a paper, to install a computer program, to open a bank account, to dig a grave, and thousands of other events. Humans may also perform accomplishments unintentionally. For example, we have "accomplished" something when we opened the wrong door of a public toilet or accidentally set the house on fire. In fact, all human accomplishments are theoretically ambiguous between these two interpretations, and often the question of whether an accomplishment was performed intentionally or unintentionally needs to be made explicit.

Like non-intentionally acting humans, non-human entities may also bring about accomplishments as in *Your chain smoking has damaged your health* or *The strike closed down the subway system*. Accomplishments may also come about due to an inherent disposition of humans or objects. Linguistically, we therefore speak of accomplishments when a child has grown up, I have recovered from a disease, the fog has lifted, the sun has set, etc. All these situations pass the linguistic tests for accomplishments: we may use the verb *finish*, as in (4a), ask a question with *How long did X take to …?*, as in (4b), and use the time-span preposition *in*, as in (4c).

(4) a. Dick has *finished* growing up.
 b. *How long did* Dick *take* to grow up?
 c. Dick grew up *in a very short space of time*.

In sentence (4a) we may, of course, also use *stop* as in *Dick stopped growing* — without *up*, but then this sentence no longer describes an accomplishment but an accomplishing activity: it suggests that Dick has stopped growing for now but may still continue to grow later on.

An accomplishment is not bound to a specific grammatical structure. The end-point at which an accomplishment concludes may take different grammatical forms: a direct object (5a), a resultative adjunct (5b), a directional prepositional phrase (5c), an adverbial particle (5d), and even a zero-form (5e).

(5) a. Howard drank *five glasses of scotch*.
 b. Margaret slammed the door *shut*.
 c. Baxter put the bottle *in the fridge*.
 d. Phil calmed *down*.
 e. The fog *lifted*.

All these forms denote, or imply, a conclusive end-point marking the completion of an event: a bounded quantity (five glasses) in (5a), the resulting state of an action (shut) in (5b), the attained goal of an act of transfer (in the fridge) in (5c), the end-point of a metaphorical motion (down) in (5d), and the physical level 'up' implied by lift in (5e). Since its completion is inherently part of an accomplishment, only entities that can serve as a boundary are compatible with this situation type. Unbounded entities cannot establish a conclusive end-point of an accomplishment. Thus, when we use the mass noun *scotch* in (5a) without a quantifying expression, as in *Howard drank scotch all evening*, we are no longer dealing with an accomplishment but with an activity (see 8.4.1 below). More generally, these observations illustrate an important characteristic of situation types: What determines a situation type is not solely a matter of aspect and the semantics of the verb or verb complex, as has often been assumed, but of the nature of the situation as a whole, including the status of its nouns as bounded or unbounded (see Chapter 5.2.2).

8.3.2 Accomplishing activities

The internal view imposed by the progressive aspect turns an accomplishment into an activity, which we will describe as an **accomplishing activity**. Like other activities, accomplishing activities can be specified by adjuncts denoting a stretch of time, such as *for hours* and *all day long* in (6).

(6) a. Ann was changing nappies *for hours*.
    b. I was laying tables *all day long*.

Accomplishing activities are not compatible with time-span expressions, which go with accomplishments. Thus we cannot say **Ann was changing a nappy in half an hour* or **I was laying the table in five minutes*. Time-span adjuncts are not possible here because they specify a bounded duration while the progressive imposes an unbounded duration of the event.

Accomplishments and accomplishing activities convey different meanings. Philosophers have observed that a bounded sentence such as *John drew a circle* entails, i.e. implies as a necessary conclusion, that a circle was drawn, whereas an unbounded sentence such as *John was drawing a circle* has no such entailment. This intriguing behaviour of unbounded, or imperfective, sentences has been described as the "imperfective paradox". The paradox is, however, easily resolved once we consider the time schema of accomplishing activities presented in Figure 8.4. The restricted viewing frame only provides a view of the cumulative phase of the accomplishment, and its completion falls outside the viewing frame. Unlike accomplishments, an accomplishing activity may therefore be broken off at any point and still count as an accomplishing activity: the event's completion may thus never occur. Since 'draw a circle' is a telic predicate, however, it invites the implicature that the drawing of the circle will be completed. Thus, if someone said "I am drawing a circle" and did not finish her drawing, we would feel deceived. As an implicature, the expectation about the event's completion may be cancelled, as illustrated in the examples under (7). When cancelling an implicature, the speaker typically uses devices that signal counter-expectation like the conjunction *but* or the adjunct *then*. These discourse markers inform the hearer that the expected course of events no longer applies.

(7) a. Ann was changing the nappy *but then* her boyfriend called and she left the baby with the dirty nappy on crying in the cot.
    b. I was laying the table when my boss called and *then* I had to spend the whole evening in the office.

The strong expectation that accomplishing activities will be completed also shows in another guise. Accomplishments are typically described in the present perfect, which invites an implicature about its result (for perfect tenses see Chapter 9.3). But notice the different meanings associated with the different aspectual forms in (8):

(8) a. Jenny *has learned* to drive.
    b. Jenny *has been learning* to drive.

The accomplishment sentence (8a) says that Jenny has finished her driving lessons, and the present perfect invites the implicature that she now knows how to drive and may legally do so. The accomplishing activity in (8b), by contrast, invites other implicatures: Jenny has not finished her driving lessons and hence does not yet know how to drive, or she has not yet taken or passed the driving test. The interpretation of this sentence is governed by the principle of relevance. If the speaker had wanted to communicate that Jenny is allowed to drive, he would have used an accomplishment sentence; the fact that the speaker focuses on the cumulative phase of the accomplishment rather than on its completion can only imply that Jenny has not yet finished her driving lessons and that, as a result, she is not allowed to drive.

8.4 Bounded activities and unbounded activities

8.4.1 Activities

Activities are solely characterised by their duration. As Binnick (1991) aptly put it, "an activity is all activity phase". Activities may involve intentionally acting humans and non-humans. Instances of activities carried out by humans are running, smiling, drinking beer, playing cards, writing letters, making noise, etc. Activities in the non-human world are usually seen as processes and include raining, the wind blowing, the sun shining, water boiling, etc. (for processes see Chapter 11.2.1.2).

An activity can be identified by a number of tests that uniquely characterise activities and which follow from the conceptual nature of this situation type:

(9) a. *Stop* making all that noise!
 b. *How long* did you play cards?
 c. The sun was shining *for half an hour*.
 d. It rained *from morning till evening*.

Since activities are atelic, they can be stopped as in (9a), and since they involve duration, they can be asked about by *how long*-questions as in (9b) and take duration adjuncts specifying a "stretch of time" such as *for half an hour* in (9c) and *from morning till evening* in (9d).

The fact that activities do not have a natural end-point has consequences for the type of direct object they take, as demonstrated in the following sentences:

(10) a. Diane wrote *poetry* all evening.   [activity]
 b. Diane wrote *poems* all evening.   [activity]
 c. Diane wrote *three poems* in one evening.   [accomplishment]

Sentences (10a) and (10b) describe activities, as can be seen from the time-stretch adjunct *all evening*. We might also ask about their duration by using a question with *how long*: *How long did you write poetry?* Their interpretation as activities is also imposed by the unbounded nature of their direct objects: the mass noun *poetry* in (10a) and the indefinite plural count noun *poems* in (10b). As shown in Chapter 4.1.2, mass nouns and indefinite plural nouns have much in common, and we now see that they also behave alike with respect to situation types. Since they express unbounded things, they cannot describe the conclusive end-point of an event (see Section 8.3.1 above). A bounded nominal like three poems in sentence (10c), on the other hand, can serve as the conclusive end-point of an event. This sentence describes an accomplishment, as can be seen from the time-span adjunct *in one evening* and the time-span question *How long did you take to write three poems?* If we combined the accomplishment in (10c) with a time-stretch adjunct, the resulting sentence is, predictably, ungrammatical: **I wrote three poems all evening.*

8.4.2 Bounded vs unbounded activities

The conceptual difference between bounded and unbounded activities is minimal: both are durational and atelic events. But the different viewing frame imposed on each of them gives rise to different grammatical behaviour and different meanings.

The importance of temporal boundaries for bounded activities is illustrated in the sentences under (11), which sound odd without a specifying context, while the unbounded activities described by the sentences under (12), which focus on the progression of the event, are fully acceptable (see also Chapter 3.1.3 and the discussion of the sentences under (6d) and (7)).

(11)   *Bounded activities*   (12)   *Unbounded activities*
    a. ?They played.   a. They were playing.
    b. ?They drank.   b. They were drinking.
    c. ?They worked.   c. They were working.

Once time expressions of temporal duration are added, the bounded activities under (11) become fully acceptable, as in *They played all morning* or *They played from morning till evening*. We may, however, also invoke other kinds of boundaries than temporal boundaries. The sentences under (13) describe activities that are bounded with respect to various conceptual domains and, as a result, are perfectly well-formed without providing any further context:

(13)   a. They played marbles.
      b. They drank scotch.
      c. They worked on their paper.

The activity described in (13a) is bounded by invoking the domain of the play, in (13b) by invoking the domain of drinks, and in (13c) by invoking the domain of work. The same activity may be bounded by different domains. For example, apart from the object of one's work in (13c), the domain may refer to space as in *He worked in the garden*, class membership as in *He worked as a taxi-driver*, or companionship as in *He worked with his colleagues*.

Bounded and unbounded activities convey subtle differences in meaning that often go beyond purely temporal notions. The following sentence pairs mainly differ with respect to implicatures invited by the type of aspect used.

(14) *Bounded activities*
    a. I *talked* to Mr Green.
    b. What *did* you *do* in my office?
    c. What *did* you *do* before you came here?
    d. Chomsky *claims* that syntax is autonomous.

(15) *Unbounded activities*
    a. I *was talking* to Mr Green.
    b. What *were* you *doing* in my office?
    c. What *were* you *doing* before you came here?
    d. Chomsky *is claiming* that syntax is autonomous.

The non-progressive aspect used in the sentences under (14) invites implicatures of factuality or determination, while the progressive aspect used in the sentences under (15) may give rise to all sorts of interpretations due to its focus on the event's progression.

Sentence (14a) suggests that I initiated the talk, that my talk with Mr Green was held with some purpose in mind, and that our conversation led to some result. Sentence (15a), by contrast, suggests that I possibly happened to meet Mr Green, that we talked for talk's sake, and that we only had some casual small talk. For these reasons, a sentence such as ?*He talked nonsense* sounds less appropriate out of context than *He was talking nonsense* and, conversely, ?*We were talking business* sounds less appropriate than *We talked business*.

Question (14b) might be asked in order to get some purely factual information about what the person actually did in my office. Question (15b), by contrast, may be asked out of interest or as a demand for an explanation, in which case it would carry a suspicious undertone regarding the intentions of the intruder.

Question (14c) asks for factual information, while question (15c) is likely to be understood as a polite enquiry about a person's previous whereabouts before she came to live here.

Sentence (14d) presents Chomsky's claims as a nearly timeless state, suggesting that this is Chomsky's permanent position, while sentence (15d) may only refer to Chomsky's claim with respect to a particular article we are looking at, suggesting that Chomsky is probably going to further develop his position by either endorsing or refuting it.

8.5 Achievements and culminating activities

8.5.1 Achievements

Achievements are punctual events and as such have no duration. The term *achievement* is used here in contrast to *accomplishment*, i.e. as a technical term, and not in its everyday understanding. It applies to terminal situations such as *He reached the finish*, which invoke a "build-up", or culminating, phase leading to a terminal point. The point of termination is profiled whereas the culminating phase is only invoked. This can be seen from the fact that achievements cannot be combined with durative adjuncts denoting a stretch of time, i.e. we can't say things like *The baby fell asleep for an hour. In The baby fell asleep, the culminating phase may include the baby's stopping crying, quietening down, and closing its eyes until it eventually drops off to sleep. The culminating phase invoked may vary according to the frame associated with the achievement. For example, falling asleep in the 'hospital' frame may result from being given sleeping tablets or an injection, while in the 'workplace' frame it may occur after vain attempts to fight one's fatigue.

Achievements occur; they are not brought about intentionally. The preceding culminating phase may, however, involve humans intentionally bringing about a result: I have "achieved" something when I cross the border, get married, catch fish, etc. The culminating phase may also involve non-intentionally acting humans: thus I have also "achieved" something when I fall asleep, notice something, lose or find something, become ill, am born or die. Finally, the culminating phase of achievements may also involve non-human entities. Linguistically, we thus also have achievements when the rain stops, the sun sets, a house catches fire, a tree falls down, the Chinese vase breaks, etc.

Since achievements are beyond a person's control, we cannot ask people to perform an achievement. Requests such as ?*Fall asleep!*, ?*Reach the summit!*, and ?*Catch the bus!* sound awkward. But we sometimes use achievement verbs in expressing requests. We might give our daughter the well-meant advice, *Get married as soon as possible!*, warn a tourist by saying *Cross the border by daylight!*, and find an ad in the paper that promises, *Win two weeks' vacation in a five-star hotel!* Such usages no longer represent achievements but accomplishments, i.e. they mean something like 'make every effort so that you will get married', etc. The requests focus on the culminating phase of an accomplishment (make every effort), in which we can take an active part in bringing about a conclusive goal (get married), which is the terminal point of an achievement (be married). The relationship between these two situation types is metonymic and has been described as RESULT FOR ACTION (LEADING TO THE RESULT).

8.5.2 Culminating activities

A punctual event cannot be extended in time. However, achievement verbs can be used with the progressive, which bestows an internal view on the event. The restricted viewing frame may apply to either the terminal point of the achievement or its preceding culminating phase. For lack of a better name we will describe both these unbounded events as **culminating activities**.

The former situation of applying a restricted viewing frame to the terminal point is illustrated in the following sentences, in which the achievement verb *arrive* is used in the progressive:

(16) a. The guests are arriving.
b. The Queen is arriving.
c. ?Uncle Joe is arriving.

We interpret sentence (16a) in the sense that the guests arrive one after the other. This "dispersive" interpretation is invited by the plural referent *the guests*. Also sentence (16b) gives rise to a dispersive, or multiplex, interpretation although the referent Queen is singular, or uniplex. Here, our knowledge of the 'royal family' frame makes us see before our eyes a scene of the Queen arriving with her court, one royal carriage after the other, as illustrated in Figure 8.5. The Queen metonymically stands for her dispersed entourage.

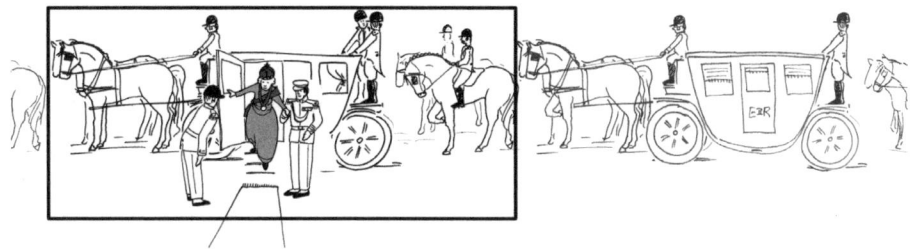

Figure 8.5. The Queen is arriving.

In order to mentally disperse a normal individual such as Uncle Joe in (16c), however, we have to imagine circumstances in which his arrival is somehow extended in time. We might, for example, picture Uncle Joe hooting the horn of his car or carrying a lot of luggage into the house. Now we do not see different people as in the Queen and her entourage, but one person coming and going repeatedly. None of these interpretations are found in the wordings themselves; they are triggered by the progressive aspect and implied on the basis of our knowledge of frames.

Situations in which a restricted viewing frame is applied to the build-up phase of an achievement are illustrated in the following sentences.

(17) a. Jennifer was (just) reaching the finish when she slipped.
 b. Our team was winning until the very end, when the opposing team scored two goals and won the game.

The end-point of the culminating activities described in these sentences falls outside the viewing frame, hence the achievements may never occur. As with accomplishing activities, the end-point of culminating activities is, however, strongly expected to come about. This is evidenced by the counter-expectation expressed by the *when*-clauses following the main clause.

Culminating activities are a special type of unbounded event. There are no unbounded achievements since achievements cannot be extended in time. The meanings that culminating activities convey come about by implicature and may be described as metonymies. The shift from a punctual event to a dispersive event as in *The Queen was arriving* involves the metonymy UNIPLEX FOR MULTIPLEX, and the shift from a punctual event to its preceding culminating phase as in *Jennifer was reaching the finish* involves the metonymy TERMINAL POINT FOR ACTIVITY (LEADING TO TERMINAL POINT).

8.6 Acts and iterative activities

Like achievements, **acts** are punctual events; but unlike achievements, acts are atelic, i.e. they do not invoke a culminating phase leading to a terminal point. Acts are also known as "semelfactive" situation types (from Latin *semel* 'once'). This term refers to their momentariness: acts come about so quickly that they are thought of as having no duration at all. We perform acts when we kick someone, knock at the door, drop a glass, when a ball bounces, a light flashes, etc.

Like achievements, acts cannot be viewed internally and are therefore of necessity bounded. However, act verbs can also be used in the progressive, as shown in sentence (18c):

(18) a. Philip kicked his sister. [one or more kicks]
b. Philip kicked his sister three times. [repetition of kicks]
c. Philip was kicking his sister. [iterative kicking]
d. *Philip was kicking his sister three times.

Sentence (18a) is ambiguous: it may describe a single act or several acts of kicking. The number of acts of kicking may be specified as in sentence (18b). Here, the three kicks constitute repetitions of the act of kicking. Each of the kicks establishes a separate event, and the kicks may even occur at separate times, e.g. one kick in the morning, another kick in the afternoon, and a third kick in the evening.

In sentence (18c) the progressive compels us to view the event as being extended in time. Since a punctual act cannot be extended in time, we interpret the event as a quick succession of acts of kicking, i.e. as an activity involving iteration, or an **iterative activity**. The separate punctual events are seen as constituting a single durational event which is internally multiplex. This also applies to progressive sentences such as *My friend is nodding his head*, *My dog is banging against the door*, *Angela is skipping in front of the class*, etc. While we may nod our head only once, we normally bang against doors and try to skip with a rope several times. However, it is only when we use the progressive aspect that we view these distinct sub-events as constituting a single iterative event.

The notion of iteration needs to be distinguished from that of repetition. Thus, sentence (18d), *Philip was kicking his sister three times*, is ungrammatical since it combines two conflicting notions: the progressive compels us to see a single event of iteration, while the quantity expression *three times* compels us to see a repetition of three distinct events.

8.7 Types of states

In Figure 8.2 we already drew attention to a basic aspectual distinction between lasting states, as in *Ann lives with her parents*, and temporary states as in *Ann is living with her parents*. Lasting states are seen with a maximal viewing frame, allowing an infinite view;

they are therefore inherently unbounded. Temporary states are seen with a restricted viewing frame, allowing an internal view; they are therefore implicitly bounded. The class of lasting states includes three subtypes: indefinitely lasting states, "habitual states", and everlasting states. Only the former two may also be construed as temporary states.

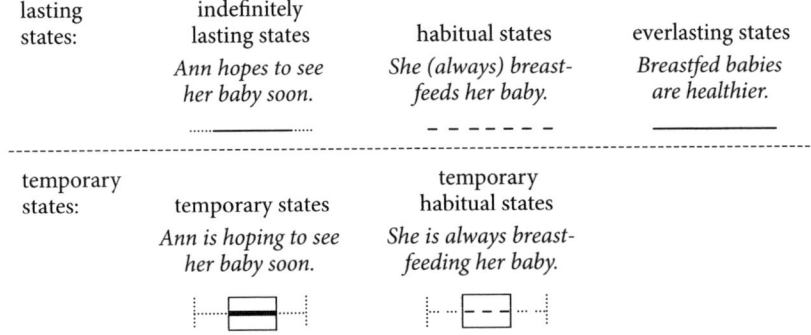

Figure 8.6. Types of lasting and temporary states and their time schemas

The distinction between the different types of states in Figure 8.6 mainly depends on the way a speaker views a given state. These types represent idealised states distinguished here for the sake of analysis, but in fact form part of a continuum from indefinitely lasting to everlasting states.

8.7.1 Indefinitely lasting states and temporary states

Indefinitely lasting states are conditions which last for an indefinite time but may eventually cease to exist. In Figure 8.6 their indefiniteness is indicated by an unbounded line shading over into dotted lines at both ends. Indefinitely lasting states can therefore be located in present, past or future time: *My life was exciting (when I first got married)*; *My life is still exciting (these days)*; and *My life will be even more exciting (when I get old)*. Indefinitely lasting states are expressed by predicative adjectives (*He is happy*) and participles (*He is shocked*), prepositional phrases (*He is in shock*), predicate nominals (*He is a teacher*), and a small but very frequently used class of so-called *stative verbs* (*He loves his wife*). The predicates which typically describe indefinitely lasting states include:

(19) a. *psychological states*: want, desire, long for, miss
 b. *emotional states*: love, hate, like, detest, be happy
 c. *mental states*: know, believe, think, hope, be doubtful
 d. *perceptual states*: see, feel, (it) feels, smells, be aware of
 e. *behavioural states*: be good to someone, be mean, be a miser
 f. *states of possession*: possess, belong, own, have
 g. *states of being*: contain, consist, exist, be tall, be a millionaire
 h. *positional states*: stand, sit, lie, rest, extend
 i. *various relational states*: involve, be similar to, be the father of

Although the states described by these predicates may only last for a short time and cease to exist after a while, they are generally seen as being homogeneous and stable for some indefinite time. Most indefinitely lasting states are seen as being infinite; hence they cannot, as a rule, be thought of as having implicit boundaries and be expressed in the progressive. Sentences such as *He is being in shock, *This bottle is containing malt whisky or *He is resembling his father are, therefore, ungrammatical.

Some of the state predicates listed in (19) can, however, be thought of as describing **temporary states** and are then used in the progressive. Compare the use of positional state verbs in the following pairs of sentences:

(20) a. My car *sits* in the garage collecting dust.
b. We are *sitting* in the garage playing cards.

(21) a. The Vietnam War Memorial *stands* on the Mall between the Lincoln Memorial and the Washington Monument.
b. We are *standing* in front of the Vietnam War Memorial.

The sentences under (20a) and (21a) describe the position of objects, which are likely to stay at the same place indefinitely, while the sentences under (20b) and (21b) describe the position of humans, who are likely to move somewhere else after a certain time. Our world knowledge tells us whether a state is likely to last indefinitely or temporarily. We know, for example, that people may sleep long, but not indefinitely; hence the situation of a person sleeping is described in the present progressive.

Many states may be described in the simple present or the present progressive and, as might be expected, convey different meanings.

(22) Lasting states
a. How do you *like* your new job?
b. I *hope* we'll get a discount.
c. I *feel* sick.

(23) Temporary states
a. How *are* you *liking* your new job?
b. I *am hoping* we'll get a discount.
c. I *am feeling* sick.

The specific meaning each sentence conveys is determined by its time schema and conversational implicatures. The speaker of question (22a) assumes that I have formed an opinion about my job, whereas the speaker of (23a) makes no such assumption; the question might be paraphrased as meaning 'by the way, have you already formed an opinion on your job?' Sentence (22b) suggests that I have firmly established hopes, while sentence (23b) may suggest that my hopes have developed spontaneously or that I even have intensive expectations. Sentence (22c) describes my overall sensation of sickness, whereas sentence (23c) describes my present awareness of this sensation.

The infinite view invoked by the non-progressive sentences in (22) makes us see the states as homogeneous, general and factual, while the internal view invoked by the progressive sentences in (23) makes us see the states as heterogeneous, specific and episodic.

The differences in meaning between these modes of viewing shows even more strikingly in the context of increase:

(24) a. I *like* my job better and better every day.
　　 b. I'm *liking* my job better and better every day.

A person's emotional state of liking something usually lasts indefinitely. The non-progressive aspect is the expected form to use, as in (24a), which conveys a factual statement about an increase in liking. The state verb *like* is normally not used in the progressive: *?I'm liking my job* sounds odd. The speaker may, however, also focus on the incremental phases of liking as they increase from day to day. This use of the progressive is not restricted to increases in emotion but is also found with changes of physical states, as in *He is resembling his father more and more*.

　　States that involve intentionally acting humans may also allow a temporary reading. This is not surprising since humans are able to change the world around them. Consider the sentences under (25), which refer either to a person's character or to a person's behaviour, as opposed to the sentences under (26), which are solely understood in a behavioural sense.

(25)　*Character or behaviour*　　(26)　*Behaviour*
　　 a.　You're obnoxious.　　　　　　 a.　You're *being* obnoxious.
　　 b.　You're a nuisance.　　　　　　 b.　You're *being* a nuisance.

As pointed out in Chapter 7.2.6, scalar adjectives in predicative position are in principle ambiguous between a permanent and temporary interpretation. This applies to the predicative adjective *obnoxious* in (25) as well as to the predicate nominal *a nuisance* in (25b). The progressive sentences under (26), however, no longer describe states but activities. We can tell this from the possibility of stopping one's behaviour. Thus, we can tell a naughty child *Stop being obnoxious, will you?*, but we can't do so with genuine states: **Stop being tall!*

8.7.2　"Habitual states" and temporary habitual states

Habitual states are, strictly speaking, not states but successions of indefinitely recurrent equivalent situations. Such situations typically apply to humans, who tend to behave in certain recurrent ways. We describe these regular patterns of behaviour as habitual, as in *My sister wears high-heeled shoes*. More rarely, we observe recurrent situations in nature, as in *The sun rises in the east*. Recurrent natural phenomena are often related to human behaviour. Especially in proverbs, we relate habitual human behaviour to natural phenomena and describe it metaphorically in terms of the non-human world, as in *A rolling stone gathers no moss* or *A new broom sweeps clean*.

　　Habitual situations are multiplex. They are typically composed of individual events that are seen in their entirety and synthesised into a single situation. In English we lose sight of the interruptions between the individual events and perceive them as forming a homogeneous, lasting state, whereas in some other languages habitual situations are grouped with events. Habitual states that hold at the present time are in English expressed in the simple present. Some kinds of habitual human states are listed below:

(27) a. Mary *smokes* a pipe. [*personal habit*]
    b. Germans *drink* a lot of beer. [*social custom*]
    c. My son-in-law *works* in London. [*occupation*]
    d. But he *lives* in Paris. [*residence*]

Habitual states display specific grammatical behaviour. Habitual situations that occurred in the past are marked by a special form, *used to* (28a), present and past habitual situations may be expressed by *keep* V-*ing* (28b), and the recent beginning of a habitual state may be indicated by *now* (28c).

(28) a. My fiancée *used to* work in a pub.
    b. She *keeps* applying for new jobs.
    c. She *now* works at McDonald's.

Used to is a grammaticised form that not only refers to people's past habits as in (28a) but also to events that regularly occurred owing to external circumstances, as in *Due to the irregular bus service, I used to arrive late for class at least three times a week*. Notice also that *used to* as a grammaticised form is differentiated by its pronunciation /juːstə/ from its lexical form /juːzd tə/, as in *This is the dagger that Macbeth used to kill Duncan*. *Keep* in its lexical sense refers to uninterrupted states; in its grammaticised sense of a habitual state as in (28b) it also allows for interruptions. The use of *now* in (28c) suggests the coming into existence of a new habitual state. Past and incipient habitual states may be combined as opposites, as in *She used to work in a pub, but now she works at McDonald's*.

Like some indefinitely lasting states, habitual states may only last temporarily. The use of the progressive makes us see an otherwise timeless habitual state (29a) as a temporary habitual state (29b). Here, the temporariness of the habitual state may also suggest that it has only recently come into existence.

(29) a. Mom *works* at the Ministry of Finance.
    b. Mom *is working* at the Ministry of Finance (for the moment).

The habitual nature of a state can also be highlighted by means of the frequency adjuncts *always, all the time, continuously* and *constantly*, which emphasise the repeated occurrences of the event:

(30) a. You *constantly* get into trouble.
    b. This car *always* breaks down.
    c. I forget people's names *all the time*.

We may also use the progressive in such habitual situations; *forever* appears almost exclusively with the progressive:

(31) a. My husband *is constantly getting* into trouble.
 b. This car *is always breaking* down.
 c. I'*m forever forgetting* people's names.

The progressive, as always, makes us focus on the progression of an event; here, it has the effect of "zooming in on" each individual event that contributes to the habitual situation as a whole. At the same time, the frequency adjunct focuses on the overall frequency of the individual events in the overall situation. If the nature of the event carries negative associations, the negative attitude it arouses gets magnified. The progressive habitual thus tends to invite inferences of irritation or even annoyance at a person's, usually the hearer's, behaviour.

8.7.3 Everlasting states

Everlasting states are phenomena whose existence or truth is timeless and unchangeable. As a result, we can only express everlasting states in the present, but not in the past or the future nor in the progressive aspect. Thus, we can say *Brighton is on the south coast*, but not **Brighton was on the south coast* or **Brighton is being on the south coast*. But even locations may not be stable and everlasting. For example, the town of Bruges once had a harbour on a sea estuary, which was later silted up, so that it is possible to say *Bruges was on the sea till the 15th century*.

Typical examples of everlasting states are physical laws (32a), definitions (32b), eternal truths (32c), generalisations that are claimed to be true (32d), and proverbial truths, i.e. generalisations that are believed to be true (32e). All of these everlasting situations have timeless validity by their very nature.

(32) a. What goes up must come down. (law of gravity)
 b. A triangle is a two-dimensional figure with three straight sides and three angles.
 c. Oil floats on water.
 d. Women are the stronger sex.
 e. Politics makes strange bedfellows.

Everlasting states are characterised by the generic nature of the overall situation, which shows up not only in the obligatory simple present form of the verb but also in the generic reference of the subject (*what(ever)*, *a triangle*, *oil*, *women*, *politics*) (for generic reference see Chapter 5.4).

8.8 Conclusion

Situation types combine with aspect in systematic ways. Table 8.1 summarises the situation types and the basic meaning associated with each type. The table does not include the wide range of meanings invited by implicature, especially in the context of the progressive aspect.

Table 8.1. Typology of situation types

	Maximal viewing frame Non-progressive aspect **Bounded events**		Restricted viewing frame Progressive aspect **Unbounded events**
accomplishment:	*Ann changed the nappy.*	accomplishing activity:	*Ann was changing the nappy.*
bounded activity:	*Ann cuddled the baby.*	unbounded activity:	*Ann was cuddling the baby.*
achievement:	*The baby fell asleep.*	culminating activity:	*The baby was falling asleep.*
act:	*The baby burped.*	iterative activity:	*The baby was burping.*
	Lasting states		**Temporary states**
indefinitely lasting state:	*How do you like your new job?*	temporary state:	*How are you liking your new job?*
habitual state:	*She works in a pub.*	temporary habitual state:	*She is working in a pub.*
everlasting state:	*Parallel lines never intersect.*	—	

8.9 Summary

Situations are, amongst others, characterised by their **time schema**, i.e. their distinct temporal structure. **Situation types** interact with aspect. **Aspect** is a grammatical form used by a speaker in taking a particular view of a situation. English distinguishes between two forms of aspect: the non-progressive and the progressive aspect. In using the **non-progressive aspect**, the speaker views a situation with a **maximal viewing frame**, in using the **progressive aspect**, the speaker views a situation with a **restricted viewing frame**. The two kinds of viewing frame lead to different time schemas depending on whether they are applied to events or states. **Events** involve changes and hence are heterogeneous; **states** do not involve changes and hence are homogeneous. In applying a maximal viewing frame to an event, we take an external view and see the event in its entirety, as in *Ann changed the nappy*; such situations are **bounded events**. In applying a maximal viewing frame to a state, as in *Ann loves the baby*, we see the state as infinite; it is an unbounded, or **lasting state**. In applying a restricted viewing frame to an event, we focus on its progression and lose sight of its boundaries, as in *Ann is changing the nappy*; such situations are **unbounded events**. In applying a restricted viewing frame to a state, we see the state internally and as implicitly bounded, as in *Ann is living with her parents*. Such states of limited duration are **temporary states**. The general time schemas defined by modes of viewing a situation are **basic aspectual classes**. We can distinguish three basic aspectual classes: bounded events viewed externally, unbounded events and states, which are viewed internally and have limited duration, and unbounded, lasting states, which are infinite.

Specific situation types are distinguished by the criteria of duration and telicity. **Duration** refers to the length of time an event lasts, **telicity** refers to the inherently conclusive end-point of an event. **Accomplishments** are bounded, durational, and telic events, as in *Ann changed the nappy*. The use of the progressive turns accomplishments into **accomplishing activities,** as in *Ann was changing the nappy*. **Activities** are durational, atelic events. They can be bounded, as in *Ann cuddled the baby*, or unbounded, as in *Ann was cuddling the baby*. **Achievements** are bounded, punctual, and telic events which imply a preceding culminating phase, as in *Ann fell asleep*. The use of the progressive turns achievements into **culminating activities**, as in *Ann was falling asleep*. **Acts** are bounded, punctual, and atelic events, as in *The baby burped*. The progressive turns acts into **iterative activities**, as in *The baby was burping*.

Three types of states can be distinguished. **Indefinitely lasting states** are conditions that last for an indefinite time, as in *I think I'll become a teacher*. To the extent that the use of the progressive is possible, it turns an indefinitely lasting state into a **temporary state**, as in *I am thinking of becoming a teacher*. **Habitual states** are recurrent events viewed as timeless states, as in *You constantly get into trouble*; the progressive turns them into **temporary habitual states**, as in *You are constantly getting into trouble*. **Everlasting states** are unchangeable, timeless situations, as in *Brighton is on the south coast*.

Further Reading

The foundations of situation types were laid by Vendler (1967) and elaborated by Dowty (1977; 1979), whose insights are reflected in the typology of situation types presented here. The notion of 'basic aspectual class' goes back to Langacker (2001).

Among the many publications on aspect and the English verb the following deserve special attention: Leech (1971), Palmer (1988), Comrie (1976), Smith (1983; 1995;²1997), Declerck (1991) and Binnick (1991). Recent approaches to aspect are reviewed in Sasse (2002). A bibliography on Tense, Aspect and Aktionsarten is found on the web at www.utsc.utoronto.ca/~binnick/TENSE/. The theoretical framework for linking things and situations is elaborated in Langacker (1991a). Descriptive cognitive applications of bounded (or perfective) and unbounded (or imperfective) situations are presented in Langacker (2001) and Cook-Gumperz & Kyratzis (2001).

The evolution of aspect in various languages is described in Dahl (1985) and Bybee, Perkins & Pagliuca (1994). Descriptions of aspect, tense and modality in various languages are offered in Bybee, Perkins & Pagliuca (1994), Hewson & Bubenik (1997), and Dahl, ed. (2000).

Study questions

1. Analyse the following sentences with respect to (i) the basic aspectual class (bounded event, unbounded event, state) and (ii) the type of situation (e.g. accomplishment) they belong to. If possible, justify your decision by using one of the diagnostic tests (type of question, preposition, *stop* vs *finish*).
    a. Beethoven composed the Moonlight sonata.
    b. Mozart received musical training from his father.
    c. Mozart's death occurred while he was composing his Requiem. (two situations)
    d. Mozart is played all over the world.
    e. Verdi achieved his first real success with *Nabucco* in 1842.
    f. Traditional opera consists of two modes of singing: recitative and aria.

2. What type of activity (culminating, etc.) or state does the progressive aspect express in the following sentences?
    a. The picture is hanging on the wall.
    b. We are losing the game.
    c. The phone is ringing.
    d. The sun is shining.
    e. I'm sitting right over there. (pointing to my seat at the bar)
    f. Where are you living?
    g. I am missing you more and more.

3. What is the difference in meaning between the following pairs of sentences?
    a. I hope someone can help me.
    a′. I am hoping someone can help me.
    b. I feel pain.
    b′. I am feeling pain.
    c. The plane took off.
    c′. The plane was taking off.
    d. You are silly.
    d′. You are being silly.
    e. I constantly receive junk mail.
    e′. I'm constantly receiving junk mail.
    f. What did you say?
    f′. What were you saying?
    g. I wrote my term paper.
    g′. I was writing my term paper.

Chapter 9

Grounding situations in time: Tense

9.0 Overview
9.1 Time and tense
9.2 Present time: Present tense and other tenses
9.3 From present anterior time to past times: Present perfect, past tense, and past perfect
9.4 From present posterior time to future times: Present prospective, future tense, and future prospective
9.5 Interplay of past and future times: Past prospective and future perfect
9.6 Summary

9.0 Overview

Like aspect, time as expressed by tense is a matter of viewing. Tense relates to the way a situation is located in time from the speaker's viewpoint. The moment of speaking serves as deictic centre and allows the speaker to refer to three time spheres: the present time sphere, the past time sphere as the time lying behind the speaker, and the future time sphere as the time lying ahead of the speaker. These three time spheres are therefore described as **deictic times**. Deictic times are typically expressed by the **simple tenses**: present tense, past tense, and future tense. The speaker may also develop notions of more **complex times** and express them as **complex tenses**. In this case the speaker adopts a viewpoint in one of the deictic times. By taking a backward-looking stance from a deictic viewpoint the speaker views **anterior times**, that is, times which occurred before a deictic time. By taking a forward-looking stance the speaker views **posterior times**, that is, times which follow a deictic time. In English, anterior times are expressed by one of the **perfect tenses** (present perfect, past perfect, and future perfect), as in *I have seen the Queen*; posterior times are expressed by various **prospective forms**, such as the *be going to*-form, as in *I was going to see the Queen*.

9.1 Time and tense

> *I'm just catching up with yesterday.*
> *By tomorrow I should be ready for today.*
> (Anonymous)

9.1.1 Time and mental spaces

Notions of time can be thought of and expressed in absolute and in relative terms. An absolute system of time would be that of calendar dates, as in *Entrance exams begin on September 15, 2007*. In everyday communication, however, we normally use relative systems of time, as in *Entrance exams begin in two weeks' time*. In our Western folk model of time we think of units of time and events as being lined up along a horizontal time line, or time axis. The fixed base for any location in time is the human observer engaging in communication. The observer/speaker occupies a position at the present moment of time: he faces the future lying in front of him on the time line and knows the past lying behind. As already mentioned in connection with time deixis in Chapter 5.3.1, units of time and events are normally understood as moving on the time line from the future via the present to the past, so that earlier events are located before later events.

Notions of time may be coded in language lexically (e.g. *today, last year, soon*) and/or grammatically by one of the tenses; the underlying model of time is the same. When a language has tense, this means that its speakers must express the time of each independent situation. Tense is thus a highly redundant marker, and not surprisingly many languages such as Chinese do not have tense.

As we saw in Chapter 3.2.2, the basic function of **tense** is to ground a situation in time. Tense, however, also relates to the situation or, more precisely, to the representation of a situation as a mental space in the speaker's and hearer's minds. We will therefore also consider some of the mental spaces that are relevant for notions of time and for situations.

The mental space that serves as the basis and starting point of any human interaction is known as the base space. The **base space** pertains to the deictic ground shared by speaker and hearer. It includes the space and time of interaction, the speech participants, and the contextual circumstances. Elements of the base space are normally taken for granted and therefore need not be made explicit in the discourse.

Part of the base space is the speech time within the ongoing discourse. **Speech time** (S) refers to the speaker's moment of speaking. The speech participants tacitly agree that this moment represents 'now'. Speech time thus provides a momentarily fixed time of orientation for anchoring the present time as well as the past time and the future time. Most importantly, speech time offers an anchor to locate the occurrence of situations in time.

The mental space surrounding a given situation is described as event space. Part of an event space is its time of occurrence, i.e. **event time** (E). As a rule, our focus of attention is on the situation described, but as we will see in the course of this chapter, it may also fall on the viewpoint from which the speaker can see the situation. The speaker normally occupies a **viewpoint** in the base space at the present time, but he may also "shift" his viewpoint to a past or a future time. The shifted viewpoint thereby serves as a reference point for accessing events in further time than the deictic times. This time of shifted viewing is therefore known as **reference time** (R).

Let us, by way of illustration, apply these notions to the following imaginary fragment of a discourse by a passenger missing her train:

(1) a. I *am* stuck here.
    b. When I *got* to the station,
    c. the train *had* already *left*.
    d. I*'ll be late* for my exam.

In (1a), the speaker opens a base space, which includes the present moment of speech, and an event space for the present situation she finds herself in. The speaker's focus of attention is on the situation described. Her viewpoint is in the base space, and the time of the situation (E) coincides with speech time (S).

In (1b), the speaker opens an event space for a past situation, which is now in focus. The speaker's viewpoint is still in the present base space.

In (1c), the speaker shifts her viewpoint to the past event of getting to the station. From this reference point (R) she looks backwards in order to situate an event (E) that is anterior to the past event. The speaker's focus may fall either on the reference time or the anterior event.

In (1d), the speaker resumes her viewpoint in the present base space and opens a space for an event that is lying ahead of her in the future. Here the focus is on the future situation.

The four situations described in (1) can be arranged on the time axis as illustrated in Figure 9.1. The heads indicate the observer, who looks into the future: the present is under her eyes (1a), the past lies behind (1b), and the future lies in front (1d). In viewing the anterior past event (1c), the observer looks back, and her line of vision is shown by the dotted line. The large box represents the base space, which includes the viewpoints at the speech time. The small box contains the shifted viewpoint serving as the reference point (R) for an anterior event.

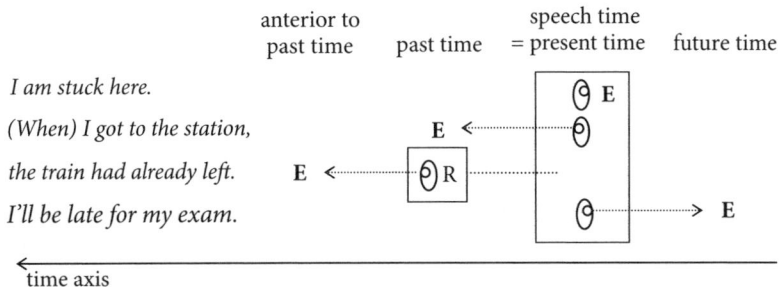

Figure 9.1. Sequence of event times on the time axis

9.1.2 Deictic and complex times: Simple and complex tenses

9.1.2.1 Deictic times: Simple tenses

> *Note to milkman:* Please leave no milk today.
> When I say today, I mean tomorrow, for I wrote
> this note yesterday … or is it today? *(Anonymous)*

Deictic times relate to speech time. This is the only moment of time that is readily available to us in our perception of time — in written language, things are more complex due to the possibility of reading a written text at a later point in time than when it was written. In spoken communication, speaker and hearer move through time, and the "I-here-now" situation changes with them. For example, the event described by *I'll have a cappuccino* is located in the future as seen from speech time; some moments later it would turn into a present event (*I am having a cappuccino*) and later into a past event (*I had a cappuccino*).

Whereas speech time always establishes the present time, event time may be either simultaneous with speech time, or be earlier or later than speech time. The three deictic times and their corresponding tenses are shown in Figure 9.2.

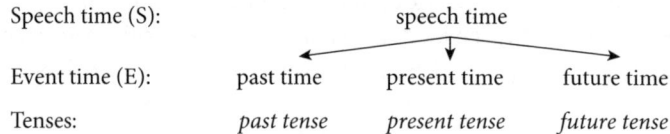

Figure 9.2. Deictic times: event times relative to speech time

The deictic times provide the basic system of three time spheres: the present, the past, and the future. They are expressed in English by **simple tenses**. The **present tense** locates a situation at, around, or including speech time, the **past tense** locates a situation at a time earlier than speech time, and the **future tense** locates a situation at a time later than speech time.

In addition to temporal information, the simple tenses convey information about the reality status of a situation. As illustrated in the model of evolving reality in Figure III.1 on p. 172, the present tense typically signals immediate reality of the situation; the past tense typically signals that the situation belongs to known reality; and the future tense indicates that the situation is to be seen in projected reality.

9.1.2.2 Complex times: Complex tenses

The three deictic times and the situations occurring at these times can serve as reference points for locating the times of further situations. The speaker shifts her viewpoint to the reference point and, from there, can either look backwards or forwards. By looking backwards from one of the three reference times, the speaker can locate *anterior* events relative to a reference time, and by looking forwards from a reference time, the speaker can locate *posterior* events. **Complex times** thus involve two temporal relations: a relation between speech time and a deictic time and a relation between the deictic time as a reference time and the time of an anterior or posterior event. Complex times are in English expressed by **complex tenses**: anterior times are expressed by the so-called perfect tenses, posterior times are expressed by several "prospective" forms, such as the *going to*-construction.

The six possibilities of conceptualising complex times via a reference time (R) and their corresponding complex tenses are diagrammed in Figure 9.3.

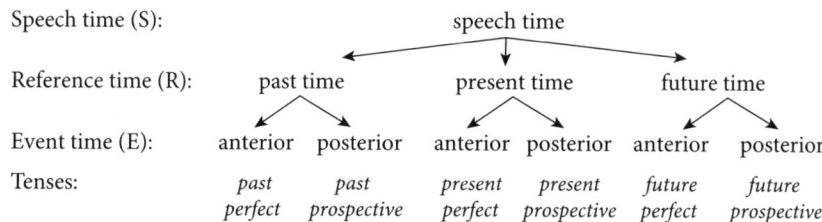

Figure 9.3. Complex times: event times relative to reference times

(i) *Anterior times: Perfect tenses*

Anterior times involve a backward-looking stance from a viewpoint at a reference time. They are expressed in English as **perfect tenses** (from Latin *perfectus* 'finished, completed'). As the term *perfect* suggests, situations described by a perfect tense occurred before a deictic reference time, which leaves the possibility that they still continue at or after reference time. The three perfect tenses are illustrated in the following examples.

(2) a. Our train *has* just left. [*present perfect*]
 b. Our train *had* left when we arrived. [*past perfect*]
 c. Our train *will have* left by the time we get there. [*future perfect*]

All three anterior situations display the same basic conceptual configuration. An event is seen as occurring before a deictic reference time: before the present in (2a), before the past in (2b), and before the future in (2c). These three anterior time configurations are represented in Figure 9.4. The ellipses indicate time spheres, the heads represent the speaker's viewpoint, the dotted arrows pointing from right to left trace the line of vision from reference time (R) back to event time (E), and S represents speech time.

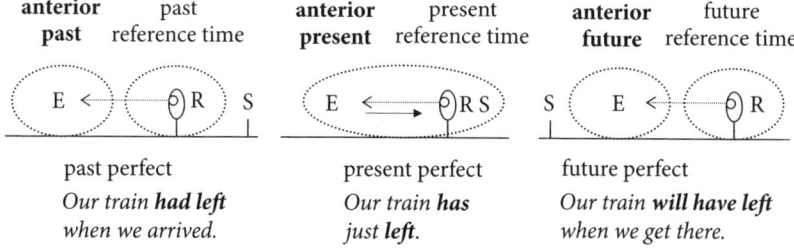

Figure 9.4. Anterior times expressed by perfect tenses

The time configuration described by the present perfect is unique among the anterior times in that it involves only one time sphere and a relation from event time to speech time, indicated in Fig. 9.4 by the solid arrow. The present perfect in sentence (2a) makes us see the past event of the train having left with respect to its present relevance, i.e. in the sense that there is no train available at present. The unique status of the present perfect is due to its present reference time: its immediacy makes the present the more prominent time — as opposed to the remoteness of non-present, i.e. past and future times.

The present perfect has both temporal and aspectual meaning: the temporal meaning of a situation's anteriority and an aspectual meaning with respect to the inherent structure of the overall situation. The anterior situation is part of the overall situation. In many grammars of English the present perfect is therefore treated as a form of aspect. However, the past perfect and the future perfect do, as a rule, not express aspect, but are normally understood in a purely temporal sense: they refer to the anterior time of a situation relative to a reference time. The overall commonality of the English perfect forms is thus to be seen in their function as tense markers.

(ii) *Posterior times: Prospective forms*
Anterior times have exact mirror images in posterior times. **Posterior times** involve a forward-looking, or prospective, stance from a viewpoint at one of the deictic reference times. They are in English coded by **prospective forms** consisting of grammaticised lexical items, in particular *be going to* and *be about to*, as in (3):

(3) a. *I'm going to* leave tomorrow. [*present prospective*]
    b. *I was going to* leave yesterday. [*past prospective*]

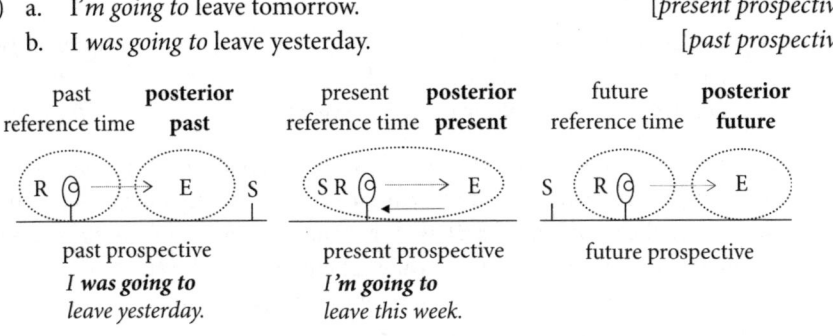

Figure 9.5. Posterior times expressed by prospective forms

As with the perfect tenses, prospective forms relate the time of an event to a deictic reference time. In sentences (3a) and (3b), the speaker forms an intention at reference time about leaving at a later time. As with the present perfect in (2a), situations described in the present prospective are felt to be of current relevance. The future prospective is rare though not impossible; therefore, no sentence is given for the future prospective in Figure 9.5. A sentence such as ?*I'll be going to leave* sounds odd: it predicts the strange situation of my making up my mind to leave at a later point in time.

9.1.3 The system of times and tenses

The system of the times coded by tenses in English and the mental spaces they belong to is presented in Table 9.1. All notions of time and tense are determined in function of one and the same base space and speech time (S), indicated as "zero time" (t_0). Event time (E) is present in each time pattern, and reference time (R) is characteristic of complex times. The units that are focused upon are printed in bold. The combination of speech time, event time, and reference time allows us to distinguish nine patterns of time and eight tenses.

Table 9.1. Patterns of time and tense

		t_{-2}	t_{-1}	t_0	t_{+1}	t_{+2}
	Deictic times: simple tenses					
Present	*Our train is leaving.*			E S		
Past	*Our train left early.*		E	S		
Future	*Our train will leave in an hour.*			S	E	
	Complex times: complex tenses					
	Anterior times: perfect tenses					
Present Perfect	*Our train has left already.*		E	R S		
Past Perfect	*Our train had left at 10 am.*	E	R	S		
Future Perfect	*Our train will have left by 10 am.*			S	E	R
	Posterior times: prospective forms					
Present Prospective	*I'm going to leave.*			S R	E	
Past Prospective	*I was going to leave.*	R	(E)	S (E)	(E)	
Future Prospective				S	R	E

(t = time, S = speech time, R = reference time, E = event time; bold print = focus)

The three deictic times are all characterised by the speaker's viewpoint in the base space (S) and the focus on the situation (**E**). As a result, the situations focused upon by the past and future tenses are seen as being detached from present time.

Complex times are characterised by a reference time (R) linking an event via the reference time to the base space. In the present perfect the speaker adopts a viewpoint in the base space, hence its reference time coincides with speech time and is focused upon (**R**). The present perfect thus describes present situations, as can be seen from the possibility of using the adjunct *now* in (4a), but not in (4b).

(4) a. Our train has left *now*.
    b. Our train had left *at 10 am* / **now*.

In sentence (4b) in the past perfect the speaker cannot focus on speech time, but may either focus on event time or on reference time: *at 10 am* may specify event time, i.e. the time when the train left (i.e. already before we arrived some time later, say, at 10.15 am), or it may specify reference time, i.e. the exact time when we arrived at the station (at 10 am) after the train had already left (at, say, 9.45 am). In Table 9.1, this ambiguity with the past and future perfect is indicated by the bold print of both event time (**E**) and reference time (**R**).

Like the present perfect, the present prospective describes a present situation, which can be seen from its co-occurrence with the adjunct *now* in (5a).

(5) a. I'm going to take the train *now*.
    b. I was going to take the train *yesterday/today/now/tomorrow*.

The past prospective as in (5b) may refer to an event anywhere in posterior time: in the past, the present or the future. In Table 9.1 this openness in interpretation is indicated by parentheses put around the three event times (**E**).

The tenses listed in Table 9.1 provide the inventory of the grammatical forms available in English for coding the time of a situation. The tenses only provide an approximate match to notions of time. Yet, we assume that the correspondences of times and tenses are, in general, valid, i.e. present situations are ideally coded by means of the present tense and, conversely, the present tense ideally refers to the present time of a situation. Whenever time and tense do not match, these mismatches are, of course, in need of explanation.

9.2 Present time: Present tense and other tenses

> *The distinction between past, present and future is only an illusion, however persistent.* (Albert Einstein)

9.2.1 Present time

The notion of present time differs depending on the basic aspectual class of the situation, i.e. whether the situation is bounded or unbounded.

9.2.1.1 *Bounded present situations (S = E): Simple present*

The present time of a bounded situation should, properly speaking, coincide with speech time, i.e. the time needed to utter the sentence describing the situation. However, most events cannot be thought of as falling exactly within the boundaries of this short span of time. An event such as going upstairs takes longer than speech time, and hence we cannot say **Dad goes up the flight of stairs*. On the other hand, a punctual event such as a glass breaking in my hand is shorter than the time necessary for describing it; hence it cannot, under normal circumstances, be expressed as **The glass breaks in my hand*, but only as *The glass broke in my hand*. It is obvious that the conceptual boundaries of most events do not neatly coincide with the temporal boundaries of uttering the speech act describing the event. Therefore in English we cannot, as a rule, use the simple present to refer to a bounded event in the present time. Yet, there are a few types of bounded events whose boundaries are conceptualised as identical with those of speech time and which are therefore expressed in the simple present. In the schematic drawing below this situation is indicated by the boundaries of speech time (S) matching those of event time (E).

(6)   ⊢ S
                                             E ⊔

a. I *admit* that was a mistake.
b. Here *comes* the bride.
c. There *goes* my dream of an acting career.
d. I *beat* two eggs like this, *add* them to the mixture, and then *heat* it up.
e. Joe *steps* up to the plate. Now he *swings* at the ball, and he *misses*! He *tries* again, but it's another miss. Now *is* the third ball, and he *hits* it. It's a homerun! He's on first, now he's on second, third, and he's safe.

The speaker of sentence (6a) does not describe a situation but, by uttering the sentence, performs the very act the sentence describes. Such utterances are known as performative speech acts, or simply performatives. **Performatives** are characterised by the simple present tense and a verb that explicitly names the speech act such as *order*, *promise*, *swear*, *suggest*, *apologise*, etc. The communicative success of a performative speech act crucially depends on its full verbalisation; hence it needs to be uttered as a whole so that the boundaries of the utterance and those of event time necessarily coincide.

Sentences (6b) and (6c) are not descriptions of situations either but have a presentational function: they draw attention to the present deictic situation, as witnessed by the deictic forms *here* and *there*.

Sentence (6d) is also used in an explicitly deictic situation, as indicated by the deictic phrase *like this*, which refers to a gesture accompanying the cook's demonstration. The cook presents his explanations as if they exactly coincided with his actions, but his explanations in fact introduce his actions.

Sentence (6e) illustrates the reverse situation: a sports commentator gives a live commentary of a series of events at a baseball game which happened right before he reported them. The use of the simple present conveys to the listening audience the feeling of being at the game and experiencing the action first hand.

With the exception of performatives, the duration of a bounded event thus only approximates that of speech time, i.e. event time and speech time are subjectively construed as coinciding. In all these situations, the speaker views the "instantaneous" event as a bounded one.

9.2.1.2 *Unbounded present situations (S ⊂ E)*

Situations that hold at present time are typically unbounded and include or surround speech time, in other words, here speech time is included in event time. The following four sentences illustrate unbounded present situations:

(7)   E   S

a. I'*m fixing* dinner now.   [*accomplishing activity*]
b. I *love* spaghetti.   [*indefinitely lasting state*]
c. Spaghetti *cooks* in eight minutes.   [*everlasting state*]
d. I *eat* spaghetti every day.   [*habitual state*]

Sentence (7a) in the present progressive describes an accomplishing activity (see Chapter 8.3.2). This unbounded event includes the present moment of speaking. Unbounded events like *fixing dinner* imply a beginning, various sub-events, and an end. This explains why we can single out any present moment of the overall activity, as in *I'm fixing dinner right now*. As we saw in the discussion of the progressive aspect in Chapter 8.1.2, an activity described in the progressive may also be suspended, i.e. it may not occur at the present moment and only surround speech time. For example, *I'm fixing dinner now* may be said when I am talking on the phone, and *I am reading a great novel currently* may even be said when I have not had the time to touch the book for a number of days.

Indefinitely lasting states as in (7b) are unbounded and unchanging by definition. Thus, my craving for spaghetti held in the past, holds at the present moment, and will probably continue into the future. Since a state is homogeneous and every moment of it is the same, it would not be informative to single out any specific moment of it by saying **I love spaghetti at the moment*. Since all the component states are identical, the present moment of a state can metonymically stand for the whole indefinite duration of the state, i.e. the present tense is well-motivated to describe states.

Everlasting states as in (7c) are timeless situations (see Chapter 8.7.3). They pertain to the way the world in general is structured. Assertions about such general situations are also valid at the present moment and therefore described in the simple present. Many genres such as scholarly discourse are thus mainly written in the simple present.

Regularly occurring habitual events as in (7d) are seen in English as states and expressed in the simple present (see Chapter 8.7.2). In fact, all "non-instantaneous" events expressed in the simple present are typically understood as habitual (see Chapter 3.1.3). Their regular occurrence makes us see habitual events as a person's or object's property. Thus, a person who eats spaghetti every day has the property of lacking a refined taste, and a person who is always smiling, as in (8a), has the property of having a cheerful disposition. At a very general level, habits are, therefore, construed as states, but their internal composition of individual events may still show up. Thus, we may relate individual occurrences of a habit, as in (8a), to another event, as in (8b).

(8) a. Sarah is always smiling.
    b. Sarah is always smiling when I see her.

9.2.1.3 Deictic shifts of present situations

Certain present situations may be conceived of as occurring in a deictic time sphere other than the present. Such deictic shifts in time tend to create special communicative effects. In the examples under (9), the speaker portrays a present situation as if it occurred in the past time:

(9) a. What *was* the topic of your paper?
    b. What *was* your name again?

The past tense in sentence (9a) may refer to a time in the past when the paper was assigned, but it may also refer to the present time. A professor may ask her student about the topic of a paper which he has been assigned to write on but has not yet handed in. Instead of using the present tense, *What is the topic of your paper*, the professor mentally shifts to the moment in the past when the topic was first agreed upon. This deictic shift has the effect of making her question sound less immediate and possibly less threatening.

We may also use the past tense with present situations that are not associated with the past time. Question (9b) does not refer to an earlier time when the person had a different name. Here, the past tense is used to create a distance from an obligation in order to attenuate a potential face threat. The past tense question sounds more polite than its present tense counterpart, *What is your name again?* The strategy of using the past tense is particularly prevalent in speech acts that impose obligations, such as *I thought you might like this present* or *I wondered if you could do me a favour*. The face threat inherent in such speech acts could be further mitigated by expressing them as unbounded situations, i.e. by using the past progressive, as in *I was wondering if you could do me a favour*.

The speaker or writer may also locate a present situation in the future, as in the following examples:

(10) a. The manuals which come with the computer *will* explain how to use it.
 b. Boys *will* be boys.

The author of sentence (10a) could also have used the present tense *explain*, but has decided to focus on the future user of the computer. Sentence (10b), *Boys will be boys*, was already discussed in Chapter 2.3.1 as an instance of a colloquial tautology, meaning something like 'boys are unruly'. The use of *will* alludes to our prediction that things will stay the way they are, i.e. to projected reality. *Will* is, however, also used as a modal verb expressing an assessment of probability (see Chapter 10.3.2.2). The sentence may, thus, also be understood in the modal sense of potential behaviour, and in this interpretation it may also be said in describing a present situation, in which boys are misbehaving.

9.3 From present anterior time to past times: Present perfect, past tense, and past perfect

English divides the time continuum from the present to the remote past into three time spheres of increasing distance from the present time. In Figure 9.6, the time spheres corresponding to the three tenses in question are represented as ellipses. The dotted arrows indicate the retrospective stance taken in viewing anterior times.

The degrees of distance from the present reflect the speaker's subjective view and are not to be understood in absolute terms. Objectively, an event described in the past tense may have occurred very recently, as in *We did Hamlet last week*, while an event in the present perfect may have occurred a much longer time ago, as in *Shakespeare has written inimitable plays*. Subjectively, however, the situation in the present perfect is felt to be mentally linked to the present time and hence closer to it than the one described in the past tense.

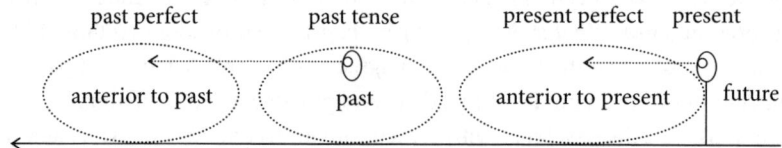

Figure 9.6. Increasing distance from the present to the past

It should be noted that British and American English often differ, particularly in the present perfect, which is noticeably less widespread in American English. We will mainly address British usage in this chapter.

9.3.1 Anterior situations viewed from the present viewpoint: Present perfect

The **present perfect** is a complex tense that involves a backward-looking stance from a viewpoint at the present moment towards an anterior situation or an anterior phase of a situation. This viewing arrangement has consequences for properties of the present perfect and its uses in English. Due to its intricacies and the difficulties it usually presents for learners of English as a foreign language, we will discuss the English present perfect more extensively.

9.3.1.1 *Meaning of the present perfect*

The present perfect is characterised by three properties which determine its general meaning: focus on the present time, current relevance, and indefiniteness.

The first property of the present perfect, its *focus on the present time*, was already touched upon in Section 9.1.2.2. The present perfect refers to the time during which a state or activity holds and which includes speech time. Sentences in the present perfect are therefore compatible with present-time adjuncts, as shown in (4a), and present tense sentences, as in (11a), but not with past tense sentences, as in (11b):

(11) a. Our train has just left and *now we're stranded here*.
      b. *Our train has just left and *we missed it*.

The auxiliary verb *have* in the present perfect grounds the situation in the present time. *Have*'s original sense of 'possession' is still discernable with transitive verbs. Thus, *I have written the letter* originally meant something like 'I have the letter written', i.e. 'I have it in its written state'. The grammaticised auxiliary *have* has the meaning of 'existence', as in French *il y a* 'there is', literally 'it there has'. The state expressed by *have* connects the present moment with the anterior situation. The anterior situation is described by a past participle, *written* or *left* in (11a). Past participles are atemporal and do not ground the situation on their own. As a result, the anterior situation (of my having written the letter or the train having left) is no longer seen as continuing through time; instead, it is scanned in summary fashion so that all its component states are viewed in their accumulated form. We thus see the whole process of letter-writing from its first line to its finished form or the process of the train leaving at once.

The second property of the present perfect, the *current relevance* of the anterior situation, is in fact the reason for looking back at the situation in the first place. We would not care to look back at some earlier event unless we felt it was somehow still "relevant", as in the case of missing one's train in (11a). The following exchange illustrates the reasoning process involved in the notion of current relevance:

(12) a. Dad: "I'm looking for my glasses. *Has* anybody *seen* them?"
 b. Son: "You*'ve* probably *left* them in the car."

Dad has apparently lost his glasses. One possible clue for finding them might be that someone has seen them. Having seen the glasses would be a relevant event for the present state and is therefore expressed in the present perfect in question (12a) — in American English this can also be said in the simple past. The son provides another potentially relevant event for the present state: Dad may have left the glasses in the car, where they may still be found. This anterior situation is therefore also expressed in the present perfect in (12b). A reply by the son in the past tense (*Probably you left them in the car again*) would, of course, also be possible but it would have a different effect. Notice that the reasoning process with the present perfect goes from the present state of affairs back to an earlier situation, which may have caused it or may explain the present state, and from there back again to the present. There may be many preceding situations that could be relevant for a given present state of affairs. However, only those past situations which the speaker subjectively views as relevant to 'now' are construed in the present perfect. The particular kind of relevance an anterior situation has for the present is thus a matter of inference.

The third property of the present perfect, the anterior situation's *indefiniteness*, follows from focusing one's attention on its present relevance. Our attention is normally only focused on one entity at a time, hence other aspects of the situation, especially its exact temporal occurrence, recede into the background. The present perfect is thus characterised by an overall indefiniteness and therefore incompatible with adjuncts that specify a definite setting. The indefiniteness of the anterior situation is particularly noticeable when a discourse topic is introduced, i.e. when a mental space for an anterior situation is opened, as in the following *yes/no*-question:

(13) a. *Have* you ever *been* to Korea? [*indefinite*]
 b. Yes, I *have been* to Korea many times. [*indefinite*]
 c. Yes, I *was* at the International Cognitive Linguistics
   Conference in Seoul in 2005. [*definite*]

Answer (13b) stays within the indefinite mental space, while answer (13c) elaborates this mental space by shifting to a definite event in the past and, concomitantly, to the past tense (for past time and past tense see 9.3.2 below).

Figure 9.7. Indefinite anterior situation and definite past situation

9.3.1.2 *Anterior situation types: Uses of the present perfect*

Depending on the type of situation, the backward-looking stance from the viewpoint at speech time gives rise to different conceptual configurations, different inferences, and different uses of the present perfect.

9.3.1.2.1 *Anterior bounded events and lasting states: Present perfect non-progressive*
(i) *Anterior bounded telic events: Resultative perfect*

The notion of telicity refers to the inherent definitive end-point of an event. In Chapter 8.2 we distinguished two types of bounded telic events: accomplishments and achievements. When a bounded telic event occurs anterior to the present moment, it must of necessity be completed. An observer who looks back at a completed event will notice its end-point first because it is closest to her on the time line. The completion of an event is also that phase which the observer will, for obvious reasons, be most interested in: it encapsulates its resultant outcome. The present perfect that is used to express this conceptual configuration is known as a **resultative perfect**.

The schematic drawings given with each type of perfect are meant to illustrate their composite meaning. The accumulated anterior event, which is expressed as a past participle, is represented as a bold line; in the sentences under (14), these are *repaired* and *passed*. Their build-up phase is drawn as a line of increasing height. The state expressed by *have* stretches from event time (E) to speech time (S) and possibly beyond. With telic events, i.e. with the resultative perfect, its meaning is that of a resultant state.

(14)
   a. Grandpa *has repaired* his old tractor. [*accomplishment*]
   b. Grandma *has passed* the driving test. [*achievement*]

The resultant state of a bounded telic event is not explicitly stated but entailed, i.e. it is "logically" concluded. The accomplishment in (14a) entails that the tractor is now in working order, and the achievement in (14b) entails that grandma is now entitled to drive a car. Entailments cannot be cancelled: thus we cannot say *#Grandpa has repaired his old tractor, but it doesn't work*. In addition to their entailments, resultative perfects also invite implicatures. An implicature that (14a) might invite is that the tractor is now ready to be driven. This assumption can be cancelled, as in *Grandpa has repaired his old tractor, but he can't drive it yet unless he gets petrol.*

(ii) *Anterior bounded atelic situations: Inferential perfect*
Bounded atelic situations are activities, acts, and temporary states. These situations lack a definitive end-point. When they occur anterior to speech time, they therefore do not entail a specific resultant state: they have merely stopped. The time of the anterior situation, or the beginning of a situation, is indefinite: the currently relevant content of the state therefore needs to be inferred. The perfect which describes this situation is sometimes described as the "experiential perfect". However, since its main characteristic is inference based on indefiniteness, we will refer to it as **inferential perfect**. The present-tense verb *have* profiles a state that begins at the time when the event itself is over (E) and continues up to the present moment (S).

(15)   E ⊢ inferred state ⟲ S

    a. The nurse *has cuddled* the baby. [anterior activity]
    b. The baby *has burped*. [anterior act]
    c. *Have* you ever *been imprisoned*? [anterior state]

The nurse's cuddling in (15a) may, looked at retrospectively, explain the baby's present state of radiant happiness. A baby's burp after drinking a bottle of milk in (15b) may indicate to its caregiver that it has relieved itself of stomach gas and is now in a state where it can be put to bed. Question (15c) may be asked by an immigration officer in order to obtain relevant information about a person before granting him a visa.

Notice that the inferential perfect is incompatible with definite time adjuncts. If the event time is specified, the situations are understood differently. Events become definite and are described in the simple past tense, as in *I started my new job last month* as opposed to *I've started my new job*. Temporary states are understood as continuing up to the present (see continuative perfect below). Thus, *I've lived in Baghdad* (without a time specification) invites the inference that I no longer live there, while *I've lived in Baghdad since the Gulf War* (with a time specification) means that I am still living there.

(iii) *Anterior recent situations: Recent perfect*
A special type of anterior atelic situation are situations that occur immediately before the present moment. These situations almost coincide with speech time and are naturally felt to be of current relevance. The perfect describing immediately preceding situations is sometimes described as "perfect of recent past"; we will refer to it for short as **recent perfect**. The immediacy of past situations needs to be explicitly signalled. This is achieved either by adjuncts indicating recency such as *just, already, now, so far, up to now*, etc., as in (16a), or by adjuncts indicating a time sphere which includes both the time of the anterior situation and speech time, as in (16b).

(16)
    a. I've *just* talked to my lawyer.
    b. I've talked to my lawyer *this morning*.

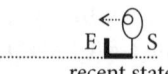
recent state

The shared and unfinished time sphere 'this morning' in (16b) is marked by the demonstrative proximal determiner *this*. Time units such as *last night* or *three days ago* fall outside an imagined present time sphere and are therefore incompatible with the immediate perfect, as in **I've talked to my lawyer last night*. In British English, and even more so in American English, anterior recent situations as in (16a) can also be expressed in the simple past, but not when they belong to the same time sphere, as in (16b).

The recent perfect is also often used in news reporting, as in *The Prime Minister has said he will not seek a fourth term in office*, a usage that is also known as "hot news perfect".

(iv) *Anterior phase of states and habits: Continuative perfect*
A situation may also include the observer's viewpoint. In this case it is not the situation as a whole that is anterior to speech time, but it is the initial phase of a situation that is anterior to its later phase. This configuration of the **continuative perfect** applies to present states or habits. Their duration up to the present must, therefore, be indicated by a time adjunct expressing duration — otherwise the whole situation, and not just an earlier phase of it, is understood to be anterior to the present moment, i.e. we would not be dealing with the continuative perfect, but with the inferential perfect. The time reference may take two forms: in looking back from his viewpoint, the observer may specify either the beginning of the state or habit or its duration up to now. The former specification is made by *since* plus a time reference to a point from which we can compute the period of time up to now; while the latter specification is made by stating the period of time up to now, from which we can compute its beginning. Sentences (17a) and (17b) illustrate these two construals with a continuative state, sentences (17c) and (17d) with a habit.

(17)
    a. We have been engaged *since Valentine's Day*.   [*beginning of state*]
    b. We have been engaged *for over a year now*.   [*period of state*]
    c. I've have worked for BA *since 2002*.   [*beginning of habit*]
    d. I've worked for BA *for six years now*.   [*period of habit*]

The continuative perfect in these sentences describes a persistent situation from its beginning to the present moment. It thus groups the anterior phase of a continuative state together with anterior situations. Other languages, such as German, group the anterior phase of a continuative state with present states. The situations described in (17a) and (17b) are thus expressed in the simple present (*Wir sind seit Valentinstag / über einem Jahr verlobt* 'we are engaged since Valentine's day / for over a year').

9.3.1.2.2 *Unbounded events and temporary states: Present perfect progressive*

The present perfect progressive combines the notions of 'progression' and 'anteriority to the present'. This means that the current relevance of an anterior situation or the anterior phase of a situation derives from focusing on its continuous or interrupted duration, not on its resultant state or its present continuation. As a result, the present perfect progressive gives rise to different inferences than the present perfect non-progressive. We only need to distinguish between two uses of the present perfect progressive: the inferential perfect progressive describing anterior unbounded events and the continuative perfect progressive describing temporary states.

(i) *Anterior unbounded events: Inferential perfect progressive*
The conceptual differences between the different types of anterior unbounded events are minimal: they are all activities viewed internally in their continuous or interrupted progression and occur at an indefinite time prior to the present moment. The *inferential perfect progressive* refers to the inferred state following an anterior unbounded event. Inferences about the current relevance of the unbounded event are therefore drawn from focusing on its durational phase. In the drawing, the durational phase of the event is indicated by the heavy line within the restricted viewing frame imposed by the progressive. The present perfect progressive is typically used with unbounded activities, as in (18a) and (18b), more rarely with accomplishing activities, as in (18c).

(18)
  a. I *have been working* all day.
  b. I *have been trying* to get Sally on the phone.
  c. Grandpa *has been repairing* his old tractor.

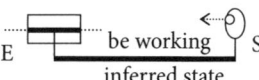

The progressive in sentence (18a) focuses on the duration of an activity; it therefore tends to evoke the idea of long and hard work, which may explain my present state of exhaustion as an indirect result of my activity. The non-progressive, *I have worked the whole day*, by contrast, focuses on the end-point of the event and may refer to a direct result in the form of a report that I have finished writing at the end of the day.

The progressive in sentence (18b) suggests several vain attempts at getting in touch with a person and invites the implicature that the message is important. The non-progressive, *I have tried to get Sally on the phone*, by contrast, may involve no more than one failed attempt of calling.

The progressive in sentence (18c) focuses on the build-up phase of a telic event. In focusing on the unbounded activity, the sentence strongly suggests that Grandpa's repair work has *not* been completed yet — otherwise the speaker would have chosen the present perfect, *Grandpa has repaired his old tractor*. Looked at retrospectively, the current relevance of this activity resides in its state of inferred incompletion and gives rise to further contextual implicatures. For example, the sentence may be uttered in response to enquiries such as "I haven't seen grandpa all day. What has he been doing?"

(ii) *Anterior phase of temporary states and habits: Continuative perfect progressive*
Like indefinitely lasting states and habits, temporary states and habits may include the present viewpoint, from where the observer is looking back at an anterior phase of this situation. As with all situations in the progressive, the focus of the *continuative perfect progressive* is on the durational phase. With temporary states and habits, the period of time they last is typically specified by adjuncts of duration, such as *over a year* in (19a) or *for the past 18 months* in (19b). Since the temporary state or habit reaches up to the present, its duration is in fact identical with that of the continuative state described by *have* and is therefore necessarily of current relevance. Its beginning, on the other hand, is defocused and need not be specified — in contrast to the continuative perfect non-progressive, where the beginning of the state or habit has to be specified, as was shown in the examples under (17).

(19)
    a. We've *been living* in tents for over a year.
    b. I've *been looking* at computers for the past 18 months.

The progressive in the temporary state (19a) implies that we are still living in tents and at the same time draws attention to the extremity of such living conditions. The non-progressive construal, *We've lived in tents for over a year*, does not imply that we are still living in tents. The progressive in the temporary habit (19b) suggests that I have regularly been looking for a computer until now and hence not yet found the right one.

9.3.2 Past time: Past tense and present tense

The past time is the deictic time preceding speech time. A situation that occurred in the past time is described in the past tense if the speaker's focus is on the past situation — if her focus is on its relevance for the present, the present perfect is used. The **past tense** grounds events and states in the present speech situation and locates them in past time as viewed from the present. As in the case of the present perfect, this viewing arrangement has consequences for the meaning of the past tense.

9.3.2.1 *Meaning of the past tense*
The past tense is characterised by three properties that distinguish it from the present perfect: focus on the past time, detachment from the present, and definiteness.

    The first property of the past tense, its *focus on the past time*, needs to be seen in contrast to the present time. We are mainly concerned with immediate reality, i.e. our mental spaces revolve around the base space. The present base space therefore usually serves as the starting point before we switch our focus of attention to mental spaces for the past. The following fragment of a discourse illustrates the switch from a focus on the present situation to a focus on a past event and back again to the present.

(20) a. Do you *know* Harry? He's *just rolling* in money.
 b. He *worked* for General Motors for 25 years.
 c. And now they've *given* him a golden handshake.

The present tense sentences in (20a) open a present-time mental space about the referent Harry and a qualifying characteristic of his. Once this mental space has been opened, it can be elaborated by adding further details. Sentence (20b) adds background information about Harry's past. This means that the speaker switches his focus to the past and opens a past-time space. At this point, the speaker could have stayed in the past space and talked, for example, about working conditions at that time. In fact, in sentence (20c) he switches his focus back to the present-time space, which allows him to relate the past event retrospectively to the present time.

The focus on the past situation relates to the second property of the past tense: its *detachment from the present*. There is a time gap between a past situation and the present, i.e. past situations are felt to be "exclusive" of the present time. Thus, the situation talked about in the past tense in (20b) is interpreted as being over, i.e. we assume that Harry no longer works for General Motors. Notice, however, that this interpretation is only implicated, since we can cancel it: *Harry worked for General Motors for 25 years, and he still has a part-time job there*. A past situation that is presented in the past tense and taken to be over is not judged on its relevance for the present. This is in strong contrast to a situation which is presented in the present perfect, like the golden handshake in (20c), which explains Harry's prosperity.

The dissociation of a past situation from the present relates to the third property of the past tense: its *definiteness*. Past situations are part of known reality and hence are typically seen as definite. The past tense has therefore been described as a "search instruction" for finding clues of definiteness in the linguistic or situational context. As is well-known, the definiteness of a past situation relates not only to its event time, which is often specified by past-time adjuncts such as *yesterday* or *a minute ago*, but also to its referents and the setting as well.

9.3.2.2 *Bounded past situations (E before S): Simple past*

Bounded situations, in particular events, are ideally suited to be located in the past time. A bounded past situation is a definite whole that is completed or over at some point in the past and then makes room for another situation to succeed it on the time line. Past situations therefore tend to form a series of events, typically in narratives. The following fragment is part of a narrative quoted in Labov & Waletzky (1967):

(21)

I *grabbed* his arm and I *twisted* it up behind his back and when I *let* go his arm there *was* a knife on the table and he just *picked* it up and *let* me have it and I *started* bleeding like a pig.

The individual events described iconically reflect their sequential order of occurrence (see Chapter 3.3.1). It is therefore not necessary to mention their order explicitly; their coordination by *and* is sufficiently clear to interpret the events as successive. Labov has argued that even two sentences describing events in the simple past are interpreted sequentially and establish a (mini)-narrative. In this excerpt, the power of the principle of sequential order can be seen in the sentence *there was a knife on the table*, which describes a state as if it was an event following the preceding *when*-clause, *when I let go his arm*. In the sequence of events, only the first event is deictically situated in the past relative to speech time; the subsequent events are situated as later relative to their preceding event as a reference point.

9.3.2.3 Unbounded past situations ($E_2 \subset E_1$)

Unbounded past situations, i.e. activities in the progressive, states and habits, naturally have a focus on their duration. One of their typical functions therefore is that of providing a background for one or more bounded events to occur, be it explicitly or only implicitly. This "incidence schema" is illustrated in the following beginning of a story about an earthquake.

(22) a. I *was living* in a trailer in Anchorage during the Good Friday earthquake,
 b. and when the earthquake *started* it *sounded* like a subway train approaching a station.
 c. Everything in the trailer *shook* and since I *was* in the kitchen I *kept* trying to push the fridge back where it *belonged*.
 d. My wife and mother-in-law *were screaming* in the front room,
 e. but I *could* not get to them due to the rolling and pitching.

Sentence (22a) describes a temporary state in the past progressive that sets the stage, i.e. opens a mental space for the story. During the state's duration, several bounded events occurred: an earthquake started (22b) and had specific effects in the house (22c). Sentence (22d) provides another unbounded activity: the women were screaming. This activity serves as the background for the event occurring in (22e).

The incidence of a bounded event in an unbounded situation is, of course, a perfect example of figure and ground. Typically, the (back)ground event is established in (22a) and (22d) before the figure event takes place in (22b,c) and (22e). This is in line with our general expectation about stories: we want to be informed about its setting first before we are given the narrative events.

It is in the nature of unbounded situations that they cannot appear in succession, but only simultaneously with others within the same complex situation. They lack boundaries which allow us to tell where one situation ends and the next one starts. Compare the different meanings conveyed by coordinated unbounded activities in the past (23a) as opposed to coordinated bounded activities (23b and c):

(23) a. We *were having* port and *listening* to music (when suddenly the door slammed shut).
 b. We *had* port and *listened* to music.
 c. We *went* for a swim and *did* some shopping.

Our drinking of port and listening to music in (23a) jointly provide the background for some event. The bounded activities in the past non-progressive in (23b), by contrast, allow for two different interpretations: they may be seen as occurring simultaneously or successively. These two interpretations are based on our knowledge of the world: we may drink wine and listen to music either at the same time or one after the other. The bounded activities described in sentence (23c), on the other hand, are normally only interpreted in the sense of succession. Our world knowledge tells us that under normal circumstances, swimming and shopping are not done at the same time, although we may, of course, imagine such a situation.

In view of their functions in discourse we may now reanalyse the differences in meaning between past activities described in the non-progressive and the progressive, which we already touched upon in Chapter 8.4.2. There we found that the non-progressive construal in sentences such as *I talked to Mr Green* sounds more factual and that the progressive construal as in *I was talking to Mr Green* sounds more casual. Such sentences do, of course, not occur in isolation, but are embedded within a discourse. The bounded past event *I talked to Mr Green* is seen within a sequence of narrative events similar to those described above in (21). Due to its completion in known reality, the bounded event is therefore interpreted as factual. The unbounded past event *I was talking to Mr Green*, by contrast, is seen as an inconclusive event. Due to the different salience of figure and ground, it is interpreted as less salient and hence as casual.

9.3.2.4 *Deictic shifts of past situations*

Certain past situations may be portrayed as occurring in the present time. This deictic shift in time produces an effect of immediacy. The following examples illustrate this well-known use of the simple present for past events:

(24) a. The day finally arrived: Forrest Gump *dies* and *goes* to Heaven.
 b. September 1st — Germany *invades* Poland.
 September 3rd — Britain, France, Australia and New Zealand *declare* war on Germany.
 September 17th — Soviet Union *invades* Poland.
 c. Reichenbach (1947: 296) *claims* that "the number of recognized grammatical tenses in English is only 6".
 d. **Stranded Britons *fly* home**.
 Six planeloads of Britons *stranded* abroad after the collapse of the travel company *arrived* back at Manchester last night.

The two sentences in (24a) are the beginning of a humorous narrative of imaginary events. The first sentence in the past tense indicates that the story is situated in the past. In shifting to the **narrative present** in the ensuing discourse, the narrator presents the events as if they are occurring in the present time and thus achieves a more immediate and lively effect.

The **historic present** in the sentences under (24b) is used to describe the chronology of important historical events at the beginning of World War II in 1939. History is part of our socio-cultural heritage, and important historical events may still be considered relevant today. The use of the historic present is characteristic of the genre of chronology and could be inserted into another text as a kind of reference.

Some domains tend to be conceptualised in a timeless or permanent present. Thus, research and discoveries in the sciences are part of the ongoing scholarly debate irrespective of the time when they were made. Hence, Reichenbach's claim in (24c) is presented in what might be called a "**scientific present**". In fact, all scientific writing tends to be in the timeless present.

Headlines of news items such as (24d) are often in the present tense, while the story itself is presented in the past tense. Headlines form the abstract of a story, and the use of the "**summary present**" in this example suggests immediacy and actuality.

9.3.3 Anterior situations viewed from a past viewpoint: Past perfect

The conception of a situation anterior to the past requires an intermediate reference time. This is achieved by shifting the viewpoint from the present base space to the deictic past, from where the speaker can take a retrospective stance towards the anterior situation. The viewpoint in the past must be fixed, which is typically achieved by the mental spaces opened for the narrative events.

The tense used to express anteriority to the past is the **past perfect**, also known by its Latin name *pluperfect* ('more than completed', i.e. double distancing). The past tense form *had* locates the overall situation of the past perfect in the past time. Since, however, past situations, and even more so past situations in the past, are over, the past perfect does not evoke relevant inferences in the same way that the present perfect does. Anterior past events typically relate to the narrative sequence of events, as illustrated in the following extract of a story:

(25) a. I *arrived* at the platform for the Tokyo express train at 10:03.
b. The train *had left* at 10:02 sharp.
c. So I *had* to wait another hour for the next train.

Sentence (25b) in the past perfect is integrated within the narrative discourse between the past tense sentences (25a) and (25c). It provides a flashback of an earlier event, which explains why I had to wait another hour. Its discourse function is thus to create coherence between two sentences. Notice also that the time specification *10:02* makes the anterior event definite.

The past perfect contrasts with the past tense, which may also refer to the time of an earlier event — provided the context offers clues about the order of the events. Compare the following sentences:

(26) a. When 007 *entered* the room, the door closed behind him.
b. When 007 *had entered* the room, the door closed behind him.

In each case, the event of entering the room precedes the event of the door's closing. However, the time elapsed between the events is felt to be shorter in sentence (26a), in which both events are located within the same past time sphere, than in sentence (26b), in which the events are located within different time spheres.

The use of the past perfect with unbounded situations parallels that of the present perfect. In both tenses, the unbounded activity or temporary state tends to provide background information, and the duration of the anterior situation invites inferences. In the present perfect, such inferences are of current relevance, as in (27a); in the past perfect, inferences pertain to the coherence of events within a narrative past space, as in (27b).

(27) a. My friends *had been drinking* all night. That's why they didn't find their way home.
b. You *have been drinking*. Look at yourself.

9.4 From present posterior time to future times: Present prospective, future tense, and future prospective

> *The nicest thing about the future is that it always starts tomorrow.* (Anonymous)

The continuum of time stretching from the present posterior to the future is to a certain extent a mirror image of the continuum from the present anterior to the past (see Fig. 9.6). We can distinguish two types of future time as reflected in the English system of tenses: the future as posterior to the present, which, like the present perfect, is strongly linked to present facts, as in *I'm going to leave*, and the deictic future, i.e. the (simple) future tense, as in *I'll leave*, which compares to the simple past. The past perfect, however, has no productive equivalent as a future posterior: it is not an established form (yet), and to many speakers not (yet) acceptable.

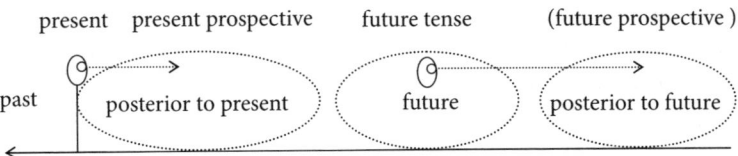

Figure 9.8. *Increasing distance from the present to the future*

The distinction of separate future time spheres is less clear-cut than that of past time spheres. Our projection of events into the future always involves a certain amount of uncertainty. Trains may not run as scheduled, and even a wedding ceremony may not proceed as planned. Future situations are therefore very much subject to people's imagination. As a result, English has a number of future tense forms expressing shades of (un)certainty about a future situation.

9.4.1 Posterior situations viewed from a present viewpoint: Present prospective forms

Situations that are posterior to the present involve a prospective viewing arrangement from a viewpoint in the base space and a focus on the present time. These situations are expressed by a variety of lexical forms, such as *be going to, be about to, be on the verge of* and *be on the point of*. Their focus on the present time can be made explicit by means of present-time adjuncts such as *now* or *today*, as in *500 employees are now going to be made redundant*. Here, the time adjunct refers to the time when the decision is made. The present situation must be conclusive enough for a future event to come about. Two notions qualify for that purpose: intentions and contingency. The *intentional future* and the *contingent future* are both expressed by the form *be going to*.

(28)
 a. I'*m going to* learn to fly. [*intentional future*]
 b. I'*m going to* be a grandmother soon. [*contingent future*]

The **intentional future** refers to future events that come about as a result of a person's present intentions or decisions. Hence the intentional future is typically used by the speaker in referring to her own intentions, i.e. in sentences with the pronouns *I* or *we*. The future meaning of the grammaticised form *be going to* derives from a model of time in which a person moves through time into the future. This variant of the metaphor of time has been described as TIME IS MOTION OVER A LANDSCAPE. Since human motion is normally goal-oriented, we easily associate motion with intention. At a further stage of grammaticalisation, the concept of motion is lost, giving rise to the meaning if intention.

The **contingent future** refers to future events which, due to our knowledge of the structure of the world, are seen as being dependent, or contingent, on phenomena that hold at the present time. When we see very black clouds in the sky, we tend to predict that it is going to rain. Likewise, in sentence (28b), our knowledge of the world tells us that a woman's pregnancy leads to the birth of a baby, so that a pregnant woman's mother "is going to" become a grandmother. In the contingent future, it is thus events that are thought of as moving into the future due to their inherent contingency.

9.4.2 Future time: Future tense forms

> *Predictions should be avoided,
> particularly those about the future.* (Mark Twain)

Like the past, the future is a deictic time that is detached from the present. Unlike past situations, however, future situations are still felt to be somehow related to the present. Even the future tense forms *will* and *shall*, which are usually cited as expressing "pure" futurity, tend to convey additional meanings. This is due to the fact that *will* and *shall* are also used as modal verbs (Chapter 10.3.2.2). Their modal meanings of 'volition' and 'insistence' relate to future situations and may also allow predictions about the future. This extension of meaning can be explained by implicature. When a person says *I will go now*, meaning 'I want to go now', the hearer may predict that the person will actually go. This implicature has become conventionalised so that *will* and *shall* can now be used as markers of a neutral, or **predicted future** with no aspect of volition involved any more. The kind of prediction they express is based on projected reality and to be understood in a rather loose, non-scientific sense.

(29) a. Scotland *will* have a little sunshine.
  b. Democracy is a device that ensures we *shall* be governed no better than we deserve. (George Bernard Shaw)

The predicted future with *will/shall* parallels the past tense: it focuses on the future situation and is exclusive of speech time. If the speaker wants to communicate that her prediction is based on evidence, she will use the contingent future with *be going to*. Thus, if the weather forecast predicts that *Scotland is going to have sunshine*, we are more confident about having a sunny weekend than if the forecast was described as in (29a). Notice also the difference in meaning between the contingent *going to*-future in sentence (28b) and the predicted *will*-future in *I will be a grandmother* (*some day*): the former, but not the latter, implies that my daughter is pregnant now.

In conjunction with the progressive, *will/shall* express a kind of predicted future which has been dubbed by Leech (1971) the **matter-of-course future**: "it indicates that a predicted event will happen independently of the will or intention of anyone concerned." Consider the future progressive in the following sentences:

(30) a. Jessy Norman's tour is almost done. She*'ll soon be leaving* for good.
  b. Don't worry, we*'ll be handling* all your problems tomorrow.

In (30a) the first sentence intimates a future course of events, which the activity expressed in the second sentence elaborates: our knowledge of the world tells us that when we are done with something, we can leave. The speaker therefore need not emphasise the conclusiveness of the future event by saying *She'll leave for good*, but may instead focus on the situation in its progression.

In downplaying the conclusiveness of a future event, the matter-of-course future suggests even greater certainty about the future event to occur than the projected future. In

(30b), our handling the problems is seen as part of a future course of events and is therefore certain to happen, while *We'll handle all your problems* may only be a promise. This use of the matter-of-course future with accomplishments as in (30b) is particularly noteworthy because, as shown before (Chapter 8.3.2 and 9.3.1.2.2), the progressive turns an accomplishment into an accomplishing activity and thus only implicates the event's completion.

9.4.3 Deictic shifts of future situations

Certain future situations are portrayed as occurring in the present deictic time sphere and expressed in the present tense. The use of the simple present with future reference is known as the "scheduled future", that of the present progressive with future reference as the "planned future". Both uses of the present tense for future situations are strongly tied to the present time.

(31) a. My train *leaves* at six p.m.   [scheduled future]
     b. We *are getting* married in spring.   [planned future]

The **scheduled future** applies to fixed, cyclic or recurrent events such as train schedules, examination dates (*The entrance exams start on September 1*), sports fixtures (*Chelsea play Manchester next Saturday*), regular sessions (*The next court session is Monday*), etc. In all these usages, the scheduled event has been arranged at or before the present time. However, the time of a scheduled future event needs to be specified by a future time adjunct. Sentences in the simple present without a temporal specification are more or less ungrammatical, such as ?*The train leaves*.

The **planned future** applies to future events for which arrangements have been made in the present. Plans and arrangements are usually made for controllable events in the near future. In using the present progressive, the speaker draws the planned event into the present time sphere and makes it become part of its duration. Hence, plans and arrangements for the foreseeable future are readily expressed in the present progressive, such as *I am getting married in a month/in half a year/early next year*, etc., whereas events in the non-foreseeable future can usually not be planned and hence are not expressed in the simple progressive, such as **I am getting married in ten years' time*.

The **background future** applies to future situations described in the present tense of temporal and conditional clauses, respectively:

(32) a. When I *see* the kids, I'll send them home.   [temporal]
     b. If I *see* the kids, I'll send them home.   [conditional]

The subordinate clauses function as the ground of the main clauses as their figure. The ground stretches from the present moment to the future point in time when the figure event occurs. What motivates the present tense of the subordinate clauses is the present moment when the ground event is established by the speaker. If, instead of the present tense, a future tense is used in a *when-* or *if-*clause, the speaker no longer sets the time frame or condition for the main clause. Thus, in saying *If it will amuse you, I'll tell you the* *story*, the speaker first seems to check whether the hearer wants to be amused, i.e. the main clause and subordinate clause are no longer causally linked.

9.4.4 Summary of uses of future forms

For the sake of clarity the uses of the future forms are summarised in Table 9.2. They are ordered along a scale according to the degree of certainty associated with the future situation. The deictic futures (a-c) convey the least degree of certainty, the present prospective forms (d, e) a high degree, and the deictic shift to the present (f) the highest degree of certainty. The background future in (g) is dependent on the complex situation.

Table 9.2. Future meanings and future forms

	future meanings	future forms	examples
a.	predicted future	*will, shall*	We'll have some sunshine.
b.	matter-of-course future	*will be -ing*	I'll be seeing you.
c.	intentional future	*be going to*	I'm going to get married.
d.	contingent future	*be going to*	It's going to rain.
e.	planned future	present progressive	I'm getting married next month.
f.	scheduled future	simple present	My train leaves at six.
g.	background future	simple present	If I see him, I'll send him home.

9.4.5 Posterior situations viewed from a future viewpoint: Future prospective

As pointed out in Section 9.1.2.2, we may conceive of situations posterior to a future reference time but only rarely feel the need to do so. The future prospective does, however, occur, especially in contexts where the sense of physical or metaphorical motion is possible, as in (33a), or in contrast to past or present prospectives, as in (33b).

(33) a. We *will be going to* see Harry Potter tonight. Yippy. We have been holding off seeing it.
b. Last night he was gonna quit his job next week. Right now he is still gonna quit his job next week. And I'm sure that tomorrow as well, he will be going to quit his job next week. But next week is another story…

In (33a), the future form *will* contributes the notion of prediction based on evolving projected reality: we had meant to see the film for quite some time. The future form *going to* contributes the notion of contingency: possibly our parents have now made plans to take us to the cinema tonight.

The future situation described in the first sentence of (33b) can only be expressed in the *be going to*-future, not as *he will be gonna quit his job next week*. This indicates that the future prospective requires a preparatory context. Its meaning is clear, though: speakers may feel the need to create a future reference point from which they can look at a time point further away in the future. It is in this sense that the future prospective is the conceptual counterpart of the past perfect.

9.5 Interplay of past and future times: Past prospective and future perfect

Past and future times may interact and give rise to complex notions of time and tense. We may look from a past reference point to a posterior situation and, conversely, from a future reference point to an anterior situation. The former temporal constellation is expressed by the *past prospective*, the latter by the *future perfect*. The following examples and their schematic representations in Figure 9.9 illustrate these complex configurations of time:

(34) a. I *was going to* finish my paper by tomorrow. [*past prospective*]
     b. I'*ll have finished* my paper by tomorrow. [*future perfect*]

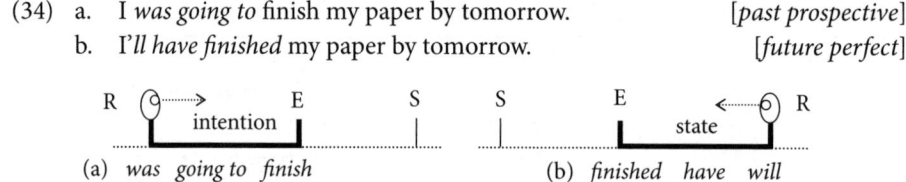

(a) was going to finish   (b) finished have will

Figure 9.9. Past prospective and future perfect

The past prospective and future perfect display near-perfect mirror images. Both complex times involve three separate units of time: speech time (S), reference time (R) and event time (E), and in both configurations R is further away from S than E. Due to the conceptual difference between known reality of the past and projected reality of the future, however, the two configurations express different notions of time.

9.5.1 Posterior situations viewed from a past viewpoint: Past prospective

In using the **past prospective**, the speaker adopts a viewpoint in the deictic past as a reference point (R) and looks forwards at a posterior situation (E). The past prospective is formed with the past form of the *be going to*-future. Like the present prospective, the past prospective has two usages: that of an intentional future, as in (34a), which focuses on the moment in the past when an intention about an event is formed, and that of a contingent future, as in (35a), which focuses on a situation in the past that relates to a later contingent situation.

The past prospective is used in reference to posterior situations in narrative contexts, as in (35a), in hypothetical conditionals, as in (35b), and in situations such as (35c) which invite the implicature that they did not materialise as originally foreseen — otherwise the speaker would have used the past tense.

(35) a. It was my turn in the high jump. I knew it *was going to* hurt.
     b. If I asked any more questions she *was going to* burst into tears.
     c. We *were going to* spend our honeymoon on a cruise in the Mediterranean (but ended up in Blackpool).

9.5.2 Anterior situations viewed from a future viewpoint: Future perfect

In using the **future perfect**, the speaker adopts a viewpoint in the deictic future as a reference point (R) and looks back at an anterior situation (E). The future perfect is formed with the future marker *will* and, like other perfect tenses, the state verb *have* and a past participle. The predicted anterior situation may be an event or a state. A state stretches up to reference time, as in (36a), and an event is followed by a resultant or inferred state, as in (36b) and (36c). The future perfect is used in reference to future situations, as in (36a), in conditional situations, as in (36b), and in generalising contexts, as in (36c).

(36) a. Next month I *will have been* Director General for 4 years.
 b. If a retailer buys jeans from a wholesaler at a cost of £10 a pair and then charges the customer £15 a pair, he *will have made* £5 profit on each pair of jeans he sells.
 c. Students who prepare a dissertation are allocated a supervisor. By this stage formal lectures *will* normally *have ceased*.

States in the future perfect may take time adjuncts with *for*, as in (36a), and events in the future perfect may take time adjuncts with *by*, as in (36b) and (36c). The time adjuncts specify the duration of the state described by *have*: with states, the state reaches from its beginning to reference time; with events, the state is inferred or results from the event and reaches from the completed event to reference time. This situation is depicted in Figure 9.9(b). The temporal preposition *by* exactly matches this situation of future perfect events: it denotes a stretch of time up to a given point in time, however minimal it may be.

The future perfect progressive is all but non-existent in authentic English. It refers to a future event anterior to a future reference point. This tense form can, of course, be a meaningful concept in sentences such as *I will have been working in the garden for most of the day before you even get out of bed*. It will not, however, be further explored here.

9.6 Summary

In the grammar of English, time is conceptualised as being located on a time axis. A fixed point on the time axis is the time of interaction between speaker and hearer. This shared deictic ground is the **base space**. The base space also serves as the **viewpoint** from which the speaker may locate the time of situations. The present moment of speaking is the **speech time**, and the time of the situation described, called **event time**, is at, before, or after speech time. These three time spheres, i.e. the present, the past and the future, are **deictic times** and are expressed by **simple tenses**: the **present tense**, the **past tense**, and the **future tense**. Tense is the grammatical expression of notions of time.

Speakers of English can also express **complex times** by shifting their viewpoint to a past or future time. From this second viewpoint and time, called **reference time**, the speaker can locate the time of a situation relative to one of the three deictic times. The speaker may take a backward-looking stance towards **anterior times** and situations, or a forward-looking stance towards **posterior times** and situations. Complex times thus involve three notions of time: speech time (S), event time (E), and reference time (R). They are expressed by **complex tenses**. Anterior situations are expressed by **perfect tenses**: the **anterior present** by the **present perfect**, the **anterior past** by the **past perfect**, and the **anterior future** by the **future perfect**. Posterior situations are expressed by **prospective forms** such as *be going to*: the posterior present by present prospective forms, the posterior past by past prospective forms and the posterior future by future prospective forms.

Situations that occur at the present time are typically expressed by the **present tense**. Bounded present events rarely coincide with the time of speaking the sentence. One such exceptional case are **performatives** (*I hereby order you to leave this room*), which explicitly name the speech act described. Present situations are normally unbounded, i.e. states, habits and activities, which include or surround speech time.

The system of English tenses distinguishes three past time spheres: spheres denoted by the present perfect, the past tense, and the past perfect. The **present perfect** refers to an anterior situation or the anterior phase of a situation; the focus, however, is on the present time. The situation is therefore seen as having current relevance. Uses of the present perfect include the **resultative perfect** (*He has passed the test*), the **inferential** perfect (*The baby has burped*), the **recent perfect** (*I've just told you*), and the **continuative perfect** (*We've been engaged for a year*). The **past tense** refers to a situation which is prior to, and exclusive of, speech time. Bounded past events (i.e. past non-progressives) typically occur sequentially, especially in narratives, unbounded past events (i.e. past progressives) typically serve as the background for bounded events as the figure (*I was living in a trailer when the earthquake started*). Past situations may also be portrayed as occurring in the present time: usages due to these shifts include the **narrative present**, the **historic present**, the **scientific present**, and the **summary present**. The **past perfect** mainly focuses on the temporal anteriority of an event (*The train had left at 10*).

The system of English future forms mainly distinguishes two future time spheres: spheres denoted by the present prospective and future tense forms. The **present prospective** is mainly expressed by *going to* and includes the **intentional future** (*I'm going to leave*) and the **contingent future** (*It's going to rain*). The **future tense** forms include the **predicted future** (*We'll have some sunshine*), and the **matter-of-course future** (*I'll be seeing you*). Future situations portrayed in the present tense include the **scheduled future** (*The train leaves at six*), the **planned future** (*I'm getting married next month*), and the **background future** (*If I see him, I'll send him home*). The rarely used **future prospective** refers to situations posterior to a future reference time (*We will be going to see the Queen*).

Past and future notions of time interact in the **past prospective** (*She was going to burst into tears*) and the **future perfect** (*He will have made a profit*).

Chapter 9. Grounding situations in time: Tense

Further Reading

Standard reference books on time and tense are Comrie (1985), Binnick (1991), Klein (1994) and Declerck (1991; 2006). Earlier insightful presentations on the English system of tenses are found in Leech (1971) and Palmer (1988) and, of course, in the various grammars of English. The metaphorical analysis of time as space goes back to Lakoff and Johnson (1980) and has been refined in Lakoff & Johnson (1999); see also Radden (2006). The framework on time and tense adopted here is based on the influential system of time developed by Reichenbach (1947) and its reanalysis in terms of mental spaces by Fauconnier (1997).

A cognitive analysis of the present tense is given in Langacker (2001). Studies of the present perfect are Inoue (1978), McCoard (1978), Klein (1992), Michaelis (1994) and Depraetere (1998). For the issue of colloquial tautologies see Gibbs (1994: 345–351). The future tense has been most extensively dealt with by Wekker (1976); specific future forms are discussed in Bybee & Pagliuca (1987), Haegeman (1989) and Nicolle (1997).

Study questions

1. Supply the appropriate tense form in the following sentences and justify your decision.
    a. I hereby (renounce) all responsibility.
    b. I've bought you a little present. I (think) you might like it.
    c. In March 1923 Lenin suffers his third stroke, loses the power of speech. In January 1924 Lenin (die).
    d. Professor Alpers (note) the tendency of modern critics to treat metaphors as primary data in understanding Shakespeare's plays.
    e. **Oil tanker (sink) off French coast**. A Maltese-registered tanker (sink) in stormy seas off north-western France last night. (newspaper article)

2. Supply the appropriate tense and aspect forms in the following sentences, describe the use of the forms, and justify your decision:
    a. I only (know) him for a minute and already (hate) him.
    b. I (sit) at the computer all day. My eyes are burning and my neck is stiff.
    c. When the phone (ring), I (sip) coffee and (watch) TV.
    d. I (be) away all week on a conference and (not arrive) home until late on Friday night. (four possibilities)
    e. It (be predicted) that, by 2025, the number of vehicles on the road (increase) by over 100 per cent.

3. Comment on the differences in meaning implied by the future tense forms in the following examples and explain which of them sounds better in the given context.
    a. Who *will* / *is going to* volunteer to clean the kitchen? — I'll do it. / I'm going to do it.
    b. I feel miserable. I'll be sick. / I'm going to be sick.

c. The graduation ceremony *is* on August 1. / *will be* on August 1.
d. Susan, *will* you pass by the post office? / *will you be passing* …
e. I'*m getting* married / I'*m going to* get married.
f. The English Theatre *presents* four plays during the coming season. / *will present* … / *will be presenting* …

Chapter 10

Grounding situations in potentiality: Modality

10.0 Overview

10.1 Modality

10.2 Modality: Modal expressions

10.3 Compelling modalities

10.4 Enabling modalities

10.5 Interaction of modality and negation

10.6 Summary

10.0 Overview

Modality is concerned with the speaker's assessment of, or attitude towards, the potentiality of a state of affairs. Modality therefore relates to different worlds. Assessments of potentiality, as in *You must be right*, relate to the world of knowledge and reasoning. This type of modality is known as **epistemic modality**. Modal attitudes apply to the world of things and social interaction. This type of modality is known as **root modality**. Root modality comprises three subtypes: deontic modality, intrinsic modality and disposition modality. **Deontic modality** is concerned with the speaker's directive attitude towards an action to be carried out, as in the obligation *You must go now*. **Intrinsic modality** is concerned with potentialities arising from intrinsic qualities of a thing or circumstances, as in *The meeting can be cancelled*, i.e. 'it is possible for the meeting to be cancelled'. **Disposition modality** is concerned with a thing's or person's intrinsic potential of being actualised; in particular abilities. Thus, when you have the ability to play the guitar you will potentially do so. Notions of modality are expressed by cognition verbs such as *I think*, modal adverbs such as *possibly*, and modal verbs such as *must*. **Modal verbs** have a special status among modal expressions: they ground a situation in potential reality.

10.1 Modality

Whenever we think of, or talk about, a situation, we assess it with respect to its status of reality. In the model of evolving reality presented in Figure III.1 (page 172) we distinguished between different types of reality. This chapter looks at situations that belong to potential reality, an area that is known as modality. **Modality** is concerned with the speaker's assessment of, or attitude towards, the potentiality of a state of affairs.

In the course of this chapter, we will define modality more precisely and distinguish different kinds of modality. The nature of modality may be best understood in contrast to similar, non-modal notions. We will, therefore, first concentrate on two of the main types of modality, epistemic and deontic modality, and consider them in connection with assertion and directive speech acts.

10.1.1 Assertion and epistemic modality

Assertion refers to the speaker's confidence in the reality status of a state of affairs as conveyed in a declarative sentence. Let us compare the assertions made by a speaker in the following fairy-tale situation. Two children get lost in the woods and come to a house built of bread with a roof made of cake and windows made of sugar. After checking the house, Hansel informs Gretel about what he has seen:

(1) a. There *is* someone living in the house. [*strong assertion*]
 b. There *isn't* anyone living in the house. [*strong assertion*]
 c. There *must* be someone living in the house. [*weak assertion*]

In sentence (1a), Hansel may have seen an old woman in the house and, on the basis of this evidence, makes a strong, or categorical, affirmative assertion and thereby grounds the situation in factual reality. In sentence (1b), Hansel has not found any evidence of a human being living in the house and hence is certain that the house is not inhabited. He expresses his certainty by making a strong negative assertion, which also grounds the situation in factual reality. In sentence (1c), Hansel may have noticed bits of evidence of a person living in the house, such as dirty dishes lying on the table and a raincoat hanging on a nail. However, he hasn't seen anybody in the house and thus can't be certain. On the basis of the evidence found he concludes that 'it is necessarily the case that there is someone living in the house'. He expresses this assessment by making a weak, or modalised, assertion. The modal verb *must* in *There must be someone living in the house* grounds the situation in potential reality.

The situation described in sentence (1c) involves epistemic modality. **Epistemic modality** is concerned with the speaker's assessment of the potentiality of a state of affairs. It is closely tied to the speaker's knowledge and inferences drawn from facts known to him, hence the term *epistemic* (from Greek *episteme* 'knowledge') — although, strictly speaking, epistemic modality refers to the speaker's lack of sufficient knowledge.

Modal assessments involve a complex interplay of mental spaces. They are partly comparable to the spaces evoked by negated assertions. Let us therefore look at negation first. The negator *not* is a space-builder that prompts us to imagine the positive counterpart of a situation. In understanding the meaning of *not anyone living in the house* in (1b), we need to imagine the house being inhabited. We thus have two mental spaces which are conceptually blended: the reality space of 'the house not being inhabited' and the counterfactual space of 'the house being inhabited'. This situation is illustrated in Figure 10.1(a).

In the epistemic assessment described in (1c), the modal verb *must* is a space-builder that prompts us to imagine three mental spaces: a reality space, in which Hansel found some evidence of the house being inhabited, a (positive) potentiality space of the house being inhabited, and a (negative) potentiality space of the house being uninhabited, which is not excluded. The information of the input spaces is fed into the blended space, which represents the epistemic assessment. As shown in Figure 10.1(b), the amount of evidence is mapped onto the degree of assessed probability on a scale between the poles of 'inhabited' and 'not inhabited'. The highest degree of inferred epistemic probability is that of 'necessity'.

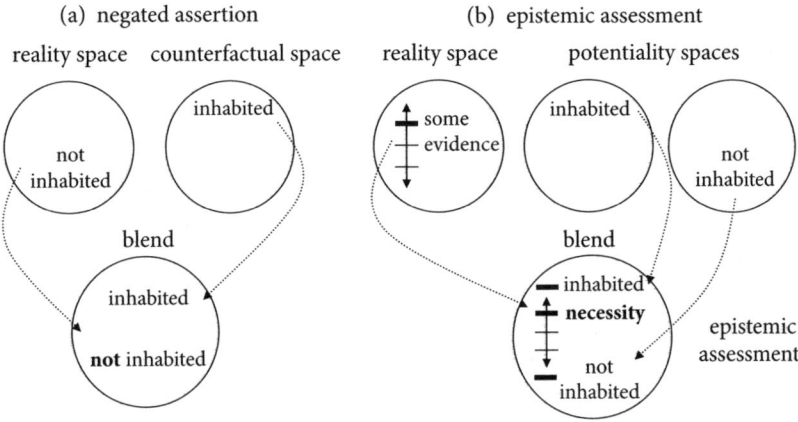

Figure 10.1. Blending in negated assertions and epistemic assessments

An epistemic assessment is based on perceptual or intuitive evidence, which the speaker processes on the basis of her knowledge or belief. In using a modal expression, the speaker assesses the probability of a situation and thereby implies that he has evidence upon which his assessment relies. We may therefore always ask for the evidence that led a person to an assessment: "What makes you think so?" Conversely, in using an evidential expression such as *look like*, the speaker profiles the evidence and invites the hearer to assess the probability of a situation. The following sentences illustrate the interdependence of epistemic modality and evidentiality:

(2) a. Peggy *must* be sick. [*epistemic modality*]
'the speaker has evidence for the claim' [*implicature*]
b. Peggy *looks* pale. [*evidential assertion*]
'Peggy's sickness is highly probable' [*implicature*]

In the modal statement (2a), the evidence for inferring that Peggy is sick might be her pale face yesterday and her absence today. In the evitential statement (2b), we might, in a given context, infer Peggy's state of health from her appearance, something we do all the time. Modal expressions as in (2a) profile an assessed probability and invoke evidence as its source, while evidential expressions as in (2b) profile the evidence and invoke an assessed probability as its result. Epistemic modality and evidentiality are thus two strategies leading to similar results.

The grammars of many languages distinguish between sources of evidence, for example, between evidence based on hearsay and evidence based on vision. In English, evidential information is only coded lexically, by means of adverbs such as *evidently*, *reportedly*, *allegedly*, copular verbs such as *seem*, *appear*, *look*, and expressions such as *I have been told*, *as everybody knows*, *I saw it with my own eyes*, and the like. For obvious reasons, evidential expressions tend to focus on the positive pole of the scale of evidence, while modal expressions cover the whole range of potentiality.

10.1.2 Directive attitude: Deontic modality

The second major type of modality is **deontic modality** (from Greek *deont-* 'binding, obligatory'). Deontic modality relates to social interaction. It is concerned with the speaker's directive attitude towards an action to be carried out. It mainly comprises the notions of 'obligation' and 'permission', i.e. speech acts in which the speaker invokes her authority or a general rule to have another person (or herself) carry out an act. Expressions of deontic modality thus can convey similar meanings as **directive speech acts**, in which the speaker "directs" the hearer to perform, or refrain from performing, a certain action, as in requests, orders, prohibitions, warnings, etc. The different types of sentences under (3) and (4) have the same directive function:

(3) a. Stand up! [*imperative mood*]
b. I *request* you to stand up. [*performative speech act*]
c. You *must* stand up. [*deontic modality*]

(4) a. I *allow* you to sit down. [*performative speech act*]
b. You *may* sit down. [*deontic modality*]

The directive speech act is expressed by the imperative mood in (3a) and by a **performative speech act** in (3b), i.e. a sentence with a performative verb, *request*, which names the speech act. The deontic modal *must* in (3c) expresses an act of obligation which is also understood in a directive sense, although less imposing. In the same vein, both the performative speech act in (4a) and the deontic verb *may* in (4b) express acts of permission. The directive usage of deontic modals is therefore sometimes described as *performative*.

A directive speech act and deontic modality are also similar in that they are made at speech time and refer to actions that are to be carried out later than speech time. Deontic modality is thus future-oriented but the outcome of an obligation imposed or a permission granted is only judged to have potential reality. In the obligation (3c), *You must stand up*, the hearer is strongly expected to stand up and hence very likely to do so; in the permission (4b), *You may stand up*, the outcome is only weakly expected and hence less likely.

Like epistemic modality, deontic modality invokes a complex interplay of mental spaces, which are normally not invoked by directive speech acts. An act of obligation such as *You must stand up* involves the following spaces: two reality spaces — general rules of conduct (behaviour in court) and a given situation (the defendant sitting), an assessment space — the speaker's assessment of the state of affairs as an infringement of a rule, and an attitude space — the speaker's attitude towards this state of affairs as requiring strong directive action (the defendant standing up). All these mental spaces contribute to the speaker's decision to express an obligation, which he assumes has a high probability of making the hearer perform the demanded act. The conceptualisation underlying this deontic act is shown in Figure 10.2.

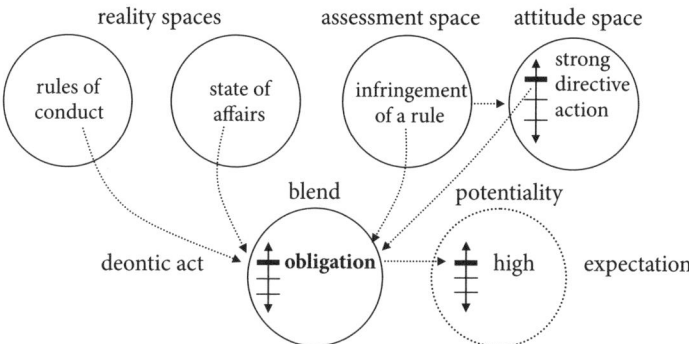

Figure 10.2. Blending in deontic modality: *You must stand up*.

Both epistemic and deontic modality involve assessments: an assessment of a given state of affairs with respect to reality in epistemic modality and an assessment of a state of affairs with respect to expected conduct in deontic modality. The role of assessment, however, differs in the two types of modality. Epistemic modality is concerned with the speaker's assessment of a state of affairs, while deontic modality is concerned with an expected behaviour derived from assessing compliance with some authority or rule. Deontic modality is thus conceptually more complex than epistemic modality but, at the same time, the deontic domain of social interaction is also experienced as more basic than the epistemic domain of reasoning.

10.1.3 Distinguishing epistemic and deontic modality

Epistemic modality mainly comprises the notions of 'necessity' and 'possibility,' deontic modality those of 'obligation' and 'permission'. These meanings are illustrated in the following uncontroversial examples:

(5) a. You *must* be right. [*necessity*]
 b. You *may* be right. [*possibility*]
 c. You *must* go home. [*obligation*]
 d. You *may* go home. [*permission*]

At least the following factors distinguish epistemic and deontic modality:

(i) *Type of situation*: Epistemic modality typically applies to states, as in (5a) and (5b). More rarely, we assess the likelihood of events, as in *She must be telling the truth*. Deontic modality, on the other hand, only applies to events, as in (5c) and (5d). Some obligations are expressed as states but are meant as actions: in *You must be in bed by 10 o'clock* the state 'be in bed' metonymically stands for the action 'go to bed', which leads to this state as its result.

(ii) *Scope of modality*: **Scope** refers to the range of a linguistic unit within which grammatical or conceptual entities are seen. In epistemic modality, the speaker assesses a proposition: the proposition 'you be right' is assessed as necessary in (5a) and as possible in (5b). These sentences can be paraphrased with a *that*-clause: 'it is necessarily/possibly the case *that you are right*'. Expressions of epistemic modality thus range over the whole proposition, i.e. they have a *wide scope*. Expressions of deontic modality, by contrast, range over parts of a proposition, in particular the hearer. Deontic sentences are paraphrasable by using the phrase *for/of X to*: 'it is required of you / permitted for you to go home'. In their focus on the hearer, expressions of deontic modality have a *narrow scope*.

(iii) *Time of situation*: Epistemic modality applies to situations that hold at the present moment, as in *Juliet may be home already*, or in the future, as in *Juliet may be home by tomorrow*. Past situations have already occurred, so their potential likelihood cannot be assessed by epistemic modals. However, since our knowledge of the past is necessarily limited, we can assess past situations in retrospect. For example, we may, at this moment, not be sure if Juliet was at home yesterday and say *Juliet may have been home last night*. Here we are taking a backward-looking stance from the present moment and consider the likelihood of an anterior situation in its continuing relevance. This is what the state verb *have* conveys. Deontic modality is, as pointed out in the preceding section, always future-oriented. We can now account for the meanings of modality conveyed by the following sentences:

(6) a. My sister may *eat* all the biscuits. [epistemic and deontic]
 b. My sister may *be eating* all the biscuits. [epistemic]
 c. My sister may *have eaten* all the biscuits. [epistemic]

Sentence (6a) allows both an epistemic and a deontic reading, where both situations are understood to occur in the future. Sentence (6b) with the progressive form refers to an unbounded event, namely an accomplishing activity, which includes the present moment. Sentence (6c) with the present perfect form refers to a state resulting from a telic event which lasts until the present moment, meaning that all the biscuits may be gone now. Both sentences thus refer to present, not to future, situations and hence are only understood in an epistemic sense.

10.2 Modality: Modal expressions

I doubt, therefore I might be.
(Anonymous)

In view of the major conceptual differences between epistemic, deontic and other types of modality, an overall definition of modality is almost impossible to find. Instead, before attempting to define modality, we will point out and discuss three common properties that characterise the various types of modality: (i) gradience, (ii) subjectivity, and (iii) force dynamics.

10.2.1 Gradience of modality

The gradient nature of modality is inherent in the phenomena it describes. In our everyday lives, we are constantly faced with unpredictable situations and cannot be certain about their likelihood: Did my wife pass the driving test? Can I travel to Iraq these days? Can I let my daughter stay with her boy friend overnight? Not surprisingly, languages provide a wealth of linguistic means which allow the speaker to express degrees and nuances of uncertainty: modal verbs like *must, may* and *should*, modal adjuncts like *perhaps, certainly* and *in all probability*, and hundreds of lexical expressions such as *it's beyond any shadow*

Table 10.1. Scales of epistemic assessment and deontic attitude

epistemic assessment		deontic attitude
	high	
Sue *must* be in bed.	↑	You *must* go to bed.
I'm *certain* Sue is in bed.		You're *supposed* to go to bed.
Sue *should* be in bed.		You *should* go to bed.
Sue is *probably* in bed.		You're *supposed* to go to bed.
Sue is *possibly* in bed.		You're *allowed* to go to bed.
Sue *may* be in bed.		You *may* go to bed.
Sue *might* be in bed.		You *can* go to bed.
Sue *can't* be in bed.	↓	You *mustn't* go to bed.
	low	

of a doubt, you had better, etc. The modal expressions in Table 10.1 illustrate a scale of epistemic assessment ranging from high to low probability and a corresponding deontic scale ranging strong to weak directive attitude.

Modal verbs are a special set among the expressions of modality: they are used in both epistemic and deontic senses, whereas most other modal expressions are restricted to either of these usages.

10.2.2 Subjectivity of modality: Modals

10.2.2.1 *Gradience in subjectivity*

A second characteristic of modality is the speaker's involvement. Modal assessments and attitudes are typically formed by the speaker and hence by their very nature involve an element of subjectivity. The speaker may, however, construe her assessment or attitude more subjectively or more objectively (see Chapter 2.1.4). Consider the following epistemic assessments:

(7)   a.   *I believe* that Ann is pregnant.   [cognition verb]
       b.   Ann is *probably* pregnant.   [modal adverb]
       c.   Ann *may* be pregnant.   [modal verb]

The speaker of sentence (7a) makes an epistemic assessment by using a complex sentence structure (see Chapter 3.3). The main clause describes the assessment while the complement clause describes the situation assessed, and both clauses are grounded in immediate reality. The modal assessment resides in the use of the personal pronoun *I* and the cognition verb *believe*. The pronoun *I* specifies the assessing speaker and the verb *believe* shows the speaker's assessment as belonging to his "belief space". It is only when the speaker expresses his own state of mind and does so at the present moment that we understand his utterance as an assessment. Reports of other people's thoughts, such as *My wife believes that Ann is pregnant*, or of the speaker's thoughts in the past, as in *I believed that Ann was pregnant*, are not modal assessments. In these descriptions, the speaker conceptualises a scene as detached from himself, like a spectator watching a play. The actors are "onstage" and the speaker views the events objectively from his seat in the auditorium. The speaker may, however, also take part in an onstage event. This is the case in sentence (7a). In using the pronoun *I*, the speaker puts himself onstage as the person that assesses the scene. Still, the speaker watches the events including his own part from outside; hence his subjective assessment is framed objectively.

Like sentence (7a), sentence (7b), *Ann is probably pregnant*, expresses an assertion grounded in immediate reality. Here, the modal assessment is expressed by the adverb *probably*, which marks the situation as uncertain — but uncertain to whom? The speaker remains "offstage", but the hearer will reasonably assume that the unnamed source of assessment is the speaker and that, moreover, his assessment is probably based on external circumstances. For example, a person asking an expert if her dog is pregnant may be informed that "if your pet has had access to the outside world while she was in heat, *she is probably pregnant*."

Sentence (7c), *Ann may be pregnant*, expresses a weak assertion. The modal *may* grounds the overall situation in potential reality. The copular verb *be* is not inflected for tense and thus has no grounding function — *Ann be pregnant* does not represent a situation of its own, but a proposition (see Chapter 3.2.4). As in the preceding sentence, the source of the modal assessment is not named, but unlike there, the modal *may* informs the hearer that the assessment is exclusively or largely the speaker's. The speaker himself remains "offstage". This construal of epistemic assessment is "maximally subjective" — a characteristic of modals that is described as *subjectification*.

The three types of modal assessment discussed above are sketched in Figure 10.3. The ellipse represents the conceptualised scene, i.e. the onstage area, and "S" the speaker, who is also the conceptualiser of the scene. The arrow pointing to the modal expression represents the speaker's modal assessment. The dotted line from "S" to the personal pronoun *I* in (a) indicates their identity.

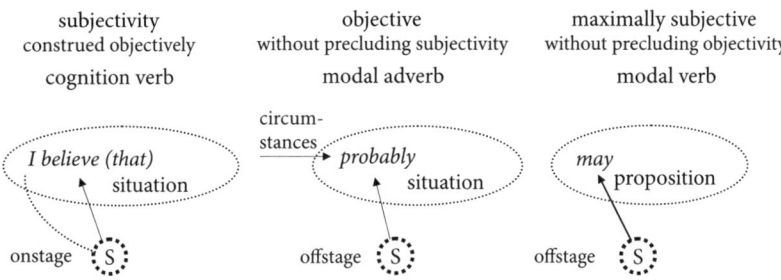

(a) *I believe Ann is pregnant.* (b) *Ann is probably pregnant.* (c) *Ann may be pregnant.*

Figure 10.3. Three types of modal assessment

The use of the cognition verb *believe* in the complementation structure imposes an objective interpretation on the speaker's subjective assessment, the use of the modal adverb *probably* tends to be understood as expressing a more objective assessment, and the use of the modal verb *may* conveys the speaker's subjective assessment.

The three types of modal assessment express increasing degrees of subjectivity. This is reflected in their syntactic structures. The complex sentence in (8a) is composed of two tensed clauses which may also be distanced by the conjunction *that*; the modal adverb *probably* in (8b) is a syntactically optional element of the simple sentence and may be fronted in the sentence (*Probably Ann is pregnant*); and the modal verb *may* in (8c) is an obligatory element of the verb phrase. Their different degrees of subjectivity also show up in their grammatical behaviour with tag questions. Tag questions ask the hearer to confirm an assertion made by the speaker. The more subjective a speaker's assessment is, the less likely the hearer is to confirm it. More subjective assessments therefore tend to become increasingly less acceptable, which explains the non-existence of the tag **mayn't I?*

(8) a. *I believe* that Ann is pregnant, isn't she?
    b. #Ann is *probably* pregnant, isn't she?
    c. *Ann *may* be pregnant, isn't she?

More generally, the three modal expressions *believe*, *probably* and *may* are instances of the following classes of modal assessment:

- *mental expressions* including cognition verbs like *believe, judge, conclude* and *doubt* and complex expressions such as *be of the opinion, have the impression, as far as I can tell*, etc.;
- *modal adjuncts* comprising adverbs like *perhaps* and *certainly*, prepositional phrases like *in all likelihood* or *of necessity*, and clauses such as *there is a good chance that*, etc.;
- *modal verbs*, or simply **modals**. Modals like *may, can* and *must* have traditionally been classified as auxiliaries together with *be, do* and *have* because their grammatical function was seen as purely subsidiary to a main verb.

The following discussion of modality will mainly be focused on the very frequently used class of modals.

10.2.2.2 The "finite only" English modals

In contrast to related languages, English has a group of modal verbs that only occur in a finite form. This group of central modals includes *may, might, can, could, must, shall, should, ought, will, would* and *need*. These modals have the function of grounding a situation in potential reality with the speaker as the fixed reference point. Compared to lexical verbs, modals lack most of their morphological and syntactic properties. They are therefore sometimes described as defective. Their structural "defects", however, relate to their grounding function and their maximal subjectivity. The structural properties of the English modals are:

- Modals lack non-finite forms (infinitive **to must*, present participle **musting*, past participle **musted*) and cannot be used in non-finite clauses (**I want him to may speak*) because of their grounding function.
- Modals lack the third person singular inflection in the present tense (**He mays*) because they do not conceptually agree with the subject of the sentence.
- Modals lack past tense forms because the speaker's assessment occurs at the present time. The only modal that has a past tense form is *can* of 'ability', as in *She could already play the piano when she was five* (see 10.4.2.1); the "distal forms" *might, could*, and *should* do not refer to past time but convey tentative modal meanings.
- Modals cannot be used as a main verb (**I can English*) because their semantic content is bleached out.
- Modals cannot co-occur with another modal (**I must may show you*) because a situation can only be grounded once. In certain dialects, though, "double modals" do occur. For example, in Texas and Arkansas one might hear *You might could be right*, and in Scottish English *You shouldn't ought to have done that*.

In addition to this central group of modals, there is a more peripheral group with finite and non-finite forms of modals including *have to, have got to, be to, be able to, be willing to, get to, be supposed to* and some others. These modals mainly express intrinsic modality (see 10.2.4.2 below). They are known as *semi-modals* and have, as nicely dubbed by Talmy (1988), "honorary modal status".

10.2.3 Force dynamics of modality

A common characteristic of epistemic and deontic modality is their "force-dynamic" basis. In Chapter 1.3.3 we identified 'force' as one of the image schemas. The notion of **force dynamics** pertains to the opposition of forces and counterforces. The phenomenon of force is ubiquitous in the physical world. For example, we feel the force of gravity when doing push-ups or the force of the head wind when riding a bicycle. We also experience force dynamics in the social world when a person in authority tells a weaker person what to do. For example, a teacher may call upon a lazy student by saying, "You *must* start working for a change now." The force-dynamic basis of modals is more perspicuous with deontic modals than with epistemic modals. Our force-dynamic analysis will therefore begin with deontic modality.

10.2.3.1 *Force dynamics of 'obligation' and 'epistemic necessity'*

An **obligation** is a binding force that is seen as compelling a person to carry out a certain action. In the obligation expressed by *You must go home*, the compelling force resides in the speaker's social authority: he imposes his will on the hearer. The hearer apparently wants to stay, i.e. his counterforce is opposed to that of the speaker but is weaker. This force-dynamic constellation is sketched in Figure 10.4(a). The speaker is identical with the imposer, which is indicated by a dotted line linking the speaker and imposer, and the speaker-imposer is offstage, i.e. he is not profiled, which is indicated by dotted circles. The speaker-imposer is the source of the force, represented by the bold "▶" sign, and his force is indicated by a bold arrow. The hearer is the agent of the action which he is obliged to carry out, and his weaker counterforce is indicated by the "<" sign. The speaker is also the conceptualiser of the scene, which is indicated by the dotted arrow pointing to the "onstage region". This force-dynamic constellation is expressed by the modal *must* of obligation.

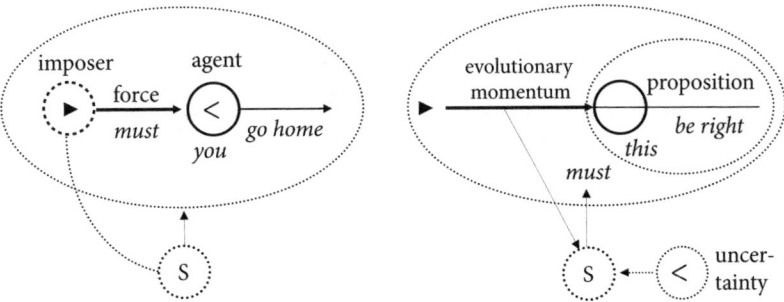

(a) Obligation: *You must go home.* (b) Epistemic necessity: *This must be right.*

Figure 10.4. Force-dynamic constellations of deontic and epistemic *must*

Figure 10.4(b) sketches the force-dynamic constellation of epistemic *must*, as in *This must be right*. This sentence expresses an **epistemic necessity**: the amount of evidence leads the speaker to the only possible conclusion that this is right. The evidence typically involves an "evolutionary momentum". Imagine a situation in which you are hooking up a new DVD-player to your TV set. You carefully follow the instructions step by step. When all the cables are connected the evolutionary momentum of your work allows you to conclude that everything is set up correctly — maybe with a little tinge of uncertainty left — and you proudly announce: "This must be right now." In the drawing the arrow pointing from the evolutionary momentum to the speaker indicates the impact it has on the speaker's assessment. The epistemic modal *must* has the whole proposition in its scope, and is therefore drawn external to the inner ellipse representing the proposition 'this be right'.

Deontic obligation and epistemic necessity display similar force-dynamic patterns. The imposer's social force corresponds to the force of the evolutionary momentum, the hearer's unwillingness to act corresponds to potential counter-evidence, and the enforced action corresponds to the epistemic conclusion reached. The parallelism between *must* of obligation and *must* of epistemic necessity is explicated in the following paraphrases:

(9) a. *You must go home.*
         'The force of my authority compels you to go home.'
     b. *This must be right.*
         'The force of available evidence compels me to conclude that this is right.'

10.2.3.2 Force dynamics of 'permission' and 'epistemic possibility'

Again we will first consider the force dynamics of deontic modality: the sense of permission as in *You may go home*. Here the speaker grants permission and the hearer seeks permission — or is supposed to seek permission. The permission-giver is more powerful than the permission-seeker, but he relinquishes his authority so that the permission-seeker can have his will. In terms of force dynamics, an act of **permission** involves a situation of enablement: the permission-giver lifts a potential barrier and thereby enables the permission-seeker to carry out his intended action. In Figure 10.5(a), the hearer is the agent and

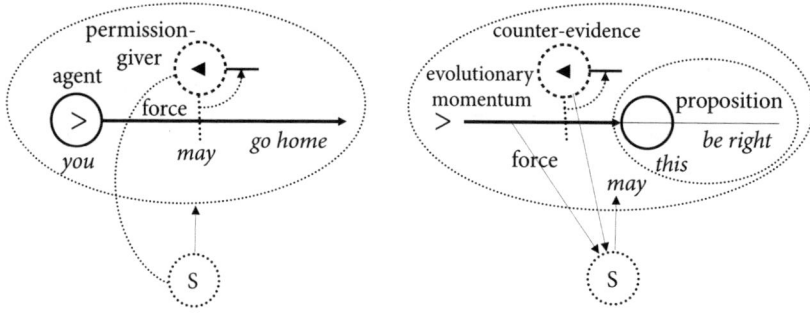

(a) Permission: *You may go home.*   (b) Epistemic possibility: *This may be right.*

Figure 10.5. Force-dynamic constellation of deontic and epistemic *may*

his weaker force is indicated by the ">" sign; the speaker is identical with the offstage permission-giver, whose stronger counterforce is indicated by the "◄" sign; by lifting the barrier, the speaker clears the way for the permission-seeking hearer to act.

Figure 10.5(b) represents the force-dynamic constellation of epistemic *may*, i.e. 'possibility', as in *This may be right*. As in epistemic *must*, the force on which an **epistemic possibility** is based is an evolutionary momentum and, as in deontic *may*, the counterforce is a potential, but lifted, barrier. A potential barrier in reasoning is lack of evidence, giving rise to uncertainty. In the above example of hooking up a DVD-player, I may have doubts about my work as a DIY-electrician and only hesitantly concede that what I have done is possibly right or possibly wrong.

The force-dynamic constellations of 'permission' and 'possibility' are also related, as explicated in the following paraphrases:

(10) a. *You may go home.*
'I relinquish the force of my authority that could bar you from going home.'
b. *This may be right.*
'I relinquish the force of potential counter-evidence that could bar me from inferring that this is right.

10.2.4 Modal polysemy and types of modality

10.2.4.1 *Polysemy of modals*

Epistemic and deontic modality are, to all intents and purposes, clearly distinct categories. Yet, in English and many other languages, the same modals are used to express different types of modality. The systematic **polysemy** of the English modals is, of course, not accidental. The preceding discussion has shown that epistemic and deontic modality are based on similar force-dynamic constellations. It is, therefore, not surprising that modal verbs systematically display deontic/epistemic polysemy. But what is the motivated link between the different modal meanings? Two explanations have been suggested.

It has been argued that the connection between the two modalities is metaphorical. According to this view, the internal domain of reasoning is metaphorically understood in terms of the external domain of socio-physical interaction. The metaphorical view is, amongst others, supported by similar cases of polysemy in lexical verbs, demonstrating that the extensions of modal meaning are a more general phenomenon. Like modal verbs, lexical verbs of permission such as *permit, grant* and *admit* can be used in an epistemic sense: *weather permitting* means as much as 'if something is possible in the weather', and *granted that* and *admitting that* mean 'acknowledging for the sake of argument'.

Metaphor relates two domains and thus involves an abrupt conceptual shift from one domain to another. Grammatical shifts, however, tend to be gradual rather than abrupt and be driven by metonymy and conversational implicature. The polysemy of present-day modals has been shown to be the result of inferential processes and pragmatic strengthening. Most of the English modals derive from lexical verbs. Their uses in certain contexts invited implicatures which, due to frequent usages, gradually came to be reinterpreted by language users as fixed senses of a modal. The original lexical meanings of the modals have been bleached but, as we will see in the following sections, traces of them are still recognisable in their present-day uses.

Two main paths of grammaticalisation can be distinguished that lead from lexical meanings to deontic and epistemic meanings: a path that leads to the *compelling modalities* of 'obligation' and 'necessity', and a path that leads to the *enabling modalities* of 'permission' and 'possibility'. These will be discussed in more detail in Sections 10.3 and 10.4. Compelling and enabling modalities crosscut with the traditional distinction into types of modality.

10.2.4.2 *Types of modality*

So far we have mainly dealt with epistemic and deontic modality. We will distinguish two more types of modality: intrinsic modality and disposition modality. **Intrinsic modality** is concerned with potentialities arising from speaker-external sources, i.e. from intrinsic qualities of a thing or circumstances, as in *The meeting can be cancelled*, which means that 'it is possible for the meeting to be cancelled'. This intrinsic possibility differs from an epistemic possibility as in *The meeting may be over*, which means that 'it is possible that the meeting is over'. Intrinsic modalities typically involve a person's or thing's intrinsic disposition, which has the potential of being actualised. If, for example, you can play the guitar, you have the possibility to do so, and very probably you will actually do so. Dispositions like my ability to play the guitar are not modal in meaning but strongly imply intrinsic modalities. We will describe such dispositions as instances of **disposition modality**. Intrinsic and disposition modalities are sometimes also referred to as "dynamic modality". Disposition modality includes the notions of 'ability' or 'propensity' and 'willingness'.

Deontic modality, intrinsic modality and disposition modality are pragmatically related and often subsumed under the term **root modality**. The word *root* suggests the primacy of non-epistemic notions over epistemic notions. The main types of modality are listed in Table 10.2. Their ordering from left to right reflects their two main paths of grammaticalisation.

Table 10.2. Main types of modality

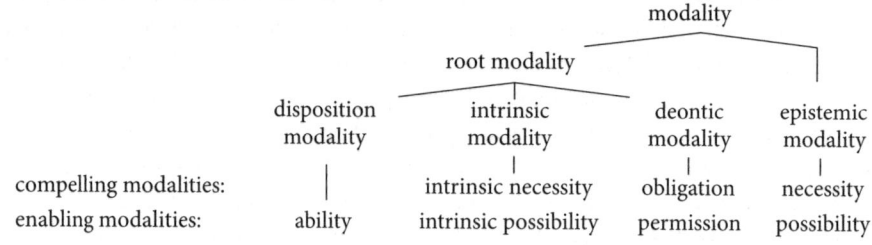

We may now offer a definition of modality that comprises characteristics of both epistemic and root modality. **Modality** is an assessment of potentiality, depending either on the speaker's judgement of the reality status of a state of affairs (epistemic modality) or on the speaker's attitude towards the realisation of a desired or expected event (root modality).

Epistemic and root modalities represent different types of modality and group together different degrees of modality within each type; compelling and enabling modalities represent different force-dynamic patterns and group together different types of modality within the same force-dynamic pattern. We will adopt the latter grouping as a structuring principle because it allows us to retrace the transition from one type of modality to another.

10.3 Compelling modalities

10.3.1 Evolution of compelling modalities

Compelling modalities involve a compelling force; they comprise obligations, prohibitions and intrinsic and epistemic necessities. They are expressed by the central modals *must, need (to)* and *should* and the semi-modals *ought to, have to* and *have got to*. These modals have evolved from different lexical origins. *Must* originally meant 'be permitted' and then came to mean 'oblige'. This transition of meaning is probably motivated by implicature. In an asymmetric interaction between a powerful and a powerless person an expression of permission is easily understood as an obligation. A judge who announces that "the next witness *may* come in" does, of course, not leave it up to the witness to come in or not.

The verbs underlying the past tense forms *should* and *ought* originally meant 'owe' in the sense of 'be indebted' and hence, in an extended sense, 'be obliged by duty'. The semi-modals *have to* and *have got to* are related to the basic meaning of *have*, 'possession'. Possession involves the state of being in control of a thing, as in *I have a car*. The obligation sense of *have to* as in *I have to drive* is a metaphorical extension of possession to social control: 'I am in the state of being in control of other people's or my own actions'.

All these modals underwent the same extension of meaning from 'obligation' to 'epistemic necessity'. Historical transitions from one meaning to another are the result of the same conceptual processes that give rise to polysemy at the synchronic level. We will therefore retrace the gradual inferential links between the senses by looking at the present-day usages of *must*:

(11) a. You *must* lock the door. [*act of obligation*]
 b. The door *must* be locked.
 c. 'it is necessary *for* the door to be locked' [*intrinsic necessity*]
 d. 'it is necessarily the case *that* the door is locked' [*epistemic necessity*]

Sentence (11a) is normally understood in its performative sense, i.e. as an act of obligation laid by the speaker upon the hearer at the present moment ('the force of my authority compels you'). It expresses a strong, subjective obligation.

Sentence (11b) is in the passive voice and does not overtly mention the person who is to perform the required action — the "doer" is in fact not relevant in this sentence. The sentence allows two interpretations. One of its meanings is about the door with respect to some general rule or regulation. This meaning is paraphrased in (11c): 'it is necessary *for* the door to be locked' (otherwise burglars may break in). The paraphrase with 'necessary for' allows us to identify an intrinsic necessity, sometimes also called deontic necessity. The force of the "necessity" arises from some intrinsic qualities of the door and some rules; in other words, the source of the compelling force is external to the speaker.

The second meaning of (11b) is about the door being locked. This meaning is paraphrased in (11d): 'it is necessarily the case *that* the door is locked'. The source of this epistemic judgement is the speaker. An epistemic necessity may be inferred from an intrinsic necessity: if it is, due to rules and regulations, in general necessary for the door to be locked, I may, in a specific situation, conclude that it must also be locked at this moment.

10.3.2 Modals of obligation, intrinsic necessity and epistemic necessity

The system of English compelling modals is quite elaborate. However, as the sentences with *must* under (11) showed, the modal verbs do not distinguish between the three types of compelling modalities but much rather between the sources of the compelling force on the one hand and degrees of its strength on the other hand. The source of the compelling force may be the speaker (or hearer) or external circumstances, i.e. intrinsic to a thing. Speaker-internal modalities are subjective, while modalities based on external sources are more or less objective. We will describe speaker-internal sources as *subjective* and, in order to avoid confusion with the objectivity associated with modal expressions other than modal verbs, describe speaker-external sources as *external*. Obligations are mostly subjective, intrinsic necessities are external, and epistemic necessities are mostly subjective. Table 10.3 presents the compelling modals within the two-dimensional grid of sources of the compelling force and their degrees of force. The modals printed in bold are the more commonly used ones within a cell.

Table 10.3. System of English compelling modals

strength	obligation	intrinsic necessity	epistemic necessity	
	subjective	external	subjective	external
strong:	**must**, have got to	**have (got) to**, must	**must**, have got to	have to
neutral:		need to	will	
weak:	should, ought to	should, (ought to)	should, ought to	

10.3.2.1 Strong compelling modalities

(i) *Obligations and intrinsic necessities:* **must**, **have to**, *and* **have got to**
Performative obligations are the strongest root modalities: they are imposed by a volitionally acting, authoritative speaker (*You must wear a tie!*) or, in questions, by the hearer (*Must I wear a tie?*). They are typically expressed by *must* and, conversely, the modal *must*

is associated with strong impositions enforced by humans. A weaker form of obligation, especially in American usage, is *have (got) to* or, more casually, *gotta*. The following sentences illustrate the different strengths associated with *must* and *have to* of obligation:

(12) a. *You must hurry up.* There's not much time left.
     b. *You have to hurry up.* There's only a very limited offer.

You must hurry up might be said by a mother urging her child to get off to school. Her obligation rests on parental authority and conveys exigency and personal concern. *You have to hurry up*, on the other hand, might be given as a piece of advice by a neighbour or found in an advertisement: it appeals to the force of circumstances, which are external to the speaker. This sentence is therefore more likely to be interpreted in the sense of an intrinsic necessity. **Intrinsic necessity** refers to a necessity arising from a thing and general rules or norms. We feel more at ease being subjected to general rules than to a person's authority. The compelling force of intrinsic necessities is therefore felt to be weaker and more readily acceptable. Like obligations, intrinsic necessities may, however, be presented more externally and hence as less compelling, or more subjectively and hence as more compelling. Consider the intrinsic necessities described by *have to* and *must* in the following contexts.

(13) a. When registering for a library card *you have to show your passport* or some other valid proof of identity.
     b. When you enter the USA, *you must show your passport* and the I-20, which is in a sealed envelope.

Here, the gravity of the circumstances determines the choice between *have to* and *must*. Issuing a library card is an almost routine matter securing the institution's property and can be entrusted to a student assistant, i.e. it is a less compelling context that prompts the use of *have to*, as in (13a). Entering the United States, on the other hand, is a serious personalised matter affecting the whole community and hence requires careful scrutiny by the immigration officers, i.e. it is a highly compelling context that prompts the use of *must*, as in (13b).

This subtle distinction in use between *must* and *have to* is the result of recent shifts in the system of compelling modal verbs, especially in spoken American English. Up to the early 19th century, the only strong obligation marker was *must*. By now the semi-modals *(have) got to* (53%) and *have to* (39%) have almost completely ousted *must* (8%). These shifts have been attributed to two major factors in American English: "colloquialisation" and "democratisation", i.e. emphasis on equality of power.

The social pressure exerted by *must* is, for obvious reasons, less pronounced in situations in which the speaker obliges himself. In *I have to go now*, the speaker views himself as being driven by some external force; in *I must go now*, the speaker urges himself to some action in a kind of self-exhortation. He views himself as being driven by two forces within himself: a stronger force, probably the rational mind, tells him to go and prevails over a weaker counterforce, possibly his emotions, which tell him to stay.

Viewing ourselves as being driven by opposing internal forces also accounts for another interesting use of *I must* in utterances involving verbs of cognition and communication, as in:

(14) a. *I must admit* I don't really follow your reasoning.
b. *We must ask* you to answer a few questions.

These constructions with *I must* or *we must* are no longer understood as expressing a modality but much rather as strong assertions : 'I admit I don't follow your reasoning' and 'we are asking you to answer a few questions'. The speaker is in fact performing the speech act he is describing, i.e. admitting, asking, confessing, protesting, etc. The performative meaning can be brought out in paraphrases with *hereby*: *I hereby admit that...* The relation between the modal meaning of *must* and its intended meaning in the sentence is metonymic: POTENTIALITY FOR ACTUALITY. The obligation meaning of *must* is, however, not obliterated but still present: it conveys that the speaker is obliged to act, thereby implying that he would prefer to be relieved from having to do so. The use of the modal in *I must* thus has a mitigating force. In pragmatics, mitigating expressions are known as *hedges*. Hedges in this function of alleviating directness have therefore been described as *hedged performatives*.

(ii) *Epistemic necessities:* **must** *and* **have (got) to**
Epistemic necessity is often described as 'logical necessity'. However, this term is misleading: if necessity was a matter of logic, the deduction reached from given premises would always have to be true (see Chapter 2.3), but this is not the case in modality. Epistemic necessity is led by inference and means that there is so much evidence for a state of affairs that it is assessed as coming very close to factual reality. As shown in Section 10.2.2, the speaker's inferential processes are of necessity subjective. At the same time, they are based on external evidence, the intrinsic force of the evolutionary momentum (see Figure 10.4(b)). In using *must*, the speaker emphasises the subjective aspect of his assessment of necessity, while in using *have to*, the speaker focuses on the external evidence determining the necessity. Necessities that are based on external circumstances are felt to be more conclusive — and make the speaker more confident — than necessities that are based on intuitive reasoning. Thus, *This has (got) to be right* sounds more compelling than *This must be right*, i.e. *have to* conveys a stronger force than *must*. The modals *must* and *have to* thus display inverse degrees of strength in obligations and epistemic necessities:

(15) a. obligation: *must* is stronger than *have to*
b. necessity: *have to* is stronger than *must*

We may use our example of hooking up a DVD-player, which we discussed in Section 10.2.3.1, to illustrate the difference in strength conveyed by *must* and *have to* of epistemic necessity. The first assessment of our work, before giving the DVD-player a try, might be "This must be right now." When, after several vain attempts, we finally detect the mistake, we are more likely to conclude "This has to be right now," because now we can reason on the basis of a longer evolutionary momentum. It goes without saying that "petty necessities" tend to be expressed by *must*, as in *This must be fun*, while "serious necessities", such as an investigation into a murder, for which solid evidence is required, tend to be expressed by *have to*, as in:

(16) He explains that only a man could have dragged the body in from the sea, so the murderer *has to* be a man.

Epistemic *have to*, and even more so *have got to*, are less commonly used than epistemic *must*. Thus, we have the seemingly paradoxical situation that *have to* has increased in popularity as the strong obligation marker at the expense of *must*, while *must* has increased in popularity as the strong marker of epistemic necessity. One reason for this asymmetry might be ecological pressure: now each modal is characterised by its own preferential niche. Leech (1971) suggests another reason for the lower frequency of *have (got) to* as a marker for necessity: there is often another, more idiomatic way of expressing what he calls "theoretical necessity". Thus, rather than saying *These lines have to be by Shakespeare*, the negative alternative *Nobody but Shakespeare could have written these lines* "comes more naturally to the tongue."

10.3.2.2 Neutral compelling modalities: **need to** and **will**

The modal verb *need to* relates to the noun *need* and the adjective *needy* and their sense of 'lacking', which, by implicature, gives rise to the idea of 'requiring what is lacking'. The verb *want*, incidentally, has the same kind of polysemy. The notions of 'lacking' and 'requiring' apply to intrinsic attributes of things or people; hence the modal *need to* is associated with a compelling force emanating from within the thing. The goal-directedness of the modal *need to* is reflected in its use with the goal preposition *to* (see Chapter 12.3.2.1). Typical usages of *need to* are:

(17) a. You *need to* upgrade your Flash Player.
      b. The brakes *need to* be replaced every 20,000 miles.

The needs described in (17) arise from the intrinsic nature of the things: software needs to be upgraded every now and then and mechanical parts wear out and need to be replaced. The implicature of taking care of the intrinsic need is probably stronger in sentence (17a) than in sentence (17b) because the hearer as the agent is explicitly addressed. Sentence (17a) is, therefore, most likely to be understood in the directive sense of a piece of advice ('I hereby advise you to …'), while sentence (17b) is likely to be understood in the sense of intrinsic necessity ('it is essential for the brakes to be replaced'). In an appropriate context, this sentence will, of course, invite the implicature of a piece of advice. Like the obligation modal *have to*, *need to* denies speaker involvement and, probably for the same social reasons as *have to*, its use has dramatically increased, especially in American English.

A second modal that hovers between the poles of strong and weak modalities is *will*. Its original sense of 'wishing' and 'desiring' has undergone a chain of motivated meaning extensions to 'volition', 'intention', 'prediction' and 'weak necessity'. 'Intention' and 'prediction' are the main aspects of meaning characterising the future tense form *will* (see Chapter 9.4.2), while 'volition' and 'weak necessity' are essentially modal notions. *Will* of volition describes a person's inner wishes and hence is an intrinsic modality (see 10.2.4.2). It is modal in that one's wishes and desires typically invite inferences about prospective actions, as in the New Year's resolution (18a). Epistemic *will*, as in (18b), describes the assessment of a probability reached by a reasonable inference.

(18) a. I WILL see my dentist this year. [*volition*]
     b. This *will* be Aunt Sophie. [*weak necessity*]

The meanings of futurity and modality are not easily distinguishable with *will*. Thus, sentence (18a) has future reference, but the emphatic WILL signals its volitional sense at the present moment. Sentence (18b) may be said at the ring of the bell and thus refers to the assessment of a present situation. Its meaning is not very different from *That must be Aunt Sophie*. However, it implies a prediction and thus shades into the future: Aunt Sophie will soon be coming through the door (see also Chapter 9.2.1.3).

10.3.2.3 Weak compelling modalities: **should** and **ought to**

> *The more you know, the more you know*
> *you ought to know.* (Anonymous)

The original sense of indebtedness of *shall* and *owe*, as in *You owe me an apology*, is still preserved in the present-day usages of *should* and *ought to*. Both modals were originally past tense forms of *shall* and *owe*, which accounts for their weakened force. The weak obligation they denote typically derives from individual wishes and desires or from general norms such as moral values. The modals are thus used for expressing both subjective obligations, as in *You should dress properly*, and external obligations, as in *Your tie should match your shirt*. People tend to share the same system of values. The force that appeals to values is therefore minimal, and the hearer is not necessarily expected to comply. Rather than imposing an obligation, *should* and *ought to* therefore describe the speaker's idea of desirability about an advisable course of action. In the ecological system of modality only one of these mild modals is needed. Especially in American English, the use of *should* has increased, while that of *ought to* has declined.

Due to its weakened force of obligation, *should* behaves differently in many ways from other root modals. Thus, *should* is not exclusively future-oriented but can also refer to general time (19a), present (19b) and past times (19c), is compatible with the progressive form (19b), and allows the use of tag questions (19d,e):

(19) a. You *should* visit your mother more regularly and more often.
     b. You *should be visiting* your mother *now*, and not just phoning her.
     c. Carol *should have* visited her mother *yesterday*. It was her birthday.
     d. Carol *should* visit her mother more regularly, *shouldn't she*?
     e. Carol *shouldn't* neglect her duties, *should she*?

The weaker force makes deontic *should* often indistinguishable from epistemic modality. Thus, the sentences below can be understood in a deontic or an epistemic sense:

(20) a. This car *should* have air-condition.
 b. This course *should* be interesting.

Sentence (20a) might mean that I, as the customer, expect that someone will install air-condition in the car or that I infer from the make of the car that it is probably equipped with air-condition. The former deontic meaning involves the metonymy RESULT FOR ACTION. Similarly, sentence (20b) might mean that the teacher should make an effort to make the course more interesting or that I infer from reading the course description that the course is probably interesting.

Only rarely are *should* and *ought to* exclusively interpreted in an epistemic sense, possibly because the notion of desirability is too dominant. A context that suggests an epistemic interpretation is illustrated in the following example:

(21) The chocolate-iced cake looks marvellous; it *should* be delicious.

Here, the interpretation of weak necessity is based on the inference from appearance to taste: food that looks good will also taste good.

10.4 Enabling modalities

10.4.1 Evolution of enabling modalities

Enabling modalities involve the unimpeded potential of a force; they comprise abilities, intrinsic possibilities, permissions and epistemic possibilities. There are only two pairs of English modals denoting enabling modalities: *may/might* and *can/could*. The original lexical meaning of *may* is 'be physically able', which is still reflected in the noun *might* and the adjective *mighty*; the original lexical meaning of *can* is 'be mentally able', which is still preserved in the verb *know*. Both verbs go back to the Indo-European base **gno-*. Abilities are dispositions of a thing (see 10.2.4.2). The following sentences illustrate paths of meaning extension from 'ability' to different other types of modality.

(22) a. I *can* drive. [ability]
 b. I *can* drive you. [intrinsic possibility]
 c. You *can/may* take me home. [permission]
 d. We *may* be leaving soon. [epistemic possibility]

The modal *can* in (22a) describes a person's general ability. Saying that "I can drive" will, in a given context, be understood as meaning 'it is possible for me to drive' and, by way of a further implicature, that I am offering a lift. The transition from the meaning of 'ability' to that of 'intrinsic possibility' and an implied 'offer' is more conspicuous in sentence (22b), which may be understood as describing an ability, an intrinsic possibility ('it is possible for me to drive you'), or an offer ('I am offering to drive you'). A well-meant offer is normally gladly accepted, i.e. a person who offers to do us a favour is usually given permission to do so. This natural inference is expressed in the permission sentence (22c). As a final inferential step we may judge the likelihood of the ensuing state of affairs. Sentence (22d), which cannot be expressed by *can* — although it might be expressed by *could*, denotes an epistemic possibility, namely that 'it is possible that we will be leaving soon'.

These stages in the evolution of enabling modals are illustrated in Table 10.4. Historically, 'intrinsic possibility' gave rise to two meaning extensions: to 'permission' and to 'epistemic possibility'.

Table 10.4. From 'ability' to 'permission' and 'epistemic possibility'

ability		intrinsic possibility		permission		epistemic possibility
can	>	can	>	can	>	can
		may	>	may	>	may

The two modals *can* and *may* have undergone different developments and still display different, often complementary, usages. *Can* has retained the original sense of 'ability' and is normally used to express 'intrinsic possibility', while *may* is normally used for 'epistemic modality'. Both *can* and *may* express 'permission' but, of course, convey different meanings of permission.

10.4.2 Modals of ability, intrinsic possibility, permission and epistemic possibility

10.4.2.1 Ability: **can, could,** and **be able to**

Abilities are salient and distinctive attributes that have the potential of being actualised as a thing's characteristic behaviour. Salient attributes of humans are, for example, being able to walk a tightrope or on one's hands, which we readily accept as abilities. Being able to walk on one's feet, on the other hand, is normally not considered a human ability unless it is seen within a frame in which walking on one's feet counts as a special achievement, such as the first steps of a one-year-old. Conceiving of a given property as an ability thus always requires a judgement about its salience relative to a frame.

An ability is inseparably linked to the thing that has this ability. Things tend to "behave" in accordance with their characteristic attributes, and they potentially or occasionally do so. Bears have the disposition to climb trees, and we expect that they will occasionally do so. Our view of things and their potential behaviour is thus guided by the conceptual metonymy DISPOSITION FOR OCCASIONAL BEHAVIOUR. According to a commonsense theory of the nature of things, things and their essential attributes are hierarchically ordered in what is known as the "Great Chain of Being". Natural physical things occupy the lowest level: they are characterised by natural physical attributes, which lead to natural physical behaviour. Natural physical behaviour is governed by physical laws; hence it is largely predictable and not salient. Therefore, we do not speak of glass as "being able to" break or of the sun as "being able to" shine. Animals occupy a medium position in this hierarchy: in addition to physical attributes, they have instinctual attributes leading to instinctual behaviour. Instinctual behaviour tends to be species-specific and hence allows us to discriminate one species from another. Humans occupy the highest level in the chain of being: in addition to having physical and instinctual attributes, they are characterised by higher-order attributes, especially intellect, morality and emotions. Human "higher-order" behaviour may vary from person to person and hence tends to be unpredictable.

It follows from this folk model of things that abilities have a different function with humans, animals and natural physical things. Individual humans can be assigned diverse abilities as in (23a), animals are mainly assigned abilities in characterising their species as in (23b), and natural physical things least qualify to be associated with abilities. One reason to think of them as having abilities is their use as a means, as in (23c).

(23) a. Phyllis *can/is able to* speak three languages.
b. Lions *can/are able to* run up to 37 mph.
c. X-rays *can/are able to* penetrate the body's tissues and bones.

Abilities can be expressed by using the modal verb *can* or its suppletive form *be able to*. The use of *can* is, however, more restricted than that of *be able to*. *Can* of ability is used to describe habitual states, which include the present moment, as in (23), and habitual states which occurred in the past, as in (24a). Only *be able to* can be used with future habitual states, as in (24b), or with an actually occurring past event, as in (24c). However, the past tense form *could* can be used with non-occurring past events, as in (24d).

(24) a. In my young days I *could/ was able to* play the Wedding March.
b. With some more practice I *will be able to* play gospels.
c. I *was even able to* compose a song.
d. I sat down at the piano but *couldn't* play any melody.

Unlike *be able to*, the modal verb *can* is strongly associated with its implied actualisation. Thus there is no contradiction in seeing a person behave differently from his abilities, as in sentence (25).

(25) Jack can be very nice, but last night he wasn't: he had too much to drink and misbehaved.

The *but*-clause in (25) does not deny the ability, but cancels the inferred modal meaning, viz. that 'it is possible for Jack to be nice' combined with strong expectations about this kind of behaviour in actual situations. In this sentence, as well as in all other sentences with *can* of ability, the notion of 'ability' shades over into that of 'intrinsic possibility'. These meanings of *can* are in fact so tightly interconnected that they are felt to convey a single unitary meaning.

10.4.2.2 *Intrinsic possibility:* **can, could, may,** *and* **might**

In the same way that we distinguished intrinsic and epistemic necessity (see 10.3.1), we need to distinguish intrinsic and epistemic possibility. The distinction between these two types of possibility is more easily recognisable because each sense is associated with its own modal verb: intrinsic possibility with *can*, and epistemic possibility with *may*.

(26) a. You *can* download PowerPoint from Microsoft.
'it is possible *for* you to download…' [*intrinsic possibility*]
b. You *may* have PowerPoint on your computer.
'it is possible *that* you have …' [*epistemic possibility*]

Sentence (26a) indicates a possibility for the hearer to do something so that a future situation will come about. The potential success of the download is dependent on the person's intrinsic abilities, in particular his computer skills, and the availability of the software. The source of an intrinsic possibility, sometimes also called root possibility, is thus inherent in a participant and hence external to the speaker. Sentence (26b) with *may* describes the speaker's assessment of a given state of affairs, i.e. the possibility results from the speaker's subjective judgement. *Can* and *may* are not interchangeable in these sentences.

Intrinsic possibility can now be defined as referring to a possibility enabled by a speaker-external source. It may apply to specific situations as in (26a), in which the external source is specified, but more commonly it is used to characterise general situations, in which the external source is left unspecified but is, nevertheless, conceptually present. Sentence (26a) may also be interpreted in this general sense and might be paraphrased as 'It is possible for anybody to download PowerPoint'. The impersonal pronoun *you* now refers to people in general. The grammatical device that typically invites general statements is, of course, the passive construction, which allows the speaker to remain vague about the agent. The use of the passive with *can* of intrinsic modality is particularly popular in academic writing. It allows the author to remain non-committal with respect to a specific source and, moreover, suggests objectivity. Phrases such as *it can be said/ noted/ observed/ argued/ claimed/ concluded*, etc. therefore abound in scholarly and bureaucratic writing:

(27) a. It *can* be argued that humans are the sum of their experiences.
b. From these figures, it *can* be concluded that bottled and tap water can be equally "healthy".

The different verbs in the passive construction convey different degrees of reliability, evidence or reservation about the potentiality of a situation. Thus, an argument (27a) requires less evidence than a conclusion (27b). The speaker may also attenuate an intrinsic possibility by using the subjective modal *may* (*It may be argued/concluded…*) or the distal form *could*: *It could be concluded* sounds more cautious than *It can be concluded*, and the spontaneous offer *We could accommodate you for a night* sounds more hospitable than *We can accommodate you for a night*.

Intrinsic possibility does not only shade over into 'ability' and 'permission', but may also shade over into reality. People often describe their actual sensations, perceptions or thoughts as if they occurred in potentiality, as in:

(28) a. I *can* see my house now.
 b. I *can* feel his breath on my neck.
 c. We *can* hear the birds chirping.
 d. I *can* remember when we first met.

The speaker *does*, in fact, see, feel, hear and remember the things talked about. The use of *can* of intrinsic possibility in these sentences thus involves the metonymy POTENTIALITY FOR ACTUALITY, which we also found in the use of *must* in phrases such as *I must admit* (see (14)). The modal verb *can*, however, does not function as a hedged performative but conceptually blends two spaces: an earlier space, in which it was not possible for the speaker to experience something, and a present space, in which she actually and unexpectedly has this experience. Thus, sentence (28a) conveys the speaker's surprise at actually seeing her house on Google Earth, which she had never thought would be possible for her to do.

10.4.2.3 *Permission:* **can**, **may** *and* **could**

Permissions express the speaker's directive attitude towards the hearer's potential action, which he "enables" to occur by relinquishing his power to prevent it (see 10.2.3.2). An act of permission is thus typically based on the speaker's authority. This subjective situation of permission-granting is expressed by use of the subjective modal *may*. Permissions may, however, also be based on external circumstances and are then expressed by the modal *can*. Two such situations of permission are depicted in Figure 10.6. The permission in *You may go now* relies on the teacher's authority, that of *You can go now* on external circumstances: the ringing of the bell.

Figure 10.6. *May* and *can* of permission

May and *can* thus evoke differences in meanings similar to those between *must* and *have to*. In the same way that the authoritative tone of obligations is mitigated by appealing to external compelling factors and using the modal *have to* (10.3.2.1), the authoritative force invoked by permissions can be softened by use of the modal *can*. As in strong compelling modals, the social forces of democratisation and colloquialisation have, especially in American English, led to a dramatic increase of *can* in expressing permissions. Thus, "typical" personal permissions such as allowing a person to stay in my apartment or use my car are now normally expressed by the colloquial *can*, as in *You can use my car*, rather than *may*, which sounds not just authoritative, but also rather stilted.

Interestingly, the force of a permission cannot be weakened by using the distal forms *might* and *could*. Possibly the sense of permission is no longer felt to be transparent because the distal forms are used to express epistemic possibility and ability. Thus, *You might go* can only express possibility and, by way of implicature, suggest performing an action.

In asking for permission, we need to balance the gravity of the request asked about against the social relation between speaker and hearer and the formality of the situation. The use of *may* is most appropriate with serious requests, high status of the hearer, and formal situations, as in *May I invite you to lunch with me tomorrow?* or *May I have your attention?*, while the use of *can* or *could* is most appropriate in casual situations, as in *Can I use your phone?* The three-way distinction between degrees of imposition provided by *may*, *can* and *could* makes the use of a further modal in asking for permissions, i.e. *might*, unnecessary. Nevertheless this form exists for very polite requests, as in *Might I use the bathroom?*, or for sarcastic requests, as in the teacher's demand, *John Smith, might I ask you what you're doing with that piece of paper*.

10.4.2.4 Epistemic possibility: *may*, *might*, *can* and *could*

Epistemic possibility pertains to the speaker's assessment of a state of affairs in the realm of potential reality. It involves considering evidence and counter-evidence which, as argued in Section 10.2.3.2, does not bar the speaker from assessing a state of affairs as possible. This process of reasoning is highly subjective and hence normally expressed by *may*. Thus, *I may have left the phone in the car* sounds fine as an epistemic assessment of my absent-mindedness, while ?*I can have left my phone in the car* forces us to think of some external circumstances that were responsible for my forgetfulness. We may, however, use the distal form *could*, which weakens the force of the external source in our assessment.

Generic situations lend themselves more readily to being assessed as "externally" possible. Thus, tobacco companies were forced to replace the warning "Smoking may damage your health" on their cigarette packets, which presented the risks of smoking as people's subjective views, by "Smoking can damage your health", which presents the risk as being based on external, scientific evidence and hence more objectively substantiated.

Can and *could* are the only modals that can be used in questions asking about an epistemic possibility, as in *Can this wait a little?* Questions such as **May this wait a little?* are, of course, excluded because the speaker is questioning the very subjective assessment he is just making.

10.5 Interaction of modality with negation

No treatment of modality would be complete without touching upon the intriguing area of its interaction with negation. Descriptions of modality in English often give the impression that the behaviour of modal verbs is erratic when they occur with negation. For example, an obligation, as in (29a), and its negation, i.e. prohibition, as in (29b), are expressed by the same modal *must*, whereas a necessity, as in (30a), and its negation, i.e. impossibility, as in (30b), are expressed by different modals.

(29) a. You *must* stay at home. [*obligation*]
     b. You *mustn't* stay at home. [*prohibition*]

(30) a. You *must* have a fever. [*necessity*]
     b. You *can't* have a fever. [*impossibility*]

Why should *mustn't* be used in (29b) but *can't* in (30b)? It has been suggested that *mustn't* is not available because its meaning is supplied by *can't*. But that begs the question why *can't* is used in the first place to denote negated necessity in English as well as in many other languages, including those that are unrelated.

10.5.1 What is special about modality and negation

The most intriguing problem in the interaction of modals and negation is the scope of negation. The negation can affect the modality or the proposition, and the negator *not* does not reveal which expression(s) are negated. The scope of negation is only visible in the paraphrases of negated modal sentences. Thus, sentence (29b) is paraphrased as 'it is necessary for you NOT to stay at home', i.e. the proposition is negated, while sentence (30b) is paraphrased as 'it is NOT possible that you have a fever', i.e. the modality is negated. We will discuss negations with root and epistemic modality separately.

10.5.2 Root modals and their negations

The negation of disposition modals is straightforward: it always applies to the modality, not to the proposition. Thus, negating my ability to swim means that 'I am not able to swim', and not that 'I am able not to swim'. The negation of intrinsic, deontic and epistemic modals is more complex: it can apply to both the modality and the proposition. The modalities of obligation and permission as well as those of necessity and possibility interact in such a way that the negation of one modality is logically equivalent to the negation of the proposition of the other modality. We will consider deontic and epistemic modality. With deontic modality, we have two equivalence relations: 'not be obliged to act' is equivalent to 'be permitted not to act', and 'not be permitted to act' is equivalent to 'be obliged not to act'.

(i) *No obligation to act = permission not to act*
If I am *not obliged* to do something I am *permitted not* to do something. These two notions are logically, but certainly not pragmatically, equivalent. 'Not be obliged to act' means that one is exempted from an obligation to act. The notion of 'obligation' is thus always present in exemptions. For example, *You need not submit a certificate* and *You don't have to pay income taxes* mean that you are exempted from some regulation that normally applies. The basis for being freed from some such obligation is external to the speaker. Therefore, the modals expressing exemptions describe them as negations of external compelling forces, i.e. *need not*, *don't have to*, and *haven't got to*. Notice that negated *need* does not, unlike its

positive counterpart (see 10.3.2.2), take the goal preposition *to* since, in lacking a force, it is no longer goal-directed.

Permitting a person not to act is a rare situation. Normally people ask for permission when they want to do something rather than to refrain from doing something. There is, in fact, no need to code this notion because an act of granting permission includes the possibility for the hearer *not* to carry out the act permitted. The concept 'be permitted not to act' is therefore not lexicalised by a modal verb of its own. Yet, this concept has its ecological niche in its contrast to 'be permitted to act'. For example, a smoking area might be designated as *You may not smoke here*, where *nót* would be stressed in speech. Needless to say, such situations have an ironic ring.

(ii) *No permission to act = obligation not to act*
If I am *not permitted* to do something, I am *obliged not* to do something. A denial or absence of permission is thus logically equivalent to a prohibition, and both notions are, in fact, close in meaning, but not interchangeable. Denials of permission are expressed by the enabling modals *may not* and *can't*, prohibitions are expressed by the compelling modal *mustn't*. All three modals invoke the force-dynamic pattern of a counterforce being blocked from taking effect, but each of them does so in its own way. In using *may not*, the speaker conveys the option of closing a barrier rather than lifting it; and in using *can't*, the speaker indicates that her denial of permission is due to external restraints. The use of the modal *mustn't* suggests that the prohibition is imposed by a strong compelling force, typically a person in authority. The following contexts illustrate these slight differences in the use of these modals.

(32) a. You *can't* come in. Not with that dog.
 b. You *may not* come in. I have nothing to say to you.
 c. You *mustn't* come in. We mustn't disturb my parents.

The denial of permission in (32a) is based on the speaker's consideration of external factors; the denial of permission in (32b) rests on the speaker's decision; and the prohibition in (32c) derives from a strong personal compelling context. Due to its external source, *can't* expresses a weaker denial of permission and hence sounds more casual than *may not*, and both refusals of permission are less forceful than *mustn't*, which conveys the same authoritative tone as *must* of obligation. The strong directive force conveyed by deontic *may not* is surprising but was also noted in its positive usage (see 10.3.1).

The system of negation in deontic modality displays a noticeable predominance of obligation over permission modals, i.e. deontic modality is "obligation-based" when combined with negation. The reverse picture emerges in negated epistemic modality, where possibility modals predominate over necessity modals, i.e. epistemic modality is "possibility-based" when combined with negation.

10.5.3 Epistemic modals and their negations

The logical equivalence relations found in epistemic modality and negation are comparable to those of deontic modality: 'not necessary' is equivalent to 'possible that not', and 'not possible' is equivalent to 'necessary that not'.

(i) *No necessity = possibility that not*
The notion 'not be necessary', i.e. "unnecessity", is coded by the same modals as its deontic counterpart 'not be obliged', i.e. *need not, don't have to,* and *haven't got to*. The two notions are also similar in their force-dynamic constellations. The deontic exemption in *You need not go* invokes a compelling force from which the hearer is exempted in the same way that the unnecessity in *It need not be true* invokes a compelling force (of evidence) from which the speaker, in her own reasoning, exempts herself.

The notions 'not be necessary' and 'be possible that not' are only logically equivalent, i.e. if something is *not necessarily* the case it is *possible that it is not* the case. Pragmatically, however, the two notions are fundamentally different. *Need not* is said in relativising an accepted fact or necessity, as in *Aging is unavoidable, but it need not be quite so inexorable*. The modal expressing 'be possible that not', *may not*, is typically used in relativising another modal statement or assumption, as in *Aging can be reversed, but it may not make you wiser*. Why should 'not be obliged' and 'be permitted not to' be near-synonymous, but 'not be necessary' and 'be possible that not' be different in meaning? In the same way that permitting a person to do something includes permitting her not to do this, the possibility that something is true includes the possibility that this is not true. However, as shown above, permitting a person not to do something is a rather anomalous situation, whereas judging a state of affairs as close to not true is perfectly normal. It is thus only natural for epistemic *may* and *may not* to denote different things: *may* conveys a higher degree of assessed likelihood than *may not*. This can be seen from the contexts in which each form may occur. *May*, but not *may not*, readily co-occurs with *yes*, as in *Yes, that may be true*, while *may not*, but not *may*, is more likely to co-occur with *no*, as in *No, that may not be true*.

(ii) *No possibility = necessity that not*
The notions 'not be possible' and 'be necessary that not' are again logically equivalent. The concept 'be necessary that not' is not lexicalised as a modal of necessity (**Jack mustn't be back home*), but may of course be expressed, as in *It is necessarily the case that Jack isn't back home*. This notion is expressed by using the equivalent negated modal of possibility, i.e. impossibility, as in *Jack can't be back home*. *Mustn't* is only used for deontic negation. Why shouldn't *mustn't* be available to express a necessity that something is not the case, and why is *can't* chosen instead? As we argued at the beginning of this chapter, the use of epistemic *must* involves an inferential process in which the evolutionary momentum compels the speaker to draw only one possible conclusion. For example, when Jack's car is parked in front of his house we infer that *he* parked it there, and when the lights in the living-room have been turned on we infer that *he* (or some member of his family) did so. The situation of Jack's not being home, on the other hand, is mainly characterised by

lack of positive evidence: his car is *not* parked in front of his house, the lights are *not* on, etc. Missing evidence does not allow us to make any strong inferences about his presence at home and hence also excludes the use of *mustn't*. However, we may also find evidence pointing to Jack's longer absence, such as junk mail piling up in his letter box and the lawn being overgrown. This kind of evidence is based on the intrinsic nature of these things. Modals that typically describe modal assessments based on speaker-external forces are, as pointed out earlier, *have to* and *can*. Negated *have to* is already preempted because it is used to denote "unnecessity". The only modal verb that qualifies to describe the concept 'not possible' as well as 'be necessary that not' is thus *can't*.

10.7 Summary

This chapter dealt with situations that are assessed as having **potential reality**. Potential reality is opposed to **factual reality** of the known past or the immediate present and **projected reality** of the future. Situations that belong to factual or projected reality can be strongly asserted, as in *Peggy is sick*. The notion of **assertion** refers to the speaker's confidence in the reality status of a state of affairs. Situations that belong to potential reality can, in spite of their possibly strong evidence, only be weakly asserted, as in *Peggy must be sick*. Such situations and their expressions in language belong to the area of modality. **Modality** is concerned with the speaker's assessment of, or attitude towards, the potentiality of a state of affairs. Notions of modality are typically expressed by **modal verbs**, which ground a situation in potential reality. Two main types of modality are normally distinguished: *epistemic modality* and *root modality*.

Epistemic modality belongs to the world of knowledge and reasoning and is concerned with the speaker's inferred assessment of the potentiality of a state of affairs, as in *You must be right*. In **epistemic necessity**, compelling evidence leaves only one possible conclusion to draw; in **epistemic possibility**, there is no counter-evidence that bars the speaker from drawing a conclusion. Epistemic modalities are paraphrased as 'it is necessarily the case/possible that'.

Root modality comprises the three subtypes of *deontic modality*, *intrinsic modality* and *disposition modality*. **Deontic modality** belongs to the world of social interaction and authority; it is concerned with the speaker's directive attitude towards an action to be carried out, as in *You must go*. Its directive function is similar to that of **directive speech acts**, in which the speaker "directs" the hearer to perform, or refrain from performing, a certain action. The use of deontic modals is similar to that of performative verbs in **performative speech acts**, which explicitly name and thereby perform the speech act, as in *I request you to go*. The two main deontic modalities are obligations and permissions. **Obligations** are binding forces that are seen as compelling a person to carry out a certain action; **permissions** express the speaker's directive attitude towards the hearer's potential action, which he "enables" to occur by relinquishing his power to prevent it.

Intrinsic modality is concerned with potentialities arising from speaker-external sources, i.e. from intrinsic qualities of a thing or circumstances. It comprises *intrinsic necessity* and *intrinsic possibility*. **Intrinsic necessity** refers to a necessity arising from a thing and general rules or norms, as in *The job must be done*, i.e. 'it is necessary for the job to be done'; **intrinsic possibility** refers to a possibility enabled by a speaker-external source, as in *The meeting can be cancelled*, i.e. 'it is possible for the meeting to be cancelled'. **Disposition modality** is concerned with a thing's intrinsic disposition which has the potential of being actualised; it includes the notions of 'ability' or 'propensity' and 'willingness'. **Abilities** are salient and distinctive attributes that have the potential of being actualised as a thing's characteristic behaviour.

The English modals are **polysemous**: most of them denote both root and epistemic modalities. Their senses are historically and synchronically related by implicatures. A common characteristic of root and epistemic modality is their *force-dynamic* basis. **Compelling modalities** involve compelling forces and comprise obligations, prohibitions and intrinsic and epistemic necessities; they are expressed by *must, have (got) to, need to, should*, and *ought to*. **Enabling modalities** involve the unimpeded potential of a force and comprise abilities, intrinsic possibilities, permissions and epistemic possibilities; they are expressed by *may, might, can* and *could*.

Modality interacts with negation in a systematic way. The negation of disposition modals always affects the modality, as in *I cannot swim*, which means 'I am not able to swim'. The negation of intrinsic, deontic and epistemic modals may affect the modality or the proposition. Thus, *You may not have a fever* means that 'it is possible that you don't have a fever', i.e. the proposition is negated, while *You can't have a fever* means that 'it is not possible that you have a fever', i.e. the modality is negated.

> **Further Reading**

Classics on English modality are Lyons (1977: Ch. 17), Perkins (1983), Coates (1983) and Palmer (²1990; 2001). Useful practical surveys of modality and modal verbs are provided in Leech (1971) and Suzuki (1989).

Cognitive-linguistic approaches to modality are found in Langacker (1991a: Ch. 6), Nuyts (2000) on epistemic modality, and Johnson (1987), Talmy (1988a/2000), Sweetser (1990), and Pelyvás (2003; 2006). The grammaticalisation of modals is discussed in Traugott (1989), Bybee, Perkins & Pagliuca (1994: Ch. 6) and Traugott & Dasher (2002: Ch. 3).

The modals of obligation and necessity are surveyed in Collins (2005), modals of strong obligation in American English are discussed in Myhill (1996), modals of possibility are contrasted in Coates (1995), and the epistemic use of *ought to* is analysed in Nordlinger & Traugott (1997). The interaction of modals with modal adverbs is studied in Hoye (1997).

Hedged performatives as pragmatic phenomenon are described in Fraser (1975); their metonymic basis has been pointed out by Panther & Thornburg (1999). The model of the Great Chain of Being is presented in Lakoff & Turner (1989: Ch. 4), where it is mainly applied to the understanding of proverbs.

> **Study Questions**

1. Point out the difference in meaning between the following pairs of sentences:
    a. (i) Sue is at home. Her car is parked in front of the house.
       (ii) Sue must be at home. Her car is parked in front of the house.
    b. (i) Tom is *perhaps* in Washington.
       (ii) Jerry *may* be in Buffalo.
    c. (i) I heard that Jennifer is walking on crutches and has her head all bandaged up.
       (ii) Jennifer must have had an accident.
    d. (i) My son *may go* to America.
       (ii) My daughter *may be going* to Australia.
       (iii) My cousins *may have gone* to New Zealand.
    e. (i) Yes, I *permit* you to store my personal data.
       (ii) Yes, you *may* store my personal data.
    f. (i) You *must* take a right turn now.
       (ii) You've *got to* take a right turn now.
       (iii) You *have to* take a right turn now
       (iv) You *need to* take a right turn now.
       (v) You *should* take a right turn now.

2. Identify and discuss the type(s) of modality in the following sentences.
    a. This car *can* run on water, alcohol or cow dung.
    b. The consumption of alcohol *may* cause you to think you *can* sing.

c. I *must* warn you that I am quite stubborn.
d. I *can* see Venus in the evening sky.
e. A group of American tourists were being guided through an ancient castle in Europe. "This place", the guide told them, "is 600 years old. Not a stone in it has been touched, nothing altered, nothing replaced in all those years."
"Wow", said one woman dryly, "they *must* have the same landlord as I have."

3. Detect the modal ambiguity in the following sentences:
   a. The table *should* be laid.
   b. Your son *must* be at school.

4. Analyse the negated modals in the following sentences by paraphrasing them and discuss differences in meaning resulting from the modal verb and the scope of negation.
   a. (i) You *mustn't* play with these children.
      (ii) You *don't have to* play with these children.
   b. (i) You *mustn't* open the door.
      (ii) You *may not* open the door.
      (iii) You *can't* open the door.

Part IV

Situations as relational units

Sentence structure

The two final Chapters 11 and 12 are concerned with the conceptual structure of situations and their expression in grammatical constructions. In Chapter 8 we distinguished types of situation with respect to their internal temporal structure. Chapters 11 and 12 will discuss situations as relational units and distinguish types of situations with respect to the conceptual entities participating in them. Conceptual entities play a specific role in the structure of a situation; these roles are known as **thematic roles**. Some such roles are the **agent**, i.e. the entity that volitionally instigates an action, and the **theme**, i.e. the entity that is affected by an action or is neutrally involved in a situation. Situations in which the roles of an agent and a theme occur together are actions. Thus, the sentence *Jilly is writing her paper* is an action in which 'Jilly' plays the role of an agent and 'her paper' that of a theme. Basic configurations of roles like that of an agent and a theme which form an action are known as **event schemas**. Event schemas make different distinctions from aspectual types of situation. Aspectually, *Jilly wrote a paper* expresses an accomplishment, and *Jilly was writing a paper* an accomplishing activity. As event schemas, however, both are instances of the action schema. Conversely, both *Jilly wrote her paper* and *Jilly recovered from her flu* describe an accomplishment aspectually; as event schemas, however, the former represents an action and the latter a process.

Chapter 11 "Event schemas: sentence patterns" looks at event schemas and the way they are coded in the basic sentence patterns of English. Event schemas characterise the conceptual core of situations. In Chapter 3.1.2 we defined the conceptual core as a relation combined with two or more conceptual entities participating in it. These entities are conceptually prominent participants, and the thematic roles they play are known as **participant roles**. In the sentence *Jilly wrote a paper*, the agent 'Jilly' and the theme 'a paper' are participant roles of the action schema. Participant roles are central to an event schema. In the structure of a sentence, they tend to be coded as obligatory elements: as a subject, direct object, indirect object, or another complement. Both the number of event schemas and the number of sentence patterns are limited. The manifold situations encountered in the world are thus reduced to a small set of event schemas and are expressed by an even smaller set of sentence patterns. The chapter relates syntactic constructions to the event schemas describing them and wants to demonstrate that the relation between the conceptual and linguistic levels is to a large extent motivated.

Chapter 12 "Space and extensions of space: complements and adjuncts" considers **non-participant roles**, i.e. roles that are not part of a situation's conceptual core. Non-participant roles mainly serve to specify the setting of a situation: the place where an event occurs, the time when it occurs, and the circumstances under which it occurs. In the structure of the sentence, setting elements are coded as adjuncts of the sentence. Thus, in *Fred got married in Las Vegas*, the adjunct *in Las Vegas* describes the spatial setting and can be omitted.

Notions of space are particularly relevant, not just in describing spatial settings, but also in providing the metaphorical source domain for many other domains, in particular 'time', 'circumstance', 'cause', 'reason', and 'purpose'. These target domains are to a considerable extent structured in terms of space. In the structure of English, this is mainly reflected in the use of spatial prepositions. Thus, the specification of time in *Fred got married on a Friday* and the specification of circumstance in *Fred got married in obscure circumstances* are based on the spatial notions of *on* and *in*, respectively. This chapter will look more closely at 'space' and its metaphorical extensions and thereby account for the use of prepositions in their spatial and non-spatial domains.

Chapter 11

Event schemas: Sentence patterns

11.0 Overview
11.1 Thematic roles and event schemas: Sentence patterns
11.2 Situations in the material world
11.3 Situations in the psychological world
11.4 Situations in the force-dynamic world
11.5 Conclusion
11.6 Summary

11.0 Overview

This chapter offers an analysis of the conceptual core of a situation and its expression as a grammatical construction. In a given conceptual core, participants are associated with a certain function, or role. The thematic roles participants play in a situation are known as participant roles. The most salient participant roles are those of an **agent**, the participant that deliberately instigates an action, a **theme**, the participant that is affected by an action or is neutrally involved in a situation, and an **experiencer**, the participant that undergoes an emotional, perceptual or mental experience. The roles participating in a conceptual core define role configurations, which become meaningful as **event schemas**. The set of event schemas includes the emotion schema, the action schema, and the transfer schema. These event schemas are expressed in a small set of sentence patterns. The basic **sentence patterns** include intransitive, transitive and ditransitive constructions. This chapter will attempt to relate event schemas to sentence patterns in a meaningful way.

11.1 Thematic roles and event schemas: Sentence patterns

11.1.1 Conceptual cores, roles and event schemas

A conceptual core was defined in Chapter 3.1.2 as a relation combined with two or more conceptual entities participating in it. Let us analyse the conceptual cores of the following sentences — elements such as determiners, modifiers, and adverbials are of course not part of the conceptual core and are disregarded here.

(1) a. *My boyfriend* kissed *another girl*. [*agent – theme*]
 b. *But my boyfriend* still loves *me*. [*experiencer – cause*]

Sentence (1a) describes the relation of kissing between two participants: 'my boyfriend', a volitionally acting human, and 'another girl', towards whom his action was directed. More generally, we can describe this event as an action and characterise the roles played by the two participants as the instigator of an action and the entity affected by this action. Such unique functions which entities hold in a situation are known as **thematic roles** — in earlier studies they were also described as 'case roles' or 'semantic roles'. The thematic role of the instigator of an action is known as the **agent**, and the role of the affected entity has been variously described as the 'theme', the 'object' or the 'patient' — we will use the term 'theme'. The **theme** is the neutral role played by a participant that is more passively involved in a situation, as an affected entity, as an entity brought into existence, as an entity that merely exists or as an entity that undergoes a change.

Sentence (1b) does not describe an action but the emotional state of love. Like the action in (1a), the emotional state in (1b) involves two participants: 'my boyfriend', who experiences an emotion, and 'me', the speaker, who is the object of his emotion and, at the same time, the stimulus or cause of that emotion. The thematic roles involved in this situation can be characterised as that of a human **experiencer** and a **cause**.

The configuration of thematic roles determines the schematic meaning of a situation. Thus, the configuration of an agent and a theme in (1a) characterises an *action schema* and the configuration of an experiencer and a cause in (1b) characterises an *emotion schema*. Such configurations of roles are known as **event schemas**. The notion 'event' is understood here to comprise both events and states, and the notion 'schema' is understood as a situation type that can be materialised in an infinite number of concrete instances of states and events.

Event schemas are intuitively meaningful, but they can also be distinguished by means of linguistic tests. Actions such as (1a), but not emotions, can be asked about by the question *What is X doing (to Y)?*, can be used in imperatives as in *Don't kiss another girl!*, and can take a purpose adjunct as in *He kissed her in order to show her his feelings*. Emotional states such as (1b), but not actions, can be asked about by the question *How does X feel (about Y)?* Another linguistic test that is often used to identify the same roles is the coordination test: the same roles may be conjoined, as the two agents in *My boyfriend kissed and hugged the girl*, which shows that the two event schemas are actions. However, we normally cannot readily conjoin different roles. Thus the agent and experiencer in **My boyfriend loves and is kissing the girl* cannot be conjoined; hence loving and kissing represent different event schemas.

Event schemas are defined by a small set of thematic roles. These conceptually prominent roles, which are typically associated with the conceptual core of a situation, are known as **participant roles**. The participant roles include the agent, the experiencer, the cause and the theme; less central participant roles are those of 'location' and 'possessor'. Thematic roles that are not part of the conceptual core of a situation are non-participant roles. **Non-participant roles** typically specify the setting of a situation and will be discussed in Chapter 12.

11.1.2 Sentence patterns

Event schemas are expressed in language by the grammatical constructions characterising basic clauses and sentences. These constructions are known as sentence patterns. **Sentence patterns** are established by obligatory constituents and have a specific syntactic function in the sentence structure. Obligatory constituents of a sentence are the subject (S), the predicate (P), the direct or prepositional object (O), the indirect object (IO), and further complements. The latter may "complement" other constituents such as the subject (C_S), the direct object (C_O), and the predicate (C_P). The following basic sentence patterns of English are well-known from traditional grammar:

Table 11.1. Basic English sentence patterns

	sentence patterns	functions	examples
i.	copulative subject-complement	S P C_S	We are an average family.
ii.	intransitive	S P	None of us works.
iii.	intransitive predicate-complement	S P C_P	We live in Venice Beach.
iv.	transitive	S P O	We have three cars.
v.	transitive object-complement	S P O C_O	Our friends consider us successful.
vi.	ditransitive	S P IO O	He is writing us enthusiastic letters.
vii.	transitive predicate-complement	S P O C_P	We have sent our son to Harvard.

Sentence patterns are largely dependent on the predicate. Predicates have a **valency**, i.e. they are characterised by a number of slots for arguments. The notion **argument** is the linguistic counterpart to the conceptual notion of participant: it refers to the obligatory constituents a predicate normally takes in a sentence. Thus, the verb *work* is normally used intransitively as in (ii): it only takes a subject argument, i.e. it is a 'one-place' predicate. All the other predicates in the above sentence patterns require at least two arguments, i.e. are two- or three-place predicates. Copular verbs like *be* in (i) require a subject complement which "completes", or specifies, the referent of the subject. Some intransitive verbs such as *live* in (iii) require a complement which is necessary to "complete" the verb or predicate of the sentence; we will describe it as a predicate complement. The four remaining sentence patterns are transitive. Transitive constructions in fact represent the most central and most frequent types of sentence pattern. Two-place transitive predicates may take a direct object as in (iv) or a prepositional object as in *Our friends rely on us*. Prepositional objects behave like direct objects: both become the subject of passive sentences, as in *We are trusted* and *We are relied on*. Both constructions are therefore subsumed under the transitive pattern. The three-place predicate *consider* in (v) requires an object complement, which is comparable to the subject complement in *We are successful*. The ditransitive construction in (vi) involves an indirect and a direct object. The three-place predicate *send* in (vii) requires a direct object and a predicate complement.

11.1.3 Sentence patterns, event schemas and "worlds of experience"

The sentence patterns form the "linguistic grid" available for expressing event schemas. Ideally, we might want to see a one-to-one correspondence between event schemas and the sentence patterns describing them. However, not every event schema is matched with a sentence pattern of its own. Moreover, the seven basic sentence patterns make different distinctions from those made by the event schemas. We may, however, expect that the relationship between event schemas and sentence patterns should not be completely arbitrary. The event schemas which will be distinguished in the ensuing sections can be subsumed under three "worlds of experience": the material world, the psychological world, and the force-dynamic world.

The *material world* is understood as the structured world of entities as they exist, change or undergo processes. The material world also includes humans who do not take an active part in shaping it.

The *psychological world* is the internal world of people's sensations, emotions, perceptions and thoughts. It is the world as experienced and conceptualised by sentient humans.

The *force-dynamic world* is the external world of action, force, and cause and their effects. In this world, human agents figure prominently as the instigators of events.

It goes without saying that these three worlds of experience are far from clear-cut; they tend to overlap and are much more likely to be understood in a prototypical sense. Here, they will mainly serve as a framework that allows us to structure the inventory of event schemas.

11.2 Situations in the material world

Situations that belong to the material world comprise the occurrence of things in states and processes, the location and motion of things, and the possession of things. These are framed in the *occurrence schema*, the *location schema*, and the *possession schema*. The common characteristic they share is that they all involve the role 'theme'.

11.2.1 Occurrence schema

The **occurrence schema** describes the state or process an entity is in. The notion 'occurrence' is understood here in the sense of the way things are or happen in the material world. Situations that belong to the occurrence schema are thus characterised by having the role 'theme' as their subject participant.

11.2.1.1 *States*

States involve a relation between a theme and an entity specifying it. Typically, two entities are related as "A is B". Grammatically, this relation is expressed by the copulative construction. The **copulative construction** consists of a subject, a copular verb (*be* or *become* or one of their near-synonyms such as *look* and *seem*), and a complement, which may be a predicative adjective (*be big*), a predicate nominal (*be a giant*), or a figurative prepositional phrase (*be in trouble*). The states expressed by the copulative construction are, however, associated with different meanings, especially those illustrated below:

(2) a. The Sahara is *actually quite fertile*. [*property assignment*]
    b. The Sahara is *a vast desert*. [*category inclusion*]
    c. The Sahara is *the world's largest desert*. [*identification*]

In (2a) the theme 'the Sahara' is assigned the property of being fertile, in (2b) 'the Sahara' is included as a member of the category 'desert', and in (2c) 'the Sahara' is identified with another thing, the world's largest desert. The assignment of properties by means of predicative adjectives was already discussed in Chapter 7.2.6, and the difference in qualification between adjectives and nouns was pointed out in Chapter 7.2.1. The difference between category inclusion and identification is less apparent — in fact, people tend to interpret the relation "A is B" as reversible, i.e. as also meaning "B is A". Relations of inclusion are, however, not reversible: we cannot, without changing its meaning, reverse sentence (2b) as *A vast desert is the Sahara*. Relations of identification, on the other hand, are reversible: thus we can also describe the content of sentence (2c) as *The world's largest desert is the Sahara*. Due to the operation of the principle of figure and ground, the reversal of a theme and an identifying participant is, of course, accompanied by differences in meaning: the theme 'the Sahara' is the figure and topic talked about in (2c), but the ground in the reversed sentence *The world's largest desert is the Sahara*.

The difference between category inclusion and identification is also marked by the choice of the determiner. In identifying relations both the theme and the identifying participant are necessarily definite — otherwise they could not be mutually identified. In order to distinguish category inclusion from identification, the ecological system of English marks the superordinate participant as indefinite, like *a vast desert* in (2b), although it must be conceptually definite to serve as category. The indefinite article may also be motivated as a kind of shorthand for 'a member of the category', so that (2b) means something like 'the Sahara is a member of the category vast desert'. The included category, on the other hand, may be definite, like 'the Sahara' in (2b), or indefinite in generic sentences such as *A collie is a dog*.

The copulative construction and the three relations associated with it are prototypical states. We may, however, conceive of many more states relating a theme and its specification. For example, the relation may be one of similarity (*resemble, compare to, be similar to*) or dissimilarity (*differ from, distinguish from*), of representation (*represent, mean, stand for*), and of any other kind of relation (*relate to, refer to, correlate with*). The prepositions *to* and *from* with some of these expressions are indicative of a conceptual affinity between states and locative relations.

Many prepositions used in figurative prepositional phrases also have a spatial origin: *We're at a standstill*; *We are in trouble*; *This is in order*; *That's out of fashion now*, etc. These usages are based on the conceptual metaphor STATES ARE LOCATIONS. The prepositional phrases no longer describe spatial situations, as can be seen from the coordination test: they can be combined with predicative adjectives, as in *The shipment is in order and correct*, but not with genuine locative expressions, as in **The shipment is in order and in London*.

11.2.1.2 Processes

Processes may involve a change of state or be steady. A change of state marks the transition from a previous state to a new state. Thus, in *The clothes dried in the sun*, the state of the clothes changed from being wet to being dry. Steady processes involve unchanging events, as in *It is raining*.

11.2.1.2.1 Changes of state: Copulative and related constructions

Changes of state may be either sudden, as in *The light turned green*, or gradual, as in *The clothes were drying in the sun*. We are normally interested in the new state. The beginning of a situation is technically known as *inchoation* (from Latin *inchoare* 'begin'), and verbs expressing a beginning are known as **inchoative verbs**. Change-of-state verbs typically convey inchoative meanings. For example, the sentence *The Sahara became a desert around 4,000 years ago* describes a change of state and focuses on the beginning of the new state 4,000 years ago.

Changes of states are comparable to states. Like states (A is B), they involve a changing relation between a theme and an entity specifying it: "A becomes B". Grammatically, this relation is also expressed by the copulative construction. The copular verb *become* is the most neutral verb expressing a change of state. More specific kinds of change are expressed by other process verbs, in particular motion verbs, as in:

(3) a. The traffic light *turned* red. [abrupt change]
 b. Beverly *fell* in love. [uncontrolled change]
 c. You never *grow* old. [gradual change]
 d. Everything *went* wrong today. [unexpected change]
 e. Our dreams have *come* true. [expected change]

The many expressions of motion for changes of state point to a general conceptual metaphor: CHANGE IS MOTION. This metaphor is more widely exploited in English than in many other languages. The particular meaning of the change of state which the motion verb metaphorically conveys is, as a rule, easily discernible: *turn* describes abrupt changes, *fall* designates sudden uncontrolled changes, and *grow* refers to gradual changes. The metaphorical usages of the deictic motion verbs *go* and *come* are less transparent but are motivated as well. Put simply, deictic *go* typically refers to motion away from the speaker and focuses on the beginning of the motion event. In a similar vein, metaphorical *go* expresses "motion" away from a normal course of events leading to unexpected and often abnormal or even unpleasant changes of state. Deictic *come* refers to motion towards the speaker and focuses on the terminal phase of a motion (see Chapter 2.1.3). Likewise, metaphorical *come* expresses an event's terminative and normal "outcome" and is usually associated with expected and gradual, often pleasant changes.

The metaphor CHANGE IS MOTION is a shorthand expression for CHANGE OF STATE IS CHANGE OF LOCATION. In this form, its relation to the metaphor STATES ARE LOCATIONS becomes apparent, which we will encounter in Section 11.2.2.2. Metaphorical expressions of motion thus tend to have counterparts in metaphorical expressions of location: *The vase fell to pieces* — *The vase is in pieces*; *The miniskirt has come into fashion again* — *The miniskirt is in fashion again*, etc.

An interesting feature of English is that many inchoative verbs are related to an adjective denoting the resultant state: *The door opened* — *The door is open*; *My shoelaces broke* — *My shoelaces are broken*; *The road widened* — *The road is wide(r)*, etc. Most adjectives, though, do not have verbal counterparts. Thus we can assign properties to a person, as in *Prince Harry is smart and ambitious*, but we cannot express the corresponding changes of state: **Prince Harry smarted and ambitioned*.

11.2.1.2.2 *Steady processes*

Steady processes are activities which involve non-humans or not intentionally acting humans as their theme. The former situation is illustrated in *The sun is shining*, the latter in *The sailor staggered down the road*. As inherently unchanging events, steady processes are not compatible with expressions that denote a change; hence ?*The sun is shining more and more* sounds bad unless it refers to a sequence of sunny days. Steady processes can be viewed as bounded or unbounded, i.e. they can be expressed in the non-progressive or progressive, as in the examples above. Typically, though, steady processes are seen as on-going and expressed in the progressive aspect. They are then seen as unbounded in the same way that states are; they can therefore be combined with predicative adjectives of states, as in:

(4) a. The sun is *bright and shining*.
    b. The sailor is *drunk and staggering down the road*.

A special type of processes are meteorological situations, which are often expressed by a construction with an "impersonal *it*". The sentences under (5) describe changes of state, the ones under (6) steady processes. Sometimes the pronoun *it* can be substituted by a full noun phrase, as in (5b) and (6b).

(5) a. *It's clearing up now.*
    b. *The weather is clearing up now.*
(6) a. *It has been raining every day.*
    b. *Happy are the dead that the rain rains on.*

It is sometimes claimed that the only function of *it* in these constructions is to fill the slot of the subject, which any sentence of English requires. The paraphrases with full noun phrases, however, show that the pronoun *it* stands for a referent — *the weather* in (5b) and *the rain* in (6b), which, of course, sounds rather poetic. The referent *it* can be said to stand for general atmospheric conditions; it serves as a circumstantial setting for the concrete meteorological situation at hand (see Chapter 12.5.1). Such a theme is therefore described as a "subject setting". Since meteorological processes often have no other participating entity beyond the process itself, an apt participant is the atmospheric background, which appears as the subject in the form of an impersonal *it*.

11.2.2 Spatial schemas: Copulative construction and related constructions

Spatial schemas describe a relation between a theme and a location or a trajectory. Like the occurrence schema, spatial schemas have a static and dynamic variant. In the static variant a theme is related to a location; this relation will be described as *location schema*. In its dynamic variant a moving theme is related to its trajectory; this relation will be described as *motion schema*.

(7) a. The ball is in the goal. [*location*]
    b. The ball rolled into the goal. [*motion*]

11.2.2.1 Location schema

Like other states, static relations characterising the **location schema** are typically expressed by the copular verb *be*. The same coding indicates that the two event schemas are felt to be closely related. Specifications of a location often refer to its function and may thus invite implicatures which are strikingly similar to the specifications described by states. Thus, sentence (7a), *The ball is in the goal*, invites the implicature that 'this *is* a goal', and Mum's announcement that "the food is on the table" implies that 'lunch is ready'.

The copular verb *be* indicates a theme's location in a neutral way; more specific locative situations may be expressed by verbs like *live* or posture verbs such as *stand*, *sit* or *lie*. However, specifying the theme's bodily position is far less common in English than in many other languages. Thus, whereas English speakers tend to say that someone or something *is* there, German speakers would have to specify that a person is *standing* in front of the mirror, that the dog is *sitting* on the sofa, and that the teddy bear is *lying* on the floor.

The thematic role **location** serves as a participant within the conceptual core and is expressed as a complement in the sentence pattern, as in (8a). Its function is different from the similar-looking situation described in (8b), where the specification of the location provides the spatial setting of a situation.

(8) a. My son is *in the bathroom*. [*participant*]
    b. My son is singing *in the bathroom*. [*spatial setting*]

In the situation described in (8b), my son's singing represents an action which takes place in the bathroom. Syntactically, the prepositional phrase functions as an optional adjunct (see Chapter 12). An adjunct, but not a complement, may be separated from the predicate by using the "*and is doing so*"-construction: *My son is singing and he is doing so in the bathroom*. This test allows us to distinguish participants of a situation, i.e. complements of a sentence, from non-participant roles or settings, i.e. adjuncts. The use of a preposition with locative complements as in (8a) is, however, indicative of the less central status of locative participants: they are distanced from the verb by the preposition.

The theme 'my son' in (8a) is a definite referent. As we saw in Chapter 5, the use of a definite article means that a mental space has already been opened for the referent. Such referents are natural discourse topics and hence well-suited to be used as subjects. Indefinite referents are less appropriate, if not impossible, as topics in subject position because first a mental space needs to be opened for them. This is achieved by means of a construction with a weak (or phonetically reduced) form of the adverb *there*. Compare the answers given to the question about where to find a petrol station:

(9) a. ⁇*A petrol station* is round the corner.
     b. *There is a petrol station* round the corner.

The use of the indefinite theme as a topic in (9a) sounds less natural than that of the *there*-construction introducing the indefinite theme in (9b). Obviously, the *there* is not, as has sometimes been claimed, a redundant copy of the locative expression but is a meaningful element: it brings an entity into awareness, i.e. it is a space-builder that provides a mental space in which the theme has an existence. In (9b), the area of the theme's existence is restricted by the locative expression *round the corner*. Without an explicit or implicit specification of the area, the theme's existence would be understood as applying universally, as in *There is no such thing as a free lunch* (= anywhere in the world) or *There are millions of stars* (= in the universe). This use of *there* is known as the 'existential *there*', and the construction in which it occurs is known as the *existential construction*. The less relevant the notion of 'location' is in an existential construction, the more the notion of 'existence' is foregrounded. This is the case in assertions such as *There is still hope* and *There is only one God*, which are almost exclusively understood in the sense of existence.

There in its existential sense is a grammaticised form of spatial *there*. The deictic adverb *there* is a stressed form, as in *Thére is the bus*; the existential *there* is an unstressed form, as in *There's a bus (to Heathrow)*. Its spatial meaning is bleached to that of an existential space-builder. The change of meaning is motivated by the conceptual metaphor EXISTENCE IS LOCATION (HERE), which is found in expressions such as *The baby has arrived*. The choice of distal *there* rather than proximal *here* is motivated by its function of opening a background space relative to which entities are foregrounded

11.2.2.2 Motion schema

> *Things in motion sooner catch the eye than what not stirs.*
> (Shakespeare, *Troilus and Cressida*)

The **motion schema** describes a theme's change along a trajectory from a place at one time to another place at a later time. A motion event is therefore directional and tends to invoke the SOURCE-PATH-GOAL image schema, i.e. a schema that involves things or people moving from a source along a path to a goal. Thus, we expect that a plane which has landed at its destination originated from some airport and followed a certain route in its flight. We thus think of motion as mainly bounded; only rarely do we think of unbounded motion without a source and/or goal, as in the case of planets, which eternally revolve around the sun, or of time, which is seen as eternally flowing from the future into the past.

Motion attracts our attention more than anything else. Even a new-born baby reacts to an object moving across its visual field. It is not surprising, therefore, that many domains are metaphorically conceptualised in terms of motion: among them are changes of state as in *He went bananas* (see 11.2.1.2.1), actions as in *Let's move on* 'do something', and many specific domains which are metaphorised by specific kinds of motion, such as LIFE IS A JOURNEY or LOVE IS A JOURNEY. Motion forms the basis of three event schemas: in its material form of a thing's motion, typically of an object (10a), in the form of an agent's self-propelled motion (10b), and in the form of a thing's motion caused by another entity (10c):

(10) a. The bottle rolled down the slope. [*object motion*]
b. We happily rolled down the slope. [*self-motion*]
c. They pushed the car down the slope. [*caused motion*]

Object motion as in (10a) is non-agentive, while self-motion (10b) and caused motion (10c) are typically agentive. The characterisation of object motion in this section thus also applies to self-motion, which will be dealt with in Section 11.4.2. Caused motion will be discussed in Section 11.4.3.

Motion is a complex event. It consists of a moving entity, its motion, a source, a path, and a goal. Typically, we also integrate aspects of 'manner' with motion events. Thus, in example (10a), the verb *roll* expresses both 'move' and 'rolling manner'. The sentence might be paraphrased as 'the bottle moved down the slope, rolling.' The conceptual integration of two such notions within one lexical form is known as *conflation*. The Germanic languages including English tend to conflate 'motion' and 'manner', as in (11a), while the Romance languages tend to express 'manner' separately, as in (11b).

(11) a. The bottle *rolled* down the slope. [*English*]
b. La botella se   fue   cuesta abajo *rodando*. [*Spanish*]
     the bottle of-itself went hill   down rolling

The conflations characterising the English and Spanish sentences in (11) are diagrammed in Figure 11.1. In the English sentence, the motion verb *rolled* conflates the meanings 'motion' and 'manner'; in its Spanish equivalent, the notions of motion ('went by itself') and manner ('rolling') are coded separately.

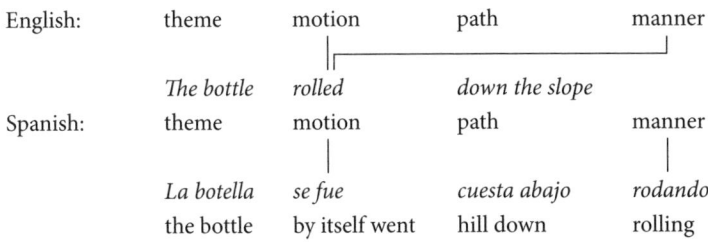

Figure 11.1. Conflation and separation of 'motion' and 'manner'

Unlike English, Spanish often conflates 'motion' and 'path' by using verbs such as *entrar* 'enter', *salir* 'exit', and *pasar* 'pass'. Thus, *The bottle floated into the cave* is rendered in Spanish as *La botella entró en la cueva flotando* 'the bottle entered the cave, floating'. The conflation of 'motion' with 'manner' in English is even more typical of self-motion (see 11.4.2).

A motion event may also be expressed by the sounds that are produced by the thing in its motion, as in:

(12) a. The fire trucks *roared* out of the firehouse.
 b. The car *screeched* to a halt.

The sounds emitted are perceptually salient within a 'motion' frame and can therefore metonymically stand for motion.

11.2.3 Possession schema: Transitive constructions

Imagine no possessions
I wonder if you can (John Lennon)

The **possession schema** describes a relation between a possessor and a theme, as in *Fiona has an iPod; Rose received an invitation for an interview; Julia lost her notes*. The **possessor** is typically a human and the thing possessed a physical object. Possession can be seen as belonging to the material world. Many languages code 'possession' as location. In Russian, Finnish and Japanese, *John has two children* would be rendered as 'At/to John are two children'. It is easy to trace a connection between location and possession: situations in which objects are always or often close to a person invite the implicature that they belong to that person; conversely, we expect that people have their possessions close to them. The conceptual affinity between 'location' and 'possession' is also reflected in the variable uses of English *be* and *have*. The notion of 'location' is typically expressed by *be*, as in *There are three opera houses in Berlin*, but may also be expressed by *have*, as in *Berlin has three opera houses*; conversely, the notion of 'possession' is typically expressed by *have*, as in *I have the book*, but may also be expressed by *be*, as in *The book is mine*.

The preferred sentence pattern used to express possession is the transitive construction, with the possessor coded as the subject and the possessed thing as the direct object. A number of transitive verbs are available to express possession, in particular *have, own, possess*, and *hold*. This coding gives prominence to the human being as the primary participant. If the natural order of possessor and thing possessed is reversed, the possessor is usually seen in a contrastive context: *The book is mine, not yours*. Apart from the copulative construction, only the verb *belong to* expresses a reversal of possessor and possessed entity.

The notion of possession subsumes two subtypes: alienable and inalienable possession. *Alienable possession* (from Latin *alienus, alius* 'other') involves ownership of things "other" than our body parts, i.e. possessions which can be separated from us such as books or bicycles. *Inalienable possession* involves an inseparable link between a possessor and a thing possessed and typically applies to one's body parts. Alienable possession thus involves two separate entities, while inalienable possession overlaps with the part/whole relation. The two types of possession are distinguished by their uses of *have* and *be*:

(13) a. He has a key.   The key is his.   [*alienable*]
     b. ?He has a nose.   ?The nose is his.   [*inalienable*]
     c. He has a straight nose. ?The straight nose is his.

Alienable possessions as in (13a) can be freely expressed by *have* or by *be*, while inalienable possession as in (13b) cannot. Body parts intrinsically belong to their owner, and every human body is composed of the same body parts. To state that a person has a nose is uninformative unless we are talking to a baby or associate the body part with a specific attribute, as in (13c) or in *He has an iron fist*. But here, too, the copulative construction sounds strange: ?*The straight nose is his* or ?*The iron fist is his*. This is due to the difficulty we have in imagining a situation where different noses or fists are contrasted. A possible contextual background for the use of *The (iron) fist is his* could be one of looking at a picture of a demonstrating crowd with raised fists and someone pointing at one of the fists.

However, the distinction between alienable and inalienable possession is far from clear-cut. For example, in some Indian cultures the vital instruments one has created for survival such as, for instance, the baskets one has woven are considered to be one's inalienable possessions. Examples like these show that the notion of possession is a culture-specific concept.

The notion of alienable possession in the Western cultures has become a key concept for various other domains: it no longer applies to material possessions only, but has been extended to social and abstract domains:

(14) a. Marcellino has *a Maserati sports car*.   [*material possession*]
     b. Alfredo has a girlfriend, but *no sisters*. [*social possession*]
     c. Cesare has *brilliant ideas*.   [*abstract possession*]

Material possessions as in (14a) are the "best" instances of 'possession'. They are the only type of possession that can be paraphrased with the verb *own*. Culturally defined links such as personal and kinship relations as in (14b) are a matter of personal commitment or social structure rather than a matter of one's possession of objects. Abstract possessions as in (14c) are reified states; still, they are seen as possessions and can be combined with material or social possessions, as in *Cesare has no money but brilliant ideas*. All these relations of possession can also be seen as states and expressed by means of the copulative construction with a possessive predicate nominal:

(15) a. The Maserati sports car *is Marcellino's*.
 b. The girlfriend *is Alfredo's*, but these are not his sisters.
 c. The sports car isn't Cesare's, but the brilliant ideas *are his*.

The notion of possession as expressed by *have* and *be* is a static one, but it can also be dynamic and relate to action. This is reflected in expressions for states of possession such as *hold a driving licence*, *hold power* and *stock holder* as well as expressions describing the dynamic transition of possession such as *take*, *get*, and *seize*. The action schema is commonly used in European languages to express possession: Spanish *tener* as in *tengo hambre* ('I am hungry', literally: 'I have hunger') goes back to Latin *tenere* 'hold', and the prototypical English verb of possession, *have*, relates to Latin *capere* 'seize' (*have* is not related to Latin *habere* 'have'). The connection between 'seizing' and 'having' something is obvious: if someone has taken all my money, I assume that he now has the money.

11.3 Situations in the psychological world

Situations that belong to the psychological world describe experiences people have or are subjected to. These experiences include emotions, perceptions, and thoughts. All these situations involve a certain amount of cognitive awareness on the part of the experiencer. The following examples illustrate typical psychological experiences:

(16) a. I *like* film music very much. [*emotion*]
 b. I distinctly *heard* the saxophone. [*perception*]
 c. I vividly *remember* the main melody. [*cognition*]

A person who experiences an emotion is normally thought of as having no or only little control over her experience. I cannot, for example, ask to have an emotion: **Let me like film music*. In the emotional state in (16a), film music is understood as having an inherent quality which stimulates joy in me.

In situation (16b), the object perceived only has a weak impact on my perception. I can, at least to a certain extent, control my perceptual experience. I can ask for a general perceptual experience: *Let me hear the music*; it is harder, though, except for a conductor, to ask for a selective perception (*?Let me hear the saxophone*) because this requires discriminating the saxophone from the other instruments in the orchestra.

In situation (16c), my memories of a melody may be stimulated by the melody but are also controlled by my cognitive abilities. We can therefore be asked to retrieve past situations from our memory (*Remember the old days*) as well as imagine taking care of future situations (*Remember to lock the door!*). The internal world of cognition is thus felt to be even less subject to external stimulation and more in control of the human experiencer.

Emotions, perceptions and cognition can be ranked on a continuum along the scales of the experiencer's control over her experience and the impact an external stimulus has on her psychological state.

Table 11.2. 'Control' and 'stimulus' in types of psychological experience

	experiencer's control	external stimulus
emotion	low	high
perception	medium	low
cognition	high	low

Given these important differences between types of psychological experience, a distinction will be made between, on the one hand, the *emotion schema*, which involves the roles of an experiencer and a cause as in (16a), and, on the other hand, the *perception/cognition schema*, which relates the roles of experiencer and theme, as in (16b and c).

11.3.1   Emotion schema

The **emotion schema** describes the emotional state or process which a sentient human experiences. Emotions are the only one of the three psychological schemas in which the experiencer can readily appear as the only argument, as in *Gloria is happy* and *Victoria became bored*. Conceptually, however, there must of course be some cause triggering the emotion. This can be seen from the possibility of asking about the cause by using questions like *What makes you happy?* or *Why are you bored?* Since we are in general more concerned with the results of causes than the causes and with humans rather than objects, the suppression of the cause is well motivated, and it is even the rule when the cause is unknown. When both the experiencer and the cause are given expression in language structure, each of them may become the primary participant and expressed as the subject of the sentence, as in the following examples:

(17)   *Experiencer – Cause*
   a.   I like Chopin.
   b.   Jenny is scared of spiders.
   c.   We're shocked at his antics.

(18)   *Cause – Experiencer*
   a.   Chopin is a pleasure to my ears.
   b.   Spiders scare Jenny.
   c.   His antics shock us.

The choice of the construction mainly depends on the discourse topic. In general, humans are given preference over non-humans as topics; hence sentences with an experiencer-subject as under (17) are preferred construals. Here we take the view of the human experiencer, who directs her attention to the stimulus. In sentences with a cause-subject as under (18), the cause of emotion is the topic. Here we focus on the stimulus rather than the human experiencer. This construction is, however, also motivated: the word order 'cause' — 'experiencer' iconically reflects the sequential order of the events: the causing event is stated before its ensuing result.

The two reversed construals of the experiencing schema are expressed by different predicates, which are known as "psych-verbs" (verbs of psychological state). Some psych-verbs take an experiencer-subject (e.g. *like, hate, fancy, detest, adore, admire*, etc.), a small number of emotion predicates take a cause-subject (e.g. *please, strike, appeal to*, etc.), and a third, very large class of emotion predicates can be construed in both ways: they can be used in *stative passives* with an experiencer-subject and a prepositional adjunct, as in (17b) and (17c), and as transitive verbs with a cause-subject and a direct object, as in (18b) and (18c). Stative passives as in (17b) and (17c) are distinguished from process passives by the preposition in the adjunct phrase: process passives take the agentive *by*-phrase as in *Jonathan was hit by Greg*, whereas stative passives take other prepositions, in particular *at* as in (17c) or (19a). If in (17c) the preposition *by* was used instead of *at*, we would understand the sentence in the sense of a process passive and interpret it differently: 'He would deliberately shock us by means of using antics.'

There are in fact not just two, but at least four, possibilities of construing emotional experiences by using the same emotion predicate:

(19) a. I'm amazed at George's stupidity. [*stative passive*]
b. George's stupidity *amazes* me. [*emotional process*]
c. George's stupidity *is amazing*. [*emotional state*]
d. It *is amazing* how stupid George is. [*extraposition*]

Sentence (19a) with the stative passive describes a person's evaluative emotional state. Here the past participle *amazed* behaves like an adjective: it can be intensified (*very amazed*) and graded (*more amazed*). The present participle *amazing* in (19c) and (19d) also behaves like an adjective: George's stupidity can be *very amazing* or *more amazing* than Henry's. While sentence (19b) mentions the person who experiences the emotion, i.e. *me*, sentence (19c) does not. This sentence therefore suggests general validity of the experience as viewed by the speaker.

The most common way of expressing the emotional situation is probably by using a complex sentence structure as in (19d). Constructions with an anticipatory *it* are known as **extraposition**. Here, the subject pronoun *it* anticipates the subordinate clause *how stupid George is*, which "really" functions as the subject of the sentence. Conceptually, the *it* is, however, not just a cataphoric pronoun for the subject clause: it opens a mental space for causes that might stimulate people's amazement, and the particular amazement meant in this situation is elaborated in the subject clause.

11.3.2 Perception/cognition schema

The **perception/cognition schema** describes an experiencer's perceptual or mental awareness of a thing. The close connection between perception and cognition is reflected in words which mean both 'perception' and 'cognition', such as *see* 'perceive, understand', *hear* 'listen to, understand' (as in *I can't hear you*), *inspect, regard, observe, look into*, and expressions such as *point of view* and *shed light on*. The transition from perception to cognition can be "seen" in the following examples:

(20) a. I see the mountains. [*percept*]
 b. I see it's raining. [*percept or concept*]
 c. I see your point. [*concept*]

In (20a) an object is perceived, in (20b) a situation of raining is either perceived or conceived when we see someone entering the house in dripping clothes, and in (20c) the content of an utterance is understood.

As shown in Table 11.2, perception and cognition involve no external causation and a higher degree of control by the experiencer than emotions, which is further reinforced by the frequent use of *can* in its sense of ability with verbs of perception, as in (21a,b,c) (see also Chapter 10.4.2.2). Hence there are only very few converse predicates, i.e. predicates that take the theme as a subject argument and the experiencer as the object argument. Converse predicates of perception tend to be coded as adjectives: *perceptible, visible, audible, palpable* and *tangible*, but English lacks adjectives such as **smellable* and **tastable* for something that can be smelled or tasted. Converse predicates of cognition are *familiar to* as in (22d) and *known to*.

(21) Experiencer – Theme (22) Theme – Experiencer
 a. I can see Venus.   a. Venus is visible to me.
 b. I can hear the flute. b. The flute is audible to me.
 c. I can smell the turkey. c. The turkey smells fine.
 d. I'm familiar with the song. d. The song is familiar to me.

11.4 Situations in the force-dynamic world

Situations that belong to the force-dynamic world describe events which are brought about by human agents or other causal entities and have effects. Force-dynamic schemas are typically goal-directed actions instigated by a human agent. We can distinguish four main force-dynamic schemas: the action schema (11.4.1), the self-motion schema (11.4.2), the caused-motion schema (11.4.3), and the transfer schema (11.4.4).

11.4.1 Action schema

We are more than anything else interested in our own and other people's deliberate actions. The **action schema** reflects this cognitive disposition: it describes events in which a human agent deliberately and responsibly acts upon another entity, the theme. Typical actions are drinking a glass of wine, writing a paper, or taking the bus. These deliberate actions are telic, or goal-directed, and were discussed in Chapter 8.3 as accomplishments. We can think of such highly energetic events in terms of a chain of energy.

11.4.1.1 *The energy chain*

In a prototypical action, the human agent generates energy and directs it to a target, where the energy is "absorbed". In this force-dynamic metaphor, the agent represents the "energy source" and the theme the "energy sink". The energy chain may also involve transmitters of energy, as in:

(23) a. The burglar forced the back door open *with a crowbar*.
     b. This bear of a man pulled three railway carriages *with his teeth*.

In sentence (23a), the energy transmitter is a crowbar. Crowbars are designed to be used as an instrument. **Instruments** are alienable possessions (see 11.2.3) which can be used in performing an action. The sentence can therefore be paraphrased as *The burglar used the crowbar to force the back door open*.

In sentence (23b), a man's body parts are expressed as energy transmitters. Body parts are one's inalienable possessions. This situation involves a flow of energy from the agent — the Belgian strongman John Massis — as the energy source via the man's body parts 'teeth' and the instrument 'rope' to the theme 'carriages' as the energy sink. Both the body parts and the instrument function as energy transmitters. The same applies to situation (23a), where the burglar must have used his hands in manipulating the crowbar. Both situations involve two energy transmitters, only one of which, however, is profiled. These situations are sketched in Figure 11.2.

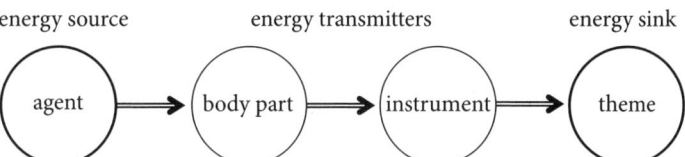

Figure 11.2. Energy chain

Only those transmitters in a chain of energy are expressed which are salient in that they do not conform to our everyday expectations. In (23a) the instrument 'crowbar' is salient, and in (23b) the body parts 'teeth'. In general, genuine instruments are felt to be more salient in the energy chain than body parts. If we only mentioned the burglar's hands in sentence (23b) and not the instrument, as in *The burglar forced the door open with his hands*, we would interpret the sentence as meaning that the burglar opened the door with his bare hands. English does not allow us to combine expressions of a body part and an instrument in the chain of energy transmission. Thus, we do not, unless jocularly, produce sentences such as **The burglar forced the back door open with his foot and a crowbar*.

Instruments as intermediate energy transmitters have a peripheral status in situations and are typically expressed as optional adjuncts. In Figure 11.2, the circles representing the energy transmitters are therefore printed in light lines, while the circles representing the energy source and the energy sink are printed in bold. These two endpoints of the energy chain are normally prominent and profiled as the two focal participants. The prototypical energy source of an action is a human agent and expressed as the subject of the sentence;

while the prototypical energy sink is a theme and expressed as the direct object. This word order of transitive sentences iconically reflects its conceptual order: a source precedes a goal.

11.4.1.2 Conceptual and grammatical transitivity

The term *transitive* is normally used in reference to grammatical constructions with a direct or prepositional object, as described in Section 11.1.2. Here we will also use the term *transitive* in reference to the meaning the transitive construction conveys. **Transitivity** (from Latin *trans-ire* 'go across') as a conceptual phenomenon is a matter of degree. Situations may conform to energetic actions at different degrees. Prototypical actions are characterised by a highly forceful energy source, a highly energetic action, and a high effect on the theme. We will first consider degrees of energetic action, then degrees of affectedness of the theme, and finally degrees of energetic agents.

11.4.1.2.1 Degrees of energetic actions

The following sentences describe actions which display decreasing degrees of energy transmitted (see also Chapter 1.1.2).

(24) a. Dorothy *tore* the letter (into pieces).
 b. Brewster *wrote* the letter.
 c. Tracy *read* the letter.
 d. Baxter *glanced at* the letter.

Tearing something into pieces as in (24a) is a physical action: it completely affects an object and can eventually lead to its destruction. We can ask about such actions by using the question *What did she do to the letter?*; we can emphasise the effect of the action by using the adverb *completely*; we can specify the resulting state of the action by using expressions such as *tear up*, *tear into pieces*, etc., as in *She completely tore the letter up into a million pieces*; and we can focus on the object that is totally affected by an action by means of the passive: *The letter was torn (by Dorothy)*. The grammatical behaviour of this sentence demonstrates the complete affectedness of the theme by a highly energetic action, i.e. the action of tearing something displays a high degree of transitivity.

Writing something as in (24b) is an action that brings an entity into existence. With verbs of creation we cannot ask the question *#What did he do to the letter?*, and we cannot describe its finished state by using *completely*: **Brewster completely wrote the letter*. However, we cannot specify the resulting state (*write up a letter*), but focus on the created object by using the passive: *The letter was written (by Brewster)*. Even if creating an object may involve quite some effort, it is seen as a less energetic action than affecting an existing object; its degree of transitivity is thus lower.

Reading something to oneself as in (24c) ranks still lower on the scale of transitivity. Reading is a purely mental action, and even if the action of reading may be intense on the part of the reader, it does not affect the book, paper or letter read. This is why many people, especially children, do not consider reading as work. With *read*, we can neither ask *#What* *did she do to the letter?*, nor use the adverb *completely* (**Tracy completely read the letter*) or specify the resultant state (**read up the letter*). *Read* also behaves differently with respect to the passive. Sentence (24c) cannot be passivised in the sense of 'read to oneself'. However, the passive sentence *The letter was read by Dorothy* can be said if the contents of the letter somehow affects people, e.g. if it is made public. The passive is fully acceptable in a context such as *The letter was read in public and later handed over to the White House*, where it has a considerable effect.

Glancing at something as in (24d) is a brief perceptual action and certainly less intense than the action of reading. The perception verb *glance* passes none of the transitivity tests: we can neither ask **What did he do to the letter?* nor use *completely* nor specify a resultant state nor turn the sentence into the passive. Its degree of transitivity is the lowest among these sentences.

The decreasing degrees of transitivity of the four sentences discussed above are summarised in Table 11.3. Sentence (24a) passes all four linguistic tests and represents a canonical action. The table shows that the passive test can best determine degrees of transitivity.

Table 11.3. Decreasing degrees of transitivity

		passive	result	*What did X do to Y?*	*completely*
a.	tear the letter	√	√	√	√
b.	write the letter	√	*	*	*
c.	read the letter	?	*	*	*
d.	glance at the letter	*?	*	*	*

The different degrees of conceptual transitivity are not overtly reflected in linguistic structure: all four situations described under (24) are coded as transitive sentences. Since the agents and themes in these sentences are equivalent or identical, their degree of transitivity is dependent on the predicate.

11.4.1.2.2 Degrees of affectedness of the theme

Degrees of transitivity can also be signalled in the way the affected entity is expressed. Consider the following pair of sentences, in which the theme is expressed as a direct object or a prepositional object.

(25) a. My boyfriend cheated *me*. [direct object]
 b. My boyfriend cheated *on me*. [prepositional object]

The use of the direct object in (25a) suggests a direct effect of the agent's action on a person. The sentence might be said in the context of my boyfriend selling me a lemon as a car. Cheating a person directly normally applies to situations in which the person is deceived by fraud. The use of a prepositional object in (25b) suggests a less direct effect of the action. The sentence might be said in the context of being unfaithful to one's partner. In this case, the boyfriend's actions are directed towards another woman and only secondarily affect his girlfriend. The direct and prepositional objects in the sentences under (25) iconically reflect directness and indirectness of effect. The direct object is in immediate proximity to the verb, while the prepositional object is separated from the verb by the preposition.

The grammar of English thus also reflects degrees of affectedness of a theme in its coding as a direct or prepositional object. In our discussion of degrees of energetic actions we already noticed that the prepositional verb *glance at* in sentence (24d) ranked lowest on the scale of transitivity. The following near-synonymous situations illustrate the differences in structural meaning between direct and prepositional object even more clearly:

(26) a. A detective *shadowed* us.   [*direct object*]
      b. A detective *spied on* us.   [*prepositional object*]

(27) a. The police *examined* the murder case.   [*direct object*]
      b. The police *looked into* the murder case.   [*prepositional object*]

Sentences (26a) and (27a) with a direct object convey more intense actions than those under (26b) and (27b) with a prepositional object. All of them, however, can be passivised, as in *We were spied on by the detective*, and can be coordinated, as in *We were shadowed and spied on by a detective*, showing that they have the same role.

The transitive construction does not only apply to typical participant roles, but may also involve non-participant roles, as in the following examples:

(28) a   The driver honked *his horn*.   [*instrument + theme*]
      b. We climbed *the Matterhorn*.   [*location + theme*]
      c. Let's talk *business*.   [*subject matter + theme*]

In each of these sentences, a non-participant role has been promoted to the conceptual core and, as a result, is seen as being affected by the action. Thus, *honking one's horn* in (28a) suggests more effort than *honking with a horn*, *climbing a mountain* in (28b) implies that we reached its top while *climbing on a mountain* may not lead us that far, and *talking business* in (28c) means having serious negotiations while *talking about business* only refers to business as a subject matter. The transitive construction thus imposes the interpretation of an affected theme, so that the non-participant roles *instrument*, *place* and *subject matter* in the sentences under (28) are fused with the role *theme*.

11.4.1.2.3   Degrees of force of the energy source

The most forceful energy sources are human agents. Only humans are in control of their actions and can use instruments. Human agents are typically expressed as the subject of a sentence. In English, much more so than in other European languages, participants other than human agents may be conceived of as the cause of an action and be coded as the subject of a sentence. These non-human subject participants tend to be seen as having human-like qualities. Depending on their force exerted on the world, there is a cline of causes. We can, however, distinguish two major types of cause as energy sources: agent-like causes and enabling causes

(i) *Agent-like causes*
Consider the roles of the subjects in the following examples:

(29) a. *Katrina* devastated New Orleans. [*natural force*]
b. *The strike* closed down the railway system. [*cause*]
c. *The experiment shows* that rats can learn the difference between Dutch and Japanese. [*means*]
d. *Guns* don't kill people; people kill people. [*instrument*]

Hurricanes as in (29a), floods, earthquakes, etc. are violent natural forces reified as things. They are even anthropomorphised by giving them human names. Grammatically, their agent-like status shows up in the same *by*-phrase that is used for agents in the passive: *New Orleans was devastated by hurricane Katrina*.

The abstract noun *strike* in (29b) describes a cause reified as a thing. *The strike* metonymically stands for workers who are on strike but, unlike striking workers, a strike cannot take an instrument (**The strike closed down the railway system with picket lines*) or be asked what it is doing (**What did the strike do?*). Yet we strongly feel that strikes are responsible for the inconvenience they cause. Similar usages of agent-like causes are frequently found with abstract nouns such as *unemployment, crime, inflation*, etc.

The abstract noun *experiment* in sentence (29c) refers to a situation reified as a thing, by means of which an unnamed agent proves something. The role which the nominal *the experiment* plays in the sentence is that of a means. The role **means** describes a thing or a situation which helps or enables an agent to bring about an event. In using situations as a means we suppress the human agent and thereby present the situation more objectively. This construction is therefore characteristic of scholarly writing, where phrases such as *the study has shown* or *these examples illustrate* abound.

Instruments are normally under the control of an agent and expressed as *with*-adjuncts. In sentence (29d), however, the instrument 'guns' is promoted to the conceptual core as the subject of the sentence. Although an agent using the gun is still implied, the instrument is seen as having a certain degree of independence from the agent and as somehow acting on its own. It is for this reason that the instrument 'guns' in the slogan (29d) can be contrasted to people and presented as an argument against gun control by conservatives. However, even promoted instruments are not at the same level as human agents: they cannot be coordinated with agents (**Guns and terrorists kill people*) or perform deliberate actions (**Guns kill people for fun*).

(ii) *Enabling conditions: The middle construction*
Enabling conditions are causal in the sense that some internal quality makes them apt to let a situation occur. The construction in which enabling causes occur is known as the **middle construction**. The subject of the middle construction expresses a theme or another role which would normally be coded as a direct object or an adjunct. The subject participant of the middle construction influences the realisation of a process but does not itself transmit any energy to the object participant. In the following examples

the subject participant is a theme which is normally expressed as the direct object of a transitive sentence.

(30) a. *This item* won't scan.
b. *Metaphors We Live By* sold 50,000 copies.

The item in sentence (30a) cannot be scanned by the salesperson, possibly because its bar code is damaged. The sentence is thus passive-like in meaning, but the salesperson cannot be expressed as in **This item won't scan by the salesperson* because the middle construction generalises on the enabling condition of the item. Since this construction is conceptually related to the passive voice but formally expressed as an active sentence, it is also known as *medio-passive*.

Sentence (30b) illustrates a similar situation. The book *Metaphors We Live By* denotes a mental entity which is given a concrete material form in each of its copies. We see some internal quality in the book as an enabling condition which influences its sale, i.e. the sales figures are due to the book's quality, not to the bookshop or the shopkeeper, which therefore cannot be expressed in the sentence (**The book sold 50,000 copies by the bookseller*). This situation might be imagined as sketched in Figure 11.3.

Figure 11.3. *The book sold 50,000 copies.*

The middle construction also applies to enabling situations which are not midway between the active and passive voice. The following examples also show the high degree of flexibility of English to allow almost any thematic role to be promoted to subject position:

(31) a. *The plane* blew a tyre. [whole]
b. *A leak* sank the ship. [part]
c. *Our new stadium* seats 80,000. [place]
d. *These caves* are dripping water. [source]

Sentence (31a) involves a whole-part configuration. The plane as a whole serves as the reference point for accessing the tyre as its active zone part that is affected by the event. The bursting tyre is related to some unidentifiable weakness of the plane, such as negligence in its servicing, as an enabling condition.

Sentence (31b) illustrates a situation in which a material defect of a part is responsible for bringing about an event affecting the whole. The hole or crack in the hull of the ship does of course not transmit any energy but allows water to enter the ship. Such enabling conditions can be paraphrased as (*the leak*) *was responsible for* or *due to* or *because of* (*a leak*), etc. We may even see the leak as a means and describe the situation as *The ship was sunk by a leak*.

The enabling condition in (31c) is the accepted capacity of the stadium, while the enabling condition in (31d) is the particular location or composition of the cave, which allows water to drip from the rock.

11.4.2 The self-motion schema

The **self-motion schema** describes an agent's instigated own motion. In English, self-motion is expressed by the intransitive construction (*Our friends left*) or the intransitive predicate-complement construction (*Our friends went to Rome*). Conceptually, however, one's own motion may be conceived as a situation of caused motion: one causes oneself to move in the same way as one causes the motion of an object. This is the way French describes one's own motion by means of the reflexive verb *s'en aller*, as in *Il s'en va* (he himself away goes = 'he is leaving').

Like object motion, self-motion invokes the SOURCE-PATH-GOAL schema. However, since people normally go to a place with a certain purpose in mind, our attention tends to be directed towards the **goal** and the **path** leading to the goal. The goal and path of one's motion can therefore always be expressed in the self-motion schema, as in (32a) and (32b), while the **source** can hardly be expressed alone (32c) or in combination with a path expression (32d), unless we focus on its length, as in (32e), or refer to a particular airport, as in *We flew from Edinburgh*.

(32) a. We drove *to Bristol*. [goal]
b. We drove *via Oxford*. [path]
c. *We drove *from Bristol*. [source]
d. *We drove *from Dover via Bristol*. [source and path]
e. We drove *200 miles from Dover*. [length of path and source]

The mention of the source of motion is only possible with *come* as in *He came from Dover*. What licenses this use of *come* is its specific semantics. As a deictic verb, *come* describes motion towards the speaker or towards the hearer (see Chapter 2.1.3). Source, path and goal are thus not on the same footing, and the salience of the goal of a motion event is part of our greater interest in the goals of human actions than in their sources.

Self-motion by animates also differs from object motion in its possibilities of conflating motion with aspects of 'manner'. In fact, most motion verbs of English apply to the self-motion of animates and are manner-of-motion verbs. The manner of motion may refer to the motor pattern (*crawl, run, march*), the speed (*dash, hurry, dawdle*), the attitude (*stroll, promenade, stagger*), the medium (*fly, swim, wade*), or the instrument used in motion (*bike, ski, kayak*). These different types of manner are of course not clearly distinguishable.

As in the case of object motion, Germanic and Romance languages lexicalise self-motion differently. Thus, in English *The boy jumped off the train*, the verb *jump* conflates 'manner' with 'motion', while in Spanish *El chico salió de el tren saltando*, the manner of jumping (*saltando*) is expressed separately and the notion of path ('off') is conflated with 'motion' in the verb *salió* 'move out'.

The different lexicalisation patterns of motion events which a language provides have considerable consequences for its speakers. The wide range of manner-of-motion verbs which are available in English allows its speakers to make fine-grained distinctions of kinds of motion, which speakers of Spanish cannot make, such as those between types of rapid bipedal motion as expressed by *run, jog, lope, sprint, dash, rush, hurry, scurry, scramble*, etc. In experiments carried out by Slobin (2005), Spanish and English speakers were asked to read and later report passages from Spanish novels which did not contain manner verbs. A passage in the English translation would be:

(33) "He picked up his bags and started to *walk* through the mud and stones of a path that led to the town. He *walked* for more than ten minutes, grateful that it was not raining, because it was only with difficulty that he was able to *advance* along the path with his heavy suitcases."

While most Spanish-speaking subjects did not specify the manner of motion, almost all English-speaking subjects used various verbs to describe the protagonist's manner of motion, i.e. they described his walking as *staggering, stumbling* or *trudging*. They also used elaborate descriptions, such as "he dodges occasional hazards in the trail", "he rocks from side to side", and "slowly edges his way down the trail". Slobin assumes that the ease of encoding 'manner' in languages like English "engenders — over time — a predisposition to attend to this domain."

11.4.3 The caused-motion schema

The **caused-motion schema** describes events in which an energetic force, typically a human agent, brings about the motion of a thing to or from a location. Situation (34a) illustrates an agent causing the motion of things to a goal, while situation (34b) involves a natural force causing the motion of a thing away from a source.

(34) a. Santa Claus puts sweets in children's stockings.
b. The storm blew the roof off the police station.

Both sentences display the transitive predicate-complement pattern, better known as the caused-motion construction. The **caused-motion construction** is characterised by a subject denoting a cause, a predicate denoting motion, a direct object denoting the moving theme, and a complement denoting the goal or source; more abstractly: X causes Y to move to/from Z'. The verbs that are used in this construction may either require all three arguments like *put* and *blow*, or require an adjunct denoting the result, as in *put away* or *blow off*, or, which is commonly the case, require two arguments and optionally take a location complement. Thus, we cannot leave out the location phrase with *put* (*Santa Claus puts sweets*) or *blow* (*The storm blew the roof*), but can easily do so with verbs which conflate 'motion' and 'manner', such as *throw, kick, push, pour*, and a host of other verbs.

A group of two-place verbs like *load, spray* and *fill* display an interesting grammatical behaviour. These verbs allow alternative construals:

(35) a. The farmer loaded *hay* on the truck. [*theme – location*]
     b. The farmer loaded *the truck* with hay. [*location – theme*]

As can be expected from energetic events, the participant that is coded as the direct object is affected by the action. In sentence (35a) the theme 'hay' is affected, and it is left open how much of the truck is loaded; in sentence (35b) the location 'the truck' is affected, which invites the implicature that the truck is fully loaded. The verbs which allow this kind of reversal conflate the notions of 'motion' and 'filling', and each of these notions may be focused upon. Sentence (35a) is an instance of the caused-motion construction and focuses on the aspect of motion, while sentence (35b) is an instance of the transitive construction and focuses on the aspect of filling — the *with*-phrase is an optional adjunct. We do not have the same alternation with genuine caused-motion verbs such as *put* (*Santa Claus puts the stockings with sweets*) or *throw* (*He threw the net with the ball*) because with them the location cannot be thought of as being affected.

The caused-motion construction may also be used with non-motional verbs:

(36) a. Fred *sneezed* the napkin right off the table.
     b. They *discussed* the problem away.

Sneeze is normally used as a one-place predicate and denotes the process of 'exhaling breath from one's mouth in a sudden, involuntary, explosive manner'. The caused-motion

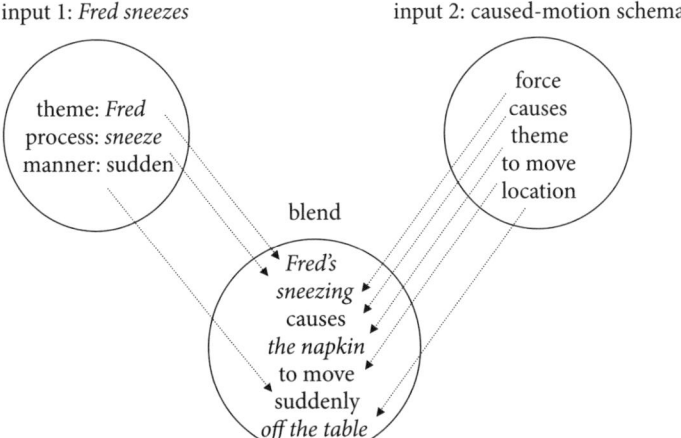

Figure 11.4. Blending in *Fred sneezed the napkin right off the table*.

construction of sentence (36a) imposes a different interpretation of *sneeze*: it is now understood to mean something like 'to use the force of one's sneezing to cause something to move away in a sudden, explosive, etc. manner'. This complex meaning emerges from blending the lexical meaning of *sneeze* and the schematic meaning of the caused-motion construction, as sketched in Figure 11.4.

Sentence (36b) shows that the caused-motion schema may also apply to metaphorical motion. Discussions are exchanges of different opinions with the goal of reaching an agreement. The caused-motion construction imposes an interpretation of *discuss* which may be paraphrased as 'by discussing cause the problem to be removed'.

11.4.4 The transfer schema

The **transfer schema** describes events in which an agent passes a thing to a recipient. Acts of transfer are often accompanied by a change of possession: the agent gives up her ownership of a thing and transfers it to the **recipient**, who becomes the new owner. This complex situation can often be expressed in two ways: as a **ditransitive construction** as in (37a), or as a caused-motion construction as in (37b).

(37) a. Phil gave his wife everything.
 b. Phil gave everything to his wife.

Both sentences are normally interpreted as having the same meanings. This is due to the fact that a prototypical act of giving involves both the transfer of a physical object and its change of ownership. The 'giving' frame thus neutralises potential differences in meaning which may arise through using different constructions. The ditransitive construction (37a) focuses on the recipient 'his wife', which is expressed as an indirect object, while the caused-motion construction (37b) focuses on the transfer of the object, which is indicated by the preposition *to* in the prepositional phrase *to his wife*. These differences in focus are diagrammed in Figure 11.5.

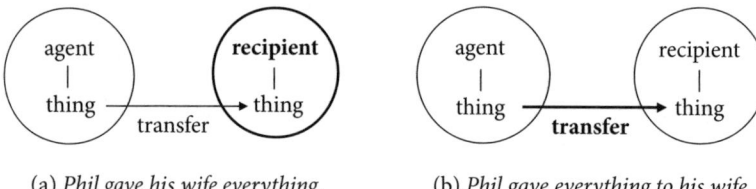

(a) *Phil gave his wife everything.* (b) *Phil gave everything to his wife.*

Figure 11.5. Ditransitive and caused-motion constructions denoting transfer

Due to their apparent interchangeability in such pairs of sentences, the two constructions are often treated as structural alternations and described as "dative shift". However, less prototypical situations of giving can no longer be expressed in alternative ways. For example, "giving" an abstract thing such as a hug is seen as relating to the recipient, as in *Phil gave his wife a big hug*, and hardly as an act of transfer, as in ?*Phil gave a big hug to his wife* (see 11.4.4.3). We therefore need to look more closely into the specific meanings imposed by the two constructions. We will first contrast situations of genuine transfer, then situations of beneficial transfer, and finally situations of metaphorical transfer.

11.4.4.1 *Physical and abstract transfer*

Many verbs of physical transfer behave like *give* and allow both construals: *offer, lend, pay, sell, send, bring, pass* and the stative verb *owe*. The only transfer verb that stands out in this group is *donate*, which can only be used in the caused-motion construction, as in *We donated £100 to charity*. The reason why **We donated charity £100* cannot be said is of course that a charity as an institution is not as much affected by the transfer as a human recipient. The same applies to verbs of sending like *send, fax* and *e-mail*, when the addressee is non-human. Thus, *?I sent Cambridge my new book manuscript* is of doubtful acceptability unless *Cambridge* is understood metonymically for a publishing house, which in its turn stands for its employees as recipients.

In acts of showing, teaching and communication, abstract things are transferred: percepts, knowledge and ideas. Here, the two constructions clearly impose differences in meaning:

(38) a. Professor White taught *me* Cognitive Grammar.
 b. Professor Schwarz taught GB *to me*.

(39) a. The manager *notified me* that I had been made redundant.
 b. The manager *pointed out to me* that the lights had to be switched off.

The ditransitive construction in (38a) suggests that the instructor's course probably had some effect on me — I may now be familiar with Cognitive Grammar, or I liked the course but may not remember much of it any more, whereas sentence (38b) only states that I was taught the theory of Government and Binding. Likewise, the communicative act in (39a) had a vital impact on the recipient, while that in (39b) may not.

Communication with its three participants speaker, hearer and message is one of the most central domains of abstract transfer. Acts of communication may focus either on the recipient or on the transmission of the message. Accordingly, two classes of verbs of communication are distinguished: those that are used with the ditransitive construction and those that are used with the caused-motion construction.

i. Verbs of communication that focus on the recipient and hence take the ditransitive construction include *tell, inform, assure, notify, remind, advise, convince, persuade, warn, promise, refuse, deny*, and *wish*.
ii. Verbs of communication that focus on the transmission of the message and hence take the caused-motion construction include *say to, report to, suggest to, acknowledge to, admit to, propose to, point out to, mention to, explain to, state to*, and *declare to*.

It should be noted here that the two groups of verbs distinguished on the basis of their grammatical behaviour apply solely to English. Other languages that allow the two construals of the transfer schema may categorise their verbs differently. For example, most of the verbs of group (ii), which take the caused-motion construction in English, take the ditransitive construction with a noun in the dative case in their German equivalents.

11.4.4.2 Beneficial transfer

Acts of transfer are usually performed for the benefit of the recipient. Interestingly, situations of selling are treated differently from those of buying. The transfer verb *sell* allows the recipient to be expressed as an indirect object (*My sister sold me her house*) or in a *to*-phrase (*My sister sold her house to me*). The verb *buy*, however, describes a beneficial situation, and the **beneficiary** may be expressed as an indirect object (*My sister bought me a house*) or in a *for*-phrase (*My sister bought a house for me*). The beneficial action itself does not involve a transfer, but there is strong expectation that the beneficiary will eventually "have" the object — therefore acts of transfer and benefaction are not felt to describe different types of situations.

The ditransitive construction does not distinguish between recipients and beneficiaries; the prepositional construction, however, does. The recipient expressed in the *to*-phrase is part of the conceptual core of the event; the beneficiary expressed in the *for*-phrase, however, is an optional participant. Grammatically, the *to*-phrase is a complement in the caused-motion construction, while the *for*-phrase is an adjunct of a transitive construction. Thus, we can separate the benefactive adjunct from the verb by paraphrasing *My sister bought a house for me* with *My sister bought a house and she did so for me*, but we can't separate a recipient phrase from the verb by paraphrasing *My sister sold the house to me* as **My sister sold the house and she did so to me*.

The "best" types of beneficial situation are those in which an agent creates a thing for a beneficiary. These situations can be expressed by the ditransitive or the prepositional construction with *for*, as in (40a, b); non-creative actions tend to be restricted to the prepositional construction, as in (40d).

(40) a. Honey, could you please fix *me* a hamburger?
 b. Honey, could you please fix a hamburger *for me*?
 c. ?Honey, could you fix *me* my drawer?
 d. Honey, could you please fix my drawer *for me*?

What counts as a creative act and hence can be expressed as a ditransitive construction is a matter of degree: it depends on the frame in which a situation is seen. In a study by Allerton (1978), speakers of English were asked to rate the acceptability of a large number of sentences with a beneficiary as an indirect object. A few of the ratings are given below.

(41) a. Could you cook me a meal? [99%]
 b. Could you paint me a room? [57%]
 c. Could you make me my bed? [37%]
 d. Could you taste me this wine? [2%]

There is a growing tendency in English to use the ditransitive construction with beneficiaries also in non-creative contexts, which suggest a stronger beneficial effect on the beneficiary:

(42) a. The waiter poured Eduardo another glass of wine.
b. The best man cut the bride and groom a piece of wedding cake.

11.4.4.3 *Metaphorical transfer*

Like the possession schema (see 11.2.3), the transfer schema is widely used as a source domain for metaphorical extensions, especially in the domain of human interaction. This follows from the nature of the transfer schema, which basically consists of two human beings transferring things. Some of the metaphorical usages of the transfer verb *give* are illustrated below:

(43) a. He gave me an idea.   [TRIGGERING THOUGHTS IS TRANSFER]
b. He gave me a fright.   [TRIGGERING EMOTIONS IS TRANSFER]
c. He gave it a look.   [DIRECTING ATTENTION IS TRANSFER]
d. He gave us a speech.   [PERFORMANCE IS TRANSFER]
e. He gave a cry.   [VOCAL OUTBURST IS TRANSFER]

The logic of these metaphors resides in our understanding of events and states as (reified) things, which can be possessed. Since I can "have" an idea, I can also "give" it to someone. But whereas objects are physically transferred and are no longer with the giver, ideas that are given to someone remain with the giver.

Many of the above expressions have counterparts with a full verb. For example, *He gave me a fright* has as a counterpart *He frightened me*. Obviously, there is an ecological need for having both constructions. Sentences with the full verb (*He frightened me*) tend to describe actions, i.e. deliberate durational events, while sentences with the functional verb *give* (*He gave me a fright*) tend to denote non-deliberate events: he is the cause of an emotion aroused in me as its experiencer (see 11.3.1). In the metaphorical situation of 'giving', the experiencer is seen as the recipient of an act of transfer. Since *give* is an achievement verb and achievements are punctual situations, the situation described by *He gave me a fright* is also punctual. Thus, *He gave me a fright* means 'he made me frightened by a sudden act'. Our focus of interest in such emotional situations is naturally on the human "experiencer-recipient". The ditransitive construction with *give* is an appropriate grammatical metaphor to describe such punctual emotions. Hence we normally say *He gave me a fright*, but not **He gave a fright to me*. The caused-motion construction can, however, also be used when the recipient is seen as less human, as in *This gave a fright to the British Government*, or when we want to give particular prominence to the act of transmission. This can be achieved by using a long postmodifier with the experiencer-recipient, as in *He gave a fright to the little old lady with the light blue 1920s cloche hat*.

The caused-motion construction is, on the other hand, the preferred construal in describing public performances like speeches as in (43d). Speeches are extended activities whose transmission is our focus. Thus, *Tony Blair gave a speech to diplomats* is the more appropriate way of describing this event than *Tony Blair gave diplomats a speech*, which almost sounds threatening.

Expressions such as *give a cry*, lastly, illustrate that, in its metaphorical usage, the transfer verb *give* can be used without naming a recipient. It is only in the metaphorical world that an object can be thought of as being transferred out into the air.

11.5 Conclusion

The main event schemas and their role configurations are summarised in Table 11.4. This list is, of course, not exhaustive but only represents the canonical event schemas which were discussed in the preceding sections. The thematic roles are abbreviated as follows: T = theme, L = location, G = goal, P = possessor, E = experiencer, C = cause, A = agent, R = recipient.

Table 11.4. Survey of canonical event schemas and their role configurations

Material world		
occurrence schemas: states	T — (T)	*be true, resemble sth.*
processes	T — (T)	*go wrong, shine*
spatial schemas: location schema	T — L	*be here*
motion schema	T — G	*go somewhere*
possession schema	P — T	*have, acquire sth.*
Psychological world		
emotion schema	E — C	*like sth.*
perception/cognition schema	E — T	*see, notice sth.*
Force-dynamic world		
action schema	A — T	*break sth.*
self-motion schema	A — G	*go somewhere*
caused-motion schema	A — T — G	*send sth. somewhere*
transfer schema	A — R — T	*give someone sth.*

11.6 Summary

This chapter has dealt with event schemas and their expressions in sentence patterns. **Event schemas** are characterised by a unique configuration of thematic roles. For example, the canonical action schema is characterised by the configuration of the roles agent and theme, as in *My boyfriend kissed a girl*. **Thematic roles** are conceptual entities associated with a unique function in a situation. The thematic roles of participants of a conceptual core are **participant roles**; they include the **agent** as the instigator of an action, the **experiencer** as the sentient human being, and the **theme** as the entity that most neutrally partakes in an event schema. Event schemas find expression in the seven basic **sentence patterns**.

Event schemas can be subsumed under three "worlds of experience": the material world, the psychological world, and the force-dynamic world. Situations in the **material world** comprise occurrences, the location and motion of things, and possessions, all of which involve the role theme. The **occurrence schemas** describe the state or process an entity is in, as in *The Sahara is fertile*. The spatial schemas comprise the **location schema**, which describes a theme's location, as in *The ball is in the goal*, and the **motion schema**, which describes a theme's motion, as in *The ball rolled into the goal*. The **possession schema** describes the relation between a possessor and a thing possessed, as in *He has the key*.

Situations in the **psychological world** include people's emotional, perceptual and mental experiences. The **emotion schema** describes the emotional state or process a human sentient experiences, as in *His stupidity amazes me*. It involves the roles of an experiencer and a cause, stimulating the emotion. Their order can typically be reversed, as in *I'm amazed at his stupidity*. Perception and cognition are closely related. The **perception/cognition schema** describes an experiencer's perceptual or mental awareness of a thing and involves the roles of an experiencer and a theme.

Situations in the **force-dynamic world** are energetic. They are brought about by a human agent or another causal entity and include actions, self-motions, caused motions and transfers. The **action schema** describes events in which a human agent deliberately and responsibly acts upon another entity, the theme. The agent generates energy and the theme is affected by the energy. Body parts and **instruments** may serve as energy transmitters within the energy chain. In English, non-human entities may also be viewed as energy sources and coded as the subject of the sentence, such as natural forces, causes, **means** and instruments. Depending on the degree of energy transmitted, actions display degrees of transitivity. A low degree of energy is generated by enabling conditions, which are expressed by the **middle construction**, as in *The book sells well*.

The **self-motion schema** describes an agent's own initiated motion and is typically conflated with aspects of 'manner', as in jumping or hurrying. The **caused-motion schema** describes events in which an energetic force brings about the motion of a thing to or from a location, as in *He put the beer in the fridge*. The **caused-motion construction** may impose its schematic meaning on non-motional verbs, as in *Fred sneezed the napkin right off the table*.

The **transfer schema** describes events in which an agent passes a thing to a **recipient**, who becomes its new owner. A transfer can be expressed by the **ditransitive construction**, as in *Please give me an aspirin*, or by the caused-motion construction, as in *I gave an aspirin to her*. The ditransitive construction involves an indirect and a direct object. The recipient of a ditransitive construction is more affected by a transfer than a recipient of a caused-motion construction. The distinction between the two types of construction is particularly pertinent with verbs of communication: verbs like *tell* focus on the recipient and take the ditransitive construction, while verbs like *say* focus on the transmission and take the caused-motion construction with *to*. The ditransitive construction also applies to **beneficiaries**, as in *I'll write you a cheque*. Beneficiaries can also be coded as adjuncts of transitive sentences, like *I'll write a check for you*. The transfer verb *give*, lastly, is widely used to describe metaphorical transfer, as in *He gave me brilliant idea*.

Further reading

The classical analysis of case roles and role configurations is Fillmore (1968; 1977); a selection of his main writings is collected in Dirven & Radden, eds. (1987). Discussions of roles and event construals are offered in Radden (1989), Croft (1991), DeLancey (1991), Palmer (1994), and Schlesinger (1995). Rich sources of verb classes and "alternations" are provided in Dixon (1991) and Levin (1993); a theoretical discussion of alternations is found in Goldberg (2002).

The use of *come* and *go* as change-of-state verbs is analysed in Radden (1996). The *there*-construction is discussed in Lakoff (1987) and Davidse (1999). The motion schema and its conflations is discussed in Talmy (1985/2000; 1991/2000), Slobin (1996) and several on-line papers by Slobin, e.g. (2005); the roles goal and source are contrasted in Ikegami (1987). Classics on transitivity are Lakoff (1977) and Hopper & Thompson (1980). The view of transitivity as an energy chain has been proposed by Langacker (1991a). The role of instruments as agents is analysed by Schlesinger (1989, 1995); the use of various roles in subject position in English is contrasted to German in Hawkins (1986). The middle construction is studied in Kemmer (1993); its link to modality is explored in Heyvaert (2003a).

The caused-motion construction is discussed in terms of construction grammar by Goldberg (1995, 1997) and in terms of blending by Fauconnier & Turner (2002), which Broccias (2003) combines with Langacker's grammar model. The English ditransitive construction and the problem of "dative alternation" is discussed in Allerton (1978), Thomson & Koide (1987), Wierzbicka (1988a), Langacker (1991a), Goldberg (1989, 1995), and Panther (1997).

Study questions

1. Which event schema and which thematic role(s) occur in the following sentence? Also try to spell out the specific subschema each time. Wherever possible, use linguistic tests to justify your decision.
    a. The suspect was an undercover CIA agent.
    b. Chess is the only game without an element of chance.
    c. The car went dead in the middle of the motorway.
    d. The door opened.
    e. This really bugs me.
    f. The burglars opened the safe.
    g. The President lied to us.
    h. He rang the money into the till.
    i. This gives me the creeps.

2. Identify the sentence pattern (transitive, intransitive, etc.) and the event schema of the following sentences and point out what is "special" about the sentences by contrasting them to similar sentences with prepositional phrases.
    a. In the evening I always surf the net.

b. I don't like the way the dog is sniffing me.
c. Mrs Walker would read us an instructive passage from the Bible.

3. Identify the thematic role played by the subject referent in the sentences, turn the sentences into the passive voice so that the role is expressed as a prepositional phrase, and indicate the impact the grammatical structure has on the meanings of the original sentence. Would you describe these situations differently in your own or another language?
    a. The FBI tapped our telephones.
    b. A dagger killed Julius Caesar.
    c. The typhoon uprooted trees.
    d. This car seats five passengers.
    e. Indian baskets never leak a drop.
    f. A survey of college students found that drug use is still widespread.
    g. My guitar broke a string.

4. Identify the type of construction (ditransitive, caused-motion) in the following examples and explain why the sentences under (a), (c) and (e) can be said, but the ones under (b), (d) and (f) are awkward or impossible.
    a. Jennifer sent a bunch of flowers to David's office.
    b. ?Jennifer sent David's office a bunch of flowers.
    c. Bernstein played us a wonderful sonata.
    d. ?Bernstein played us the piano.
    e. The dressmaker designed me a lovely dress.
    f. ?The dressmaker shortened me the dress.

Chapter 12

Space and extensions of space

Complements and adjuncts

12.0 Overview
12.1 Space and extensions of space: Non-participant roles
12.2 Physical space
12.3 Topology of space
12.4 Topology of spatial time
12.5 Abstract space
12.6 Summary

12.0 Overview

This chapter is concerned with non-participant roles, i.e. thematic roles that typically do not participate in event schemas. These peripheral roles describe notions of **space**, **time**, **circumstance**, **cause**, **reason**, **purpose**, and some other abstract domains, which cannot be discussed here. In the structure of English, non-participant roles normally function as adjuncts which specify the setting. They tend to be expressed by prepositional phrases whose prepositions primarily denote spatial relations. Space is one of the most basic and tangible domains of experience. It is characterised by an elaborate system of spatial relations. By metaphorically extending the senses of spatial prepositions, the domain of time and other abstract domains are conceived of and expressed in a variety of space-like ways. The analysis of prepositions of space and their motivated extensions amply demonstrates the pervasiveness of conceptual metaphor in grammar.

12.1 Space and extensions of space: Non-participant roles

Next to the experience of our bodies, our interaction with objects in physical space is among the most basic experiences. Most of the image schemas are based on spatial relations and many basic conceptual metaphors are derived from them, such as TIME IS SPACE or CHANGE IS MOTION. These spatial metaphors are most noticeable at the lexical level in expressions such as *the coming week* or *turn twenty*. At the grammatical level, spatial metaphors are particularly apparent in the use of prepositions.

Most prepositions denote spatial relations as their basic and historically primary meanings, and their uses in abstract domains are metaphorical extensions of spatial meanings. Seeing and describing time, circumstances, cause, reason or purpose in terms of space is so natural that we have to think twice before we realise that we are dealing with metaphor. We have rich conceptions of space, and when we project spatial notions onto abstract domains we tend to preserve the topology of space even if it does not apply to the target domain. For example, literally it does not make sense to speak of *in the morning* or *out of curiosity* because these domains are not three-dimensional. In their metaphorical usages, however, spatial prepositions allow us to make finer distinctions in the abstract domains which we would not be able to make if we could not make use of the spatial metaphor.

We will, therefore, first look at the way we conceive of physical space and describe it in English by means of spatial prepositions and then consider those abstract domains which make ample use of spatial prepositions. We describe these domains metaphorically as 'space': 'temporal space' and 'abstract space'. For lack of "space" in this book, our presentation of abstract space is restricted to the domains 'circumstance', 'cause', 'reason' and 'purpose'.

12.2 Physical space

12.2.1 Reference frames in physical space

A recurrent everyday problem is determining and describing the location of objects and situations. What are needed for this task are stable frames of reference. One method of locating objects and situations in physical space is by using an absolute reference frame. *Absolute reference frames* make use of unchanging locations such as prominent environmental landmarks like islands or mountains, of universal anchoring points such as the rising or setting sun, or of the system of coordinates or postal addresses. Another possibility is using relative reference frames, which most cultures and their languages have opted for. In using *relative reference frames*, physical space and objects in space are specified relative to one or more reference objects. Let us illustrate these possibilities of specifying a location by the ways in which a person may describe the location of the Museum of Modern Art in New York.

(1) a. The Museum is at 11 West 53rd Street. [*absolute*]
 b. It is right in front of you. [*relative deictic*]
 c. It is between Fifth and Sixth avenues. [*relative non-deictic*]

Sentence (1a) describes the location of MoMA in an absolute way by giving its postal address. For everyday purposes, we prefer to describe locations with respect to objects as reference points, as in (1b) and (1c). Description (1b) specifies the location of the museum by using the hearer and her momentary location as a reference point, i.e. it makes use of the deictic situation. The use of a *deictic reference frame* is restricted to the physical space surrounding speaker and hearer. Description (1c) relies on a *non-deictic reference frame*: it relates the location of the museum to two well-known avenues as reference points. The presentation of space in this chapter will mainly concentrate on non-deictic relative reference frames.

12.2.2 Trajector, landmark and spatial region

In using a non-deictic reference point, we specify the location of a thing relative to one or more things which the speaker assumes are identifiable to the hearer. In the cognitive-linguistic literature on space, the thing to be located is usually described as the **trajector** and the thing that serves as the reference point as the **landmark**. These terms correspond to the notions of figure and ground, which we introduced in Chapter 2.1.8. A trajector is a spatial figure and a landmark is a spatial ground.

Languages can express the spatial relation between a trajector and a landmark in various formal ways: by means of verbs such as *contain*, *surround* or *include*, by means of body part terms such as *back* for 'behind', *head* for 'on top of', or *heart* for 'inside', as in *the heart of the city*, by means of case suffixes to a noun as in Finnish or Hungarian, and by means of prepositions as in English. Let us consider a simple case of a spatial relation: a wife telling her husband where he left his tie, which he is desperately looking for:

(2) Your tie is on the kitchen table.

In this sentence *your tie* describes the trajector and *the kitchen table* the landmark. In our discussion of schematic relations in Chapter 7.3.3 we pointed out that image-schematic meanings are typically expressed by prepositions. The preposition *on* evokes the contact schema, which instructs the hearer that the tie is in contact with the kitchen table. Due to his knowledge of the 'table' frame, our husband assumes that his tie is to be found on the top of the table. Technically, the spatial area where a trajector is located relative to a landmark is known as a **region** or "search domain". *The table* as a whole is conventionally used to stand for one of its active zone parts: the table top (for active zone see Chapter 1.2.3.1). This is the part of the table which we normally interact with. We therefore also assume that the table is in its normal, upright position. If for some reason or other the table was tilted or upside down and the tie was lying on one of its legs or its under-side, we would not say *Your tie is on the table* but specify the particular part of the landmark and say *Your tie is on the leg of the table* or *Your tie is on the under-side of the table*.

The relation between a trajector and a landmark is asymmetrical. We prefer to describe the spatial relation between a table and a tie lying on it as in sentence (2) rather than saying ?*The table is under the tie*, where the larger table is the trajector and the smaller tie the landmark. The relation between the tie and the table is static. The asymmetry between trajector and landmark is even more pronounced in motion events, i.e. dynamic relations, as in (3).

(3) a. The cat jumped onto the dinner table.
    b. James, will you move the dinner table a bit more under the chandelier?

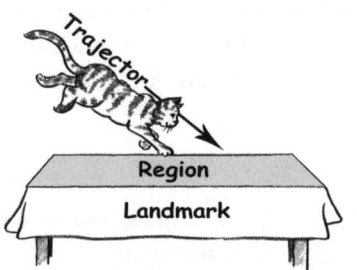

Figure 12.1. *The cat jumped onto the table.*

In situation (3a), the trajector 'cat' is in motion with the top region of the landmark 'dinner table' as its goal. Trajectors are normally smaller than their landmarks, and in situations of motion, the trajectors, not the landmarks, move. We can hardly reverse trajector and landmark and describe the situation as **The table received the cat.*

In situation (3b), the dinner table is the trajector, and the goal of its motion is the region vertically below the chandelier and its immediate vicinity. Here, the trajector is the larger entity and the landmark the smaller entity. As in (3a), we cannot reverse their relation. However, due to its smaller size, the landmark must at least have a certain salience. This can truly be said of a chandelier, but it would, for example, be less normal to say *Move the dinner table under the lamp.*

Trajector and landmark are not just in a spatial relation to each other but are typically also seen in a particular functional relation within a stereotypical frame and/or domain (see also Chapter 7.3.3). The situation of a dinner table under the chandelier might invoke a 'romantic dinner' frame. The spatial situation of cars on a highway invokes the 'driving' frame, with roads typically functioning as landmarks and cars as their trajectors, as in (4a). If we were confronted with a spatial situation of cars on a train, as in (4b), we would have to see their functions within a different frame.

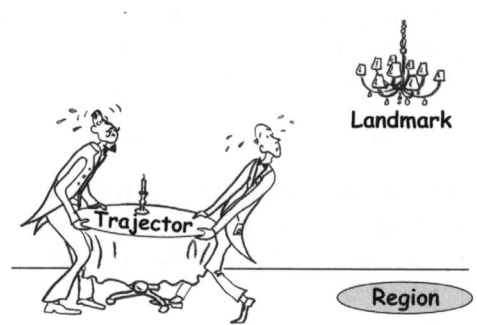

Figure 12.2. *Will you move the table under the chandelier?*

(4) a. The car is now on the highway.
    b. The car is now on the train.

Sentence (4a) invokes the normal 'driving' frame and makes us enrich the situation in the sense of the car moving on the highway. Sentence (4b), however, is not understood in the sense of a car moving on the train but much rather invokes a highly specialised frame: the one of piggyback transport by railroad. *The car* is still the trajector in the spatial relation but, due to this particular frame, is no longer seen as moving on its own.

12.3 Topology of space

The notion 'topology of space' shall be understood here as our commonsense structuring of physical space and entities in physical space as reflected in language. We will first consider three basic types of spatial relations and then discuss the two basic strategies of locating entities in space in English: dimension of a landmark and orientation between landmarks.

12.3.1 Location, direction, and extent and their expression in English

(i) *Location*: As pointed out in Chapter 11.2.2, in static spatial relations as in the sentences under (2) and (4) the **location** of a stationary trajector is specified relative to a landmark. The trajector may be a thing or a situation. In *The kids are in the attic* the trajector is a thing, and in *The kids are playing in the attic* the trajector is an event. In either case, the location is asked about by a *where*-question: *Where are the kids?* The prepositions used in prepositional phrases expressing a location are known as positional or **locative prepositions**.

(ii) *Direction*: In dynamic spatial relations as in the sentences under (3) the **direction** of a moving trajector is specified relative to a landmark. Our understanding of motion events is based on the image schema SOURCE-PATH-GOAL (see Chapter 11.2.2.2). The direction is typically specified with respect to a goal, more rarely with respect to a source, and very rarely with respect to the path. Directions are asked about by questions with *where (to)?* and *where from?* — other languages may have a separate question word for directions. The prepositions used in expressing direction are known as **directional prepositions**.

(iii) *Extent*: An extent involves not a relation between a trajector and a landmark, but a relation between a thing and its measured property. An **extent** describes a measured length (or width or depth) or the distance of things in space. Lengths are typically measured in a static relation, distances in a dynamic relation.

(5) Extent in a static relation [*length*]
    a. *How long* is the Grand Canyon?
    b. – It is *almost 300 miles* **long**.
    c. – It stretches **for** / **over** *almost 300 miles*.

(6) Extent in a dynamic relation [*distance covered in motion*]
    a. *How far* did you go? / *Where* did you go?
    b. – We went **from** Buena Vista **(up) to** Cottonwood.

(7) Extent in a static relation seen as dynamic [*distance in fictive motion*]
    a. *How far* does the road go? / *Where* does the road go?
    b. – The road goes **from** Buena Vista **(up) to** Cottonwood.

The extent of a thing in space normally applies to static relations. It is asked about by questions with *how long* (*wide*, *deep*, etc.) as in (5a), and its length is specified by means of a measure phrase with *long* (5b) or *for* or *over* (5c).

We may also specify the extent of a thing in a dynamic situation of physical motion, as in (6). The extent is asked about by a question with *how far* (6a) and specified by an extent phrase with *from ... to* (6b), or only *to* when the starting point is implied. The extent designates the distance covered by walking or driving the whole length of the route from one end to the other end, i.e. it is directional. Sentence (6b) might also be given as an answer to a *where*-question, asking for the location of our physical motion.

A distance may also be specified by construing a static relation as dynamic. In question (7a) and answer (7b), the road is presented as if it was moving. Since the road itself does not move, we imagine a trajector moving along the road and thereby measure the distance between its end-points. In Chapter 2.1.6 we referred to the construal of a static scene in terms of motion as fictive motion. This interpretation is not just imposed by the motion verb *go*, but also triggered by the distance marker *far* and the directional prepositions *from* and *to*. Situations without a motion verb such as *How far is the moon from the earth?* are also seen as directional.

In the structure of the sentence, all three types of extent phrases are (obligatory) complements: Sentence (5c) cannot be reduced to **It stretches*, sentence (6b) cannot, in the sense of extent, be phrased as **We went*, and sentence (7b) cannot be shortened to **The road goes*.

Location, direction, and extent represent the three basic types of spatial relations. They and their subtypes can be distinguished by the question words used to ask about them and the prepositions used to specify them.

Table 12.1. Types of spatial relations

location	direction		extent	
static	dynamic	static	dynamic	static–dynamic
		length		directional extent
where?	where (from)?	how long?	how far, where?	
in, etc.	into, etc.	for, over	from ... to	

The system of English spatial prepositions is not organised along these three types of spatial relations but makes use of topological properties of landmarks. Locations, directions and extents are specified by referring either to the *dimension* of a landmark or to the *orientation* established between two or more landmarks. As will be seen in the ensuing sections, English has a rich inventory of dimensional and orientational prepositions, but only the few extensional prepositions *from...to, for*, and *over*, whose spatial usages will not be discussed any further. The three types of spatial relations distinguished above and the two topological properties of dimension and orientation form the basic framework within which the spatial prepositions of English are set. This framework is shown in Table 12.2.

Table 12.2. Spatial relations, topological properties, and spatial prepositions

	location	direction	extent
dimension:		dimensional prepositions	
orientation:		orientational prepositions	

The following sections will be devoted to the subtle distinctions made within the topologies of dimension and orientation and their expressions as dimensional and orientational prepositions in English.

12.3.2 Spatial dimensions: Dimensional prepositions

We can roughly determine the spatial region where a thing is to be found by specifying the **dimension** of a landmark, i.e. its geometric shape. Notions of spatial dimension are expressed in English by topological, or **dimensional prepositions** such as *on* and *in*. In specifying a dimension of a landmark, we narrow down the potential regions where the trajector is to be found. The dimension of the trajector is irrelevant. Thus, irrespective of whether the object that I am holding in my hand is elongated, flat, or a container, it is always *in* my hand. Most physical objects come in a clearly recognisable shape, but often we have to give it a shape in our mind. Consider the following examples:

(8) a. A large flock of pigeons is perched **on** the tree.
    b. There is an owl perched **in** the tree.

In description (8a), the two-dimensional preposition *on* evokes a scene of pigeons perched on the top of the tree and on the ends of its branches. The region where the birds are to be found is thus an imaginary outer "surface" of the tree. In description (8b), the three-dimensional preposition *in* makes us see the owl perched on a branch near the stem. Here, the region where the bird is to be found is the "inside" of the tree. Objectively speaking, a tree neither has a surface nor an inside. The geometric dimensions we assign to the object are purely mental constructs.

The Euclidian system of space distinguishes three dimensions: one dimension for length, two dimensions for length and width, and three dimensions for length, width and depth. The basic dimensional prepositions of English also include zero-dimensionality. The dimensions expressed by the three basic dimensional prepositions *at*, *on* and *in* in English are:

(9) zero-dimensional   *at the corner*   [*point*]
     one-dimensional   *on the border*   [*line*]
     two-dimensional   *on the table*   [*surface*]
     three-dimensional   *in the bottle*   [*container*]

The preposition *at* describes landmarks seen as points, the preposition *on* groups together landmarks seen as lines (*on the border*) and surfaces (*on the table*), and the preposition *in* refers to landmarks seen as containers. In addition to purely geometrical dimensions, functional relations between the landmark and the trajector are also relevant, or even more so.

A zero-dimensional space is a point and has no shape of its own. Points are, however, highly useful as points of recognition and hence allow a wide range of reference points to locate a trajector, as in *I'll wait at the bus stop*.

One- and two-dimensional spaces share the property that trajectors may be in contact, or come into contact, with them as landmarks. With a one-dimensional landmark, the trajector is in a sideways contact with the landmark, as in *on the edge*, with a two-dimensional landmark, the trajector is typically seen as being in vertical contact with the landmark, as in *on the table*.

Three-dimensional spaces characterise containers. The preposition *in*, however, does not refer to the three-dimensional shape of a landmark but to its interior cavity, which some three-dimensional objects like bottles have. The interior of a physical object is relevant to us because it establishes a container.

All three dimensional prepositions are thus characterised by the landmark's interaction with a trajector. These relationships are often also meaningful as image schemas: *on* invokes the CONTACT-schema, and *in* the CONTAINER-schema.

Most dimensional prepositions of English are by themselves not locative or directional: almost all of them can be used in both static and dynamic relations. Still, locative prepositions are typically used in static relations, whereas directional prepositions typically apply to dynamic relations. The basic dimensional prepositions can be arranged according to their dimensionality on the one hand and their normal use as locative or directional on the other hand, as shown in Table 12.3. The preposition that prototypically represents each slot is printed in bold.

Table 12.3. The basic dimensional prepositions of English

	location		direction	
dimensions	PLACE	SOURCE	GOAL	PATH
0-dimensional POINT	**at**, by, near, close to, with	**from**, away from	**to**, at, for, towards	**by**, past, via
1- & 2-dimensional LINE / SURFACE	**on**, on top of	**off** (of)	**on(to)**, against	**along**, about, around
3-dimensional CONTAINMENT	**in**, within, inside, between, among	**out of**, outside of	**in(to)**	**through**, throughout

In our understanding of the physical world an object can only be in one place at a time. We may, however, describe the place or path of a thing by means of multiple spatial expressions:

(10) a. I'll meet you **at** the coffee shop **on** 125th Street **in** Harlem.
　　 b. You enter the house **by** the backyard **past** the flower beds and **through** the backdoor.

Multiple locative expressions as in (10a) serve to identify the same place by naming increasingly larger locations — we may, of course, also zoom in on the same place by naming increasingly smaller locations. Multiple path expressions as in (10b), on the other hand, allow the hearer to scan a path. Since the sequence of the landmarks along a given path is iconically ordered, path expressions cannot be reversed.

The following description of the basic dimensional prepositions will be restricted to prepositions of place, source, and goal.

12.3.2.1 *Zero-dimensionality: Points and indeterminacy*

Strictly speaking, zero-dimensionality only applies to points. Points are prototypically referred to by the preposition *at*, and these points can only be non-human landmarks, not humans. Thus we may say *Bill waited at the entrance*, but not **Bill waited at Helen*, unless Helen is a statue. Zero-dimensionality is, however, also understood in the sense of indeterminacy or irrelevance of a landmark's shape. As shown in Table 12.2, English has a number of prepositions at its disposal that specify a region in the vicinity of a landmark. The particular spatial dimension remains unspecified with these prepositions; they much rather focus on the kind of relation that holds between the trajector and the landmark: *by* expresses the notion of 'connection', *near* and *close to* express 'proximity', and *with* describes 'accompaniment'. These prepositions are used with both animate and inanimate landmarks. The notion of 'accompaniment' is a typically human characteristic: the use of *with* in reference to inanimate things is therefore either ungrammatical, as in **Howard waited with the entrance*, or interpreted metaphorically, as in *The kitchen comes with a refrigerator, a dishwasher, a microwave and a wine cooler*. Due to the accompaniment preposition *with*, all these kitchen appliances may be seen as metaphorical companions.

In motion events, the source and goal of a trajector's motion are also normally indeterminate with respect to their shape. Source and goal do not, however, have the same conceptual salience (see Chapter 11.4.2). We are generally more concerned with the goal of a motion event than with its source. This tendency is reflected in the finer distinctions made by four zero-dimensional goal prepositions: *to, at, for,* and *towards*. *To* suggests reaching a goal, *at* and *for* refer to a person's intention of reaching a goal, and *toward(s)* describes motion in the direction of a goal. The contrast between the goal described by *to* and the target described by *at* is illustrated in the following pair of sentences:

(11) a. Eileen threw the ball **to** Cyril. [goal]
 b. Eileen threw the ball (right) **at** Cyril. [target]

Sentence (11a) might be said in the context of a ball game in reference to a player's pass to a team-mate; it thus suggests cooperativeness. Sentence (11b), by contrast, invites implicatures of hostility and aggressiveness: Eileen probably intended to hit Cyril. This implicature is induced by the dimensional sense of *at*: as in its locative use, directional *at* construes the landmark as a point. An agent's action is thus directed towards a point-like goal, i.e. a **target**. A target may be an object or a human being, as in (11b) — in this respect directional *at* differs from locative *at*, which, as said above, is not used with humans.

12.3.2.2 One- and two-dimensionality: contact and support

As already mentioned in Section 12.3.2, landmarks in the shape of a line or surface tend to be seen in contact with the trajector. Let us consider some situations of a trajector's contact with the surface of an object. The most natural situation of contact is established by the force of gravity. Gravity makes a trajector vertically rest upon a landmark, which counteracts to this force by supporting the trajector, as in *the book on the table*. Situations in which a trajector touches a landmark sideways (12a) or from below (12c) are seen as instances of contact and expressed by *on* only if the trajector as a whole is somehow attached to the landmark. Compare (12a) vs (12b) and (12c) vs (12d):

(12) a. The ladder is **on** *the wall*. [= hung up on the wall]
 b. The ladder is standing **against** *the wall*. [= leaning against it]
 c. The lamp is **on** *the ceiling*. [= fixed to the ceiling]
 d. The lamp is hanging **from** *the ceiling*. [= on a hook and chain]

The goal of a motion bringing a trajector into contact with a landmark is expressed by *on* or *onto*, the source of a motion bringing about the separation of a trajector from the surface of a landmark is expressed by *off* or *off of*:

(13) a. James put the Bible **on** *the table*.
 b. James put the Bible **onto** *the highest shelf*.
 c. James brushed the crumbs **off** *the table*.
 d. James lifted the cast iron pot **off of** *the stove*.

The construal of a motion event with either *on* or *onto*, as in (13a) and (13b), gives rise to different implicatures. *On* suggests a neutral situation of contact: the goal is taken to be within easy reach, which is normally the case with ordinary tables. *Onto* is a compound preposition, in which *to* expresses motion to a goal and *on* the resulting state of contact. In separately highlighting the phase of the trajector's motion to the goal, *onto* makes us see the goal as somewhat more distant, less easy to reach, and possibly even requiring some effort. A similar distinction applies to the use of *off* versus *off of*. *Off* as in (13c) describes 'separation' in a neutral way, while *off of* in colloquial American English as in (13d) suggests more effort in separating an entity from a landmark.

12.3.2.3 Three-dimensionality: Containment

A container is not a mere receptacle, but also has the function of holding objects or substances in it. Therefore, according to the things contained, containment may involve the total enclosure of the trajector, as in the examples under (14a), or only partial enclosure, as in the examples under (14b–d).

(14) a. a hot potato in his mouth; the soup in the bowl
 b. a cigarette in his mouth; the flower in the vase
 c. the car in the driveway; the players in the field
 d. a hole in the sock; the highlights in the show

The notion of containment presupposes boundaries. The examples under (14c) show that 'boundedness' may override 'dimensionality': surfaces that have well-demarcated boundaries are conceived of as containers. The examples under (14d) show that the notion of containment may also apply to cases where the trajector is not a separate object but a profiled part of the landmark. Here, the notion of containment borders on that of part and whole: thus, we speak of *the heel of the sock* and *the best part of the show*.

As with contact-related motion (13), motion into a container and motion out of a container allow two construals, as shown in the following examples.

(15) a. Mark jumped **in** the water.
  b. Mark jumped **into** the water.
  c. Mark took some change **from** his pocket.
  d. Mark fished some cash **out of** his pocket.

Like *on* (13a) and *onto* (13b), the goal prepositions *in* and *into* express closer and more distant goals respectively. Thus, sentence (15a) may be used in describing a situation of someone jumping from the bank of a river or lake, while sentence (15b) could be said of someone jumping from a diving-board. As a result, *into* here suggests deeper penetration.

Situations of emergence from a container that are seen as involving no intensity are coded by the zero-dimensional source preposition *from* as in (15c), i.e. the trajector's source of motion is shifted from the interior of the container to its outside edge. The complex source preposition *out of* in (15d) corresponds to the goal preposition *into*: it makes us see the trajector's emergence from the depth of a container and hence suggests greater effort.

12.3.3 Spatial orientations: Orientational prepositions

A second strategy which can be applied in determining a spatial region involves two landmarks. The two landmarks are mentally linked so that they form a line of **orientation**. We use this strategy when we want to point out a star in the night-time sky. Stars appear to us as zero-dimensional so that the strategy of using dimensionality is not applicable. But we might project an imaginary line into the sky by linking two bright stars as landmarks, for example the stars at the end of the bowl of the Plough (AmE Big Dipper). By extending the length of this line of orientation we can now specify the position of the North Star.

Notions involving spatial orientation are typically expressed by projective, or **orientational prepositions** such as *behind* and *below*. The two reference points may be explicitly mentioned, as in sentence (16a), where the line of orientation is established by the two landmarks *the curtain* and *the balcony*. As a rule, however, only one of the two reference points is expressed in English while the second one remains implicit, as in (16b). In sentence (16c), none of the reference points is expressed at all.

(16) a. A man stood *behind the curtain* from the balcony.
    b. A man stood *behind the curtain*.
    c. Another man followed *behind*.

In sentence (16a), the region where the man is standing is found by tracing an orientational line from the balcony as the viewpoint through the curtain into the room. Sentence (16b) involves a deictic or contextually given viewpoint: the man is to be found by tracing an orientational line from that viewpoint through the curtain to a region behind it. These two orientational arrangements are illustrated in Figure 12.3.

(a) *A man stood behind the curtain from the balcony.*   (b) *A man stood behind the curtain.*
Figure 12.3. Spatial orientation with two and one explicit reference points

Sentence (16c) may be understood deictically or non-deictically. In its deictic arrangement, the observer traces a line from her location to the first man and a region behind this man. In its non-deictic arrangement, the orientational line is determined by the men's direction of motion, i.e. it is inherent to our canonical way of motion facing forwards. The man following behind is therefore to be found in the region behind the first man relative to his direction of motion. These orientational arrangements are illustrated in Figure 12.4.

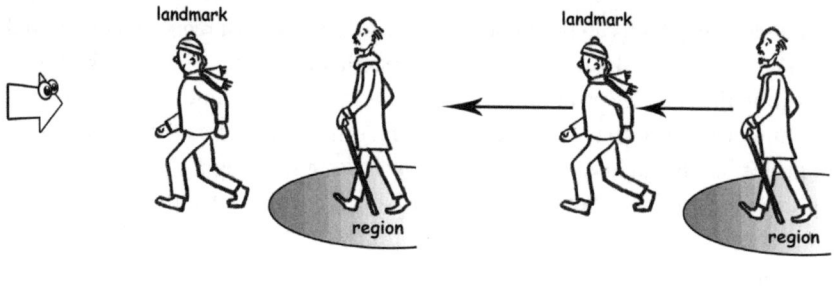

(c) *Another man followed behind.*   (d) *Another man followed behind.*
      (deictic)   (non-deictic)
Figure 12.4. Spatial orientation: the orientational preposition *behind*

In our spatial orientation we make use of three coordinates, which, however, are of different importance to us. Verticality is the most important coordinate: it is at the basis of the ubiquitous UP–DOWN image schema. Horizontality comes next in importance: it is at the basis of the FRONT–BACK image schema. The least important coordinate is that of LEFT–RIGHT.

Many people experience difficulty in telling 'left' from 'right' but hardly anybody will confuse 'up' and 'down' or 'front' and 'back'. The English prepositions describing vertical and horizontal orientations are shown in Figure 12.5.

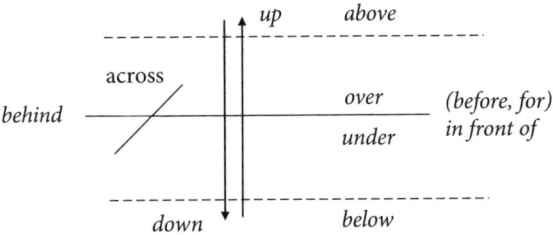

Figure 12.5. The basic orientational prepositions of English

The vertical coordinate is more significant in our everyday experience than the horizontal one. Not surprisingly, its conceptual salience is reflected in the finer distinctions made by prepositions denoting verticality. Along the vertical orientation three types of distinction are made: the designation of a path towards the upper or lower end-point of a landmark (17a), the designation of a region vertically above or below a landmark (17b), and the designation of a region other than vertically above or below a landmark (17c):

(17) a. The monkey climbed **up** / **down** the tree.
 b. The bridge goes **over** the river.
 The river goes **under** the bridge.
 c. Mount A is 800 feet **above** Mount B.
 Mount B is 800 feet **below** Mount A.

The prepositions *up* or *down* describing the situation in (17a) designate vertical paths. With paths, vertical orientation may extend as far as near-horizontal orientation. Thus, the path in *go up the stairs* may be at an angle of 45 degrees, and it is almost, or even completely, horizontal in *go up the road*, as illustrated in Figure 12.6.

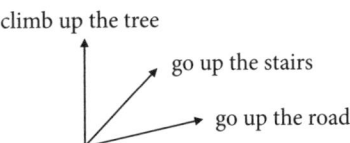

Figure 12.6. Degrees of verticality as expressed by *up*

The regions specified by *over* and *under*, as in (17b), and *above* and *below*, as in (17c), are mutually exclusive. The region covered by *over* is vertically superior to the landmark; conversely, the region covered by *under* is vertically inferior to the landmark. The regions specified by *above* and *below*, by contrast, are not vertically aligned with the landmark, but are established by comparison of two different vertical levels. Thus, the region covered by *above* is higher than the level of a landmark but prototypically excludes the vertical region covered by *over*. The reverse situation applies to *below*.

Figure 12.7. *Over* and *under*; *above* and *below*

On the horizontal plane the system of English prepositions distinguishes between FRONT–BACK (18a–c) and LEFT–RIGHT (18d) orientations:

(18) a. The flag is **in front of / behind** us.
b. The case is (brought) **before** the court
c. We left **for** New York.
d. The castle is **to the right / to the left** of you.

The complex preposition *in front of* (18a) has largely superseded the older forms *before* and *for*. *Before* in its spatial sense is still used in a few fixed phrases as in (18b), and *for* in its spatial sense is restricted to the meaning of 'destination'. **Destinations** are spatial goals that persons intend to reach, as in (18c). The people may also be expressed metonymically as places, as in *Whole villages left for America*. Due to our bodily make-up, we attach more importance to the front than to the back and more importance to FRONT–BACK orientation than to LEFT–RIGHT orientation.

Compared to the set of dimensional prepositions, the set of orientational prepositions is less elaborate. They are fewer in number and they make fewer internal distinctions. The same orientational prepositions can often be used to specify a location (19a), a motion along a path (19b), and a motion to an end-point (19c):

(19) a. He lives *under the bridge*. [location]
b. He walked *under the bridge* (from side to side). [path]
c. He walked *under the bridge* (and stopped there). [goal]

In its goal-directional use in (19c), the preposition *under* is conceptually composed of 'to' and 'under', where 'under' describes a region lower than the landmark where the motion ends. With source-directional prepositions, the region would be expressed on its own, as in *He walked from under the bridge*. Interestingly, the preposition *under* behaves differently from *over*: *He walked over the bridge* can only mean that he crossed the bridge from side to side and not that he stopped walking midway on the bridge.

Most dimensional and orientational path prepositions can, however, be used in a static relation in reference to the end-point of a path:

(20) a. My bonnie is **over** the ocean.
b. The beach is **down** the street.
c. The bathroom is **through** the kitchen.

All these sentences describe a location which would be reached if we took a route from our deictic position to its end-point. Thus, in example (20b), when we go down the street all the way from where we are now we would end up at the beach. We do not actually move but only mentally scan the path. Since our focus is on the end-point of the path, the path metonymically stands for its end-point. The metonymy applies to the SOURCE-PATH-GOAL image schema and has therefore been described by Lakoff (1987) as "image-schema transformation". It is motivated by our tendency "to follow the path of a moving object until it comes to a rest, and then to focus on where it is" (p. 442).

12.4 Topology of spatial time

12.4.1 Topologies of space and time

Notions of time are probably universally conceptualised in terms of space. The metaphor TIME IS SPACE also accounts for many of the temporal uses of basically spatial prepositions of English. In order to comprehend the motivation for these metaphorical extensions of meaning, we will first consider the correspondences between the topologies of space and time in Table 12.4.

Table 12.4. Correspondences between physical space and temporal space

		physical space	temporal space
(i)	dimensions:	three dimensions	one dimension: time axis
	orientations:	three orientations	one orientation: horizontal
(ii)	trajector:	object or event	event
(iii)	landmark:	object	period or event
(iv)	search domain:	spatial region	time sphere
(v)	static relation:	location in space	location in time
(vi)	dynamic relation:	motion: direction	mental scanning: duration

i. Physical space is three-dimensional and hence provides three coordinates of orientation. Time is thought of as a one-dimensional time-axis with a horizontal front-back orientation; more rarely, time is also conceptualised as having a vertical orientation, as in *The new year is coming up*, where *up* refers to future time.
ii. A spatial trajector is an object (*The bottle is on the table*) or an event (*She dances on the table*). A temporal trajector to be located on the time axis is a situation, typically an event, as the engagement in *We got engaged on Valentine's Day*, which occurred during the period of Valentine's Day.
iii. The spatial landmark is an object. The temporal landmark is a period, such as *Valentine's Day*, or another situation, as in *We got engaged when our baby was born*.
iv. The search domain for a spatial trajector is a spatial region, which is determined relative to the landmark. The search domain for an event is a time sphere, which is determined relative to a period. In *We got engaged on Valentine's Day*, the temporal search

domain is the whole of Valentine's Day, but the event of exchanging our engagement vows only lasted for a brief moment of this day.

v. In a static spatial relation, the trajector occupies a fixed location in space, as in *I usually work in the library*. In a static temporal relation, a situation occurs at a fixed location in time, as in *I usually work in the morning*, where my work is "located" within the time frame of the morning.

vi. In a dynamic spatial relation, the trajector moves along a path in a certain direction, as in *We travelled from coast to coast*. In a dynamic temporal relation, a situation is mentally scanned through its duration in a certain direction, as in *We travelled from morning to evening*, where the duration of our journey is scanned in the direction from the morning to the evening.

Apart from their inherent differences with respect to dimensionality, space and time show striking parallelisms so that it is only natural to relate the two domains conceptually. It also makes economical sense to use the same conceptual framework for both domains, and there is a biological predisposition towards projecting SPACE onto TIME — rather than TIME onto SPACE. As expressed by Lakoff (1993), "we have detectors for motion and detectors for objects/locations. We do not have detectors for time (whatever that could mean)" (p. 218).

12.4.2 Location in time and duration

When we specify notions of time, we almost always do so with respect to situations. Lexical specifications of time provide the hearer with more precise information than grammatical specifications of time, i.e. aspect and tense. Lexical specifications of time of course need to be in conformity with grammatical specifications of time. Let us consider the specifications of time given in the following sentences.

(21) a. The next Olympic Games will take place in Beijing *in 2008*.
 b. The Olympic Games last *for 17 days*.
 c. The Olympic Games take place/last *from August 8th to 24th*.

In sentence (21a), the tense form *will* locates the time of the forthcoming Olympic Games in the future time sphere, and the lexical specification *in 2008* indicates the time more precisely by means of absolute calendrical dating. The year 2008 is included in the future time sphere and hence compatible with the future tense form — at least as long as the sentence is uttered before the Games take place. We can ask about the time by using a *when*-question: *When will the next Olympic Games take place?* and expect to be given a lexical specification, not a grammatical one. The prepositional phrase *in 2008* specifies the temporal location of the event on the time axis in the same way that *in Beijing* specifies its location in space. We will describe specifications that locate a situation at a point of time or in a period as **location time**. Since location times can be asked about by *when*-questions, they are sometimes also described as "time-when".

In sentence (21b), *for 17 days* describes a period that specifies the duration of the Olympic Games. **Duration** refers to the length of time a situation lasts. Duration corresponds to spatial extent, as presented in example (5). Both duration and extent are specified by measured units, both are expressed by the preposition *for*, and both are asked about by *how long*-questions: *How long is the Grand Canyon?* and *How long will the Olympic Games last?* The adjective *long* in *how long* also hints at the spatial origin of the notion of duration.

In sentence (21c), the time of the Games is specified by two absolute points in time, *August 8th* and *August 24th*. We can ask about the time by using a *when*-question: *When will the next Olympic Games take place?* — *From August 8th to August 24th*. The time specification thus describes the event's location time. But we can also ask about the time by using a duration question with *how long*: *How long will the Olympic Games last?* — *From August 8th to August 24th*. The duration of the event is of course inferable from the fixed calendrical dates. We compute its duration by mentally scanning the period from the beginning to the end — in fact we often count the days with the help of our fingers. The duration is directional — we certainly would not count the days backwards. Sentence (21c) would in fact be the answer people expect to be given to this question. It allows them to locate the event in absolute time and to infer its duration.

The three types of time specification discussed above are schematically sketched in Figure 12.8, where "S" represents speech time.

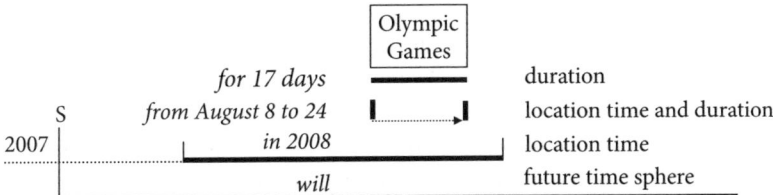

Figure 12.8. Specifications of an event's time and duration

The three types of time specification are exactly parallel to three types of place specification listed in Table 12.1. Location time corresponds to location in space, static duration corresponds to static extent, and directional duration corresponds to directional extent. The questions asked about them and the prepositions used in the prepositional phrases of time are listed in Table 12.5

Table 12.5. Correspondences of spatial and temporal relations

space:	location in space	static extent	directional extent
	where? — in, etc.	how long? — for	how far? where? — from... to
time:	location in time	static duration	directional duration
	when? — in, etc.	how long? — for	how long? when? — from... to

The correspondences between spatial and temporal relations also carry over to their grammatical realisations. Like expressions of the spatial location of an event, expressions of the location time are adjuncts describing the setting. Temporal adjuncts may be expressed as adverbs such as *soon*, as subordinate clauses such as *after I graduated*, and as prepositional phrases. As peripheral elements of the sentence, they can be separated from the grammatical core: they can be fronted, as in (22a), and "extraposed" by *it is … that/when*, which is, however, more commonly done with past events, as in (22b).

(22) a. *In 2008*, the Olympic Games will take place in Beijing.
 b. *It was in 2004* that the last Olympic Games took place.

Duration, like an extent, is part of the situation. Both extent and duration expressions are therefore integrated into the structure of the sentence as complements. They can neither be omitted (**The Olympic Games last*) nor normally be fronted (?*For 17 days the Olympic Games last*) or extraposed (?*It is for 17 days that the Olympic Games will last*).

A comparison of Tables 12.3 and 12.5 reveals that the spatial relations involving goal and source of motion are not matched by temporal relations. This may come as a surprise since we conceive of time as moving. But it is just because time and events on the time axis are in a perpetual flow that asking questions such as ?*Where has your birthday gone?* or ?*Where has your birthday come from?* makes no sense — although we may ask the rhetorical question *Where have all the years gone?*

12.4.3 Location times: Locative phrases

In order to locate a situation in time we can apply different strategies. Fixed events are appropriately located in time by means of absolute time units such as days. In prepositional phrases, these time units are specified by means of dimensional prepositions, as in (23a). Non-fixed events may be located in time by specifying a period as in (23b) or a period combined with a point in time as in (23c). Both types of non-fixed times are mainly seen in terms of orientations and paths.

(23) a. I wrote my paper **on** *Friday*. ["dimensional" time]
 b. Then I slept **over** *the weekend*. [period]
 c. I have to submit the paper **by** *Monday*. [period plus time point]

12.4.3.1 Fixed times: Dimensional phrases

Like spatial landmarks, time units can be associated with dimensions and expressed by dimensional prepositions. Typical temporal usages of dimensional prepositions are illustrated by the sentences under (24) and diagrammed in Figure 12.8, where the times of the event (E) are indicated by a vertical line.

(24) a. Victoria arrived *at Waterloo Station* **at** *7 pm*.
 b. David was waiting for her *on platform 3* **on** *Sunday*.
 c. They had champagne *in the VIP lounge* **in** *the evening*.
 d. They left **between** *three and four o'clock*.

Figure 12.9. "Dimensional" times: *at*, *on*, *in* and *between*

The preposition *at* in its temporal use in (24a) specifies a point in time in the same way that spatial *at* specifies a point in space. The point in time coincides with the time of the event. The event can thus only be a punctual event, i.e. an achievement or an act. Time points can readily be pinpointed on the time line, especially when they refer to clock times, as in *at 7 o'clock sharp*.

Fixed times other than points specify time spheres which tend to include the time of the event. Thus, we normally understand sentence (24b) to mean that David spent only a limited amount of time waiting for Victoria to arrive on Sunday and not the whole day — although this interpretation is possible as well.

The preposition *on* in its temporal use in (24b) mainly specifies days. Thus we have *on my birthday*, *on New Year's Day*, *on Christmas Day*, etc. as well as, metonymically for the whole day, *on Christmas Eve* and *on Monday morning*. Days are particularly salient calendrical units "on" which our routine activities are organised. We may still perceive some similarity between spatial and temporal *on*: in the same way that spatial *on* describes contact of a trajector with a landmark, temporal *on* describes contact of our activities with the most prominent units of time.

The preposition *in* in its temporal use in (24c) applies to bounded time units, i.e. time spans. Time spans are the natural equivalents of bounded spaces, i.e. containers. The temporal prepositions *on* and *in* describe complementary notions of time. All units of time other than days are conceptualised as time spans, i.e. units larger than a day such as weeks, months, years, centuries, etc., as well as units smaller than a day such as mornings, afternoons, hours, minutes, seconds, etc. All these time spans have in common that they have been created by man in organising time for specific purposes.

The preposition *between* in its temporal use in (24d) describes an interval separating two time points in the same way that spatial *between* describes an intermediate space separating two landmarks. The temporal prepositions *between* and *in* may describe the same time sphere but differ in their focus: *in* focuses on the time span, *between* focuses on the time points delimiting the time span.

In using the dimensional prepositions *at*, *on*, *in* and *between*, the speaker commits herself to a fixed sphere of time. The speaker may, however, also express approximation about the time sphere by means of the path prepositions *about* and *around*. In physical space, *about* and *around* describe the paths of indeterminate motion relative to a landmark. *About* (from Old English *a-būtan* 'on (the) outside') refers to dispersed motion in any direction relative to a landmark, as in (25a), while *around* refers to circular motion around a landmark, as in (26a). Used for time, *about* and *around* express time spheres approximating a reference time but display subtle differences in meaning which reflect their spatial origin:

(25) a. I wandered *about the town*. [*dispersed motion*]
     b. I'll be home *at about midnight*. [*approximate time including 'now'*]

(26) a. I ran *around the lake*. [*circular motion*]
     b. I'll see you *around Christmas*. [*approximate time excluding 'now'*]

Time expressions with *about* as in (25b) specify a time sphere that approximates and includes a given point in time. This is why this notion of approximate time can be expressed by means of the complex preposition *at about* or *round about*. Time expressions with *around* in (26b), on the other hand, specify a wider time sphere before or after a time unit and probably exclude this time unit; hence this notion of approximate time is normally not combined with *at*.

12.4.3.2 Non-fixed times: Orientational phrases

(i) Periods: *over* and *during*

Non-fixed periods typically lack clearly-defined boundaries. They are specified either by vague units of time like weekends or events:

(27) a. We'll talk about marriage *over* the weekend.
     b. Don't fall asleep *during* the lecture.

The orientational preposition *over* refers to a period that is surveyed as a whole, as if seen from a bird's eye view. Such periods are typically larger time units like years, months, weeks and weekends; smaller units such as a single day, hours and minutes are normally not compatible with *over* in the sense of a period. Thus, in *He worked over a day*, the form *over* can only mean 'more than'; conversely, *under* means 'less than' as in *He worked under 20 hours a week*. These senses relate to the metaphor MORE IS UP/LESS IS DOWN. Periods which occur with *over* may also be specified metonymically by means of events that have a fairly well-defined duration, such as Christmas, breakfast, dinner, or lunch. The time of the event that occurs "over" the period is understood to extend over a considerable length of the time.

During is one of the few exclusively temporal prepositions. In spite of its common stem with the noun *duration*, it does not, properly speaking, express duration. Phrases with *during* cannot answer *how long*-questions but only *when*-questions. The preposition *during* derives from the present participle of the Middle English verb *duren* 'last'. Only situations can be said to last, not fixed time units:. we rarely or never speak of ?*during this minute* or ?*during 2010*. *During* is used with vague time expressions such as *the 18th century* and abstract nominals such as *the lecture, pregnancy* or *my lifetime*. Here, the reified event metonymically stands for the period it lasts. *During* has a much wider application than *over*. This can be seen from the different ways events may be located within the period specified by *during*. The event may either occur at a given point within the period, as in (27b), or stretch over the whole period or over part of it. Both interpretations are possible in *He slept during the lecture*.

(ii) *Periods combined with time point:* **ago, in; before, after; past, by**

> Was there a time Now Why east wind chills A grief ago
> (Dylan Thomas, *Twenty-five Poems*, 1936)

A period may be bounded on the time-axis at one end. This point in time of course needs to be anchored as a reference time. Situations in the deictic past and future are anchored relative to speech time, as in the sentences under (28). The arrow from speech time to event time indicates the flow of time from the future via the present into the past.

(28) a. I graduated *two years* **ago**.
  b. I'll graduate **in** *two years' time*.

The temporal distance between speech time (S) and event time (E) needs to be specified by measure terms — hence the oddity of **a grief ago*. The end of the interval marks the end-point or beginning of the event time. The postposition *ago* in (28a) invokes the disappeared flow of time from the present into the past, which is indicated by the dotted arrow. This spatial image is encapsulated in the form *ago*, a reduced past participle derived from Middle English *agone* 'gone away'. The origin of *ago* also explains its exceptional position following the time nominal: 'two years have passed'.

The time pattern invoked by the preposition *in* in (28b) is not a complete mirror image of the time pattern invoked by *ago*. The *in*-phrase describes the measured distance between speech time and a future point in time. However, the preposition *in* is not directional and hence does not invoke a time flow but rather a static time span. As a result, the interval needs to be definite. Thus, we speak of *some time ago*, but not of **in some time*.

The speaker can of course make use of other temporal reference points than speech time. These may be events or dates, as in the following examples:

(29) a. We took a swim **before** breakfast.
  b. and went scuba diving **after** breakfast.

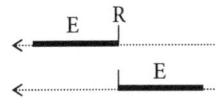

The events are bounded at one end by a non-deictic reference point (R = time of breakfast) and extend over an indefinite time sphere in anterior or posterior time (see Chapter 9).

The reference point that establishes one boundary of a period may also be an absolute calendrical time. Absolute points in time are often set as delimitations or deadlines, as in the following examples:

(30) a. You got home **past** midnight.
  b. You have to be in bed **by** midnight.

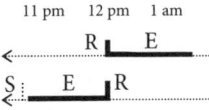

In (30a), the time sphere specified by *past midnight* is understood to follow the reference point 'midnight', i.e. your coming home occurred some time after 12 pm, whereas in (30b), the time sphere specified by *by midnight* is understood to precede this reference point, i.e. your going to bed has to occur at any time before or at 12 pm. This event is typically a future accomplishment which a person is to complete within a period bounded by the present moment (S) and the set date. Sentence (30b) seems to describe a state, i.e. an atelic situation, but is in fact also understood in the sense of an accomplishment: the hearer is meant to perform certain actions such as brushing his teeth and putting on his pyjamas so that, as a result, he will be in bed by midnight. The sentence thus counts as an accomplishment by virtue of the metonymy RESULT FOR ACTION.

12.4.3.3 Duration: Duration phrases

Specifications of duration are inseparably tied to a situation and, of course, only apply to situations that have duration. In Chapter 8 we distinguished between bounded and unbounded durational situation types. The only bounded durational situations are accomplishments. Accomplishments are asked about by using the question *How long does/did X take to …?*, as in *How long did Ann take to change the nappy?*, and their duration is specified by means of *in*-phrases: *She changed the nappy in less than a minute* (see Chapter 8.3.1). Here the span of time *in less than a minute* refers to the event's duration from its beginning to its conclusive end-point.

We typically associate duration with unbounded situations, i.e. activities, states and habitual states. These situations are asked about with *how long*-questions, as in *How long did you play cards?* (see Chapter 8.4). Their duration can be specified by expressing their length of time, i.e. a stretch of time, as in (31a), or by expressing their beginning and/or end-points, which allows the hearer to compute their duration, as in (31b). Sentence (31c) shows that both duration specifications can also be combined.

(31) a. I slept *for twelve hours*. [*stretch of time*]
 b. I slept *from midnight to midday*. [*beginning and end-point*]
 c. I slept *for twelve hours from midnight to midday*.

There is, of course, no contradiction in specifying the duration of a situation such as my sleeping, which in itself is unbounded.

12.4.3.3.1 Duration as a stretch of time: **for** and **through**

Stretches of time can be conceptualised as static or directional. In English, they are expressed by phrases with *for* and *through(out)*, as in (32).

(32) a. We slept *for twelve hours*.
 b. We partied *through(out) the night*.

Durations expressed by *for* as in (32a) are conceived of in the same way as spatial extents, as illustrated in sentence (5), *The Grand Canyon stretches for almost 300 miles*. Both require units of measurement: miles, kilometres or yards for space, and years, days or hours for time. Vaguely defined units of time are hardly compatible with durations described by *for*. Thus we rarely speak of ?*working for a season* or ?*travelling for a spring*. The temporal sense of *for* derives from its originally spatial sense 'in front of'. This orientational sense of *for* can be seen in usages such as *We are going to Australia for a month*, where the period *a month* does not refer to the duration of the journey but to the projected duration of our stay after our arrival in Australia. The duration of our stay is thus metaphorically conceptualised as lying ahead of us.

Durations that are vaguely defined as in (32b) are conceived of as directional. The path preposition *through* invokes the image of motion through a conduit. Since time is conceived of as flowing, the image of water flowing through a conduit provides a particularly well-suited metaphor to render the unidirectionality of time and the continuous nature of activities. The completeness of a scanned duration may be reinforced by using the modifiers *right* or *all* (*right/all through the night*) or the complex preposition *throughout*. The preposition *out* appropriately suggests completion by focusing on the final point of a motion through a conduit, i.e. the point where a moving thing reaches the exterior.

12.4.3.3.2 *Duration computed from a beginning and an end-point:* ***from…to****, **since** and **till/until***

A situation's duration may be specified by stating both its beginning and end-point, as in (31b) and (33a) below, or by stating only its beginning as in (33b) or only its end-point as in (33c).

(33) a. It rained ***from*** Friday ***to*** Sunday.
 b. It has rained twenty inches ***since*** Friday.
 c. It rained ***till*** / ***until*** Sunday.

The temporal specification of duration by means of *from…to* parallels the construal of a spatial extent in terms of fictive motion, as in *The road goes from A to B* (see example (7)). In the same way that we can mentally scan a spatial extent, we can scan a period of time. However, while we can reverse the direction of scanning in space and describe the road as going from B to A, we cannot reverse the direction of scanned time. We can describe a period of time as *from today to tomorrow*, but not as **from tomorrow to today* — although we can see two time points independently of each other in the reversed order, as in *We had to change our tickets from tomorrow to today*.

Neither temporal *from* nor *to* can normally occur in isolation: both **It rained from Friday* and **It rained to Sunday* sound odd. Since an event's duration can only be computed when two points in time are available, the missing second reference point must be accessible from the deictic situation or the current discourse. The uniquely temporal preposition *since* profiles an event's starting point, from which duration is mentally scanned to the later deictic moment of speech time, as in (33b). This time pattern is matched by the present perfect (see Chapter 9.3.1.2.1(iv)). Especially in narratives, the complex preposition *from…on* is also used to refer to a duration that starts at some point in time, as in *It rained from then on*.

The uniquely temporal prepositions *till* and *until* profile a situation's end-point whose beginning is retrievable or indefinite. Both reference points can be in any deictic time sphere: in the past as in (33c), in the present as in *It has been raining till now*, and in the future as in *It will rain till Sunday*. Time expressions with *until* only apply to unbounded situations. It may therefore come as a surprise that phrases with *until* occur with bounded events that are negated, as in *I won't come back until next year*. Other languages express this situation in an affirmative way, i.e. as 'I will only come back next year', which focus on the punctual event of my coming back. In English, the focus is on the period preceding the punctual event, i.e. the state when the event has not yet occurred. The duration of this unbounded situation is therefore appropriately described by *until*.

The end-point of a duration may also be specified by the complex preposition *up to*, as in *Regattas were scheduled right up to Christmas*. The orientational preposition *up* emphasises the totality of an event's duration. The upward orientation denoted by *up* may be seen in analogy to spatial *up* as in *They live up the road*, where *up* describes near-horizontal orientation. The notion of upward motion metaphorically translates into the length of time.

12.5 Abstract space

Abstract space is understood here in the sense of domains other than 'space' and 'time' which are systematically conceptualised in terms of physical space. This applies to the abstract domains of 'circumstance', 'cause', 'reason', and 'purpose'. We conceive of these notions as situations of their own, and they are often expressed as subordinate clauses. However, they are also, possibly even most frequently, expressed as prepositional phrases with abstract nouns. These reified nouns metonymically stand for situations. Thus, in sentence (36b), *He went on trial for murder*, the noun *murder* stands for 'being suspected of murder'.

12.5.1 Circumstances: Circumstantial phrases

Circumstances are understood in the sense of external conditions which surround and possibly affect a situation as its setting. Circumstances are normally inseparably tied to a place and a time, as in the following example:

(34) The hikers lost their way *in the snowstorm*.

The setting phrase *in the snowstorm* may be seen as referring to the location of the event and asked about by a *where*-question, or as referring to its location time and asked about by a *when*-question, or as referring to its circumstances and asked about by *how* or *how come*-questions: *How come they lost their way?* A more elaborate and formal way of asking about circumstances would be *under what circumstances?*, as in *Exactly where, when and under what circumstances did he meet his death?*

Circumstantial situations may be construed in different ways by means of different prepositions. Typically, circumstances are construed as containers "including" the nuclear event, as in sentence (34). The choice of the circumstantial preposition is dependent on the overall situation.

(35) a. **At** *Mario's flattering remark*, Helen's face brightened.
  b. **On** *entering my house*, I uttered a fervent "Thank God".
  c. We spent a romantic evening **by** *candlelight*.
  d. I can't concentrate **with** *all this noise*.
  e. **Under** *these circumstances* we can't accept your offer.

The point preposition *at* in (35a) indicates a reflex reaction, the contact preposition *on* in (35b) conveys the sense of conscious self-reflection, the connection preposition *by* in (35c) suggests functional co-presence of a romantic evening and a room lit by candlelight, the accompaniment preposition *with* in (35d) implies the simultaneity and interaction of two events and hence invites the implicature of cause, and the orientational preposition *under* in (35e) evokes the UP–DOWN schema. As suggested by the expression *under these circumstances*, the circumstances are seen as dominating and determining the nuclear event (cf. the example *Amanda was overcome by grief* discussed in Chapter 1.3.3).

12.5.2 Causal notions: Cause, reason, and purpose

The notions of causality considered here comprise 'cause', 'reason', and 'purpose'. The relation between one of these causal notions and a nuclear event can be established at two different levels: at the contents level, that is at the level of physical reality as in (36a), or at the epistemic level (see Chapter 10.1.1), that is at the mental level of awareness of some other event, as in (36b) and (36c). This difference is captured in the notions of 'cause', on the one hand, and 'reason' and 'purpose', on the other.

(36) a. The bride's mother cried **for** *joy*. (= *because of*) [cause]
  b. He went on trial **for** *murder*. (= *on account of*) [reason]
  c. He's crying **for** *help*. (= *in order to get*) [purpose]

'Cause', 'reason', and 'purpose' are clearly distinct notions. At the same time, all of them serve to provide causal explanations for changes of state or events. Hence, the borderlines between them are blurred, and their meanings tend to shade into one another. Thus the word *cause* in the expression *This is for a good cause* is meant in the sense of 'purpose', as in its German equivalent *Dies ist für einen guten Zweck* 'This is for a good purpose'. The conceptual affinity between 'cause', 'reason', and 'purpose' is reflected in the use of the same preposition *for* in the prepositional phrases, the use of the *why*-question in asking about them (*Why did he...?*), and the use of the *because*-clause for all three notions. But the differences are equally real.

Causes are situations which trigger off another physical or psychological situation as their effect. Causes can be paraphrased by *because of*, *as a result of*, and *due to*.

Reasons are situations which are adduced as an explanation or justification for the occurrence of a situation. The causal link between these situations only exists in the mind of the speaker and reflects her judgement, i.e. it does not need to be factual. Reasons can typically be paraphrased by *on account of*.

Purposes are situations which refer to a goal which is intended or hoped to be attained by means of one's actions. Purposes are projected into posterior time and, like reasons, only exist in the mind of the speaker. Purposes can typically be paraphrased by *in order to*.

Causes, reasons, and purposes are normally peripheral participants of a situation, but are more closely integrated into the core of a situation than spatial, temporal and circumstantial settings. Their intermediate status is reflected in their syntactic behaviour. Like other setting elements, expressions of cause, reason, and purpose function as adjuncts but, unlike prototypical setting elements, they can hardly be moved to the front of a sentence (*With joy the bride's mother cried*) or extraposed (**It was with joy that the bride's mother cried*).

12.5.2.1 Causes

Causes are inherently related to their effects: there is no cause without an effect and no effect without a cause. Causes are therefore seen as affecting a situation more immediately than circumstances, whose causal connection is only inferred, as in the example of the snowstorm in sentence (34). The specific notions of causation as denoted by primarily spatial prepositions pertain to (i) direct and indirect causes, (ii) causes triggering emotions, and (iii) emotions triggering reactions.

(i) Direct and indirect causes

Causes precede effects. Hence the most natural way of conceiving of cause and effect is in terms of the SOURCE-PATH-GOAL schema. Causes may appear in chains of causation, in which the effect of a cause may become the cause for another effect, etc. English reflects the idea of chains of causation in the distinction between direct and indirect causes. *Direct causes* are expressed by the preposition *of*. The preposition *of* is historically a reduced variant of spatial *off*, i.e. it derives from the sense of 'separation'. Possibly the notion of 'contact' accounts for its sense of direct cause, as in (37a). *Indirect causes* are expressed by the preposition *from*. Since the source of a motion is the point that is farthest from the goal, the source preposition *from* is well-suited to express ultimate, i.e. typically indirect, causes, as in (37b).

(37) a. He died **of** heart-failure. [direct cause]
b. He died **from** an overdose of drugs. [indirect cause]

Heart-failure is a disease that may be the direct or immediate cause leading to a person's death. This situation therefore tends to be described by using the preposition *of*. Taking an overdose of drugs only indirectly leads to one's death. This situation therefore tends to be expressed by using the preposition *from*. As a further contrast, *He died with AIDS* is considered correct for such a case, as AIDS is not the direct cause of death, but is seen as an accompanying condition which may or may not be directly responsible for the cause of death.

Direct and indirect causation may be seen as poles on a cline of directness of causal impact. Intermediate degrees of causation are in English appropriately expressed by the path prepositions *by* and *through*, as in:

(38) a. The country is hit **by** crime. [*means*]
     b. Many young drivers are killed **through** accidents. [*determinate cause*]

The preposition *by* in (38a) construes a cause as a means controlled by an agent. The ultimate cause of a crime is the implicit agent 'criminals'. The conduit preposition *through* construes a cause as a "channelled", or determinate, means in a chain of causation. Thus, the accidents described in (38b) may result from the young driver's careless driving as the ultimate cause.

(ii) *Causes triggering emotions*
The following examples illustrate causes that trigger a particular emotional reaction.

(39) a. Sally got angry **at** her daughter's tone of voice. [*targeting*]
     b. I am happy **about** stricter smoking policies. [*indeterminate*]
     c. We often laughed **over** this story. [*repetitive*]

Causes expressed by the target preposition *at* trigger a chain of two causal relations. First, a stimulus such as the daughter's tone of voice in (39a) triggers the emotion of anger in Sally and, secondly, the state of emotion makes Sally target her anger at the person who is responsible for her anger, i.e. her daughter. We cannot make inanimate entities responsible for causing something unless we personify them; hence the oddity of ?*I was angry at the snowstorm*. Natural phenomena like snowstorms may give rise to an indeterminate emotional reaction. Such causes are, as in example (39b), expressed by the preposition *about*: *I was angry about the snowstorm*. Causes expressed by the orientational preposition *over* as in (39c) trigger reactions which, in accordance with the temporal meaning of *over* as in (27a), tend to be long or repetitive.

(iii) *Emotions triggering reactions*
A type of cause that is of particular interest to humans is our emotions and the effect they have with respect to physiological or other reactions. In its use of prepositions English provides at least four construals of viewing emotional causality, as illustrated in the following examples:

(40) a. He jumped back **in** fear. [*intense emotion*]
     b. He went red **with** anger. [*concomitant emotion*]
     c. He ran away **out of** fear (of punishment). [*motive*]
     d. I could have died **for** shame. [*reasoning*]

Emotions expressed by the container preposition *in* are intense and trigger reactions which are beyond a person's control as in (40a). This causal sense of *in* is motivated by the image schema of containment and the restraints it imposes upon the entity contained. Weak emotions are not compatible with the containment schema. Thus, we do not ?*tremble in sadness* but *with sadness*.

Emotions expressed by the accompaniment preposition *with* are seen as co-occurring with their physiological reactions. They bring about one of a limited range of reactions normally associated with them, such as turning red with anger as in (40b), beaming with joy or screaming with pain. Emotions that do not trigger reactions that normally "accompany" them are therefore not expressed by *with*. Thus, we do not ?*smash the computer with anger* but *in anger*.

Emotions expressed by the emergence preposition *out of* focus on the person's active and controlled part in determining her reaction. Thus, in sentence (40c), the boy's fear of punishment is the motive for his deliberate escape. Emotions which do not leave room for a person's active part are not compatible with the notion of emergence. Hence we do not say that **She grew white out of fury* but *white with fury*.

Emotions expressed by the orientational preposition *for* involve an element of reasoning. They may occur in hypothetical contexts as in (40d) and with positive emotions such as joy, which allow for a wide range of possible reactions such as dancing, hopping or crying for joy. All of these reactions are still controllable or even rational. The preposition *for* sounds rather odd with negative emotions. Thus, *He laughed for pain* might only be said of a masochist. The motivation for the use of *for* may be seen in its close relation to 'reason'.

12.5.2.2 Reasons

Reasons differ from causes in that they are concerned with real or conceived states of affairs adduced as an explanation for a given situation. Reasons may be based either on inferences drawn from perceptual information or on norms provided by our culture. In the former case, reasons tend to be expressed by *because*, as in *She must be at home, because her car is parked in front of the house*; in the latter case, reasons may be expressed by *for*. Thus, a driver's drunken driving constitutes a culturally sanctioned reason for arresting this person (41a), and a good exam is traditionally considered a reason for complimenting or rewarding a person (41b).

(41) a. The driver was arrested **for** *drunken driving*.
b. Grandma complimented her niece **on** *her good grades*.

The link between a situation and the reason for its being is understood to be rational or sensible by the members of a given culture. The use of the orientational preposition *for* as in (41a) might be motivated by a spatio-temporal situation: the driver's drunken driving occurred "before" his arrest and hence is seen as its causal source.

Reasons expressed by the preposition *on* as in (41b) typically apply to people's achievements which draw ritualised appreciations in the form of congratulations and compliments. Here, the reason is based on, or "supported" by, the achieved event.

12.5.2.3 Purposes

Purposes are situations that are often metaphorically conceptualised as destinations. In the same way that destinations are goals to be reached by our motion, purposes are goals to be achieved by our actions. Destinations and purposes are linked in our experience: in order to attain a purpose we often have to go to a certain place, as in *We'll have to take a taxi (in order) to get to the concert in time*. Here, the subordinate conjunction (*in order*) *to* expresses the idea of a goal. In prepositional phrases, the orientational preposition *for* suggests frontness — as well as a benefaction gained from reaching the purpose.

(42) a. We ran *for our lives*.
 b. Please click here *for more information*!

Sentence (42a) describes a motion event whose destination is the desired situation of having our lives saved. Sentence (42b) describes an action that has to be performed to achieve a benefit, i.e. the receiving of more information.

12.6 Summary

Our interaction with objects in physical space is among the most basic experiences. This explains why the domain of 'space' serves as the metaphorical source for many other domains, in particular 'time' and certain abstract domains. In English, notions of physical, temporal and abstract space are typically expressed as prepositional phrases. The prepositions used in these different domains are largely identical, i.e. the primarily spatial meanings of the prepositions have been metaphorically extended.

The domain of **physical space** is mainly relevant for specifying the location of things and events in space. The things and events which are to be located are described as **trajectors**; the things that serve as reference points for their location are described as **landmarks**. Landmarks determine the spatial **region** where a trajector is to be found. In the spatial situation *The cat is on the table*, *the cat* describes the trajector, *the table* the landmark, and *on* specifies a relation of contact between the trajector and the region of the table top.

Three basic types of spatial relation are distinguished: location, direction and extent. **Location** applies to static trajector-landmark relations. Locations are typically expressed by **locative prepositions** and are asked about by *where*-questions: *Where is the cat? — On the table*. **Direction** applies to dynamic trajector-landmark relations, i.e. to motion events. Directions are typically expressed by **directional prepositions** and are asked about by *where*- or *where from*-questions: *Where are you going? — To the university*. **Extent** applies to the measured length or distance of a thing in space, as in *The beach stretches for five miles*.

The spatial regions in which a thing is to be found are in English specified by means of the topological properties **dimension** and **orientation** of the landmark. Accordingly, we have dimensional and orientational prepositions. **Dimensional prepositions** distinguish between points (zero-dimensional), lines and surfaces (one- and two-dimensional), and containers (three-dimensional). These three dimensions combine with **place** (*at, on, in*), **source** (*from, off, out of*), **goal** (*to, on(to), in(to)*), and **path** (*by, along, through*). Points, surfaces and containers tend to be associated with functional aspects. For example, points often stand for recognition points or targets and surfaces suggest contact and support. **Orientational prepositions** distinguish between the axes of **verticality** (*up–down, over–under, above–below*), **horizontality** (*before–behind*), and left–right.

The domain of **temporal space** is largely structured in terms of spatial topologies. Time expressions are used to specify a situation's location in time or its duration. "**Location times**" serve as the setting of a situation and are asked about by *when*-questions: *When will the next Olympic Games be?* Fixed location times are specified by dimensional prepositions (*on Sunday*); non-fixed location times are specified by orientational prepositions, either by means of a period (*over the weekend*) or a period combined with a time point (*two years ago*). **Durations** form part of the situation and are asked about by *how long*-questions: *How long will the Olympic Games last?* Durations can be conceptualised as a static stretch of time, as in *I slept for twelve hours*, or dynamically by mentally scanning a period of time, as in *It rained from Friday to Saturday*.

Domains of **abstract space** include 'circumstance', 'cause', 'reason', and 'purpose'. **Circumstances** belong to the setting of a situation: they describe external conditions surrounding the situation. The meanings of the causal notions 'cause', 'reason' and 'purpose' tend to shade into one another. **Causes** refer to causal phenomena in physical reality. Subtle distinctions of causes are made by the choice of preposition: *of* expresses 'direct causes', *from* 'indirect causes', *by* 'means', *through* 'determinate causes', *at* 'targeting causes', *over* 'repetitive causes', *about* 'indeterminate causes', *in* 'intense emotional causes', *with* 'concomitant emotional causes', *out of* 'motives', and *for* 'reasoned causes'. **Reasons** are seen either within a spatio-temporal front–back orientation and expressed by *for* or as being based on a person's achievement and expressed by *on*. **Purposes** are metaphorically seen as destinations and expressed by the preposition *for*.

Further reading

General aspects of language and space are presented in Svorou (1994) and Levinson (2003). Cognitive accounts of prepositional meanings and their extensions are Talmy (1983/2000), Herskovits (1985, 1986), and Tyler & Evans (2003). Among the many studies of selected prepositions only a few can be mentioned here: Brugman (1988), Lakoff (1987) and Tyler & Evans (2001) on *over*, Boers (1996) on orientational prepositions, Beitel, Gibbs & Sanders (1997) on *on*, Bennett (1975) and Wierzbicka (1993) on temporal prepositions, and Dirven (1995, 1997) and Radden (1985, 1998) on prepositions of causality.

Study questions

1. Which active zones of the landmarks are meant in the examples below and how are they motivated? (see Section 12.2.2). The first three examples are adopted from Herskovits (1985).
   a. *the child in the back of the car*
   b. *the house above the building*
   c. *the key under the rug*
   d. *the submarine under the water*
   e. *the roots of the tree under the earth*

2. Supply the appropriate preposition and analyse the spatial relation.
   a. *There is a huge spider … the ceiling.*
   b. *The heart of England stretches … the Midlands … the North West.*
   c. *Can you get me a bottle of beer … the fridge?*
   d. *I work in New York but live … the river in New Jersey.*

3. Which orientational arrangements do the following sentences involve and how do they affect the region where the trajector is to be found?
   a. *There are burglars behind the house.*
   b. *The treasure chest is hidden behind the tree.*
   c. *The left arm of our armchair has come off.*
   d. *Your love letters are in the left drawer of my desk.*
   e. *Watch out, there are children in front of the car.* (three possibilities)

4. Supply the appropriate preposition in the following sentences and justify your choice.
   a. *Jack got married … a Saturday morning.*
   b. *Phil got married … the early morning.*
   c. *The shops will be open … 9 pm.* (at least two possibilities)
   d. *The shops will open … 9 am.* (two possibilities)

5. Supply the appropriate causal preposition and justify your choice.
   a. *Mozart may have died … eating undercooked pork.*

b. *Shakespeare probably died ... cancer.*
c. *He smashed the computer ... anger.*
d. *His heart fluttered ... fright.*
e. *He cried ... pride when hearing the Star-Spangled Banner.*
f. *I couldn't sleep ... fear that this could be my last course in linguistics.*

Glossary

This glossary provides condensed definitions of linguistic terms which the authors consider essential for an understanding of Cognitive Grammar. These are the terms that are printed in bold throughout the text; terms printed in italics are not included in the glossary. The entries listed in the glossary are intended to be used for quick references and cross-references. The definitions closely follow the wording and their discussion in the chapter where the terms are introduced, and the linguistic terms can only be understood within the overall framework of the book, not as self-contained entries as found in dictionaries. The user should be aware of the fact that the definitions reflect the authors' view of cognitive grammar and may differ from usages given by other scholars.

Abilities are salient and distinctive attributes that have the potential of being actualised as a thing's characteristic behaviour. (10.4.2.1)

Accomplishing activities are unbounded telic events whose conclusive end-point is expected to come about, such as *Ann is changing the nappy*. (8.2.1.2; 8.3.2)

Accomplishments are bounded telic events that require a certain duration for their completion and focus on their conclusive end-point, such as *Ann changed the nappy*. (8.2.1.1; 8.3.1)

Achievements are bounded punctual events that invoke a preceding culminating phase leading to the punctual event at its terminal point, such as *The baby fell asleep*. (8.2.1.1; 8.5.1)

The **action schema** describes events in which a human agent deliberately acts upon another participant, typically the theme, as in *She tore the letter*. (11.4.1)

The **active zone** of an entity is that part within a frame that is crucially involved in a given situation, e.g. the engine in *Can you start the car?* (1.2.3.1)

Activities are atelic events that have duration, such as *Ann cuddled the baby*. Activities may be bounded or unbounded. (8.2.1.1; 8.2.1.2; 8.4)

Acts are bounded, punctual, and atelic events, such as *The baby burped*. (8.2.1.1; 8.6)

Adjectives are members of a grammatical category that typically designate properties. (7.2.1; 7.2.2)

Adjuncts are optional grammatical constituents within the structure of a sentence. (3.2.1)

Agent (A) is the thematic role describing the human instigator of an event. (11.1.1)

Amount quantification contrasts with *number quantification* and refers to the magnitude of a substance instance; it is expressed by amount quantifiers such as *much*. (4.1.3; 6.1.3; 6.3.2)

Amount quantifiers, or mass-noun quantifiers, describe the quantity of substance instances and are used with mass nouns as in *much work*. (6.1.3)

Anaphoric reference applies to an instance of a thing for which a mental space has already been opened in prior discourse, like the pronoun *it* in *I saw the game. It was terrible.* (5.3.2)

Anterior times involve a backward-looking stance from a viewpoint at one of the deictic times; anterior times are expressed as perfect tenses. (9.1.2.2(i))

Argument, see **valency**

Aspect is the grammatical form used by a speaker in taking a particular view of a situation. See **progressive** and **non-progressive aspect**. (Part III; 8.1.2)

Assertion refers to the speaker's confidence about the truth of a situation as conveyed in a declarative sentence. (10.1.1)

Atelic, see **telicity**

Attention refers to the selective focusing, or "windowing", on certain elements of a scene; e.g. in *The horse cost $500*, attention is focused on the goods and the money. (2.1.7)

Attributive adjectives are modifiers of a noun that qualify the thing or instance they designate by means of a property. (7.2.3)

The **background future** refers to future situations described in the present tense of temporal and conditional clauses, as in *If I see the kids I'll send them home*. (9.4.3)

A **base** is the immediate larger conceptual content characterising a **profiled** expression, such as the content 'book' for the expression *page*. (2.1.9)

The **base space** is the mental space that serves as the basis and starting point of any human interaction. (9.1.1)

Basic aspectual classes are general time schemas that are relevant for aspectual distinctions; they include bounded events, unbounded events, temporary states, and lasting states. (8.1.2)

The **basic level** is the most salient level in the middle of a taxonomy. (1.2.1)

Basic-level terms, i.e. categories located at the basic level of a taxonomy, are simple in form, frequently used, acquired early, and evoke rich images, such as 'car'. (1.2.1)

Beneficiary (B) is the thematic role describing the human being for whose benefit an action is performed, e.g. *her father* in *She bought a nice present for her father*. (11.4.4.2)

Blending refers to the conceptual integration of two or more mental spaces into a newly created "blended space"; e.g. the word *brunch*, in which the mental spaces 'breakfast' and 'lunch' are blended. (2.2.2)

Bounded, or *perfective*, **events** are viewed externally and in their entirety; they are expressed in the non-progressive aspect, such as *Ann cuddled the baby*. (8.1.2; 8.2.1.1)

Boundedness of a conceptual unit refers to its limits in space, time or other domains. (4.1.2.1); boundedness of a situation refers to its having a beginning and an end. (8.1.2)

Cataphoric reference applies to an instance for which a mental space is opened to be filled in subsequent discourse, as in *Let me tell you this*. (5.3.2)

Categorisation is the process of establishing categories within a classification system, e.g. the category 'airmail' within the system of types of mail. (1.1.1)

A **category** is the conceptualisation of a collection of relevant, and hence meaningful, similar experiences, e.g. the collection of experiences conceptualised as 'fog'. (1.1.1)

Cause (C) is the thematic role describing a stimulating cause as in *He loves her* (11.1.1;

11.3.1), or the reified participant that brings about an effect, as in *The baby is crying for joy*. (12.5.2)

The **caused-motion construction** is a transitive predicate-complement pattern which typically describes the caused motion of a thing to or from a location, as in *He put the sweets in the stockings*. (11.4.3)

The **caused-motion schema** describes events in which an energetic force brings about the motion of a thing to or from a location. (11.4.3)

Circumstances are situations which, as a situation's setting, surround, and possibly affect, this situation, as in *The hikers lost their way in the snowstorm*. (12.5.1)

A **class** is a collection of similar individual elements that are understood as forming a type and having a name, like the collection of all tigers in the world. (5.4.1)

A **clause** describes a situation that is combined with another situation in a complex sentence. A clause contains a grammatical core, but not necessarily the grounding elements tense and modals; such tenseless clauses are described as non-finite or atemporal. (3.3.1)

Collective nouns denote multiplex objects that group together individual elements as members of a composed set, e.g. *football team*. (4.3.2.1)

Collective quantifiers invoke a full set by denoting all its individual elements collectively, as in *all doctors*. (6.2.1; 6.2.2)

Compelling modalities involve compelling forces; they mainly comprise obligations, prohibitions, and intrinsic and epistemic necessities. (10.3)

Complements are obligatory grammatical constituents of a sentence other than the predicate, in particular the subject and objects. (3.2.1)

Complementary properties are properties that evoke their opposite, such as 'faithful' and 'unfaithful'. (7.2.1)

Complementation refers to a tight conceptual link of two situations by means of fully integrating a clause into the grammatical nucleus of the main clause, as in *I saw the burglar run away*. (3.3.2)

Complex sentences describe more than one situation and consist of two or more structurally combined clauses. (3.3.1)

Complex tenses denote complex times and include the perfect tenses and prospective forms. (9.1.2.2)

Complex times involve a relation between a deictic time as a reference time and the time of an anterior or posterior event. (9.1.2.2)

The **composition** of a conceptual unit refers to the internal arrangement of its parts which gives it its identity. (4.1.2.2)

Conceptual blending, see **blending**

A **conceptual core** is a relation combined with conceptual entities participating in it; e.g. the relation 'kick' and the two conceptual entities 'Joe' and 'garbage can'. (3.1.2)

Conceptual entities comprise things, relations, and their combination in situations treated as things, i.e. they are conceptual units which are expressed as noun phrases and clauses. (3.1.2)

Construal refers to the speaker's choice among alternative ways of conceptualising and describing a scene; e.g. the choice between *half full* and *half empty* in describing the contents of a bottle. (2.1)

The **contingent future** refers to future events which are dependent on phenomena that are observable at the present time, as in *It's going to rain*. (9.4.1)

The **continuative perfect** refers to the anterior phase of a present state or habit, as in *We have been engaged over a year now*. (9.3.1.2.1)

Conversational implicature, see **implicature**

Co-ordination by *and* refers to a slightly stronger linking of two independent sentences than juxtaposition. (3.3.2)

The **copulative construction** consists of a subject, a copular verb (*be, look, seem,* etc.), and a predicative adjective or nominal as a complement. (11.2.1.1)

Count nouns denote bounded, internally heterogeneous and multipliable objects; they can therefore be pluralised. (4.1.3)

Countability of a conceptual unit refers to its ability to be conceptually replicated. (4.1.2.3)

Culminating activities are unbounded telic events that extend in time the terminal point of an achievement or focus on its build-up phase, such as *The baby is falling asleep.* (8.2.1.2; 8.5.2)

Deadverbial adjectives are adjectives that relate to the manner of an action, as in *hard worker.* (7.2.4)

Definite reference applies to an instance of a category which the speaker knows and assumes is already accessible to the hearer, either from his background knowledge or inferable from the discourse. (5.1.2; 5.3)

Deictic reference applies to an instance which is accessible in the speech situation. (5.3.1)

Deictic times relate to speech time and include the present, the past, and the future. (9.1.2.1)

Denominal adjectives are adjectives that relate to participants of a situation, as in *presidential decision.* (7.2.4)

Deontic modality belongs to the world of social interaction and authority; it is mainly concerned with the speaker's directive attitude towards an action to be carried out, as in *You must leave.* (10.1.2)

Destinations are spatial goals that people intend to reach; destinations are specified by *for,* as in *We left for America.* (12.3.3)

Determiners form a small class of function words (*the, a, no, this, every, each, either,* etc.) which ground the thing denoted by the noun in the current discourse, e.g. *this man.* (3.2.2)

Determining adjectives specify a thing or ground a referent, as in *a true asset.* (7.2.4)

Dimension refers to the geometric shape of things. (12.3.2)

Dimensional prepositions specify a dimensional property of a landmark, such as the three-dimensionality of a landmark denoted by *in.* (12.3.2)

Direction refers to dynamic spatial relations between a moving trajector and a landmark, as in *The cat jumped on(to) the table*; directions are asked about by *where-* or *where from-*questions. (12.3.1)

Directional prepositions specify the direction of a trajector relative to a landmark, as in *The cat jumped on(to) the table.* (12.3.1)

Directive speech acts are requests by the speaker asking the hearer to perform, or refrain from performing, a certain action, such as orders, prohibitions, etc. (10.1.2)

Disposition modality is concerned with the disposition of things or people that have the potential of being actualised; they include the notions of 'ability' or 'propensity' and 'willingness.' (10.2.4.2)

Distributive quantifiers invoke a full set by denoting each single element of the set, as in *every doctor.* (6.2.1; 6.2.3)

Distributiveness refers to the individual focus on all elements of a set. (6.2.1)

The **ditransitive construction** is characterised by "double objects": an indirect and a direct object; it typically expresses events of transfer, as in *I gave her a ring.* (11.4.4)

Domains are the general fields to which a category or frame belongs in a given situation; e.g. a knife may belong to the domain of 'eating' or 'fighting'. (1.2.3.2)

Duration refers to the length of time a situation lasts; durations are asked about by *how long*-questions. (8.2.1.1; 12.4.2)

Ecology in language refers to its nature as a system in which the existence of each linguistic category depends on its neighbouring categories, i.e. a category occupies an "ecological niche"; e.g. the ecological niche of the non-progressive aspect of English is defined relative to the progressive aspect. (1.1.1)

The **emotion schema** describes an emotional state or process which a human sentient experiences. (11.3.1)

Enabling modalities involve the unimpeded potential of a force; they comprise abilities, intrinsic possibilities, permissions and epistemic possibilities. (10.4)

Episodic situations are events and states that are thought of as holding for a limited length of time only; e.g. the situation of attacking someone. (4.4.3)

Epistemic modality belongs to the world of knowledge and reasoning; it is concerned with the speaker's inferred assessments of the potentiality of a state of affairs, as in *You may be right*. (10.1.1)

Epistemic necessity refers to the only possible conclusion reached by the speaker on the basis of compelling evidence, as in *This must be right*. (10.2.3.1, 10.3.2)

Epistemic possibility refers to a speaker's conclusion that is not barred by counter-evidence, as in *This may be true*. (10.2.3.2, 10.4.2.4)

Epithets are non-restrictive qualifications of things, such as *rosy-fingered* (*dawn*). (7.1.1)

Event schemas are types of situation which are characterised by a unique configuration of participant roles, such as the action schema. (11.1.1)

Event time (E) refers to the time of occurrence of a situation. (9.1.1)

Events are dynamic and hence changeable situations, such as *Ann cuddled the baby*. (8.1.2)

Everlasting states are natural phenomena or laws whose existence or truth is timeless and unchangeable, such as *Brighton is on the south coast*. (8.7.3)

Experiencer (E) is the thematic role describing a sentient human who entertains an emotion, a perception or a conception. (11.1.1)

Extraposition is a construction in which the "anticipatory pronoun" *it* refers to the clause following the verb of a sentence, as in *It is amazing how stupid George is*. (11.3.1)

An **extent** refers to the measured length or distance of a thing in space or time. (12.3.1)

Factual reality refers to the world that is experienced as real; it comprises the known past and the immediate present. (Part III)

Fictive motion refers to the construal of a static scene as motional, as in *The gate leads into the garden*. (2.1.6)

The **figure** of a scene is / are the salient and well-delineated element(s) which stand(s) out against a non-salient **ground**. (2.1.8; 3.3.1)

Finite and **non-finite**, see **clause** and **sentence**.

Force dynamics refers to the opposition of forces and counterforces in the physical world as well as in abstract domains such as deontic and epistemic modality. (10.2.3)

Framed uniqueness is a type of unique reference in which a referent can be uniquely identified due to our knowledge of frames, as in *Let's go to the seaside*. (5.3.3.3)

Frames are packages of knowledge about a coherent segment of experience; e.g. the 'book' frame contains components such as pages, contents, copies, etc. (1.2.3.1)

Full-set quantifiers describe the quantity of a full set as in *all doctors*. (6.2)

The **future perfect** refers to a predicted situation or phase of a situation anterior to a future reference time, as in *I'll have finished my paper by tomorrow*. (9.5.2)

The **future prospective** refers to future events posterior to a future reference time, as in *He will be going to quit his job*. (9.4.4)

The **future tense** grounds a situation at a time later than speech time. (9.1.2.1; 9.4)

Generality refers to the speaker's choice of describing a situation in lesser detail, e.g. by means of higher-level categories such as 'vehicle'. See also **specificity**. (2.1.2)

Generic reference is used in generalising about a class. (5.1.1; 5.4)

Goal (G) is the role describing the endpoint of a motion event. (11.4.2)

The **grammatical core** of a sentence is the skeletal part of the sentence which combines subject, predicate, and complement(s) if present. (3.2.1)

Grammaticalisation refers to the process of developing grammatical forms and meanings from lexical forms and meanings; e.g. the verbal participle *supposing* is used in the grammatical sense of a condition. (2.3.2)

The **ground** of a scene is/are the non-salient element(s) of a scene which serve(s) as the background for a salient **figure**. (2.1.8)

Grounding refers to the speaker's act of "anchoring" a situation in the speech situation by means of grounding elements such as tense and determiners. (3.2.2)

Habitual states are successions of indefinitely recurrent equivalent situations, which are, in English, conceived of as states, such as *Mary smokes a pipe*. (8.7.2)

The **historic present** is the use of the simple present to refer to past events in a chronological history. (9.3.2.4)

Hybrid nouns are nouns in which aspects of different types of things are blended; e.g. the mass noun *furniture*, in which aspects of objects and substances are blended, and the collective noun *team*, which blends aspects of multiplexity and uniplexity. (4.3)

Iconicity in language refers to the reflection of conceptual structure in linguistic structure. (3.3.1)

Image schemas are basic, schematic structures that are directly meaningful, such as the CONTAINER schema. (1.3.3)

Implicatures are inferences drawn by the hearer in order to recover the speaker's intended meaning of an utterance. (2.3.1)

Inchoative verbs express the beginning of a situation, as in *Beverly fell in love*. (11.2.1.2.1)

Indefinite reference applies to an instance which the speaker assumes is not accessible to the hearer so that he must first open a mental space for it. (5.1.2; 5.2)

Indefinitely lasting states are conditions that last for an indefinite time but may eventually cease to exist, such as *I love skiing*. (8.7.1)

Individuative reference applies to an individual instance of a thing. (5.1.1)

Inferences are cognitive operations in which conclusions are drawn from a set of premises. (2.3)

The **inferential perfect** refers to the inferred state following an anterior bounded atelic situation, as in *The nurse has cuddled the baby*. (9.3.1.2.1)

Inherent uniqueness is a type of unique reference in which the referents are understood to be the only instances for their kind, as in proper names. (5.3.3.1)

An **instance** of a thing is a token of a type. Instances may be chosen as a referent, e.g. a particular tree. An instance may also consist of different elements and hence be expressed by a plural phrase, e.g. *three trees*. (4.1.1)

Instrument (I) is the thematic role describing the implement used by an agent in bringing about an action. (11.4.1.1)

The **intentional future** refers to future events that come about as a result of a person's present intentions or decisions, as in *I'm going to learn to fly.* (9.4.1)

Intrinsic modality is concerned with potentialities arising from speaker-external sources, i.e. from intrinsic qualities of a thing or circumstances. It comprises intrinsic necessity and intrinsic possibility. (10.2.4.2)

Intrinsic necessity refers to a necessity arising from a thing and general rules or norms, as in *The job must be done* 'it is necessary for the job to be done.' (10.3.2.1)

Intrinsic possibility refers to a possibility enabled by a speaker-external source, as in *The meeting can be cancelled* 'it is possible to cancel the meeting.' (10.4.2.2)

Intrinsic relations between two entities are determined by inherent relational properties of the things related. In English, intrinsic relations are signalled by the preposition *of*, as in *the end of the tunnel*. (7.3.2)

Iterative activities are quick successions of punctual acts, such as *The baby is burping.* (8.2.1.2; 8.6)

Juxtaposition refers to the loose linking of two independent sentences, which is signalled by falling intonation and an intonation break. (3.3.2.)

Landmarks are "ground" entities in a spatial relation which define the region where a trajector is to be found. (12.2.2)

Lasting states are inherently unbounded and seen as infinite; they include indefinitely lasting states, habitual states, and everlasting states. (8.1.2; 8.7)

Location (L) describes the place of a trajector relative to a landmark, as in *They are in the garden.* (11.2.2; 12.3.1)

The **location schema** describes the relation between a thing and the place where it is. (11.2.2.1)

A **location time** is the period at or during which a situation occurs; location times are asked about by *when*-questions. (12.4.2)

Locative prepositions specify the location of a trajector relative to a landmark, as in *The cat is on the table.* (12.3.1)

Mapping is the projection of one set of conceptual entities onto another set of conceptual entities; see **metonymy** and **metaphor**. (1.3.1)

Mass nouns denote unbounded, internally homogeneous and non-multipliable substances. Mass nouns can therefore not be pluralised. (4.1.3)

The **matter-of-course future** in the future progressive refers to a future event that will happen as part of a course of events, as in *I'll be seeing you.* (9.4.2)

Means is the role describing a thing or situation which enables an agent to bring about an event. (11.4.1.2.3)

Mental scanning is a construal of a situation with respect to its phasing in time. See also **sequential scanning** and **summary scanning**. (2.1.5)

Mental spaces are small conceptual packages constructed as we think and talk and used for purposes of local understanding and action. (2.2)

Metaphor is a conceptual shift in which the structure of one domain is mapped onto that of another domain, as in the use of *brain* in *the brain of a computer*. (1.3.1; 1.3.3)

Metonymy is a conceptual shift in which one conceptual entity is mapped onto another within the same frame or domain, as in the use of *brains* for 'intelligent persons'. (1.3.1; 1.3.2)

The **middle construction** blends properties of the active and passive voice: its verb is in the active voice and, as in the passive construction, the theme or another participant role is promoted to the subject position and seen as enabling the situation described, as in *This book sells well.* (11.4.1.2.3)

Modal verbs, or **modals**, are a class of "defective" verbs that ground a situation in potential reality, such as *may* in *This may be true.* (10.2.2.1)

Modality is concerned with assessments of potentiality, depending either on the speaker's judgement of the reality status of a state of affairs (epistemic modality) or on the speaker's attitude towards the realisation of a desired or expected event (root modality). (Part III; 10.1, 10.2.4.2)

Modifiers are qualifying expressions that are grammatically dependent on a head noun. (7.1)

The **motion schema** describes a theme's change of place along a trajectory. (11.2.2.2)

Necessity, see **epistemic necessity** and **intrinsic necessity**.

Nominal, see **noun phrase**.

Nominalisation is the morphological process of deriving an abstract noun from a verb, an adjective or a noun; e.g. the derivation of *friendship* from *friend*. (4.4.1)

The **narrative present** refers to past situations that are portrayed as occurring in the present time, as in *Forrest Gump dies and goes to Heaven.* (9.3.2.4)

Non-participant roles are thematic roles which normally do not function as participants of an event schema, but typically belong to the setting. (11.1.1; 12.1)

Non-partitive quantification refers to a magnitude which is not explicitly related to a full set, as in *most apples* or *many apples*. (6.1.2).

The **non-progressive aspect** is expressed by simple verb forms. It is used to describe bounded events and lasting states. (8.1.2)

Non-restrictive qualification, or epithetical qualification, provides additional, typically expressive information about a thing or instance of a thing, as in *the wide ocean*, which is always wide. (7.1.1)

Non-restrictive relative clauses provide purely qualitative information about a referent that is already identified, as in *My friend, who lives in Tokyo, is coming to see me*, which only involves one friend. (7.4.2)

Non-specific reference is a type of indefinite reference that refers to imaginary, or virtual, instances, as in *I wish there was a taxi.* (5.2.2)

A **noun phrase** is a grammatical unit that denotes an instance of a thing in a situation. (3.2.1)

The **nucleus** of a sentence consists of the grammatical core and grounding elements. (3.2.2)

Number quantification, as opposed to amount quantification, refers to the magnitude of an object instance; it is expressed by number quantifiers such as *many*. (4.1.3; 6.1.3; 6.3.2)

Number quantifiers describe the quantity of object instances and are used with count nouns, as in *many jobs*. (6.1.3)

The **object** of a verb phrase is the noun phrase denoting the secondary participant, or ground, in a situation. (3.2.1)

Objectivity refers to the construal of a scene as detached from the speaker (see also **subjectivity**). (2.1.4)

Obligations are binding forces that are seen as compelling a person to carry out a certain action. (10.2.3.1; 10.3.2)

The **occurrence schema** describes the state or process an entity is in. (11.2.1)

Ontological metaphors involve a conceptual shift in which a relational concept (e.g. 'be married') is reified as a thing ('marriage'). (4.4.1)

Orientation pertains to spatial relations established by two landmarks as reference points. (12.3.3)

Orientational prepositions specify a region relative to two landmarks, as in *behind the curtain from the balcony*. (12.3.3)

Qualified uniqueness is a type of uniqueness in which a referent's uniqueness is established by descriptive qualification, as in *My coat is the green one*. (5.3.3.2)

Participant roles are the conceptually prominent roles which are typically associated with the conceptual core of a situation and constitute an event schema: the agent, the experiencer, the cause, and the theme. (11.1.1)

Participants are conceptual entities which form part of a situation's conceptual core and play a specific role, e.g. the participant 'he' plays the role of an agent in *He is reading*. (3.2.1)

Partitive quantification refers to the magnitude of a subset relative to a named full set, as in *most of my apples*. (6.1.2; 6.4.1)

Partonomies are conceptual hierarchies which are established by *part of*-relations between categories, e.g. 'wheels' and 'engine' as parts of a 'car'. (1.2.2)

The **past perfect** refers to a situation anterior to a past reference time, as in *When I arrived, the train had left*. (9.3.3)

The **past prospective** refers to situations posterior to a past reference time, especially used in narratives, as in *She was going to burst into tears*. (9.5.1)

The **past tense** grounds a situation at a time before speech time. (9.1.2.1; 9.3.2)

Path is the role describing the trajectory of a motion event. (11.4.2)

The **perception/cognition schema** describes an experiencer's perceptual or mental awareness of a thing. (11.3.2)

Perfect tenses denote the time of events which are anterior to a deictic reference time. (9.1.2.2)

Performatives are speech acts which explicitly name and thereby "perform" the speech act, as in *I hereby order you to leave this room*. (9.2.1.1; 10.1.2)

A **permission** refers to the speaker's directive attitude towards the hearer's potential action, which he "enables" to occur by relinquishing his power to prevent it, as in *You may go*. (10.2.3.2; 10.4.2.3)

The **planned future** in the present progressive refers to future events for which arrangements have been made in the present, as in *I am getting married in a month*. (9.4.3)

Pluralia tantum are inherently plural nouns which express multiplex objects or loosely amassed things; e.g. *measles*. (4.3.2.2)

Polysemy is the phenomenon of an expression having two or more senses which are related in a motivated fashion, e.g. the deontic and epistemic senses of modal auxiliaries. (10.2.4)

The **possession schema** describes a situation holding between a possessor and a thing possessed. (11.2.3)

Possessive relations relate a possessor to a thing possessed. In English, the possessor is expressed as a pronoun or genitive noun preceding the noun expressing the possessed thing, as in *my father's house*. (7.3.1)

Possessor (P) is the thematic role describing the human being who owns and controls a thing. (11.2.3)

Possibility, see **epistemic possibility** and **intrinsic possibility**.

Posterior times involve a forward-looking stance from a viewpoint at one of the deictic reference times; posterior times are expressed as prospective forms. (9.1.2.2)

Postnominal modifiers typically express occasional or temporary qualifications, as in *a star visible tonight*. (7.1.2)

Potential reality is thought of as having a certain probability of being or becoming reality. Situations in potential reality belong to the area of modality. (Part III; 10.1.1)

The **predicate** of a sentence is the unit (a verb or copula + adjective) that denotes a relation in a situation and states something about the subject participant. (3.2.1)

The **predicted future** conveys a prediction based on projected reality, as in *Scotland will have a little sunshine*. (9.4.2)

Predicative adjectives assign a property to a thing or instance of a thing, as in *The stars are visible*. (7.2.3; 7.2.6)

Prenominal modifiers typically describe permanent or characteristic qualifications, as in *visible star*. (7.1.2)

The **present perfect** refers to a situation or phase of a situation anterior to the present time; its focus is on the present time, as in *Have you seen my glasses?* (9.3.1)

The **present tense** grounds a situation at, around or including speech time. (9.1.2.1; 9.2)

Principle of relevance, see **relevance**

Processes involve a change of state, as in *He grew old*, or an unchanging event, as in *It is raining*. (11.2.1.2)

Profiling refers to designating a conceptual unit by means of a linguistic expression. (2.1.9)

The **progressive aspect** is expressed by a construction with *be V-ing*. It characterises situations as 'unbounded within implicit boundaries' and makes us view them internally as they unfold. (8.1.2)

Projected reality relates to future situations seen as evolving from past and present reality. (Part III; 9.4)

Proper names are inherently unique by virtue of denoting the only instance of their kind, such as *Trafalgar Square*. (5.3.3.1)

Properties are single qualitative features that are related or relatable to a thing or an instance of a thing. Properties are typically expressed as adjectives, as in *a brilliant detective*. See also **scalar** and **complementary properties**. (7.2)

A **proposition** is that part of the meaning of a sentence or clause that is constant, irrespective of the form it takes. (3.2.4)

Prospective forms denote the time of events which are posterior to a deictic reference time, in particular *be going to* and *be about to*. (9.1.2.2)

Prototypes are those members of a category that are felt to be the "best", or most typical, members of their category, e.g. 'saloon' within the category 'car'. (1.1.2)

Proximity/distance (principle of proximity/distance): this iconic principle says that units which belong together conceptually are more closely integrated syntactically. (3.3.1)

Purposes are situations which refer to a goal that is intended to be attained by means of one's actions, as in *He's crying for help*. (12.5.2)

Qualifications are attributes that specify things, instances of a thing, or situations. (7.1)

Qualified uniqueness is unique reference achieved by restrictive descriptive qualification, as in *My coat is the green one*. (5.3.3.2)

Qualifying properties, see **properties**.

Qualifying relations specify things or instances of a thing by means of relations; they are expressed as genitive or prepositional phrases, as in *the detective with a waxed moustache*. (7.3)

Qualifying situations specify things or instances of a thing by means of situations; they are expressed as participial phrases or relative clauses, as in *a detective who has come to England*. (7.4)

Quantification refers to the specification of the magnitude of an instance, as in *three tests*. (6.1)

Quantifiers denote the quantity, or magnitude, of an instance, as in *many books*. (6.1)

Quantity refers to the magnitude of an instance, e.g. the magnitude *three* in *three tests*. (6.1)

Quantity (principle of quantity): this iconic principle says that something that carries more meaning is given more wording and, conversely, something that carries less meaning is given less wording; e.g. 'more than one' of a thing is marked by the addition of a plural suffix. (5.3.2)

Reasons are situations which, as a situation's setting, are adduced as an explanation or justification for the occurrence of this situation, as in *He went on trial for murder*. (12.5.2)

The **recent perfect** refers to the state following an immediately preceding anterior event, as in *I've just talked to my lawyer*. (9.3.1.2.1)

Recipient (R) is the role describing the human being who receives a thing and normally becomes its new owner. (11.4.4)

Reference is a mental operation by means of which the speaker communicates which particular referent she has in mind and is talking about. (5.1.1)

The **reference mass** of a thing is all its potential instances in the world. (5.1.1)

Reference points are salient conceptual entities which provide mental access to less salient conceptual entities, as in *my father's car*. (1.3.2; 5.3.3.2)

Reference time (R) refers to a time which serves a reference point for locating times other than deictic times. (9.1.1)

Referents are instances of a thing the speaker has in mind in a communicative situation and tries to call up in the hearer's mind. (5.1.1)

Referring expressions are noun phrases which ground referents in the current discourse. (5.1.1)

Regions are spatial areas where a trajector is located relative to a landmark, like the region 'table top' in *The tie is on the table*. (12.2.2)

Reification is a conceptual shift converting a relational concept into a thing, e.g. 'marriage' from 'be married'. See also **nominalisation**. (4.4.1)

Relations are dependent conceptual units which link two or more things, i.e. autonomous conceptual entities. They typically have a lower degree of time stability than things. Relations are typically expressed as verbs, adjectives, prepositions, etc. (3.1)

Relative clauses express qualifications by means of situations. See **restrictive** and **non-restrictive relative clauses**. (7.4)

Relevance: this principle says that an optimal act of communication creates adequate contextual effects for a minimum of processing effort. (2.3.1)

Restrictive qualification subcategorises a thing as in *a feminist writer* or restricts a referent within its reference mass, as in *the woman with the shiny earrings*. (7.1.1)

Restrictive relative clauses restrict the range of a thing or a potential referent, as in *the friend who lives in Tokyo*, which involves more than one referent. (7.4.1)

The **resultative perfect** refers to the resultant state of an anterior telic event, as in *He has repaired the tractor*. (9.3.1.2.1)

Root modality is concerned with the world of things and social interaction; it comprises deontic modality, intrinsic modality and disposition modality. (10.2.4.2)

Scalar adjectives, or gradable adjectives, are gradable, intensifiable, and can be used both attributively and predicatively, as in *an expensive car* or *The car is expensive*. (7.2.4)

Scalar properties relate to an open-ended scale which involves an implicit norm, such as *expensive*. (7.2.1; 7.2.4)

Scalar quantification refers to a magnitude along a scale; it is expressed by scalar quantifiers such as *many*. (6.1.1; 6.3)

Scalar quantifiers describe quantities along a scale and are used with both count nouns and mass nouns as in *many jobs* and *much work*. (6.1.1)

The **scheduled future** is the use of the simple present tense to refer to a fixed, cyclic or recurrent event, as in *The entrance exams start on September 1*. (9.4.3)

Schematic relations between two entities are based on an abstract schema. In English, schematic relations are typically expressed by prepositions, as in *the plates on the dinner table*. (7.3.3)

The **scientific present** refers to scientific writing in the timeless present, as in *Reichenbach claims that the number of tenses in English is only 6*. (9.3.2.4)

Scope refers to the range of a linguistic unit within which grammatical or conceptual entities are seen. (10.1.3)

Selective quantifiers invoke a full set by denoting one or more random members as representative for the set, as *any doctor*. (6.2.1; 6.2.4)

The **self-motion schema** describes an agent's own instigated motion. (11.4.2)

Semantic bleaching is a shift to weaker meanings, as in *at a certain time*, which expresses vague time. (5.2.2.1)

The **sentence** is the smallest independent grammatical unit; it consists of a grammatical nucleus, grounding elements, and possibly adjuncts and adverbials. Due to its grounding element tense, a sentence is described as finite or temporal. (3.2.4)

Sentence patterns are the basic grammatical constructions which form simple clauses and sentences. (11.1.2)

Sequential order (principle of sequential order): this iconic principle says that the order of events in the conceived world is mirrored in language, as in *I came, I saw, I conquered*. (3.3.1)

Sequential scanning is a mode of viewing a situation in its successive phases. In language, sequential scanning applies to temporal situations, i.e. to situations which are described by a tensed verb. See also **summary scanning**. (2.1.5, 4.4.1)

A **set** is a collection of elements that forms a whole, as in *all novels*. (5.2; 6.1.1)

Set quantification refers to the magnitude of a subset relative to a full set; it is expressed by set quantifiers such as *all*. (6.1.1; 6.2)

Set quantifiers describe quantities relative to a set and are mainly used with count nouns as in *most novels*. (6.1.1)

Setting refers to the space, time and circumstances in which a situation is set. (3.2.3)

Simple tenses denote deictic times and include the present, past and future tenses. Some grammars only recognise the synthetic tenses present and past as simple ones. (9.1.2.1)

Situations are events that happen or states that things are in. Technically, situations can consist of a conceptual core, a time schema, and grounding and setting elements. (3.2; 8.1.1)

Situation types such as accomplishments, activities, etc. are defined by a unique time schema and interact with aspect. (8.1)

Source (S) is the role describing the starting point of a motion event. (11.4.2)

The **source domain** of a metaphorical mapping is that conceptual domain in terms of which a **target domain** is understood. E.g. in *the brain of a computer*, the target domain 'electronics' is understood in terms of the source domain 'human being'. (1.3.1)

Space-builders are expressions that open or refer back to a mental space; e.g. *I think* opens a potentiality space. (2.2.1)

Spatial schemas describe a relation between a theme and a location or trajectory. (11.2.2)

Specific reference is a type of indefinite reference that applies to a factually existing instance, as in *There is a taxi*. (5.2.2)

Specificity (or granularity) refers to the speaker's construal of a conceptualisation in greater detail. See also **generality**. (2.1.2)

Speech time (S) refers to the deictic centre as the present moment of speaking. (9.1.1)

States are static and hence unchangeable situations; they comprise lasting and temporary states (8.1.2; 8.7). As an event schema, a state involves a relation between a theme and an entity specifying it. (11.2.1.1)

Steady situations are states and events that are thought of as lasting indefinitely; e.g. the situation of knowing in *I know her*. (4.4.3)

The **subject** of a sentence is the noun phrase denoting the primary participant, or figure, in a situation, from whose perspective the situation is viewed. (3.2.1)

Subjectivity refers to the construal of a scene in which the speaker is involved. See also **objectivity**. (2.1.4)

Subordination refers to the tighter linking of two situations by means of a subordinate clause and a subordinating conjunction such as *when*. (3.3.2)

A **subset** is a collection of elements that forms part of a set, as in *most novels*. (6.1.1)

Subset quantifiers describe the quantity of subsets relative to a full set, as in *most doctors*. (6.2; 6.2.5)

Summary scanning is a mode of viewing a situation in which all its phases are activated simultaneously. It applies to atemporal situations, i.e. to situations whose descriptions do not contain a tensed verb but are expressed by infinitives, gerunds or abstract nouns. See also **sequential scanning**. (2.1.5; 4.4.1)

The **summary present** gives an abstract of past narrative events in the present tense, as in the genre of headlines, as in *Vicar elopes with housekeeper's daughter*. (9.3.2.4)

Target domain, see **source domain**.

Targets are point-like landmarks towards which an agent's action is directed; targets are specified by the preposition *at*, as in *shoot at the burglar*. (12.3.2.1)

Taxonomies are conceptual hierarchies which are established by *kind of*-relations between higher and lower categories, e.g. 'car' is a kind of 'vehicle'. (1.2.1)

Telicity refers to an event's property of having an inherently conclusive end-point. Telic events are accomplishments and achievements, atelic situations are activities, acts and states. (8.2.1.1)

Temporal and **atemporal**, see **clause** and **sentence**.

Temporary states are states that are thought of as lasting for a limited duration, such as *How are you liking your new job?* (8.1.2; 8.7.1)

Tense is a grammatical expression of notions of time; its main function is to ground a situation in time. (Part III; 9.1.1)

Thematic roles are conceptual entities associated with a unique function in a situation, for example the agent as the instigator of an action. See also **participant roles**. (11.1.1)

Theme (T) is the thematic role that most neutrally partakes in a relation. It describes an entity which exists, is brought into existence, undergoes a change, or is affected in a situation. (11.1.1)

Things are autonomous conceptual entities that extend over a region in some domain. Prototypical things tend to have conceptual stability in space and time. Things are typically expressed as nouns. (3.1, 4.1.1)

Time schemas are general patterns defining the internal temporal structure of types of situations, such as the time schema of achievements. (8.1.1)

A **token**, or **instance**, is an element of a type. (4.1.1)

Trajectors are "figure" entities in a spatial relation whose position is defined relative to a landmark, such as *the tie* in *The tie is on the table*. (12.2.2)

The **transfer schema** describes an agent's transfer of a thing to a recipient, who becomes the new owner of the thing, as in *He gave his fiancee a wedding ring*. (11.4.4)

Transitivity refers to the degree to which situations conform to the canonical action schema; transitivity is prototypically expressed in the form of a transitive construction. (11.4.1.2)

A **type** is an abstract class of elements, e.g. 'tree', instances are tokens, e.g. 'this tree'. (4.1.1)

Unbounded, or *imperfective*, events are viewed internally and in their progression; they are expressed in the progressive aspect, such as *Ann is cuddling the baby*. (8.1.2; 8.2.1.2)

Unbounded activities focus on the event's progression, which tends to invite implicatures, such as casualness in *I was talking to Mr Green*. (8.2.1.2; 8.4.2)

Unique reference applies to an instance that is commonly known due to its singularity. Unique reference includes inherent uniqueness, qualifying uniqueness, and framed uniqueness. (5.3.3)

Valency refers to the number of **arguments** a predicate takes; e.g. the verb *love* takes two arguments, or is a two-place verb. (11.1.2)

The **verb phrase** is that part of a sentence which includes the predicate and, if present, its object and / or possibly other complements. (3.2.1)

A **viewing frame** provides a view of a scene or part of a scene that is immediately accessible to the observer. In language, the notion of viewing frame is particularly relevant for characterising aspectual classes. (2.1.1; 8.1.2)

Viewpoint refers to the point of view adopted by the speaker in construing a scene or locating a situation in time. (2.1.3; 9.1.1)

References

Allan, Keith. 1980. Nouns and countability. *Language* 56: 541–567.
Allerton, David J. 1978. Generating indirect objects in English. *Journal of Linguistics* 14: 21–33.
Ariel, Mira. 1998. The linguistic status of the "here" and "now". *Cognitive Linguistics* 9: 189–237.
Ariel, Mira. 2004. Most. *Language* 80: 658–606.
Barcelona, Antonio (ed.). 2000. *Metaphor and Metonymy at the Crossroads: A Cognitive Perspective.* Berlin: Mouton de Gruyter.
Beitel, Dinara A., Raymond W. Gibbs and Paul Sanders. 1997. The embodied approach to the polysemy of the spatial preposition *on*. In: Cuyckens, Hubert and Britta Zawada (eds.), *Polysemy in Cognitive Linguistics,* 241–260. Amsterdam: John Benjamins.
Bennett, David C. 1975. *Spatial and Temporal Uses of English Prepositions: An Essay in Stratificational Semantics.* London: Longman.
Berezowski, Leszek. 1997. Iconic motivation for the definite article in English geographical proper names. *Studia Anglica Posnaniensia* 32: 127–144.
Berezowski, Leszek. 2001. *Articles and Proper Names.* Wrocław: Wydawn. Uniw. Wrocławskiego.
Binnick, Robert I. 1991. *Time and the Verb: A Guide to Tense and Aspect.* Oxford: OUP.
Birner, Betty and Gregory Ward. 1994. Uniqueness, familiarity, and the definite article in English. *Berkeley Linguistics Society* 20: 93–102.
Blakemore, Diane. 1992. *Understanding Utterances: An Introduction to Pragmatics.* Oxford: Blackwell.
Bloomfield, Leonard. 1933. *Language.* New York NY: Henry Holt and Company.
Boers, Frank. 1986. *Spatial Prepositions and Metaphor: A Cognitive-semantic Journey along the UP–DOWN and the FRONT–BACK Dimensions.* Tübingen: Gunter Narr.
Bolinger, Dwight. 1967. Adjectives in English: Attribution and predication. *Lingua* 18: 1–34.
Bolinger, Dwight. 1977. *Meaning and Form.* London: Longman.
Brisard, Frank (ed.). 2003. *Grounding: The Epistemic Footing of Deixis and Reference.* Berlin: Mouton de Gruyter.
Broccias, Cristiano. 2003. *The English Change Network: Forcing Changes into Schemas.* Berlin: Mouton de Gruyter.
Brugman, Claudia. 1988. *The Story of 'over': Polysemy, Semantics and the Structure of the Lexicon.* New York NY: Garland.
Bunt, Harry C. 1985. *Mass Terms and Model-Theoretic Semantics.* Cambridge: CUP.
Bybee, Joan L. and William Pagliuca. 1987. The evolution of future meaning. In: Ramat, Anna Giacalone, Onofrio Carruba and Giuliano Bernini (eds.), *Papers from the 7th International Conference on Historical Linguistics,* 109–122. Amsterdam: John Benjamins.
Bybee, Joan L., Revere Perkins and William Pagliuca. 1994. *The Evolution of Grammar: Tense, Aspect and Modality in the Languages of the World.* Chicago IL: The University of Chicago Press.

Carston, Robyn and Seiji Uchida (eds.). 1998. *Relevance Theory: Applications and Implications*. Amsterdam: John Benjamins.

Chafe, Wallace L. 1976. Givenness, contrastiveness, definiteness, subjects, topics, and point of view. In: Li, Charles N. (ed.), *Subject and Topic*, 25–55. New York NY: Academic Press.

Chafe, Wallace L. 1994. *Discourse, Consciousness, and Time*. Chicago IL: The University of Chicago Press.

Chesterman, Andrew. 1991. *On Definiteness: A Study with Special Reference to English and Finnish*. Cambridge: CUP.

Christophersen, Paul. 1939. *The Articles: A Study of Their Theory and Use in English*. Copenhagen: Ejnar Munksgaard.

Clark, Herbert. 1977. Bridging. In: Johnson-Laird, P.N. and P.C. Wason (eds.), *Thinking: Readings in Cognitive Science*, 411–420. Cambridge: CUP.

Clark, Eve and Herbert Clark. 1979. When nouns surface as verbs. *Language* 55: 767–811.

Clark, Herbert and Catherine R. Marshall. 1992. Definite reference and mutual knowledge. In: Clark, Herbert H. (ed.), *Arenas of Language Use*, 9–77. Chicago IL: The University of Chicago Press.

Coates, Jennifer. 1983. *The Semantics of the Modal Auxiliaries*. London: Croom Helm.

Coates, Jennifer. 1995. The expression of root and epistemic possibility in English. In: Bybee, Joan L. and Suzanne Fleischman (eds.), *Modality in Grammar and Discourse*, 55–66. Amsterdam: John Benjamins.

Collins, Peter C. 2005. The modals and quasi-modals of obligation and necessity in Australian English and other Englishes. *English World-Wide* 26: 249–273.

Comrie, Bernard. 1976. *Aspect*. Cambridge: CUP.

Comrie, Bernard. 1985. *Tense*. Cambridge: CUP.

Cook-Gumperz, Jenny and Amy Kyratzis. 2001. Pretend play: Trial ground for the simple present. In: Pütz, Martin, Susanne Niemeier and René Dirven (eds.), *Applied Cognitive Linguistics I: Theory and Language Acquisition*, 41–62. Berlin: Mouton de Gruyter.

Croft, William. 1983. Quantifier scope, ambiguity and definiteness. *Chicago Linguistic Society* 9: 25–36.

Croft, William. 1991. *Syntactic Categories and Grammatical Relations*. Chicago IL: The University of Chicago Press.

Croft, William. 1993. The role of domains in the interpretation of metaphors and metonymies. *Cognitive Linguistics* 4: 335–370.

Croft, William, Chiaki Taoka and Esther J. Wood. 2001. Argument linking and the commercial transaction frame in English, Russian and Japanese. *Language Sciences* 23: 579–602.

Croft, William and D. Alan Cruse. 2004. *Cognitive Linguistics*. Cambridge: CUP.

Cushing, Steven. 1982. *Quantifier Meanings: A Study in the Dimensions of Semantic Competence*. Amsterdam: North-Holland.

Dahl, Östen. 1985. *Tense and Aspect Systems*. Oxford: Blackwell.

Dahl, Östen (ed.). 2000. *Tense and Aspect in the Languages of Europe*. Berlin: Mouton de Gruyter.

Davidse, Kristin. 1999. The semantics of cardinal versus enumerative existential constructions. *Cognitive Linguistics* 10: 203–250.

Davidse, Kristin. 2004. The interaction of quantification and identification in English determiners. In: Achard, Michel and Suzanne Kemmer (eds.), *Language, Culture, and Mind*, 507–534. Stanford CA: CSLI Publications.

Declerck, Renaat. 1986. The manifold interpretation of generic sentences. *Lingua* 68: 149–188.

Declerck, Renaat. 1991. *Tense in English: Its Structure and Use in Discourse*. London: Routledge.

Declerck, Renaat. 2006. *The Grammar of the English Verb Phrase*. Vol 1: *The Grammar of the English Tense System: A Comprehensive Analysis*. Berlin: Mouton de Gruyter.

DeLancey, Scott. 1991. Event construal and case role assignment. *Berkeley Linguistics Society* 17: 338–353.

Depraetere, Ilse. 1998. On the resultative character of present perfect sentences. *Journal of Pragmatics* 29: 597–613.

Depraetere, Ilse. 2003. On verbal concord with collective nouns in British English. *English Language and Linguistics* 7: 85–127.

Dik, Simon C. 1989. *The Theory of Functional Grammar*. Part 1: *The Structure of the Clause*. Dordrecht: Foris.

Dirven, René and Günter Radden (eds.). 1987. *Fillmore's Case Grammar: A Reader*. Heidelberg: Julius Groos Verlag.

Dirven, René. 1995. The construal of cause: The case of cause prepositions. In: Taylor, John R. and Robert E. MacLaury (eds.), *Language and the Cognitive Construal of the World*, 95–118. Berlin: Mouton de Gruyter.

Dirven, René. 1997. Emotions as cause and the cause of emotions. In: Niemeier, Susanne and René Dirven (eds.), *The Language of Emotions: Conceptualization, Expression and Theoretical Foundation*, 55–83. Amsterdam: John Benjamins.

Dirven, René and Ralf Pörings (eds.). 2002. *Metaphor and Metonymy in Comparison and Contrast*. Berlin: Mouton de Gruyter.

Dirven, René and Marjolijn Verspoor (eds.). 1998, ²2004. *Cognitive Exploration of Language and Linguistics*. Amsterdam: John Benjamins.

Dixon, R.M.W. 1991. *A New Approach to English Grammar, on Semantic Principles*. Oxford: Clarendon Press.

Dowty, David R. 1977. Toward a semantic analysis of verb aspect and the English "imperfective" progressive. *Linguistics and Philosophy* 1: 45–77.

Dowty, David R. 1979. *Word Meaning and Montague Grammar: The Semantics of Verbs and Times in Generative Semantics and in Montague's PTQ*. Dordrecht: Reidel.

Dryer, Matthew S. 1989. Article-noun order. *Chicago Linguistic Society* 25: 83–97.

Epstein, Richard. 1996. Viewpoint and the definite article. In: Goldberg, Adele E. (ed.), *Conceptual Structure, Discourse and Language*, 99–111. Stanford CA: CSLI Publications.

Epstein, Richard. 2001. The definite article, accessibility, and the construction of discourse referents. *Cognitive Linguistics* 12: 333–378.

Evans, Vyvyan and Melanie Green. 2006. *Cognitive Linguistics: An Introduction*. Edinburgh: Edinburgh University Press.

Evans, Vyvyan, Benjamin K. Bergen and Jorg Zinken (eds.). 2007. *The Cognitive Linguistics Reader: Advances in Cognitive Linguistics*. Hereford: Equinox.

Fauconnier, Gilles. 1985. *Mental Spaces*. Cambridge: CUP. Reprinted 1994.

Fauconnier, Gilles. 1997. *Mappings in Thought and Language*. Cambridge: CUP.

Fauconnier, Gilles and Eve Sweetser (eds.). 1996. *Spaces, Worlds and Grammars*. Chicago IL: The University of Chicago Press.

Fauconnier, Gilles and Mark Turner. 1996. Blending as a central process of grammar. In: Goldberg, Adele E. (ed.), *Conceptual Structure, Discourse and Language*, 113–131. Stanford CA: CSLI Publications.

Fauconnier, Gilles and Mark Turner. 2002. *The Way We Think: Conceptual Blending and the Mind's Hidden Complexities*. New York NY: Basic Books.

Ferris, Connor. 1993. *The Meaning of Syntax: A Study in the Adjectives of English*. London: Longman.
Fillmore, Charles J. 1968. The case for case. In: Bach, Emmon and Robert T. Harms, (eds.), *Universals in Linguistic Theory*, 1–88. New York NY: Holt, Rinehart and Winston.
Fillmore, Charles J. 1977. Scenes-and-frames semantics. In: Zampolli, Antonio (ed.), *Linguistic Structures Processing*, 55–81. Amsterdam: North-Holland.
Fillmore, Charles J. 1982. Frame semantics. In: The Linguistic Society of Korea (ed.), *Linguistics in the Morning Calm*, 111–137. Seoul: Hanshin Publishing Co.
Fillmore, Charles J. 1997. *Lectures on Deixis*. Stanford CA: CSLI Publications.
Fillmore, Charles J. and Beryl T. S. Atkins. 1992. Toward a frame-based lexicon: The semantics of 'risk' and its neighbours. In: Lehrer, Adrienne and Eva Feder Kittay, (eds.), *Frames, Fields and Contrasts: New Essays in Semantic and Lexical Organization*, 75–102. Hillsdale NJ: Lawrence Erlbaum.
Fischer, Olga and Max Nänny (eds.). 2001. *The Motivated Sign: Iconicity in Language and Literature 2*. Amsterdam: John Benjamins.
Fox, Barbara A. and Sandra A. Thompson. 1990. A discourse explanation of the grammar of relative clauses in English conversation. *Language* 66: 297–316.
Fraser, Bruce. 1975. Hedged performatives. In Cole, Peter and Jerry L. Morgan (eds.), *Syntax and Semantics*, Vol. 3: *Speech Acts*, 187–210. New York: Academic Press.
Geeraerts, Dirk (ed.). 2006. *Cognitive Linguistics: Basic Readings*. (Cognitive Linguistics Research 34). Berlin: Mouton de Gruyter.
Geeraerts, Dirk and Hubert Cuyckens (eds.). 2007. *Handbook of Cognitive Linguistics*. New York NY: OUP.
Geisler, Christer. 1995. *Relative Infinitives in English*. Stockholm: Almqvist & Wiksell.
Gentner, Dedre. 1981. Some interesting differences between verbs and nouns. *Cognition and Brain Theory* 4: 161–178.
Gibbs, Raymond W. 1994. *The Poetics of Mind: Figurative Thought, Language and Understanding*. Cambridge: CUP.
Gibbs, Raymond W. and Herbert Colston. 1995. The cognitive psychological reality of image-schemas and their transformations. *Cognitive Linguistics* 6: 347–378.
Gibbs, Raymond W. and Gerard J. Steen (eds.). 1997. *Metaphor in Cognitive Linguistics*. Amsterdam: John Benjamins.
Gibson, Edward et al. 2005. Reading relative clauses in English. *Cognitive Linguistics* 16: 313–353.
Givón, Talmy. 1984. *Syntax: A Functional-Typological Introduction*. 2 vols. Amsterdam: John Benjamins.
Givón, Talmy. 1993. *English Grammar*. 2 vols. Amsterdam: John Benjamins.
Goldberg, Adele E. 1989. A unified account of the semantics of the English ditransitive. *Berkeley Linguistics Society* 15: 79–90.
Goldberg, Adele E. 1995. *Constructions: A Construction Grammar Approach to Argument Structure*. Chicago and London: The University of Chicago Press.
Goldberg, Adele E. 1997. The relationship between verbs and constructions. In: Verspoor, Marjolijn, Kee Dong Lee and Eve Sweetser (eds.), *Lexical and Syntactical Constructions and the Construction of Meaning*, 383–398. Amsterdam: John Benjamins.
Goldberg, Adele E. 2002. Surface generalizations: an alternative to alternations. *Cognitive Linguistics* 13: 327–356.

Goldberg, Adele E. and Farrell Ackerman. 1996. Constraints on adjectival past participles. In: Goldberg, Adele E. (ed.), *Conceptual Structure, Discourse and Language*, 17–30. Stanford CA: CSLI Publications.

Górska, Elżbieta. 1994. Moonless nights and smoke-free cities, or what can be without what? A cognitive study of privative adjectives in English. *Folia Linguistica* 28: 413–435.

Grice, H. Paul. 1975. Logic and conversation. In: Cole, Peter and Jerry L. Morgan (eds.), *Syntax and Semantics*, Volume 3: *Speech Acts*, 41–58. New York NY: Academic Press.

Gundel, Jeanette K. 1996. Relevance theory meets the givenness hierarchy: An account of inferrables. In: Fretheim, Thorstein and Jeannette K. Gundel (eds.), *Reference and Referent Accessibility*, 141–153. Amsterdam: John Benjamins.

Haegeman, Liliane. 1989. *Be going* and *will*: A pragmatic account. *Journal of Linguistics* 25: 291–317.

Haiman, John (ed.). 1985. *Iconicity in Syntax*. Amsterdam: John Benjamins.

Halliday, M.A.K. and Ruqaiya Hasan. 1976. *Cohesion in English*. London: Longman.

Hampe, Beate (in cooperation with Joseph E. Grady) (eds.). 2005. *From Perception to Meaning: Image Schemas in Cognitive Linguistics*. Berlin: Mouton de Gruyter.

Hawkins, John A. 1978. *Definiteness and Indefiniteness: A Study in Reference and Grammaticality Prediction*. London: Croom Helm.

Hawkins, John A. 1986. *A Comparative Typology of English and German: Unifying the Contrasts*. London: Croom Helm.

Hawkins, John A. 1991. On (in)definite articles: Implicatures and (un)grammaticality prediction. *Journal of Linguistics* 27: 405–442.

Hayase, Naoko. 1997. The role of figure, ground, and coercion in aspectual interpretation. In: Verspoor, Marjolijn, Kee Dong Lee and Eve Sweetser (eds.), *Lexical and Syntactical Constructions and the Construction of Meaning*, 33–50. Amsterdam: John Benjamins.

Heine, Bernd, Ulrike Claudi and Friederike Hünnemeyer. 1991. *Grammaticalization: A Conceptual Framework*. Chicago and London: The University of Chicago Press.

Heine, Bernd and Tania Kuteva. 2002. *World Lexicon of Grammaticalization*. Cambridge: CUP.

Herskovits, Annette. 1985. Semantics and pragmatics of locative expressions. *Cognitive Science* 9: 341–378.

Herskovits, Annette. 1986. *Language and Spatial Cognition: An Interdisciplinary Study of Prepositions in English*. Cambridge: CUP.

Hewson, John. 1972. *Article and Noun in English*. The Hague: Mouton.

Hewson, John and Vit Bubenik. 1997. *Tense and Aspect in Indo-European Languages*. Amsterdam: John Benjamins.

Heyvaert, Liesbet. 2003a. *A Cognitive-Functional Approach to Nominalization in English*. Berlin: Mouton de Gruyter.

Heyvaert, Liesbet. 2003b. Nominalization as grammatical metaphor: On the need for a radically systemic and metafunctional approach. In: Simon-Vandenbergen, Anne-Marie, Miriam Taverniers and Louise Ravelli (eds.), *Grammatical Metaphor: Views from Systemic-Functional Linguistics*, 65–100. Amsterdam: John Benjamins.

Heyvaert, Liesbet. 2004. Towards a symbolic typology of '-ing' nominalizations. In: Achard, Michel and Suzanne Kemmer (eds.), *Language, Culture, and Mind*, 493–506. Stanford CA: CSLI Publications.

Hopper, Paul J. and Sandra A. Thompson. 1980. Transitivity in grammar and discourse. *Language* 56: 251–299.

Hopper, Paul J. and Sandra A. Thompson. 1985. The iconicity of the universal categories 'noun' and 'verb'. In: Haiman, John (ed.), *Iconicity in Syntax*, 151–183. Amsterdam: John Benjamins.

Hopper, Paul J. and Elizabeth Closs Traugott. ²2003. *Grammaticalization*. Cambridge: CUP.

Horowitz, Franklin. 1989. ESL and prototype theory: Zero vs. definite article with place names. *IRAL* 27: 81–98.

Hoye, Leo. 1997. *Adverbs and Modality in English*. London: Longman.

Huddleston, Rodney and Geoffrey K Pullum. 2002. *The Cambridge Grammar of the English Language*. Cambridge: CUP.

Ikegami, Yoshihiko. 1987. 'Source' vs. 'Goal': A case of linguistic asymmetry. In: Dirven, René and Günter Radden (eds.), *Concepts of Case*, 122–146. Tübingen: Narr.

Inoue, Kyoko. 1978. An analysis of the English present perfect. *Linguistics* 17: 561–589.

Jespersen, Otto. 1924. *The Philosophy of Grammar*. New York NY: Henry Holt and Company.

Jespersen, Otto. 1949. *A Modern English Grammar on Historical Principles*. Part VII: *Syntax*. London: George Allen & Unwin.

Johnson, Mark. 1987. *The Body in the Mind: The Bodily Basis of Meaning, Imagination and Reason*. Chicago IL: The University of Chicago Press.

Johnson-Laird, P.N. and P.C. Wason (eds.). 1977. *Thinking: Readings in Cognitive Science*. Cambridge: CUP.

Kemmer, Suzanne. 1993. *The Middle Voice*. Amsterdam: John Benjamins.

Klein, Wolfgang. 1992. The present perfect puzzle. *Language* 68: 525–552.

Klein, Wolfgang. 1994. *Time in Language*. London: Routledge.

Kövecses, Zoltán. 1990. *Emotion Concepts*. New York NY: Springer Verlag.

Kövecses, Zoltán. 2002. *Metaphor: A Practical Introduction*. Oxford: OUP.

Kövecses, Zoltán. 2005. *Metaphor in Culture: Universality and Variation*. Cambridge: CUP.

Krifka, Manfred, et al. 1995. Genericity: An introduction. In: Gregory N. Carlson and Francis Jeffry Pelletier (eds.), *The Generic Book*, 1–124. Chicago IL: The University of Chicago Press.

Kristiansen, Gitte, Michel Achard, René Dirven, and Francisco Ruiz de Mendoza (eds.). 2006. *Cognitive Linguistics: Current Applications, Future Perspectives*. Berlin: Mouton de Gruyter.

Krzeszowski, Tomasz P. 1993. The axiological parameter in preconceptual image schemata. In: Geiger, Richard A. and Brygida Rudzka-Ostyn (eds.), *Conceptualizations and Mental Processing in Language*, 307–329. Berlin: Mouton de Gruyter.

Labov, William. 1985. The several logics of quantification. *Berkeley Linguistics Society* 11: 175–195.

Labov, William and Joshua Waletzky. 1967. Narrative analysis: Oral versions of personal experience. In Helm, June (ed.), *Essays on the Verbal and Visual Arts: Proceedings of the 1966 Annual Spring Meeting of the American Ethnological Society*, 11-44. Seattle and London: American Ethnological Society.

Lakoff, George. 1977. Linguistic gestalts. *Chicago Linguistic Society* 13: 236–287.

Lakoff, George. 1987. *Women, Fire, and Dangerous Things: What Categories Reveal about the Mind*. Chicago: The University of Chicago Press.

Lakoff, George. 1993. The contemporary theory of metaphor. In Ortony, Andrew (ed.), *Metaphor and Thought*, 2nd ed., 202–251. New York NY: CUP.

Lakoff, George. 2004. *Don't Think of an Elephant! Know Your Values and Frame the Debate*. White River Junction, Vermont: Chelsea Green Publishing.

Lakoff, George and Mark Johnson. 1980, ²2003. *Metaphors We Live By*. Chicago IL: The University of Chicago Press.

Lakoff, George and Mark Johnson, 1999. *Philosophy in the Flesh: The Embodied Mind and Its Challenge to Western Thought*. New York NY: Basic Books.

Lakoff, George and Mark Turner. 1989. *More than Cool Reason: A Field Guide to Poetic Metaphor*. Chicago IL: The University of Chicago Press.

Lakoff, Robin. 1969. Some reasons why there can't be any *some-any* rule. *Language* 45: 608–615.

Lakoff, Robin. 1974. Remarks on *this* and *that*. *Berkeley Studies in Syntax and Semantics* 1: XVII-1–12.

Landsberg, Marge E. (ed.). 1995. *Syntactic Iconicity and Linguistic Freezes: The Human Dimension*. Berlin: Mouton de Gruyter.

Langacker, Ronald W. 1987a. *Foundations of Cognitive Grammar*. Vol. I: *Theoretical Prerequisites*. Stanford CA: Stanford University Press.

Langacker, Ronald W. 1987b. Nouns and verbs. *Language* 63: 53–96.

Langacker, Ronald W. 1990. Subjectification. *Cognitive Linguistics* 1: 5–38.

Langacker, Ronald W. 1991a. *Foundations of Cognitive Grammar*. Vol. II: *Descriptive Application*. Stanford CA: Stanford University Press.

Langacker, Ronald W. 1991b. *Concept, Image, and Symbol: The Cognitive Basis of Grammar*. Berlin: Mouton de Gruyter.

Langacker, Ronald W. 1992. The symbolic nature of cognitive grammar: the meaning of 'of' and 'of'-periphrasis. In: Pütz, Martin (ed.), *Thirty Years of Linguistic Evolution*, 483–502. Amsterdam: John Benjamins.

Langacker, Ronald W. 1993. Reference-point constructions. *Cognitive Linguistics* 4: 1–38; revised version in Langacker 2000, 171–202.

Langacker, Ronald W. 1995. Possession and possessive constructions. In: Taylor, John R. and Robert E. MacLaury (eds.), *Language and the Cognitive Construal of the World*, 51–79. Berlin: Mouton de Gruyter.

Langacker, Ronald W. 2000. *Grammar and Conceptualization*. Berlin: Mouton de Gruyter.

Langacker, Ronald W. 2001. The English present tense. *English Language and Linguistics* 5: 251–272. Also available at http://mind.ucsd.edu/syllabi/05–06/cogs200/English%20Present.pdf

Langacker, Ronald W. 2002. Deixis and subjectivity. In: Brisard, Frank (ed.), *Grounding: The Epistemic Footing of Deixis and Reference*, 1–28. Berlin: Mouton de Gruyter.

Langacker, Ronald W. 2003. One any. *Korean Linguistics* 8: 65–105.

Lawler, John M. 1989. Lexical semantics in the commercial transaction frame: Value, worth, cost and price. *Studies in Language* 13: 381–404.

Lee, David. 2001. *Cognitive Linguistics: An Introduction*. Oxford: OUP.

Leech, Geoffrey N. 1971. *Meaning and the English Verb*. London: Longman.

Lees, Robert B. 1960. *The Grammar of English Nominalizations*. Bloomington IN: Indiana University Research Center.

Levi, Judith N. 1973. Where do all those other adjectives come from? In: *Chicago Linguistic Society* 9: 332–354.

Levin, Beth. 1993. *English Verb Classes and Alternations: A Preliminary Investigation*. Chicago IL: The University of Chicago Press.

Levinson, Stephen C. 2003. *Space in Language and Cognition: Explorations in Cognitive Diversity*. Cambridge: CUP.

Lyons, Christopher. 1999. *Definiteness*. Cambridge: CUP.

Lyons, John. 1977. *Semantics*. Vol. 2. Cambridge: CUP.

Mann, William C. and Sandra A. Thompson. 1988. Rhetorical structure theory: Toward a functional theory of text organization. *Text* 8: 243–281.

Markman, Ellen M. 1985. Why superordinate category terms can be mass nouns. *Cognition* 19: 31–53.

Matlock, Teenie. 2004a. The conceptual motivation of fictive motion. In: Radden, Günter and Klaus-Uwe Panther (eds.), *Studies in Linguistic Motivation*, 221–248. Berlin: Mouton de Gruyter.

Matlock, Teenie. 2004b. Fictive motion as cognitive simulation. *Memory and Cognition* 32: 1389–1400.

Matlock, Teenie, Michael Ramscar and Lera Boroditsky. 2005. On the experiential link between spatial and temporal language. *Cognitive Science* 29: 655–664. Also at http://www-psych.stanford.edu/~michael/papers/mrb-cogscij-final.pdf.

McCawley, James D. 1977. Lexicographic notes on English quantifiers. *Chicago Linguistic Society* 13: 372–383.

McCoard, Robert. 1978. *The English Perfect: Tense-Choice and Pragmatic Inferences*. Amsterdam: North-Holland.

Michaelis, Laura A. 1994. The ambiguity of the English perfect. *Journal of Linguistics* 30: 111–157.

Middleton, Erica L., Edward J. Wisniewski, Kelly A. Trindel and Mutsumi Imai. 2004. Separating the chaff from the oats: Evidence for a conceptual distinction between count noun and mass noun aggregates. *Journal of Memory and Language* 50: 371–394.

Miki, Etsuzo. 1996. Evocation and tautologies. *Journal of Pragmatics* 25: 635–648.

Moravcsik, J.M.E. 1973. Mass terms in English. In: Hintikka, Jaakko (ed.), *Approaches to Natural Language*, 263–285. Dordrecht: Reidel.

Mufwene, Salikoko. 1984. Non-individuation and the count/mass distinction. *Chicago Linguistic Society* 20: 221–238.

Myhill, John. 1996. The development of the strong obligation system in American English. *American Speech* 71: 339–388.

Nicolle, Steve. 1997. A relevance-theoretic account of *be going to*. *Journal of Linguistics* 33: 355–377.

Nikiforidou, Kiki. 1999. Nominalizations, metonymy and lexicographic practice. In: de Stadler, Leon and Christoph Eyrich (eds.), *Issues in Cognitive Linguistics*, 141–163. Berlin: Mouton de Gruyter.

Nordlinger, Rachel and Elizabeth Closs Traugott. 1997. Scope and the development of epistemic modality: Evidence from *ought to*. *English Language and Linguistics* 1: 295–318.

Nuyts, Jan. 2000. *Epistemic Modality, Language, and Conceptualization: A Cognitive-Pragmatic Perspective*. Amsterdam: John Benjamins.

Palmer, Frank R. 1988. *The English Verb*. 2nd ed. London: Longman.

Palmer, Frank R. ²1990. *Modality and the English Modals*. London: Longman.

Palmer, Frank R. 1994. *Grammatical Roles and Relations*. Cambridge: CUP.

Palmer, Frank R. 2001. *Mood and Modality*. Cambridge: CUP.

Panther, Klaus-Uwe. 1997. Dative alternation from a cognitive perspective. In: Smieja, Birgit and Meike Tasch (eds.), *Human Contact through Language and Linguistics*, 107–126. Frankfurt: Peter Lang.

Panther, Klaus-Uwe and Günter Radden (eds.). 1999. *Metonymy in Language and Thought*. Amsterdam: John Benjamins.

Panther, Klaus-Uwe and Linda Thornburg. 1999. The potentiality for actuality metonymy in English and Hungarian. In: Panther, Klaus-Uwe and Günter Radden (eds.), *Metonymy in Language and Thought*, 333–357. Amsterdam: John Benjamins.

Pelletier, Francis (ed.). 1979. *Mass Terms: Some Philosophical Problems*. Dordrecht: Reidel.

Pelyvás, Péter. 2003. Metaphorical extension of *may* and *must* into the epistemic domain. In Barcelona, Antonio (ed.), *Metaphor and Metonymy at the Crossroads*, 233–250. Berlin: Mouton de Gruyter.

Pelyvás, Péter. 2006. Subjectification in (expressions of) epistemic modality and the development of the grounding predication. In: Athanasiadou, Angeliki, Costas Canakis and Bert Cornillie (eds.), *Subjectification: Various Paths to Subjectivity*, 121–149. Berlin: Mouton de Gruyter.

Perkins, Michael R. 1983. *Modal Expressions in English*. London: Francis Pinter.

Posner, Roland. 1986. Iconicity in syntax: The natural order of attributes. In: Bouissac, Paul, Michael Herzfeld and Roland Posner (eds.), *Iconicity: Festschrift for Thomas A. Sebeok*, 305–337. Tübingen: Stauffenberg.

Post, Michael 1986. A prototype approach to denominal adjectives. In: Kastovsky, Dieter and Aleksander Szwedek (eds.), *Linguistics across Historical and Geographical Boundaries: In the Honour of Jacek Fisiak on the Occasion of his 50th Birthday*. 2 vols., 1003–1013. Berlin: Mouton de Gruyter.

Prideaux, Gary D. and William J. Baker (eds.). 1986. *Strategies and Structures: The Processing of Relative Clauses*. Amsterdam: John Benjamins.

Prince, Ellen F. 1981. Toward a new taxonomy of given-new information. In: Cole, Peter (ed.), *Radical Pragmatics*, 223–255. New York NY: Academic Press.

Prince, Ellen F. 1995. On *kind*-sentences, resumptive pronouns, and relative clauses. In: Guy, Gregory R., John G.. Baugh, Deborah Schiffrin and Crawford Feagin (eds.), *Towards a Social Science of Language: A Festschrift for William Labov*, 223–235. Cambridge: CUP.

Quirk, Randolph, et. al. 1985. *A Comprehensive Grammar of the English Language*. London: Longmans.

Radden, Günter. 1985. Spatial metaphors underlying prepositions of causality. In: Paprotté, Wolf and René Dirven (eds.), *The Ubiquity of Metaphor*, 177–205. Amsterdam: John Benjamins.

Radden, Günter. 1989. Semantic roles. In: Dirven, René (ed.), *A User's Grammar of English: Word, Sentence, Text, Interaction*, 421–472. Frankfurt: Lang.

Radden, Günter. 1996. Motion metaphorized: The case of 'coming' and 'going'. In: Casad, Eugene H. (ed.), *Cognitive Linguistics in the Redwoods: The Expansion of a New Paradigm in Linguistics*, 423–458. Berlin: Mouton de Gruyter.

Radden, Günter. 1998. The conceptualisation of emotional causality by means of prepositional phrases. In: Athanasiadou, Angeliki and Elżbieta Tabakowska (eds.), *Speaking of Emotions: Conceptualisation and Expression*, 273–294. Berlin: Mouton de Gruyter.

Radden, Günter. 2006. Where time meets space. In: Benczes, Réka and Szilvia Csábi, (eds.), *The Metaphors of Sixty: Papers Presented on the Occasion of the 60th Birthday of Zoltán Kövecses*, 210–235. Budapest: Eötvös Loránd University.

Reichenbach, Hans. 1947. *Elements of Symbolic Logic*. New York NY: Macmillan.

Rosch, Eleanor. 1977. Human categorization. In: Warren, Neil (ed.), *Studies in Cross-Cultural Psychology*. Vol. 1, 3–49. New York NY: Academic Press.

Rosch, Eleanor. 1978. Principles of categorization. In: Rosch, Eleanor and Barbara B. Lloyd (eds.), *Cognition and Categorization*, 27–48. Hillsdale NJ: Lawrence Erlbaum.

Rosch, Eleanor. 1999. Reclaiming concepts. *Journal of Consciousness Studies* 8: 61–77.

Rouchota, Villy and Andreas H. Jucker (eds.). 1998. *Current Issues in Relevance Theory*. Amsterdam: John Benjamins.

Sasse, Hans-Jürgen. 2002. Recent activity in the theory of aspect: accomplishments, achievements, or just non-progressive state? *Linguistic Typology* 6: 199–271.

Schlesinger, Izchak M. 1989. Instruments as agents: on the nature of semantic relations. *Journal of Linguistics* 25: 189–210.

Schlesinger, Izchak M. 1995. *Cognitive Space and Linguistic Case: Semantic and Syntactic Categories in English*. Cambridge: CUP.

Schmid, Hans-Jörg. 2000. *English Abstract Nouns as Conceptual Shells: From Corpus to Linguistics.* Berlin: Mouton de Gruyter.

Sheffer, Ronald E. Jr. 1996. Roles, values and possessives: Deictic adjectives in the noun phrase. In: Goldberg, Adele E. (ed.), *Conceptual Structure, Discourse and Language*, 435–447. Stanford CA: CSLI Publications.

Simone, Raffaele (ed.). 1995. *Iconicity in Language.* Amsterdam: John Benjamins.

Sinha, Chris. 1999. Grounding, mapping, and acts of meaning. In: Janssen, Theo and Gisela Redeker (eds.), *Cognitive Linguistics: Foundations, Scope, and Methodology*, 223–255. Berlin: Mouton de Gruyter.

Slobin, Dan I. 1996. Two ways to travel: verbs of motion in English and Spanish. In Shibatani, Masayoshi and Sandra A. Thompson (eds.), *Grammatical Constructions: Their Form and Meaning*, 195–219. Oxford: OUP.

Slobin, Dan I. 2005. Linguistic representations of motion events: What is signifier and what is signified? In Maeder, Constantino, Olga Fischer and William J. Herlofsky (eds.), *Iconicity Inside Out: Iconicity in Language and Literature 4*, 307–322. Amsterdam: John Benjamins.

Smith, Carlota S. 1983. A theory of aspectual choice. *Language* 59: 479–501.

Smith, Carlota S. 1995. The relation between aspectual viewpoint and situation types: Aspectual systems in universal grammar and in languages of the world. http://eric.ed.gov/ERICDocs/data/ericdocs2/content_storage_01/0000000b/80/26/e0/a5.pdf

Smith, Carlota S. ²1997. *The Parameter of Aspect.* Dordrecht: Kluwer.

Sperber, Dan and Deirdre Wilson. 1986. *Relevance: Communication and Cognition.* Oxford: Blackwell.

Suzuki, Nathanael Yuji. 1989. Modality. In: Dirven, René (ed.), *A User's Grammar of English: Word, Sentence, Text, Interaction*, 275–309. Frankfurt: Lang.

Svensson, Patrik. 1998. *Number and Countability in English Nouns: An Embodied Model.* Umeå, Sweden: Umeå University.

Svorou, Soteria. 1994. *The Grammar of Space.* Amsterdam: John Benjamins.

Sweetser, Eve E. 1990. *From Etymology to Pragmatics: Metaphorical and Cultural Aspects of Semantic Structure.* Cambridge: CUP.

Sweetser, Eve E. 1999. Compositionality and blending: Semantic composition in a cognitively realistic framework. In: Janssen, Theo and Gisela Redeker (eds.), *Cognitive Linguistics: Foundations, Scope, and Methodology*, 129–162. Berlin: Mouton de Gruyter.

Tabakowska, Elżbieta. 1980. Existential presuppositions and the choice of head NP determiner in English restrictive relative clauses. In: van der Auwera, Johan (ed.), *The Semantics of Determiners*, 189–210. London: Croom Helm.

Talmy. Leonard. 1978. Figure and ground in complex sentences. In: Greenberg, Joseph H. (ed.), *Universals of Human Language.* Vol. 4: *Syntax*, 625–649. Stanford, CA: Stanford University Press. Revised version as: Figure and ground in language. In: Talmy 2000 Vol. I, 311–344.

Talmy, Leonard. 1983. How language structures space. In: Pick, Herbert and Linda Acredolo (eds.), *Spatial Orientation: Theory, Research, and Application*, 225–282. New York NY: Plenum. Revised version in Talmy 2000 Vol. I, 177–254.

Talmy, Leonard 1985. Lexicalization patterns: Semantic structure in lexical forms. In: Shopen, Timothy (ed.), *Language Typology and Lexical Description: Vol. 3. Grammatical Categories and the Lexicon*, 36–149. Cambridge: CUP. Revised version in Talmy 2000 Vol. II, 21–146.

Talmy, Leonard. 1988a. Force dynamics in language and cognition. *Cognitive Science* 12: 49–100. Revised version in Talmy 2000 Vol. II, 409–470.

Talmy, Leonard. 1988b. The relation of grammar to cognition. In: Rudzka-Ostyn, Brygida (ed.), *Topics in Cognitive Linguistics*, 165–205. Amsterdam: John Benjamins. Revised version in Talmy 2000 Vol. I, 21–96.

Talmy, Leonard. 1991. Path to realization: A typology of event conflation. *Berkeley Linguistics Society* 17: 480–519. Revised as: A typology of event integration. In Talmy 2000 Vol. II, 213–288.

Talmy, Leonard. 1996a. The windowing of attention in language. In: Shibatani, Masayoshi and Sandra Thompson (eds.), *Grammatical Constructions: Their Form and Meaning*, 235–287. Oxford: OUP. Revised version in Talmy 2000 Vol. I, 257–309.

Talmy, Leonard. 1996b. Fictive motion in language and 'ception'. In: Bloom, Paul, Mary A. Peterson, Lynn Nadel and Merrill F. Garrett (eds.), *Language and Space*, 211–276. Cambridge MA: The MIT Press. Revised version in Talmy 2000 Vol. I, 99–175.

Talmy, Leonard. 2000. *Toward a Cognitive Semantics*. Vol. I: *Concept Structuring Systems*. Cambridge MA: The MIT Press.

Talmy, Leonard. 2000. *Toward a Cognitive Semantics*. Vol. II: *Typology and Process in Concept*. Cambridge MA: The MIT Press.

Taylor, John R. 1992. Old problems: Adjectives in cognitive grammar. *Cognitive Linguistics* 3: 1–36.

Taylor, John. 1994. 'Subjective' and 'objective' readings of possessor nominals. *Cognitive Linguistics* 5: 201–242.

Taylor, John. 1995, ^{3}2004. *Linguistic Categorization: Prototypes in Linguistic Theory*. Oxford: Clarendon Press.

Taylor, John. 1996, ^{2}2006. *Possessives in English: An Exploration in Cognitive Grammar*. Oxford: Clarendon Press.

Taylor, John 2002. *Cognitive Grammar*. Oxford: OUP.

Taylor, John. 2004. The ecology of constructions. In: Radden, Günter and Klaus-Uwe Panther (eds.), *Studies in Linguistic Motivation*, 49–73. Berlin: Mouton de Gruyter.

Tfouni, L. V. and R. L. Klatzky. 1986. A discourse analysis of deixis: Pragmatic, cognitive and semantic factors in the comprehension of *this*, *that*, *here* and *there*. *Journal of Child Language* 10: 123–133.

Thompson, Sandra A. 1989. A discourse approach to the cross-linguistic category 'adjective.' In: Corrigan, Roberta L., Fred R. Eckman, and Michael Noonan (eds.), *Linguistic Categorization*, 245–265. Amsterdam: John Benjamins.

Thompson, Sandra A. and Yuko Koide. 1987. Iconicity and 'indirect objects' in English. *Journal of Pragmatics* 11: 399–406.

Traugott, Elizabeth Closs. 1989. On the rise of epistemic meanings in English: An example of subjectification in semantic change. *Language* 65: 31–55.

Traugott, Elizabeth Closs and Richard B. Dasher. 2002. *Regularity in Semantic Change*. Cambridge: CUP.

Traugott, Elizabeth Closs and Bernd Heine (eds.). 1993. *Approaches to Grammaticalization*, 2 vols. Amsterdam: John Benjamins.

Tsohatzidis, Savas L. (ed.). 1990. *Meanings and Prototypes: Studies in Linguistic Categorization*. London: Routledge.

Tyler, Andrea and Vyvyan Evans. 2001. Reconsidering prepositional polysemy networks: The case of 'over'. *Language* 77: 724–765.

Tyler, Andrea and Vyvyan Evans. 2003. *The Semantics of English Prepositions: Spatial Scenes, Embodied Meaning and Cognition*. Cambridge: CUP.

Ungerer, Friedrich and Hans-Jörg Schmid. ^{2}2006. *An Introduction to Cognitive Linguistics*. London: Longman.

van der Auwera, Johan (ed.) 1980. *The Semantics of Determiners*. London: Croom Helm.
van Hoek, Karen. 1997. *Anaphora and Conceptual Structure*. Chicago IL: The University of Chicago Press.
Vendler, Zeno. 1961. Order of adjectives. *Transformations and Discourse Analysis Papers*: 1–16. Philadelphia PA: University of Pennsylvania.
Vendler, Zeno. 1967. *Linguistics in Philosophy*. Ithaca NY: Cornell University Press.
Vendler, Zeno. 1968. *Adjectives and Nominalizations*. The Hague: Mouton.
Violi, Patrizia. 2004. Embodiment at the crossroads between cognition and semiosis. *Recherches en Communication* 19: 199–234.
Wallace, Stephen. 1982. Figure and ground: The interrelationships of linguistic categories. In: Hopper, Paul (ed.), *Tense-Aspect: Between Semantics and Pragmatics*, 201–223. Amsterdam: John Benjamins.
Wekker, Herman Chr. 1976. *The Expression of Future Time in Contemporary British English*. Amsterdam: North-Holland.
Wierzbicka, Anna. 1985. Oats and wheat: The fallacy of arbitrariness. In: Haiman, John (ed.), *Iconicity in Syntax*, 311–342. Amsterdam: Benjamins.
Wierzbicka, Anna. 1988a. *The Semantics of Grammar*. Amsterdam: John Benjamins.
Wierzbicka, Anna. 1988b. What's in a noun (Or: how do nouns differ in meaning from adjectives?). *Studies in Language* 10: 287–313.
Wierzbicka, Anna. 1993. Why do we say *in April, on Thursday, at 10 o'clock?* In search of an explanation? *Studies in Language* 17: 437–454.
Wilckens, Mark A. 1992. *Grammatical Number in English Nouns*. Amsterdam: John Benjamins.
Yus, Francisco. Relevance Theory Online Bibliographic Service. http://www.ua.es/personal/francisco.yus/rt.html
Zerubavel, Eviatar. 1991. *The Fine Line: Making Distinctions in Everyday Life*. Chicago IL: The University of Chicago Press.

Index

A

ability, 233, 242, 246, 253, **254**-6, 258-9, 263, 284
abstract noun, *see* noun
accompaniment, 311, 327, 329
accomplishment, **180**-6, 188, 196-7, 214, 226, 267, 284, 324
achievement, **180**-2, 187-90, 197, 214, 254, 297, 321, 332
act, 180, 182, **190**, 196-7
    punctual, 182, 190
action, 157, 209, 237-8, 252, 267, 270, 272, 277-8, 284-9, 291, 296-9, 324, 328, 330
action schema, 267, 269-70, 281, **284**, 298-9
active zone, **10**-1, 17-9, 290, 305, 333
activity, 176, **180**-1, 185-7, 196-7, 215, 217, 220-1, 223, 225, 230, 275, 297, 321, 324-5
    accomplishing, **181**, 184-5, 189, 196-7, 209-10, 218, 226, 239, 267
    bounded, **181**, 185-7, 196-7, 220-1
    culminating, **181**, 187-9, 196-7
    iterative, 181, **182**, 190, 196-7
    unbounded, **181**, 185-7, 196-7, 217, 220-1, 223
adjective, 41-4, 46-7, 56, 79, 84, 93, 95, 101, 104, 110, 141-2, 144-7, **148**-57, 159, 164, 166, 168, 251, 253, 275, 283-4, 319
    attributive, 129, **149**, 151, 166
    behavioural, 157
    deadverbial, **151**-2, 154, 166
    denominal, 150-1, **152**, 154, 156, 166, 168
    determining, 104, 118, **151**-4, 156, 166
    evaluative, 154
    functions of, 149-50
    nominalised, 110
    non-restrictive, 146
    postmodifier, 145, 150, 154, 156
    predicative, **150**, 156-7, 167-8, 191, 193, 273-5
    premodifier, 145-6, 150-1, 153-6, 169
    restrictive, 146
    scalar, **150**-1, 154, 157, 166, 193
    types of, 150, 166
adjunct, 31, **48**, 50, 154-5, 57, 182-6, 194-5, 207-8, 216, 218-9, 224, 226, 229, 239, 242, 268, 270, 277, 283, 289, 293, 296, 304, 320, 328
adverb, 42, 56, 93, 116, 118, 122, 132-3, 151, 240, 277, 286-7, 236, 242, 320
    approximative, 118
    deictic, 277
    intensifying, 118, 133
    modal, 233, 240-2, 264
advice, 157, 249, 251
affirmative (context), 91-3, 128, 131-2, 168, 234, 326

agent, 47, 56, 152, 169, 243-4, 251, 256, 267, 269, **270**, 272, 278, 284-9, 291-2, 294, 296, 298-300, 329
all, 115, 117-9, 121-2, **123**-5, 127-9, 134-8
amassed object, *see* object
amount quantification, *see* quantification
amount quantifier, *see* quantifier
anaphoric reference, *see* reference
anterior, 203, 211-18, 222-3, 227, 229, *see also* event, situation, present, situation, time
antonym, 151
any (determiner), 90-4, 128
any (quantifier), 117-8, 121-2, 127-8, 136, 138-9
apposition, 144
argument, **271**, 282, 284
article, 66-7, 83, 92, 93, 100-2, 132, 138, 154
    absence of, 66-7, 83
    definite, 49, 67, 88-9, 100-2, 104-5, 113, 124, 135, 154, 277
    indefinite, 36, 49, 67, 90, 92-3, 132, 273
    zero, 100-2
articleless, 92, 129
as-clause, 55
aspect, 5, 11, 23, 46, 171, 173-5, **176**-7, 183, 187, 195-6, 198, 201, 206, 231, 318
    non-progressive, 5, 22, 46, 174-75, **176**-9, 187, 193, 196, 214, 217-8, 221, 230, 275

progressive, 5, 22, 46, 157, 173–6, **177**–80, 184, 187–90, 192–8, 210–1, 217–8, 220–1, 225–7, 229–30, 239, 252, 275
aspect marker, 173
aspectual class, **176–9**, 196, 198, 208
aspectual meaning, 177, 206
assertion, 92, 210, **234**, 236, 240–1, 262, 277
  negated, 92, 234–5
  strong, 234, 250
  weak, 234, 241
assessment, 25, 50, 173–4, 211, 233–5, 237, 239–42, 244, 250, 252, 256, 258, 262
atelic, 179–81, 185–6, 190, 197, 215, 324
atemporal, 53, 80, 144–5, 155, 212
attention, 14, **26**–9, 55, 64, 87, 88–9, 92, 96, 116, 124, 126, 129, 202–3, 209, 213, 218, 278, 282, 291, 297
  windowing of, 22, **26**–9, 37–8
attitude, 195, 232–4, 236–7, 239–40, 246, 257, 262, 291
  directive attitude, 233, 236, 240, 257, 262
attributive adjective, *see* adjective

B
background, 28, 33, 50, 55, 74–5, 126, 147–8, 213, 220–1, 230, 276–7, 280
  information, 1, 164, 166, 219, 223,
  backward-looking stance, 201, 205, 212, 214, 230, 238
base, **30**, 37
base space, **202**–3, 207, 218, 222, 224, 229
basic aspectual class, *see* aspectual class
basic level, **8**–9, 17, 23, 69–70
be able to, 242, 254–5
be going to, 98, 201, 206, 224–5, 227–8, 230

because-clause, 327
behavioural adjective, *see* adjective
BELIEFS ARE POSSESSIONS, 16
beneficiary, **296**–7, 299
bleaching, 36, 95, 151, 242, 246, 277
blended space, 31–2, 37, 235
blending, **31**–2, 37–8, 57, 71–8, 108, 147–8, 158, 165, 235, 237, 278, 293–4, 300, *see also* category
body part, 12–3, 280, 285, 299, 305
bounded, 69–73, 80–1, 100–1, 179, 183, 190, 196–8, 208, 275, 278, 321, 323–4, *see also* activity, event, instance, quantity, situation, bounded time, thing
boundedness, **64**, 66, 83, 100, 179, 183, 313
but-clause, 254

C
can, 239, 242, 253–8, 263
can't, cannot, 239, 259–63
cancel, *see* implicature
cataphoric reference, *see* reference
categorisation, 5–7, 12, 17–18, 42, 47, 61, 68, 71, 80, 147, 156, 167, 295
category, 1, **3**–9, 11–12, 17, 23, 42, 61, 63, 65, 69–70, 83, 88–9, 99–100, 106, 109, 135, 142, 144, 146–9, 151, 153, 162, 164, 166, 171, 174, 179, 273
  blended, 73–4
  extension of, 12
  grammatical, 6–7, 17, 23, 42, 171
  inclusion of, 273
  lexical, 4–7, 15, 23
  linguistic, 1, 3–5, 12, 17, 18, 46, 63, 83, 94
category-property continuum, 146
causation, 36, 284, 328–9
  chain of, 328

cause, 17, 268, 270, 272, 282–3, 288–9, 292–3, 297–9, 303–4, 326, **327**–30, 332
  agent-like, 288–9
  determinate, 329, 332
  direct, 328, 332
  emotional, 332
  enabling, 288–9
  indeterminate, 332
  indirect, 328, 332
  reasoned, 332
  repetitive, 332
  targeting, 332
caused motion, 278, 291, 299
  caused-motion construction, **292**–7, 299, 300–1
  caused-motion schema, 284, **292**–4, 298–9
CAUSES ARE FORCES, 16
chain of energy, 284–5
CHANGE IS MOTION, 16, 274–5, 304
change of state, 17, 274–5, 278, 327, see also verb
circumstance, 2, 50, 103, 156, 172, 176, 189, 194, 202, 208, 221, 233, 240, 246, 248–50, 257–8, 263, 268, 303–4, **326**–8, 332
class, 105, **106**–112, 122–3, 149
class predicate, 108
clause, 31, 43, 51, **52**–3, 55–7, 93, 100, 144, 153, 155, 161–5, 189, 220, 226, 240–2, 255, 271, 283, 327
collection, 3–4, 75–6, 85, 91, 100, 106, 117, 121, 136, 138
collective construal, 75
collective noun, *see* noun
collective quantifier, *see* quantifier, *see also* set
collectivity, 121–2, 124, 126, 129
common name, 89
comparative clause, 93
compelling modality, *see* modality
complement, **47**–48, 50–1, 56–7, 119, 155, 240, 267, 271, 273, 276–7, 291–3, 296, 308, 320

Index   363

complementation, 52, **55**–7, 241
complement clause, 56, 240
complex sentence, *see* sentence
complex situation, *see* situation
complex tense, *see* tense
complex time, *see* time
compound, 4, 12, 146, 163, 312
composition, 64, **65**–6, 69, 73, 75–6, 81, 83, 100, 135–6, 210
conceptual blending, *see* blending
conceptual continuum, 5, 6, 83
conceptual core, 1, 41–2, **43**–8, 50, 53, 56, 58, 78, 80, 176, 267–71, 276, 288–9, 296, 298
conceptual distance, 53–4, 56
conceptual domain, *see* domain
conceptual entity, 12, 14, 17, **43**, 45–7, 56, 58, 63, 106, 238, 267, 269, 298
conceptual frame, *see* frame
conceptual integration, *see* blending
conceptual link, 52, 54–5, 57, 72, 158–60
conceptual metaphor, *see* metaphor
conceptual metonymy, *see* metonymy
conceptual shift, 1, 12–4, 17, 63, 78–9, 245
conceptual unit, 1–2, 17, 30, 41–3, 46–7, 53, 56–7, 79–80, 83, 135, 143, 149, 176
concrete noun, *see* noun
conditional clause, 31, 93, 226
conflation, 278–9, 291–3
conjunction, 31, 36, 42–3, 52, 56, 95, 122, 124–5, 133, 150, 154, 159, 162, 165, 184, 225, 241, 330
connection, 16, 311, 327
CONNECTION IS CONTACT, 16
construal, 1, 21, **22**–5, 26, 27, 37–8, 54–5, 57, 72, 74–5,
107–8, 124, 152, 216, 218, 221, 241, 293, 295, 300, 308, 312–3, 325, 329
dimensions of, 22, 37–8
group, 75
individual, 75–6
preferred, 282, 297
contact, 106, 116, 159, 305, 310, 312–3, 321, 327–8, 331
CONTACT schema, 16, 159, 305, 310
CONTAINER FOR CONTENTS, 14
CONTAINER schema, 16–7, 159
containment, 158, 167, 312–3, 329
contextual effect, 34–5, 37, 45, 52
conventionalisation, 14, 35, 37, 72–3, 225
conversational implicature, *see* implicature
converse predicate, 284
co-ordination, 52, **54**–5, 57
coordination test, 270, 274
copula, 43, 47, 142
copular verb, see verb
copulative construction, **273**–4, 276, 280–1
could, 31, 35, 95, 242, 253–8, 263
count noun, *see* noun
countability, 64, **65**–70, 83
counter-expectation, 54, 184, 189
counterfactual, 31–2, 147–8, 172, 235
counterforce, 243, 245, 249, 260
current discourse, 21, 49–50, 56, 61, 88–9, 96, 106, 111–2, 325
current relevance, *see* relevance

D
definite article, *see* article
definite determiner, *see* determiner
definite plural, 107, 109–10, 124
definite reference, *see* reference
definite singular, 105, 107, 109–10, 114
definiteness, 90, 104, 107, 112–3, 124, 138, 218–9
deictic centre, 24, 97, 201
deictic ground, 202, 229
deictic shift, 210, 221, 226
deictic time, *see* time
deictic verb, *see* verb
democratisation, 249, 257
denominal adjective, *see* adjective
deontic modality, *see* modality
destination, **316**, 330–2
determiner, **49**, 51, 56, 61, 67, 88, 91–3, 95, 107, 118–9, 128–9, 132, 136, 138, 154, 216, 270, 273
  definite, 100, 107, 118, 129, 136, 153, 161
  demonstrative, 95
  indefinite, 91, 92, 93, 94, 129
  possessive, 88
dimension, 146, 307–8, **309**, 311, 331
dimensional preposition, *see* preposition
direction, 97, 117, 138, 158, **307**–11, 314, 317–8, 321, 325, 331
directional, 183, 278, 308, 310–1, 316, 319, 323–5
directional extent, 308, 319
directional preposition, see preposition
dispersive, 189
disposition, 246, 263, *see also* modality
DISPOSITION FOR OCCASIONAL BEHAVIOUR, 254
distance, 53–4, 56, 68, 173, 211–2, 223, 307–8, 323, 331, 241, *see also* principle of proximity/distance
distributiveness, **121**–2, 124, 129
ditransitive construction, 269, 271, **294**–7, 299, 300
domain, 8–9, **11**–3, 15–8, 44–6, 58, 61, 63–4, 71–4,

76, 78, 82–3, 138, 149, 153, 160, 169, 186, 222, 237, 245, 268, 278, 280, 292, 295, 297, 303–4, 306, 317–8, 326, 331–2
abstract, 16, 280, 303–4, 326, 331
source, **13**, 16–7, 19, 133, 268, 297
target, **13**, 17, 268, 304
duration, 79, 176, **179**–82, 184–7, 190, 196–7, 209–10, 216–8, 220, 223–4, 226, 229, 317–8, **319**–20, 322, 324–6, 332
limited, 81, 177–9, 196

E
each, 117, 119, 121–2, 125–7, 136, 138–9
ecological niche, 4–5, 17, 260
ecological system, **4**–5, 17, 18, 252, 273
ecology, 177, 251, 297
emotion schema, 269–70, **282**, 298–9
emotional causality, 329
EMOTIONS ARE OPPONENTS, 16
enabling cause, *see* cause
enabling condition, 289–91, 299
enabling modality, *see* modality
end-point, 176, 178–83, 186, 189, 197, 214, 215, 217, 308, 315–7, 323–6
energetic action, 286, 288
energetic event, 284, 293
energetic force, 292, 299
energy, 9, 285, 289, 291, 299
chain, 284–5, 299–300
sink, 285–6
source, 180, 285–6, 288, 299
transmitter, 285–6, 299
enrichment, 33, 306
entailment, 184, 214–5
entrenchment, 16, 146, 158
EPISODIC EVENTS ARE OBJECTS, 82
episodic situation, *see* situation

EPISODIC STATES ARE OBJECTS, 82
epistemic assessment, *see* assessment
epistemic modality, *see* modality
epistemic necessity, *see* necessity
epistemic possibility, *see* possibility
epistemic probability, *see* probability
epithet, 143, 146
equivalence, 259–61
eternal truth, 195
event, 47, 50, 81–3, **177**–82
anterior, 203–5, 214–7, 222
atelic, 180–1, 186, 197
bounded, 82, 175, 177, **178**–82, 196, 198, 208–9, 214, 220–1, 230, 326
dispersive, 189
durational, 182
episodic, 82, 132, 159
habitual, 5, 210
motion, 278, 292, 306–7, 311, 331
punctual, 15, 179–82, 187–90, 197, 208, 321, 326
posterior, 204
steady, 82
telic, 179–82, 197
temporary, 155
unbounded 175, 177, **178**–81, 188–9, 196, 198, 210, 217, 221, 230, 239
types of, 179–82, 208
EVENT FOR ITS RESULT, 82
event schema, 176, 267, 269, **270**–2, 276, 278, 298–300, 303
event time, **202**–5, 207–9, 214–5, 219, 228–30, 323
every, 117–9, 121–2, 125–7, 136, 138–9
evidentiality, 235–6
evolutionary momentum, 172, 244–5, 250–1, 261
exemption, 259

EXISTENCE IS LOCATION (HERE), 277
existential construction, 277
experiencer, 269, **270**, 281–4, 297–9
extension
of categories, 3, 12, 15, 17, 35
of meaning, 12, 127, 225, 245, 247, 251, 253–4, 268, 333
metaphorical, 247, 268, 297, 304, 317
of space, 176, 268, 303–4
spatial, 101, 133
extent, **307**–9, 319–20, 324–5, 331
extraposition, **283**, 320, 328

F
factual, 31, 49, 94–5, 127, 148, 171–2, 187, 192–3, 221, 234, 250, 262, 327
factual reality, *see* reality
factuality, 56, 187
few, 66, 117–9, 130–4, 136–7
fictive motion, 22, **26**, 32, 37–8, 307–8, 325
figure, **28**–9, 43–4, 46–8, 53–5, 226, 230
figure and ground, 22, **28**–9, 37–8, 43, 50, 54–5, 57, 220–1, 305, *see also* principle of figure and ground
figure event 29, 220, 226
figure/ground alignment, 28
figure/ground reversal, 29
finish, 155, 180, 182–5, 198, 286
finite, 51, 172, 242
fixed location, *see* location
fixed time, *see* time
force, 239, 243–5, 247–53, 257–63, 272, 284–5, 288–9, 292–4, 298–9, 312
force dynamics, 239, **243**–5, 247, 260–1, 263, 272, 284, 285, 299
force-dynamic world, 272, 284, 298–9
FORCE schema, 17, 284
foreground, 54–5, 74–5, 277
forward-looking stance, 201, 230

frame, 8–9, **10**–5, 17–8, 27–31, 34, 38, 44, 49, 52, 58, 90, 92, 95, 98, 104–5, 112, 119, 124, 130, 147–8, 160, 169, 188–9, 226, 254, 279, 294, 296, 305–6, 318
framed uniqueness, see uniqueness
FRONT-BACK orientation, 317
FRONT-BACK schema, 17, 159
full set, 115, 117–22, 124–5, 128, 130, 134, 136
future
 anterior, 205, 230
 background, **226**–7, 230
 contingent, **224**–5, 227–8, 230
 intentional, **224**, 227–8, 230
 matter-of-course, **225**–6, 230
 planned, **226**–7, 230
 predicted, **225**, 277, 230
 scheduled, **226**–7, 230
future form, 227, 230–1
future perfect, see perfect
future progressive, 225
future prospective, 206–7, 223, 227–8, 230
future tense, 172, 201, **204**, 207, 223–6, 229–31, 252, 318
future tense form, 172–3, 224–5, 230–1, 252, 318
future time, 17, 23, 191, 201–6, 223–6, 228–30, 317–8

G
generality, 22, **23**, 37, 104
generic, 32, 107–8, 110–4, 123–4, 158, 195, 258, 273
generic reference, see reference
genitive phrase, 141, 144–5, 157, 167
genitive suffix, 157–8
goal, 24, 27, 152–3, 169, 182–3, 188, 224, 251, 260, 276, 278, 284, 286, **291**–2, 294, 298–300, 306–7, 310–3, 316, 320, 328, 331
goal preposition, see preposition
gradable, 149–51, 166

grammatical core, 47, **48**–50, 52, 56–8, 320
grammatical integration, 53–4, 56–7
grammaticalisation, **35**–8, 93, 132, 151, 194, 206, 212. 224, 246, 264, 277
ground, **28**–30, 43–7, 53–6, 220, 226, 229, 305, see also figure
grounding, 1, **48**–2, 56–8, 61, 67, 87–9, 106, 110–1, 116, 118–9, 152, 154, 173–4, 176, 201, 212, 218, 233–4, 240–2
grounding element, 48, 49, 50, 52, 57, 58, 88, 89, 118, 119, 176
grounding function, 118, 241, 242

H
habit, 5, 44–6, 176, 194, 210, 216, 218, 220, 230
habitual behaviour, 45, 47
habitual event, see event
habitual state, see state
half, 121, 128–9, 136, 151
have to, 242, 247–51, 257, 259, 261–2
head, 119, 160–7, 190, 243, 264, 305
head noun, 119, 141–4, 146, 148, 154, 158, 162, 166–7
head of relative clause, 161–2, 165
headless relative clause, 162–3
hedged performative, see performative
heterogeneous, 65, 69, 73, 81–3, 149, 177–8, 192, 196
hierarchy (conceptual), 8, 17
homogeneous, 65, 67–70, 73, 81, 83, 102, 123, 161, 177, 192, 196, 210
horizontality, 314, 331
hybrid noun, see noun
hyperbole, 122, 133
hyperonym, 8
hyponym, 8
hyponymy, 8
hypothetical, 36, 94, 96, 228, 330

I
iconic, 53, 55, 103, 158, 163, 165, 173–4, 220, 282, 286, 288, 311
 order, 55, 58, 103, 173, 220
 principle, see principle
iconicity, **53**, 57–8, 168
identification, 61, 159, 166, 273
if-clause, 226
image schema, **16**–8, 159, 167, 243, 303, 307, 310, 314, 329
image-schematic, 17, 19, 159, 305
imperfective, 178, 184, 198
imperfective paradox, 184
implicature, 21, 33, **34**–9, 54–5, 152, 184–5, 187, 189, 192, 195, 214, 217, 225, 228, 236, 245, 247, 251, 253, 258, 263, 276, 279, 293, 311–2, 327
 cancelling of, 184, 219
implicit boundaries, 177–9, 181, 192
implicit ground entity, 44, 46
implicit norm, 44, 117, 120, 130–2, 147
inalienable possession, see possession
incidence schema, 220
indefinite determiner, see determiner
indefinite plural, 107–10, 123, 129, 186
indefinite reference, see reference
indefinite singular, 92, 107–8, 110, 114
indefinitely lasting state, see state
indefiniteness, 90–3, 107–8, 113, 191, 212–3, 215
indirect object, 267, 271, 294, 296
individuative reference, see reference
inference, 21, **33**–4, 37, 113, 166, 195, 213, 215, 217, 222–4, 234, 250, 252–4, 262, 330

inferred uniqueness, *see* uniqueness
infinitive, 26, 56, 242
inherent uniqueness, *see* uniqueness
input space, 31–2, 37, 75, 147, 235
instance, 47, 61–3, **64**, 87–90, 92, 94, 96, 99–109, 111–3, 115–6, 119–20, 125, 130–2, 136–7, 141–3, 146, 153–4, 156, 162
  bounded, 132, 183
  of a category, 17, 106, 111
  of a thing, 47, 61, 64, 87–8, 90, 111, 115–6, 136, 141–3, 146, 161, 166
  of a substance, 69, 102, 120, 131, 137
  of an object, 67, 69–70, 120, 131–2, 137
instigator, 270, 298
INSTITUTION FOR PERSON, 14
instrument, 280–1, **285**, 288–9, 291, 299–300
intensifiable, 149–51, 166
intensifier, 118, 151, 153
internal composition, *see* composition
internally heterogeneous, *see* heterogenous
internally homogeneous, *see* homogeneous
intonation break, 54, 56
intrinsic modality, *see* modality
intrinsic necessity, *see* necessity
intrinsic possibility, *see* possibility
intrinsic quality, *see* quality
intrinsic relation, *see* relation
irreality, 172
iteration, 190

J
juxtaposition, 52, **54**–5, 57, 144

K
kind of-relation, 8, 17, 70
known reality, *see* reality

L
landmark, 304, **305**–13, 315–6, 317, 320–1, 331, 333
lasting state, *see* state
LIFE IS A JOURNEY, 278
little, 117–8, 120, 131–3, 137
location, 100, 162, 195, 202, 270, 272, 275, **276**, 279, 288, 291–3, 298–9, 304–5, **307**–9, 311, 314, 316–20, 326, 331–2
  fixed, 318, 332
location schema, 272, 276, 299
location time, **318**–20, 326, 332
  non-fixed, 332
locative preposition, *see* preposition
logic, 33, 122–3, 250, 297
LOVE IS A JOURNEY, 278
LOVE IS MADNESS, 16

M
main clause, 29, 52, 55–7, 165, 167, 189, 226–7, 240
manner, 151–2, 156, 169, 278, 291–2
many, 66, 115–21, 123, 130–7
mapping, **12**–3, 17, 235
  metaphorical, 13
mass noun, *see* noun
material world, 272, 279, 299
may, 25, 49, 173–4, 237–42, 244–7, 253–8, 260–1, 263
may not, 260–1, 263
means, **289**, 291, 299, 329, 331, 332
medio-passive, 290
member, 4, 7–8, 17, 65, 70, 74–6, 83, 102, 106, 112, 146, 164, 261, 273, 330
  peripheral, 7, 69
  prototypical, 7, 17, 69, 109
mental scanning, 22, **26**, 37, 317, 319, 332
mental space, 1, 21, **30**–31, 37–8, 89–90, 95, 98–9, 104, 107, 147, 165, 202, 207, 213, 218–20, 222, 231, 235, 237, 277, 283
metaphor, 1, 3, 12, **13**–9, 85, 99, 151, 153, 193, 245, 247, 268, 274–5, 277–8, 285, 294, 297–9, 303–4, 311, 317, 322, 325–6, 330–2
  dead, 15
  ontological, 78, 82, 84–5
  of time, 224, 227, 231, 326
metaphorical expression, 15–16, 275
metaphorical mapping, *see* mapping
metaphorical quantifier, *see* quantifier
metaphorical shift, 13, 78
metaphorical source, *see* source
metaphorical transfer, *see* transfer
meteorological situation, 275–6
metonymic expression, 14–5
metonymic mapping, *see* mapping
metonymic reasoning, *see* reasoning
metonymic reference point, 14
metonymic shift, 13, 72–3, 82
metonymy, 1, 3, **12**–5, 17–9, 33, 72, 99, 101, 110, 112, 129, 148, 188–9, 210, 238, 245, 250, 253–4, 257, 264, 279, 289, 295, 316–7, 321–2, 324, 326
  grammatical, 15
middle construction, **289**–90, 299–300
might, 239, 242, 255, 263
miscommunication, 34–5, 61, 116
mitigation, 211, 250, 257
modal (verb), *see* verb
modal assessment, *see* assessment
modal attitude, *see* attitude
modal expression, 172–3, 233, 236, 239–40, 242, 248
modality, 25, 51, 95, 171–4, 176, 198, 232–3, **234**–265, 300
  compelling, 246, **247**–53, 263
  deontic, 233–4, **236**–8, 243–6, 259–63

disposition, 233, **246**, 262–3
enabling, 246–7, **253**–8, 263
epistemic, 233, **234**–9, 246, 253–4, 259–64
interaction with negation, 258–62
intrinsic, 233, 243, 246, 252, 256, 262, 263
root, 233, **246**, 262
types of, 234, 237, 239, 245–7, 253, 262
model of evolving reality, *see* reality
model of time, *see* time
modifier, 61, 103, **141**–5, 149, 155, 160, 166, 168, 270, 325
genitival, 158
non-restrictve, 142, 144
qualifying, 101, 103, 143–5, 161
postnominal, **144**, 166, *see also* postmodifier
prenominal, **144**, 166, *see also* premodifier
restrictive, 142
types of, 142–3
MORE IS UP, 16, 322
most, 115, 117–21, 128–30, 134–38
motion event, *see* event
MOTION schema, 16, 17, 276–7, **278**–9, 298–300
motion verb, *see* verb
motivation, 36, 53, 56–7, 68, 76, 98, 127, 173, 210, 226, 245, 247, 251, 268, 273, 274, 277, 282, 303, 317, 329–30, 333
much, 66, 115, 117, 120–2, 131–2, 137
multiplex, 65–7, 68, 70–1, 74, 76–7, 83, 100, 116, 123, 131, 135, 189–90, 193
must, 233–9, 242–5, 247–52, 257–63
mustn't, 239, 259–262

N
narrative present, *see* present
natural force, 289, 299

necessity, 160, 190, 214, 235, 238, 242, 244, 246, 248–53, 258–61, 263–4
epistemic, 243, **244**, 247–8, 250–1, 255, 262
intrinsic, 246–8, **249**, 251, 263
weak, 251–3
need to, 248, 250–1, 263
need not, 259, 261
negation, 93, 95, 132, 235, 258–61, 263
negative, 15, 33, 131, 146, 151, 195, 234–5, 251, 330
negative expectation, 91–3, 128, 132
nominal, **47**, 148, 186, 289, 322–3, *see also* noun phrase
nominalisation, 78, **79**, 84–5, 110
non-affirmative (context), 91–5, 128, 132
non-factual, 127
non.participant role, **268**, 271, 277, 288, 303
non-partitive construction, **119**
non-progressive, *see* aspect
non-reality, 88, 94
non-restrictive relative clause, *see* relative clause
non-specific reference, *see* reference
non-specific referent, *see* referent
noun, 7, 41–2, 61, 166
abstract, 63–4, **78**–85, 92, 102, 159, 289, 326
collective, **74**–6, 83, 85, 125
concrete, 78, 80, 83–4, 149
count, 6, 15, 23, 61–5, **66**–72, 76–7, 79–85, 91–3, 120, 123, 125, 129–32, 186
hybrid, **71**–8, 83
mass, 6, 15, 23, 61, 63–65, **66**–72, 79–85, 91–2, 100, 102, 120, 123, 129–32, 183, 186
types of, 23, 66

noun phrase, **47**, 49, 61, 64, 88, 99, 119, 146, *see also* nominal
complex, 144, 157, 159, 160
nucleus, **49**–51, 56, 58
number quantification, *see* quantification
number quantifier, *see* quantifier
numeral, 36, 66–7, 76, 83, 92–3, 117, 132

O
object, **47**–8, 56, 61, 63–78, 83,
abstract, 80
amassed, 76–7
dual, 77
multiple, 77
uniplex, 77
object complement, 271
OBJECT FOR SUBSTANCE, 15
object motion, 278, 291, 292
objectivity, 22, **25**, 37–8, 248, 256
objects viewed as substances, 73, 83
object-substance continuum, 71, 73–4, 83
obligation, 31, 211, 233, 236–8, **243**–4, 246–52, 257–60, 262–4
occasional property, *see* property
occurrence, 116, 194, 202, 210, 213, 220, 272, 299, 327
occurrence schema, **272**, 276, 298–9
of-phrase, 102, 120, 136, 168
one-place predicate, *see* predicate
opposite, 147, 166, 194
order
grammatically fixed, 55
of events, 29, 55, 57
of premodifier adjectives, 153–54
of quantifiers, 136
orientation, 133, 202, 307–9, **313**–7, 320, 326, 331–2
orientational preposition, *see* preposition

ought to, 242, 247–8, 252–3, 263–4

P
PART FOR WHOLE, 14
part of-relation, 9, 17, 30
part/whole relation, *see* relation
participant, 25, 27–9, **47**–51, 53, 56–8, 90, 102, 105, 142, 149, 151–2, 159, 176, 202, 256, 267–73, 276–7, 280, 282, 288–9, 290, 293, 295–6, 298, 303, 328
participant role, 176, 267–9, **270**–71, 277, 288, 298, 303
participial phrase, 144–5
participle, 145, 149, 154–6, 191
 past, 53, 155–6, 168, 212, 214, 229, 242, 283, 323
 present, 36, 56, 155–6, 242, 283, 322
partitive construction, 71, 115–6, 119, 129, 134–7
partitive quantification, *see* quantification
partonomy, 8, **9**, 11,17
part of a whole, 10, 167
passive, 7, 247, 256, 271, 283, 286–90, 301
 process, 283
 stative, 283
passive construction, 256
past anterior, 203, 205, 230
past participle, *see* participle
past perfect, *see* perfect
past progressive, 211, 220, 230
past prospective, 206, 208, 228, 230
past situation, 213, 215, 219, 220, 221, 222, 225, 230, 238, 281
past tense, 45, 49, 50, 173, 201, **204**, 211–3, 215, 218–9, 222–3, 225, 228–30, 242, 247, 252, 255
past time, 49, 152, 201–5, 210–1, 213, 218–9, 222–4, 230, 242, 252

path, 26, 278–9, **291**–2, 307, 310–1, 315–8, 320–1, 325, 331
path preposition, *see* preposition
perception, 22–4, 29, 53, 57, 64, 68, 171, 204, 235, 279, 281–4, 287, 299
perception/cognition schema, 282–3, 299
perfect
 continuative, 215, **216**–8, 230
 future, 201, 205–6, 208, 228, **229**–30
 hot news, 216
 inferential, **215**–7, 230
 past, 31, 201, 205–7, 211, 222–3, 228, 230
 present, 184–5, 201, 205–8, 211, **212**–9, 222–3, 230–1, 239, 325
 recent, **215**, 216, 230
 resultative, **214**, 230
perfect progressive
 future, 229
 present, 217–8
perfect tense, 184, 201, **205**–7, 229–30
performative, **209**–30, 237, 247–8, 250
 hedged, 250, 257, 264
performative speech act, *see* speech act
performative verb, *see* verb
period, 81, 216, 218, 317–20, 322–6, 332
permission, 83, 236–8, 244–7, 253–4, 256, **257**–60, 262–3
perspective, 22, 25, 27, 47, 74
physiological reaction, 329
place, 2, 50, 97, 101, 103, 162, 176, 268, 278, 288, 290–1, 310–1, 316, 326, 330–1
PLACE FOR INSTITUTION, 101
plural, 6, 61, 66–8, 72, 74, 76–7, 81, 83–4, 91–2, 100, 107–10, 112, 114–6, 121, 123, 162, 186, 189
plural agreement, 77, 83–4, 110, 121
pluralia tantum, **76**–7, 83, 84

point, 309–11, 313, 319, 321, 331
polarity item, 93–4, 113
 negative, 93–4
 positive, 94
polysemy, 82, 122
polysemy of modals, 245–7, 251, 263
positive, 33, 131–4, 151, 235–6, 260, 62, 330
positive expectation, 91–4, 128, 132–3
possessed, 15, 157–8, 160, 279–80, 297, 299
possession, 144–5, 191, 212, 247, 272, 279–81, 294, 299
 alienable, 280, 285
 inalienable, 280, 285
POSSESSION FOR OWNER, 14
possession schema, 272, **279**–81, 297–9
possession verb, 8
possessive, 113, 158, 168
possessive construction, 103
possessive determiner, *see* determiner
possessive pronoun, *see* pronoun
possessive relation, *see* relation
possessor, 157–8, 167, 279–80, 298–9
possibility, 238, 245–6, 256, 258–61, 263–4
 epistemic, 244, **245**–6, 253–6, **258**, 262–3
 intrinsic, 246, 253–5, **256**–7, 263
post hoc, ergo propter hoc, 36, 54
postdeterminer, 136, 137, *see also* determiner
posterior event, *see* event
posterior situation, *see* situation
posterior time, *see* time
postmodifier, 145, *see also* modifier
postnominal modifier, *see* modifier
postnominal position, 141, 144–5, 149, 156, 167

potential reality, *see* reality 49, 93, **171**–3, 233–4, 237, 241–2, 258, 262
potential referent, *see* referent
potentiality, 172, 173, 174, 233–7, 246, 256, 262
POTENTIALITY FOR ACTUALITY, 250, 257
potentiality space, 31, 56, 235
pragmatic strengthening, 35, 245
pragmatics, 33, 250
preceding discourse, 98, 112, 135, 165
predeterminer, 129, 136–7, *see also* determiner
predicate, **47**–51, 56, 79, 149–50, 155, 184, 191–2, 271–2, 277, 283–4, 287, 292
  converse, 284
  one-place, 293
  three-place, 271–2
  two-place, 271, 293
predicate-complement, 271–2, 291–2
predicate nominal, 119, 142, 153, 191, 193, 273, 281
predicate noun, 144, 153
premodifier, 145–6, 149, 150, 151, 153, 154, 155, 156, 169, *see also* modifier
prenominal modifier, *see* modifier
prenominal position, 116, 129, 141, 144–5, 155
preposition, 4, 36, 42–3, 56, 93, 157–60, 167, 182–3, 198, 229, 251, 260, 268, 273–4, 277, 283, 288, 294, 303–5, 307–23, 325–33
  complex preposition, 316, 322, 325–6
  dimensional, 308, **309**–1, 316, 320–1, 331–2
  directional, 307, **308**, 310, 316, 331
  extensional, 308
  goal, 251, 260, 311, 313
  locative, **307**, 310, 331
  orientational, 308–9, **313**–6, 322, 326–7, 329–33
  path, 316, 321, 325, 328
  point, 327
  spatial, 268, 303, 308–9, 317, 328
prepositional object, 4, 271, 286–8
prepositional phrase, 29, 31, 119, 135, 141, 144–5, 157, 167, 183, 191, 242, 273–4, 277, 294, 300–1, 303, 307, 318–9, 320, 326–7, 331
present
  anterior present, 205, 230
  historic, 222, 230
  narrative, 222, 230
  scientific, 222, 230
  summary, 222, 230
  timeless, 222
present anterior, 211, 223
present participle, *see* participle
present perfect, *see* perfect
present progressive, 5, 192, 210, 226–7
present prospective, 206, 208, 223–4, 227, 228, 230
present tense, 5, 26, 45, 94, 172–3, 201, 203, **204**–19, 222, 226, 229–31, 242
present time, 5, 31, 97, 123, 172, 194, 201–5, 207–19, 221–2, 224, 226, 230, 242
principle of figure and ground, 43, **53**, 57, 273
principle of proximity/distance, **53**, 56–7, 136, 154, 173
principle of quantity, **98**, 132
principle of relevance, **35**, 37, 45, 185
principle of sequential order, **53**–4, 57, 220
probability, 211, 235–7, 239–40, 252
process, 82, 185, 267, 272, 274–6, 282–3, 289, 293, 298–9
  cognitive, 1, 3, 5, 12, 17, 177, 247
  inferential, 21, 245, 250. 261
  steady, 274–5
processing, 14, 32, 35, 80, 103, 153, 158, 163, 235
processing effort, 35, 37
profiling, 22, **30**, 37, 75, 79, 117, 119, 160, 178, 187, 215, 235–6, 243, 285, 313, 325
progressive, *see* aspect
prohibition, 236, 247, 258–60, 263
projected reality, *see* reality
prominence, 12, 22, 28–9, 37, 76–7, 206, 267, 270, 272, 280, 285, 297, 304, 321
pronoun, 25, 75, 93, 96, 98, 116, 119, 128, 153, 162–3, 224, 240–1, 275–6, 283
  demonstrative, 36, 162
  impersonal, 256
  of laziness, 98
  possessive, 49, 75, 157
  relative, 75, 161–5
proper name, 89, 99, **100**–1, 112–3, 161
property, 9, 12, 30, 32, 44–6, 61, 68–9, 71, 80, 83, 103, 106, 110–1, 141, 144–5, **146**–52, 154–7, 161, 165–7, 176, 210, 212–3, 218–9, 239, 242, 249, 254, 307
  assigned, 150, 156–7, 167, 273, 275
  characteristic, 144, 149–54, 156
  complementary, **147**–8, 151, 166
  functions of, 149–50
  inherent, 167
  occasional, 149–50, 156, 167
  qualifying, 141, 144, 166, 168
  recategorised, 152
  scalar, **147**, 151–2, 154, 156, 166, 254
  specifying, 152–3
  stable, 110, 167
  topological, 308–10, 331
PROPERTY OF A THING FOR THE THING, 110
PROPERTY OF AN INSTRUMENT FOR PROPERTY OF A PERSON USING THE INSTRUMENT, 148
proposition, **51**–2, 56, 238, 241, 244, 259, 263

Index

prospective form, 201, 206, 230
prototype, **7**–8, 17, 63, 153
prototype structure, 8, 63, 153
prototypical, 7, 9, 17, 42, 66, 69, 74, 78, 83, 104, 109–10, 150, 156, 272–3, 281, 285–6, 294, 328
prototypical member, *see* member
proximity, 53, 163, 288, *see also* principle of proximity/distance
pseudo-adjective, 151
psychological state, 191
psychological world, 272, 281, 299
punctual event, *see* event
punctual situation, *see* situation 297
purpose, 268, 270, 291, 303–4, 326–7, **328**, 330–2

Q

qualification, 61–2, 103, **141**–6, 150, 157, 160–2, 165–6, 168, 273
   function of, 142
   non-restrictive, **143**, 166
   intrinsic, 233, 246, 248, 263
   restrictive, **142**–143, 166
   temporary, 141, 166
   types of, 103, 142–5, 157, 160, 168
qualified uniqueness, 99, **103**
qualifying modifier, *see* modifier
qualifying property, *see* property
qualifying relation, 141, 144, 145, **157**–8, 169
   types of, 157–8, 160, 167
qualifying situation, 141, 144, **161**, 163, 167
quantification, 61, 67, 115, **116**–22, 127–8, 134–6, 138, 151
   amount 67, 117, **120**–1, 130–1, 133, 137
   distributive, 127
   non-partitive quantification, **119**, 121

number, 67, **120**–1, 131, 133, 137
partitive, 117, **119**–21, 134, 136
scalar, 115, **117**–21, 130–7
set, 115, **117**–30, 135–8
types of, 67, 115–21, 136
universal, 123
quantifier, 61, 66–8, 83, 115–7, 119–39, 162
   amount, **120**, 131, 137
   collective, **121**–2, 124–5, 136
   distributive, **121**–2, 125, 136
   full-set quantifier, **121**–2, 163
   lexical, 116, 133–4
   metaphorical, 133–4
   number, **120**, 131, 137
   partitive, 135
   scalar, 61, 115, **117**–20, 129–34, 136–7
   selective, **122**, 136
   set, 61, 115, **117**–23, 127–30, 134, 136–9, 163
   subset, **121**, 128–30, 135–6, 138
   types of, 134, 136
   universal, 123
quantity, 16, 67, 77, 108, 115–21, 124, 128–36, 130, 134, 136, 151, 183, 190, *see also* principle of quantity
   bounded, 70, 73, 183

R

reality, 5–6, 8, 30–1, 75, 88, 94, 96, 171, 237, 256, 327, 332, *see also* irreality and non-reality
   conceived, 53
   conception of, 6–7
   evolving, 170–2, 204. 234
   factual, 49, 94, **171**–3, 234, 250, 262
   future, 173
   immediate, 171–3, 204, 218, 240
   known, 171–3, 204, 219, 221, 228

   model of evolving, 171–2, 204, 234
   objective, 6
   past, 50
   potential, 49, 93, **171**–3, 233–4, 237, 241–2, 258, 262
   projected, **171**–3, 204, 211, 225, 227–8, 262
   types of, 172–3, 234
   virtual, 94–5
   world of, 88, 96, 172
reality space, 31–2, 56, 94, 96, 147–8, 235, 237
reality status, 49, 51, 88, 93, 104, 152, 171–3, 176, 204, 234, 246, 262
reason, 36, 162, 268, 303, 326, **327**–30, 332
reasoning, 213, 233, 237, 245, 250, 258, 261–2, 329–30
   deductive 33
   metonymical 33, 107
recategorisation, 145, 151–2, 156
recipient, 152, **294**–9
reference, 49, 51, 61, 64, 66–7, 76, 87, **88**–91, 94, 97–100, 103, 105–8, 110–3, 115, 117–9, 133, 135, 138, 142–3, 147, 158, 160–2, 166–7, 176, 195, 203–8, 216, 220, 222, 226–31, 242, 252, 290, 304–5, 310, 313, 323, 325, 331
   act of, 87–9, 111, 116
   anaphoric, **98**–9, 112–3, 135, 138
   cataphoric, 98, **99**
   definite, 87, **90**–1, 96–8, 112, 124
   deictic, **97**, 112, 205–6
   discourse, 98–9, 112
   generic, 87, 89, **90**, 105–112, 114, 123, 195
   indefinite, 87, **90**–6, 112
   individuative, **89**–90, 106–9, 111
   non-specific, **94**–6, 104, 112–3
   specific, **94**–5, 112, 133
   types of, 89–91, 94, 111, 113, 138

unique reference, 97, **99**–105, 112
reference frame, 304–5
　absolute, 304
　deictic, 305
　non-deictic, 304–5
　relative, 304–5
reference mass, 61, 88–9, 91, 94, 116–8, 142–3, 161–2, 166
reference point, **14**–5, 17, 49, 103, 113, 118, 133, 147, 158, 160, 167, 203–4, 220, 227–9, 242, 290, 305, 310, 313, 323, 325, 331
reference time, **203**–8, 222, 227–30, 321, 323
referent, 49, 50 64, 87, **88**–101, 103–7, 111–2, 118–9, 124, 129, 132–6, 142–4, 151–4, 158, 161–2, 164–7, 189, 219, 271, 276–7, 301
　anaphoric, 98–9, 165
　articleless, 92
　definite, 50, 95–6, 99, 104, 124, 129, 144, 165, 277
　discourse, 165
　generic, 106–7
　indefinite, 91, 98–9, 129, 161, 277
　individuative, 90
　non-specific, 95–6, 104, 132
　potential, 158, 161, 165
　specific, 95–6, 104, 132–3
　unique, 101, 103–5, 161
referential failure, 88
referring expression, 61, 87–90, 94, 96–7, 100, 102, 105–7, 109, 111, 113–6
region, 63–4, 243
　spatial, 97, 305–6, 309, 311, 313–7, 331, 333
reification, 63, 77, **78**–2, 82, 84–5, 102,
reified event, 82–3, 322
reified noun, 132, 326
reified situation, 82, 102, 289
reified state, 82–3, 280
reified thing, 78–83, 159, 289, 297

relation, 1, 16–7, 28, 30, 41–4, 46–50, 52, 54–6, 58, 78–80, 110, 119, 121, 126–8, 134, 136, 141, 144, 149, 157–60, 166, 168–9, 204–5, 250, 258–9, 261 267–70, 273–6, 279–80, 299, 303, 305, 306–11, 318, 320, 327, 329–31, 333
　conceptual, 43, 79
　dynamic, 306–7, 310
　intrinsic, 157–58, **159**–60, 167
　part/whole, 159, 280
　possessive, 157, **158**, 160, 165, 167
　qualifying, 157–8, 160, 167
　schematic, 157–8, **159**–60, 167, 169, 305
　spatial, 307–8, 331
　static, 276, 307–8, 310, 316
　temporal, 54–5, 204, 318–20, 323
relational concept, 42, 63, 78–9, 81, 84, 157–9, 176, 191, 267
relational expression, 43, 71, 157
relational noun, 159
relational term, 159
relational unit, 42, 267
relative clause, 100, 141, 144–5, 153, **161**–8
　non-restrictive, 161, **164**–7
　restrictive, **161**–7
relative pronoun, *see* pronoun
relevance, 69, 213, 218–9, 238
　current, 206, 212–3, 215, 217–8, 223, 230
relevance theory, 35, 38, *see also* principle of relevance
repetition, 190
request, 35, 157, 236, 258, 262
restricted viewing frame, *see* viewing frame
restrictive qualification, *see* qualification
restrictive relative clause, *see* relative clause
RESULT FOR ACTION, 15, 188, 253, 324

reversal, 29, 55, 273, 280, 293
role configuration, 176, 267, 269–70, 290, 298, 300
root modality, *see* modality

S
salience, 9, 14–5, 17, 26, 28, 37, 53–4, 76, 100, 103, 110, 158–9 221, 254, 263, 269, 279, 285, 291, 306, 311, 315, 321
scalar property, *see* property
scalar quantification, *see* quantification
scalar quantifier, *see* quantifier
scale, 44, 61, 77, 115, 117–20, 130–1, 133–4, 136, 147, 150–1, 227, 235–6, 240, 286, 288
scanning, 26, 80, 290, 311, 317, 325, *see also* mental scanning and sequential scanning
scene, 21–9, 32, 37, 46, 160, 189, 240–1, 243, 308–9
schematic meaning, 145, 159–60, 162, 270, 294, 299
scope, 138, **238**, 244, 259, 265
search domain, 305, 317
self-motion schema, 284, **291**–2, 299
semantic bleaching, *see* bleaching
semelfactive, 190
semi-modal, 243, 247, 249
sentence, 47–9, **50**–51
　complex, 2, 29, 41, **52**–3, 55, 57, 163, 240–1, 283
sentence pattern, 267, 269, **271**–2, 276, 279, 298, 300
sentient human, 272, 282, 298
sequential order, 53, 55, 57, 220, 282, *see* principle of sequential order
sequential scanning, **26**, 80
set, 61, 70, 74, 83, 91–4, 96, 98, 104, 106, 108–9, 112, 115, 117–30, 132, 134–9, 159, 163, 165, 167, 182–3, 240, 244, 267, 269–70, 308, 316, 323–4
　collective, 123, 125–7

distributive, 125, 127
restricted, 119, 123–4, 134
selective, 127
uniplex collective, 123, 125
universal, 119, 123
set quantification, *see* quantification
set quantifier, *see* quantifier
setting, 16–7, **50**, 53, 57–8, 152, 176, 213, 219–20, 268, 271, 276, 303–4, 326, 328, 332
setting element, 50, 58, 176, 268, 328
shared knowledge, 10, 112
should, 239, 242, 247, 252–3, 263
simple present, 5, 45–6, 192, 194–5, 208–10, 216, 221, 226
simple tenses, 201, **204**, 207, 229
situation, 41–2, **47**–51, 56, 171–6, 196, 267–69
 anterior phase of, 212, 216–8, 230
 anterior, 205–6, 212–7, 222–3, 228–30, 238
 bounded, 208, 215, 219, 324
 complex, 53–4, 57, 220, 227, 294
 episodic, **81**–2, 84, 132, 159
 posterior, 224, 227–8, 230
 steady, **81**, 84
 time of, 229
 timeless, 210
 unbounded, 208–9, 211, 220, 223, 230, 324, 326
situation type, 174–175, **176**, 179–81, 183, 195–8
some, 92, 94–5, 121, 128–31
source (spatial), 278, 290, **291**–2, 300, 307, 310–3, 320, 328, 330–1
source (metaphorical), 17, 268, 331
source domain, *see* domain

SOURCE-PATH-GOAL schema, 278, 291, 307, 317, 328
space, 11, 80–1, 176, 186, 303- 318, *see also* base space, blended space, input space, mental space, potentiality space, reality space
 abstract, 304, 326–32
 physical, 303–5, 307, 317, 321, 326, 331
 temporal, 304, 317–8, 332
 topology of, 304, 307–317
space-builder, **31**–2, 37, 95, 235, 277
spatial schema, **276**–9, 298–9
speaker involvement, 240, 251
specific reference, *see* reference
specificity, 22, **23**, 37
speech act, 157, 208–9, 211, 230, 236
 directive, 234, **236**–7, 262
 performative, 209, 236, 250, 262
speech community, 4, 99, 102, 112
speech time, 174, 202–5, 207–10, 212, 214–6, 218, 220, 225, 228–30, 237, 319, 323, 325
state, 17, 47, 56, 78, 80–3, 155–6, 161, 171, 175–9, 190–7, 210, 212–6, 218, 220, 228–30, 238, 270, 272, **273**–6, 298–9, 324, *see also* change of state
 anterior, 215
 anterior phase of, 216–7
 continuative, 216, 218
 emotional, 83, 191, 270
 everlasting, 191, **195**, 197, 209–10
 habitual, 191, **193**–4, 197, 209, 255, 324
 indefinitely lasting, **191**–2, 194, 197, 209–10, 218
 inferred, 215, 217

 lasting, 175, 177–8, **179**, 190–2, 194, 196–7, 214
 perceptual, 191
 recent, 216
 resultant, 214–5, 217, 275, 287
 resulting, 183, 286, 312
 steady, 82–3
 temporary, 175, **179**, 190–3, 196–7, 215, 217–8, 220, 223
 temporary habitual, 191, 193–7
 timeless state, 187, 194, 197
 types of, 179, 190–7
 unbounded, 81, 177–9, 196, 210
STATES ARE CONTAINERS, 16
STATES ARE LOCATIONS, 274–5
STEADY EVENTS ARE SUBSTANCES, 82
steady situation, *see* situation
stop, 44–5, 180, 182–3, 185, 188, 193, 198, 215
subject, 27–9, **47**–8, 50–1, 53, 56, 75–6, 107, 142, 159, 163–4, 195, 242, 267, 271–3, 276–7, 279, 282–5, 288–90, 292, 299–301
subject clause, 283
subject complement, 271
subject matter, 288
subject participant, 28, 47, 52, 142, 159, 272, 288–90,
subjectification, 241
subjectivity, 22, **25**, 37–8, 49, 239, 240–1
 maximal, 25, 241–2
subordinate (term), 8–9, 23, 72
subordinate clause, 29, 52, 55, 57, 226–7, 283, 320, 326
subordinating conjunction, 36, 55
subordination, 52, 55, 57
subset, 115, **117**–9, 121, 128–30, 134–6, 138, 151, 163
substance, 15–6, 61, 53–73, 78, 80–1, 83, 102, 120, 123, 125, 128, 130–2, 137, 177

substances viewed as objects, 71, 83, 125
summary scanning, **26**, 80
superordinate, 8–9, 23, 48, 69, 70–2, 109, 123, 162, 273
support, 312, 331
surface, 309–10, 312–3, 331

T
tag question, 241, 252
target (conceptual), 14, 103, 158
target (spatial), 285, 311, 329, 331
target domain, *see* domain
target preposition, 329
tautology, 33, 38, 76, 231
taxonomy, **8**–9, 11, 17, 23, 69–70
telic, 178–82, 184, 197, 214, 217, 239. 284
telicity, **179**, 180–1, 197, 214
temporal, 29, 31, 36, 50, 52–5, 57, 79–81, 144, 161, 171, 176–7, 186–7, 196, 204, 206, 208, 213, 226, 228–30, 267, 304, 317–25, 328–33
temporary state, *see* state
tense, 26, 49–50, 52, 56, **171**–4, 198, 201–2, 205–9, 211–3, 215, 218–9, 222, 226, 228–31, 241–2, 318
   complex, 201, 204, **205**, 230
tense form, 172–3, 230
terminal point, 180, 187–90
TERMINAL POINT FOR ACTIVITY (LEADING TO TERMINAL POINT), 189
textual coherence, 52
that-clause, 56, 238
THE FUTURE IS IN FRONT, 16
thematic role, **267**, 269–71, 276, 290, 298, 3003, see also participant role
theme, 47, 152, **267**, 269–70, 273–7, 279, 282, 284–90, 292–3, 298–9
there-construction, 277, 300
thing, 41, **42**, 47–9, 56–8, 61–2, **63**–6, 68–4,
   bounded, 68, 72, 74, 81
   types of, 61, 63–4, 179
   unbounded, 74, 81, 186

time, 171–4, 201–231
   anterior, 173, 200–1, **205**–6, 211, 230, 323
   bounded, 184, 321
   calendrical, 323
   complex, 201, **204**–5, 207, 228–30
   configuration of, 205, 214, 216, 228
   deictic, 97, 201, 203, **204**, 207, 218, 225–6, 229
   fixed time, 202, 320–2
   location in, 26, 202, 317–9, 332
   model of, 98, 202, 224
   posterior, 201, 205, **206**–8, 230
   unbounded, 184
time axis, 20–3, 229, 317–8, 320
TIME IS MONEY, 16
TIME IS MOTION OVER A LANDSCAPE, 224
TIME IS SPACE, 304, 317
time point, 204, 219, 226, 228–9, 318–23, 325, 332
time schema, **176**, 178, 180–1, 184, 191, 192, 196
time span, 182–4, 186, 208, 321, 323-
time sphere, 201, 204–5, 210–1, 215–6, 223, 226, 229, 317–8, 321–3, 325
time stretch, 184–5, 188, 229, 324, 332
token, **64**, 87, 88, 90, 106, 107, see also type
TOKENS FOR A TYPE, 107
topic, 213, 273, 277, 282
topology of space, *see* space
toponym, 100
trajector, **305**–13, 317–8, 321, 331
trajectory, 276, 278
transfer, 183, 249, 269, 284, 294–9
   beneficial, 295–6
   metaphorical, 295, 297, 299
transfer schema, 269, 284, **294**–5, 297, 299
transitive construction, 269, 271, 279, 286, 288, 293, 296

transitive verb, *see* verb
transitivity, 8, **286**–8, 300
type, 7, **64**, 87–8, 106–7, 116,
type-token, 64

U
unbounded, 65, 68–9, 73–4, 81, 83, 101–2, 132, 161, 183, 191, 221, 230, 239, 275, 278, *see also* activity, event, situation, thing, time
uncountable, 68–9, 83, 102, 123
underspecification, 46
UNDERSTANDING IS SEEING, 16
understatement, 133
uniplex, 65, 67, 71, 74, 76–8, 83, 116, 123, 125, 132, 189
UNIPLEX FOR MULTIPLEX, 189
uniplex-multiplex continuum, 71, 74, 77–8, 83
uniqueness, 100, 103–5, 111, 153, 161
   framed, 99, **104**
   functional, 104–5
   inferred, 104
   inherent, 99, **100**–3, 161
UP–DOWN schema, 16, 314, 327
used to, 194

V
valency, 271
verb, 7–8, 27–8, 42, 44–5, 47–8, 56, 58, 78–9, 93, 148–9, 155, 253, 271, 292–6
   achievement, 188, 297
   action, 8
   caused-motion, 293
   change-of-state verb, 274, 300
   copular, 150, 156, 236, 241, 271, 273–4, 276, 271, 273–4, 276,
   cognition, 233, 240–2, 250
   communication, 250, 295, 299, 295, 299
   creation, 286
   deictic 24–5, 291
   emotion, 8, 283
   inchoative, **274**–5

intransitive, 7, 43–5, 271
manner-of-motion, 291–2
modal, 25, 31, 36, 49–52, 56, 95, 172–4, 211, 225, 232, 233–5, 237, 239–41, **242**–7, 249–65
motion, 24, 274, 278, 291 293, 308
perception, 284, 287
performative, 236, 262
possession, 8, 280–1
posture, 276
prepositional, 288
process, 274
"psych", 283
reflexive, 291
state, 192–3, 228, 238
stative, 191, 295
transfer, 295–9
transitive, 7–8, 44–5, 212, 280, 283

verb agreement, 75–8, 83
verb phrase, **47**–8, 241
verticality, 77, 159, 314, 315, 331
view, 23, 25, 175, 176, 196
   external, 174, 177–8, 196
   infinite, 177–8, 190, 192
   internal, 174, 177–8, 184, 188, 191–2
viewing frame, 22–3, 37, 46, 175, **177**–8, 181, 184, 186, 189, 196
   maximal, 22, 64, 175, 177–8, 190, 196
   restricted, 22, 46, 175, 177, 181, 184, 188–9, 191, 196, 217
viewpoint, 22, **23**–5, 27, 37, 201–7, 212, 214, 216, 218, 222, 224, 227–9, 314
   shifted, 24, 202–3, 222
   speaker's, 24, 201, 203, 205, 207
   hearer's, 24–5
virtual, 26, 94–6, 112

W

when-clause, 189, 220, 226
whole and part, 158. 290
WHOLE FOR PART, 14
will, 211, 225–9, 252
word class, 41, 56, 58, 61, 79, 149
word order, 48, 168, 282, 286
world of experience, 272, 299

Z

zero-form, 92, 163–4, 183

In the series *Cognitive Linguistics in Practice* the following titles have been published thus far or are scheduled for publication:

1   **DIRVEN, René and Marjolijn H. VERSPOOR (eds.):** Cognitive Exploration of Language and Linguistics. **Second revised edition**. In collaboration with Johan De Caluwé, Dirk Geeraerts, Cliff Goddard, Stef Grondelaers, Ralf Pörings, Günter Radden, Willy Serniclaes, Marcello Soffritti, Wilbert Spooren, John R. Taylor, Ignacio Vazquez, Anna Wierzbicka and Margaret E. Winters. 2004. xii, 277 pp.
2   **RADDEN, Günter and René DIRVEN:** Cognitive English Grammar. 2007. xiii, 374 pp.